ADVANCING EQUITY PLANNING NOW

ADVANCING EQUITY PLANNING NOW

Edited by
Norman Krumholz and
Kathryn Wertheim Hexter

CORNELL UNIVERSITY PRESS   ITHACA AND LONDON

First published 2018 by Cornell University Press

Printed in the United States of America

Library of Congress Cataloging-in-Publication Data

Names: Krumholz, Norman, editor. | Hexter, Kathryn Wertheim, editor. | Bates, Lisa K. Growth without displacement.
Title: Advancing equity planning now / edited by Norman Krumholz and Kathryn Wertheim Hexter.
Description: Ithaca : Cornell University Press, 2018. | Papers originally presented at a conference held in November 2015 at the Levin College of Urban Affairs, Cleveland State University. | Includes bibliographical references and index.
Identifiers: LCCN 2018026557 (print) | LCCN 2018027620 (ebook) | ISBN 9781501730382 (epub/mobi) | ISBN 9781501730399 (pdf) | ISBN 9781501730375 | ISBN 9781501730375 (pbk. ; alk. paper)
Subjects: LCSH: City planning—United States—Congresses. | Regional planning—United States—Congresses. | Urban policy—United States—Congresses. | Social justice—United States—Congresses.
Classification: LCC HT167 (ebook) | LCC HT167 .A573 2018 (print) | DDC 307.1/2160973—dc23
LC record available at https://lccn.loc.gov/2018026557

We dedicate this book to the memory of our colleague, Susan Christopherson, formerly at Cornell University's Department of Planning. Her energy, keen insight, and wise guidance helped shape this book. Sadly, she passed away in 2016. We also dedicate this book to our families for their encouragement, support, and embrace of the importance of this work.

Contents

Foreword

By Ronn Richard, President and Chief Executive Officer, Cleveland Foundation

"For many of us in the city planning field, [Norm] Krumholz has been that small voice in our heads reminding us of why we entered the field—namely, to help create a better world and to create a better quality of life for those who are sometimes left behind by what others have defined as progress. We could choose to ignore that voice, but we could not deny that we had heard its message."
            —Retired Cleveland Planning Director Robert Brown, "Rebel with a
                    Plan: Norm Krumholz and 'Equity Planning' in Cleveland"

This path-breaking book espouses the principles of inclusive planning and attests to the dedication of that framework's most ardent champion: Norman Krumholz, professor emeritus at Cleveland State University's Maxine Goodman Levin College of Urban Affairs. I am honored to have the first word in service to these two aims, because for more than a century, the Cleveland Foundation—the world's first community foundation—has focused on issues of diversity, inclusion, and equity as embodied in Norm's work.

In funding this publication, the Cleveland Foundation sustains a long-held commitment to address these deeply rooted, complex issues affecting our community's most underserved neighborhoods. We view this book as a blueprint to enhance the lives of the disadvantaged in every area our work touches: housing, employment, education, economic development, health and human services, transportation, and recreation, to name a few.

At the core of every initiative that we and our many public, nonprofit, and private partners support is the intent to provide Greater Cleveland's underserved citizens with one element they consistently lack: access. In this spirit, we have:

- Worked to shape a high-performing school system for Cleveland's children from their earliest years and to ensure that more students enter college and succeed.
- Recognized the importance of out-of-school time with MyCom (My Commitment, My Community), which connects young people with

caring adults and high-quality, neighborhood-based programs and services in a safe, supportive environment.

- Invested to revitalize all of Cleveland's neighborhoods. Case in point: investment in seven low-income neighborhoods that adjoin the city's institution district of University Circle, where we have pursued inclusive growth and personal well-being for residents via job, housing, transportation, and community health initiatives. Here, we have helped fund the Evergreen Cooperatives: employee-owned businesses that recruit and train local workers.
- Nurtured job creation and economic growth throughout the core city and worked to align our region's education and training programs with viable career opportunities that provide family-sustaining wages for Greater Cleveland residents.
- Established a Mastery Arts Initiative that aims to meaningfully connect every child in every underserved Cleveland neighborhood to the arts, including theater, photography, dance, and music.

This is not tinkering around the edges. The thread that binds all these enterprises is a determination to effect systemic change—a determination to widen access for all those individuals who are not at the table when decisions that impact their lives are made.

This inclusion has been Norm Krumholz's life's work. He has successfully practiced equity planning under three Cleveland mayors, while also trying to encourage all planning professionals not only to plan the physical city, but also to try to move resources, political power, and participation toward lower-income disadvantaged people of the city and region.

Norm earned his master's degree in planning at Cornell University in 1965. Four years later, he came to Cleveland to serve as city planning director—and sparked a national dialogue as he and his staff redefined the planner's role with a focus on social policy that extended well beyond traditional land use and design issues.

After leaving city government in 1979, Norm began his teaching career at Cleveland State University. He served on the Cleveland Planning Commission and was president of the American Planning Association; the APA conferred their National Planning Award for Distinguished Leadership to him in 1990. Among his many other honors, I am proud to note that in 2001 he received the Cleveland Foundation's Homer C. Wadsworth Award, which recognizes creative, visionary local leaders.

In the classroom, Norm continues to inspire future city planners. We hope this book will magnify his reach by:

- Embedding equity planning in the curricula of planning schools nationwide, to encourage the next generation of civic leaders to embrace this approach;
- Fostering changes in national policy, with an eye toward expediting the implementation of equity planning locally; and
- Accelerating these needed changes on a broad scale.

To disseminate these ideas as widely as possible, we are immediately making this book available online via open access, at no cost to readers and researchers. The decision to fund worldwide accessibility to this book is in keeping with the tenet of accessibility that is at the heart of equity planning.

In closing, I would like to salute Clevelander Joseph Keithley, a Cornell engineering graduate with a passion for landscape architecture, who convened the Cleveland-Cornell partnership that made this book possible. Joe is a generous Cleveland Foundation donor who served with distinction for a decade on our board of directors; he has worked tirelessly to strengthen the ties between his alma mater and his community and to enhance equity in Greater Cleveland. He has also been an avid proponent of this project from the start.

I give my thanks as well to the esteemed contributors to this book. They represent a mix of scholars and practitioners with different perspectives, ages, and races. Some are recognized senior scholars, while some are emerging voices with fresh ideas. All are considering how we can shape the environment to create a more just and equitable world. Their insights could not be more timely, as our divided nation wrestles with rampant income disparity, racial injustice, and socioeconomic dislocation. These challenges make a powerful argument for a renewed emphasis on equity planning.

Acknowledgments

This book would not have been written at all if not for the inspired idea brought to us in 2015 by Lillian Kuri, vice president of Strategic Grantmaking, Arts and Urban Design Initiatives, The Cleveland Foundation. She envisioned a book that would restore the concept of equity into the planning profession and celebrate and recognize Cleveland's historic role in equity planning. Her vision shaped the structure of the book and led to a fruitful collaboration between Cleveland State University's Maxine Goodman Levin College of Urban Affairs and Cornell University's Department of Urban Planning. The two schools have a long, scholarly association. Cornell's students often use Cleveland as a "living laboratory" for their studies. Moreover, Norman Krumholz is a Cornell alum and co-authored the award-winning book *Making Equity Planning Work* with John Forester, a Cornell professor and a contributor to this book.

We are grateful to our collaborators at Cornell University's Department of Urban Planning. The book and symposium were cocreated by the late Susan Christopherson, professor and former chair of the department. Sadly, Susan passed away in 2016 before this book was completed, but she and Peter Wissoker, a PhD student (now doctorate) in Cornell's planning program, worked closely with us on the difficult tasks of selecting authors to include in the book and critiquing the early drafts of the chapters. Peter Wissoker, drawing from his previous editorial experience with Cornell University Press, offered valuable advice on organizing and editing the book. Susan was instrumental in ensuring that the book included contributions from young scholars of equity planning as well as seasoned professionals and scholars. She also played a lead role in facilitating the symposium.

The development of the book spanned the administrations of two deans at the Levin College, and we are grateful to both former Dean Ned Hill and current Dean Roland Anglin for supporting our work on the book. We are also grateful to our colleague, Molly Schnoke of the Levin College's Forum Program, for organizing the symposium that brought all of the authors together to discuss the theme and structure for the book. We were fortunate to have research and technical help from three outstanding graduate assistants in the Center for Community Planning and Development at Levin College during the two and a half years we worked on this book—Joyce P. Huang, Nicholas Downer, and Liam Robinson. Both Joyce and Nick are now working as equity planners in Cleveland.

Finally, we acknowledge all of the planners, philanthropists, community development professionals, elected public servants, and community activists who work every day as advocates for higher quality places and greater equity for those who are disadvantaged. Recently, their work has become increasingly difficult, but ever more critical, as our nationally elected leaders pursue a path of increasing inequality. However, we remain hopeful. As the authors in this book demonstrate, it is possible to take an alternate path—one that offers more selections to those who have few, if any choices—and to redistribute resources, political power, and participation toward the lower-income disadvantaged populations.

ADVANCING EQUITY
PLANNING NOW

Introduction

Norman Krumholz

This is a book about equity planning, a process by which professional city and regional planners plan the physical city but also, in their day-to-day practice, try to move resources, political power, and participation toward the disadvantaged, lower-income people of their cities and regions. They are called "equity planners" because they seek greater equity among different groups as a result of their work and prioritize the needs of the poor. While the work of most city planners is rarely consciously redistributive, equity planners conceive their potential contributions in broad social and economic terms. They try to provide the poor with more resources and some countervailing power that, like universal suffrage and majority rule, create a more equal and just democratic society.

Many observers place the birth of equity planning in the 1960s when crowds in the streets of American cities protested the demolitions and displacements of urban renewal and highway programs. These traumatic events, and the antiwar and civil rights movements which occurred at about the same time, challenged the belief in top-down planning by value-free experts and demanded a more socially involved process. The events of the 1960s provided great support for equity planning, but the practice actually had its roots in the nineteenth-century industrial city.

History

It was during the Progressive Era (1880–1915) when the respectable urban bourgeois discovered the slum city beneath their urban world. The larger cities, centers of manufacturing and distribution, had grown explosively through immigration without proper planning or regulation. They had become choked with slums that had become breeding grounds for crime, disease, and human misery. Progressive leaders believed that such conditions could be corrected by modern housing and health planning.

The settlement house movement was one of their first efforts at neighborhood improvement. In the immigrant neighborhoods of dozens of major cities settlement houses, such as Hull House in Chicago and Henry Street Settlement in New York City, were established. The settlement house workers were not city planners, but their advocacy for better housing, larger parks, and other improvements in the slums helped provide the needed reform that underpinned the nascent city planning profession.

Some of the Progressive Era reformers carried their reform work into the New Deal. For example, Mary Kingsbury Simkhovitch helped establish Greenwich House in New York City at the turn of the last century; during the 1930s, she helped draft the Wagner-Steagall Housing Act of 1937 that provided for the first federal public housing. Many early Progressive Era leaders were strongly impressed by the ideas of the Englishman Ebenezer Howard. Howard, who loathed the industrial city, proposed a scheme of land development into a regional pattern of small, self-contained cities. These "garden cities" would enjoy all the advantages of the core city—including nearby jobs, industry, and social opportunities—while also enjoying the opportunities of the countryside—such as gardens, fresh air, and the common ownership of land. Dozens of new towns, built on Howard's model of the garden city (only without the common ownership of land), were built in the United Kingdom in the twentieth century.

Other early planners also sought improved housing and egalitarian models of city development. Frederick Law Olmsted proposed the building of urban parks so that the poor—as well as the rich—might have a rural-like landscape to escape from urban life. Patrick Geddes, a Scottish biologist, drew up dozens of town plans in India and elsewhere based on a cooperative model of city evolution. Frank Lloyd Wright, who was bitterly opposed to socialism, still offered each resident of his low-density Broadacre City scheme an acre of land, a house, and at least one car.

Following the ideas of Ebenezer Howard and other planners, a small group of American visionaries formed in 1923 to plan entire regions to achieve social objectives. The Regional Planning Association of America (RPAA) expounded their vision of small self-sufficient communities scattered throughout regions in ecological balance with rich natural resources. In the 1930s their ideas on regional planning and environmental conservation led to the Tennessee Valley Authority, the Civilian Conservation Corps, and the fourteen-state Appalachian Trail. Other important reformers and equity planners during the New Deal of the 1930s included Rexford Tugwell and his Resettlement Administration, which built the three Greenbelt Towns patterned after Howard's garden cities, and the planners of the National Resources Planning Board, which is America's first effort at national planning.

The civil rights revolution of the 1950s and 1960s provided outstanding examples of organization, struggle, heroism, and ultimate achievement in the face of the bitter resistance determined to hold onto three hundred years of subjugation and racial discrimination. The victories of the civil rights revolution continue to serve as a model for equity planning and for all other efforts at progressive reform.

Reformers were also active on the labor front with aggressive organizing and frequent strikes among low-paid workers in the garment and other industries. These great labor battles included the 1886 Bay View Massacre in Wisconsin, the 1892 Homestead strike in Pittsburgh, and the 1914 Ludlow Massacre in Colorado. Many of these labor actions ended in violent defeat for the workers; yet the defeats, in their very brutality, forged a sense of solidarity that eventually produced great labor victories, such as the eight-hour workday enshrined into federal law during the Depression and the passage of the 1935 National Labor Relations Act (also known as the Wagner Act) that guarantees the right to strike and remains labor's greatest means of leverage. The same year the American Federation of Labor fully chartered A. Philip Randolph's Brotherhood of Sleeping Car Porters, a black union. By the mid-1950s, more than a third of all American workers belonged to a union; they were instrumental in creating the middle class while helping to save our society from individual materialism and the threat of political oligarchy.

More recent examples of equity planning include Paul Davidoff, a lawyer, planner, and educator who has made the most substantial contribution to the theory and practice of equity (or advocacy) planning. Davidoff urged the preparation of alternative plans for all groups holding special values about their communities' future. Using legal analogies, the merits of these alternative plans were to be debated so that the best plan emerged from the debate. Davidoff's ideas on planning theory and practice were taken up by planning practitioners and educators with strong, cumulative effects.

In the 1960s, President Lyndon Johnson expanded the government role in social welfare from education to health care and economic opportunity. In the process, Johnson's War on Poverty essentially reassigned responsibility for the poor from mainstream planning to the growing subfield of community development. The conservative reaction from the Reagan Revolution of the 1980s resulted in the virtual abandonment of the poor. In response, planners mobilized.

Across many planning subfields there was an emerging consciousness of how existing power structures affected the poor, as well as a sense of obligation to incorporate the poor into planning. A social equity agenda became embedded into many plans, policies, and programs.

By the 2000s, the community development movement of the 1960s had matured into a community development industry, with support for community development corporations coming from the federal government, banks, foundations, and other members of the corporate establishment. The new generation focused on building assets for the poor, developing mixed-income housing, revitalizing commercial corridors, and negotiating Community Benefits Agreements (CBAs) with developers active in their neighborhoods. Over the length of its history, equity planning has expanded; more and more planners have adopted these approaches because they believe that planning along these lines holds the promise of better lives for the most troubled residents of their cities.

This book reframes the traditional planning debates to inform decisions that affect city residents. It illustrates a variety of techniques and managerial protocols for the planning profession. It challenges not only the ideologies that underlie planning decisions but also the application of those ideologies under various political, social, and economic conditions. It is a guide for managing and balancing the planning process toward more equitable outcomes.

Despite periodic glimmers of successful equity planning, like the low-income housing inclusionary zoning ordinance in Montgomery County (Maryland), the tax-sharing scheme in the Twin Cities of Minneapolis and St. Paul, and Portland, Oregon's environment-preserving land-use and transportation plans, planning in U.S. cities has focused on growth. For decades, academics and journalists have described cities as relentlessly driven to favor the better-off over the poor, thus contributing to the impoverishment of people and neighborhoods, neglect of infrastructure (except in downtown areas), and reductions of essential neighborhood services. Cities, it is said, must respond this way because of the dialectics of growth and the constant need for new jobs and taxes. As a result, cities have usually responded to declines and recessions by attempting to stimulate new investment and developing heavily subsidized real-estate projects in downtown areas. On the ground, "trickle down" was supported by such federal programs as urban renewal, urban development action grants, and empowerment zones. The politicians and civic leaders implementing these plans hoped that the benefits of their efforts would somehow "trickle down" to those in the lower reaches.

To an extent, these efforts have been successful; new hotels, office buildings, convention centers, and stadiums have been built, and city skylines have been redesigned. But the benefits have not "trickled down"; that is, they have not improved poor neighborhoods or reduced poverty, unemployment, or dependency.

In fact, the less-advantaged city residents must now endure a sharply lower quality of life than that which is enjoyed by most Americans. In the face of power, the powerless are removed or neglected.

The relative lack of interest by many city planners in these tragic social-equity issues has led scholars to rhetorically wonder: "Do planners hate the poor? . . . Despite the idealistic rationales for planners' actions, the lure of building large projects seems irresistible no matter what the cost in human suffering" (Teitz and Chapple 2013). Planners have a good reason to be interested in building large projects; after all, cities need investment, jobs, and taxes. But as professionals involved in building better cities, planners also have a good reason to look up and down the economic ladder. Economic stratification and the rise of the super-rich class threatens our mobility, our economy, and our democracy. Americans are growing increasingly separated from each other along class lines in virtually all aspects of life: where they are born, where they grow up, where they go to school, who they marry, what their children do, how long they live, and how they die. Building a national and local community based on fairness and mutual obligations is virtually impossible when Americans have so little shared experience.

An alternative approach to the problems of the central city and the "trickle down" approach is equity planning—a reorientation of physical planning that places equity at its heart. Instead of aiming for "trickle down" effects, this policy directs planning and program benefits directly to the deprived residents of the city. This approach was pioneered by official planners in Cleveland in the 1970s, and variations of the same theme have been documented in Chicago, Jersey City, Santa Monica, and other cities. In these cities, planners have pressed for broader citizen participation, regional fair-share plans for low-income housing, rent control, transit accessibility, and other measures to aid poor and working-class residents.

Planners are also turning to Community Benefits Agreements (CBAs). CBAs are legally binding contracts between two or more private-sector parties—a developer and a community-labor coalition, for example—to ensure that an economic development project benefits vulnerable community residents as well as the developer. CBAs usually focus on the issue of jobs; first-source hiring provisions are written into the contract. CBAs also typically focus on the quality of jobs, often including requirements that many of the jobs pay a certain wage level and provide for health care. If the project involves the demolition of housing, CBAs may require the developer to create affordable housing or contribute to an affordable housing corporation. Los Angeles, New York City, and Denver are three of many cities that are promoting CBAs in order to broaden the number of groups benefiting from redevelopment.

Two Examples of Equity Planning: Cleveland and Chicago

Cleveland

From 1969 to 1979, the Cleveland City Planning Commission worked in a highly visible way to achieve equity objectives. During this period, advocacy planning became less of a hortatory theory and more of a tangible effort undertaken within the political system and directed toward and achieving real ends. The Cleveland planners set out their overarching goal for equity planning in their Policy Planning Report of 1975. It directed the planning commission's efforts to one simply stated goal: equity requires that locally responsible government institutions give priority to promotion of a wider range of choices for those Cleveland residents who have few if any choices (Krumholz et al. 1975, Krumholz 1982). The planners also discussed five clarifying points. First, the goal was to provide as wide a range of alternatives and opportunities as possible, leaving individuals free to define their own needs and priorities. Second, the goal called for a more equitable society, not merely a more efficient political or economic system; efficiency was important but given a secondary role. Third, the goal focused on the crucial role played by legal, political, social, and economic institutions in promoting and sustaining inequities and urged reform in these institutions. Fourth, the goal was to direct and guide all the efforts of the commission staff, identifying those issues which took priority and asking the question, "who benefits and who pays?" in all aspects of the staff's analytical framework. Fifth, the staff was not seeking a consensus; instead, they were seeking to identify the usually opposing interests between the more and less favored and keeping the consequences of inequitable decisions for the future of Cleveland before decision makers.

The planners justified the selection of their equity-oriented goal by appeals to tradition, citing religious and political figures throughout the ages who called for helping the poor and distressed; by reason, citing the work of philosopher John Rawls (1974), who argued to have the kind of society that free and rational people would establish to protect their own self-interest; and by necessity, citing the many inequalities in income and opportunity that separated the people of Cleveland from those of the suburbs, region, and nation.

In carrying out their work, the planners realized that their agency was a weak platform to call for reform. Accordingly, they adopted a number of strategies, including coalition building, leaking, and framing, to move their agenda forward. They created or joined coalitions wherever they could with planners who agreed with them in other agencies, with like-minded politicians, with foundation officials, and especially with community organizations. For example, they joined an antihighway coalition, which included staff planners from the regional agency who quietly disagreed with their own board's support of the highway, to stop a proposed freeway. They joined a business-based coalition to lobby progressive tax-foreclosure changes through the Ohio legislature. They joined an environmental coalition to facilitate the transfer of Cleveland's run-down lakefront parks to the Ohio Department of Natural Resources. Cleveland's planners also leaked information to the press to clarify their policies and to curry favor. Leaking information is regarded in some quarters as unethical, but it is widespread at all levels of government. Other leaks were used to discredit or hurt rivals in the public sphere or to serve as trial balloons to test the popularity of an idea. A significant leak can get a story onto the front page and therefore strengthen a mayor's (or a planner's) agenda.

Properly framing an issue as positive or negative is one of the most important keys to a planner's power. Cleveland's planners tried to be careful of their audience's background and interests during presentations. When opposing a taxpayer-funded sports stadium, for example, it was never "build the stadium or lose the team"; it was "here is the impact of the stadium expenditure on the essential needs of the neighborhoods." When proposing the expansion of the city-owned electric power company, it was never "power to the people," but "this is a good business proposition that will produce lower rates, jobs, and taxes."

In the ten years of the equity planning experiment during which three different mayors presided, the efforts of Cleveland's planners resulted in thousands of units of new public housing in the city. They also resulted in successful and progressive changes in Ohio's property laws, improvements in public service delivery, enhancement of transit services to the transit-dependent population of the city, the rescue of lakefront parks, and many other improvements.

As an example of their work with community organizations, the planners worked closely with the Commission on Catholic Community Action, helping nurture into existence and providing support for nine neighborhood-based advocacy groups. These groups later transformed themselves into a number of community development corporations (CDCs) that now cover the entire city and work to improve poor neighborhoods abandoned by the private market. Many of these CDCs, often staffed by trained city planners, have made dramatic differences in reversing declines in many inner-city neighborhoods. In support of these CDCs, the professional planning staff broadly defined its role to include providing advocates for the poor with data, analysis, and strategies. They provided CDCs with data not only to support anti-redlining campaigns, but also to challenge under the Community Reinvestment Act banks closing branches in poor neighborhoods and "redlining" parts of the city. They conducted research and wrote reports on such issues as subprime lending that they turned over to the CDCs for protest actions. In what might be called "entrepreneurial networking," Cleveland's planners forged links, built alliances, and cooperated with and strengthened local advocacy groups without worrying about their right to do so.

The planners also developed a four-point work program to help Cleveland (and other cities) to provide a reasonable level of services even as fiscal resources shrink.

1. Imposition of restraints: Don't buy every proposal for large-scale redevelopment, and be certain the ones you buy offer a sure prospect of benefits for the maximum possible number of residents and neighborhoods;
2. Creative investments: make the investments needed to keep current physical assets in good repair, to help existing systems work more efficiently, and to leverage public funds to achieve these goals;
3. Constructive shrinkage of responsibilities: identify city responsibilities, such as public transit and lakefront parks, that states and metropolitan regions can not only take over but also find it in their self-interest to do so;
4. Build strong community organizations: these organizations should be fostered as useful allies to emphasize their neighborhoods' needs. They should also bring a skeptical eye to politically appealing but expensive proposals for new investment that are based on unreasonable growth assumptions.

Chicago

During the 1980s, Chicago adopted a model of equity planning in its economic development and planning departments, under the leadership of Robert Mier and some of his colleagues from the University of Illinois at Chicago. Mier and his associates helped build the political coalition of Latinos and blacks that elected Harold Washington as the city's first black mayor in 1982. Mayor Washington then hired them into executive positions in City Hall where they explicitly included "redistributive and social justice goals within the government's policy planning and implementation framework" (Giloth 2007, Clavel 1991). They also involved themselves in extensive interaction between city hall and the neighborhoods, broadening the base of political support as well as diversifying decision making. And they reflected on their experiences and wrote thoughtfully about them (Mier 1993).

Mier, who served as commissioner of economic development, and his associates wrote the "Chicago Economic Development Plan" that proposed to use the city's tax incentives, public financing, and infrastructure improvements to generate jobs for Chicago residents, with emphasis on unemployed residents. Specific hiring targets were set for minority and female employment; 60 percent of the city's purchasing was directed to Chicago businesses, 25 percent was for minority and female-owned firms. Job-generating manufacturing facilities were to be protected by a special zoning provision from conversion into residential condominiums.

The plan also proposed to encourage a model of balanced and "linked" growth between downtown Chicago and the city's neighborhoods. It offered public support to private developers interested in building projects in "strong" market areas of the city, but only if they would agree to contribute to a low-income housing trust fund or otherwise assist neighborhood-based community development corporations to build projects in "weaker" areas.

Cleveland and Chicago represent two cities that pioneered the development of equity planning and accomplished important improvements in their communities. At the same time, it is important to point out that significant problems remain. Focusing on Cleveland, one must conclude that while equity planning provided some important and tangible support for low- and moderate-income people in the city, it was not enough to overcome industrial decline, racial segregation, poverty, and the collapse of the housing and financial markets that began in 2007. By most measures, the city and its people continued to be troubled. Population continues its downward trend, dropping to 396,000 in 2010—a figure almost equal to the city's population in 1900; a majority of its residents are minority group members. Cleveland is ranked the fifth most racially segregated. while the city's poverty rate is second highest behind only Detroit in the United States. Racial disparities continue to be troubling; the median family income of white families in Cuyahoga County was $48,768 in 2010 while the median income for black families was $31,088. Regional efforts to control growth and equalize tax burdens have been weak, with the five-county metropolitan planning organization confining its activities to transportation and environmental studies. No agency, local or regional, has addressed the severe housing, job-related, or income-related problems of concentrated poverty or racial segregation. Equity planning, then, has been a limited means of addressing some of the city's problems while other issues like poverty and race have not been seriously addressed.

This is not a criticism of planning. No urban planners, no matter how expert their practice, can reverse industrial decline or change the political economy of their cities. Only broad social and political movements can accomplish that. But urban planners can make a substantial difference in the quality of life of their cities if they focus less on large-scale downtown redevelopment projects like convention centers, stadiums, and the like and more on fixing the basics—safe streets, good schools, fair taxes, efficient services—and giving highest priority to improving the lives of their poor and near-poor residents who make up a larger and larger proportion of their population. This is not a radical proposal. It is simply providing appropriate service with regard to the reality of conditions in the city and the inherently exploitative nature of the American metropolitan development process, which sorts out people by economic class and consigns the poorest and darkest to the central city or first-ring suburbs. On a more pragmatic level, it is acceptance of the fact that until the social and economic problems of the poor are abated, older industrial cities are not going to attract significant amounts of new private investment.

While more and more cities and agencies seem to be embracing the principals of equity planning, and while the practices of equity planning are slowly being absorbed and adopted by official planning agencies, equity planning is becoming the prime focus of many of the new nonprofit community-based groups that are multiplying rapidly and are set to expand greatly in the future. These groups represent urban planning activity outside official planning agencies. They have been strengthened by civil rights laws and other changes in state and federal legislation as well as new regulations over the past fifty years. They include neighborhood-based community development organizations, public interest research groups, organizations concerned with the environment, groups focused on food accessibility and workforce development, and many other groups. They also include philanthropy from community and private foundations with public interest agendas. Most of these organizations employ urban planners as members of their staffs and follow basic equity planning principles in their work including problem identification, data collection and analysis, and policy recommendations. They reflect a deepening of consciousness regarding social-equity issues and are creating new opportunities for equity planning.

This book makes the case that urban planners have a unique professional responsibility to be a more powerful voice for equity in decision making. From its inception, the rise of modern urban planning was a reformist project motivated by the need to correct the evils of the industrial city. Planners are uniquely positioned to gather and synthesize relevant information from often-competing actors and perspectives to frame conclusions and recommendations for decision makers. Using real-world examples, our contributors seek to influence today's practicing planners as well as the educators who are preparing the planners of the future. Hopefully, this book will inspire these present and future planners and inform politicians and those concerned with social change by demonstrating how planners have worked to support equitable outcomes in cases around the country. In these cases, our contributors, many of them practicing planners, have used their understanding of urban and regional structures and processes to address the pressing issues of our times—poverty, environmental deterioration, the lack of employment opportunities, the need to invest in infrastructure, the looming crisis of an aging population, and other crucially important matters. This book demonstrates how, at a time of impoverished governments, faltering economies, and federal neglect, planners have been freer to build alliances with collaborating organizations and propose their own equitable solutions. Everyone is looking for workable proposals that can make the most of the resources that can be tapped.

There is a particularly urgent need for equity planning at the present time given the rising concerns about issues ranging from increasing income inequality to global warming. Issues of equity, race, inclusion, participation, ownership, and access remain unresolved in many communities around the world. The persistence of injustice is especially evident in the world's cities—dramatic inequality, unequal environmental burdens, and uneven access to opportunity—and demands a continued search for ideas and solutions. In the United States, inequality of income, wealth, and opportunity is very high compared to that in other developed democracies and appears to be growing. Until recently, the dominant neoliberal economic belief was that a rising tide would lift all boats and that income disparities would eventually stabilize without significant policy changes. But this belief was shaken by the recent global economic crisis, which began in 2008, and it is widely feared that economic forces and absent regulation by the federal government will concentrate more and more wealth into fewer and fewer hands, thereby stifling class mobility and leading to oligarchy.

The reaction has been growing slowly. The "Occupy Wall Street" movement in New York and in dozens of other U.S. cities and around the world shone a spotlight on the huge increase in wealth and income enjoyed by the top 1 percent of the population, while incomes for the remaining 99 percent stagnated. Our "Gini Coefficient,"[1] which separates the rich and the poor, is comparable to that of China, but the United States is a large, developed economy, while China is a developing country where huge gaps inevitably rise between rich and poor. Thomas Piketty's book *Capital in the Twenty-First Century* became an unlikely best seller. The theme of inequality of income and opportunity helped Massachusetts Senator Elizabeth Warren defeat her incumbent rival in 2014, and inequality was a powerful plank in the Democratic platform in the 2016 presidential election. Taken all together, "inequality," with its fears of stagnation for the 99 percent and of limited class mobility and democracy, is and will continue to be a major concern for the future.

Dozens of new books and hundreds of articles on this theme have been printed in the last few years. By offering a range of lessons and innovations in planning theory and practice, this book hopes to make a uniquely important contribution to the inequality/opportunity discussion. It can be a discursive tool that planners and policy makers can use to more effectively advance equity in the political arena. At the same time, it may help support the thesis that economic restructuring and globalization, without regulation to mitigate negative effects, inevitably results in ratcheting down the government's role in social safety net programs, low-income housing, and social equality. It may also encourage progressive planners to embed policies that promote greater equity into comprehensive land-use plans, require regional "fair-share" affordable housing programs, and use regional transportation plans and programs to connect inner-city poor to suburban housing and job opportunities.

Organizing the Book

A mix of planning scholars and practitioners were selected as contributors. They have different perspectives, ages, disciplines, and races, yet all have an interest in planning and policy issues to promote social equity. Some authors are recognized senior scholars in their fields, while some are emerging new voices with fresh ideas. Each author was asked to write a chapter about the practical application of equity planning in his or her area of expertise. Authors were asked to stress how equity planning must speak to all levels of government. They were also asked to take into consideration interconnections and interdependencies among disciplines as well as the intended and unintended consequences of public decisions and the fundamental question in equity planning: who benefits and who pays?

All authors, as well as thirty-five Cleveland-area planning and policy professionals, were invited to a symposium at the Levin College of Urban Affairs, Cleveland State University in November 2015, where the authors presented their chapters, discussed the concept of equity planning as it related to their specific areas of expertise and to the themes of the book, shared feedback, and garnered insights to strengthen their chapters. Each chapter was then subject to rigorous review and editing.

The chapters in this book were written to serve contemporary urban policy and planning practitioners as well as students and professors. The book is divided into four sections, three of which reflect the local, regional, and national context for equity planning. It concludes with a look to the future, including innovations in the teaching and practice of equity planning.

The first section presents three personal narratives from academics and practitioners who have woven equity planning into their work on local plans and programs. Lisa Bates, an academic with one foot in the academy and one foot in the community, describes her work in Portland, Oregon, where planning for growth has specifically aimed to minimize displacement. Even in relatively enlightened

Portland, Bates points out the difficulty of fully including minority voices and how to make those voices resonate. Her keen analysis of the process provides insights into the successes and setbacks as well as effective strategies for building coalitions that can hold planners accountable for equity goals in a rapidly gentrifying city. Bates describes the inside-outside game of outsider advocates prodding professional planners to adopt city policies that promote equity.

Mark McDermott, an experienced housing and community development professional, offers a personal reflection on building the principles of equity planning into programs for neighborhood change in Cleveland. He chronicles the rise of the community development movement in Cleveland and nationally, illustrating how the basic concepts of equity planning greatly influenced this movement, which grew out of the closely related civil rights movement and community organizing in the 1960s and 1970s. As the industry evolved, organizers became community developers—community being the operative word as they worked with and for neighborhood residents to offer better choices to those who had been left behind by systems that perpetuate poverty. The evolution of the industry was supported by local government, philanthropic, and faith leaders—a strong coalition of advocates and funders. Using a combination of newly passed civil rights laws, regulations, and coercion, they gained the support and eventually the respect and involvement of the banking and corporate community.

The final chapter in this section is by Majora Carter, a long-time resident/activist and nonprofit real estate developer. Carter uses the lessons she learned after returning to her childhood home, the South Bronx, to make the case that it is possible for neighborhoods to regenerate without displacement. She offers an example of a successful struggle to achieve environmental equity in a troubled neighborhood, as well as a set of recommendations drawn from her own development experiences of working to benefit existing residents and to attract new residents. Her approach to managing neighborhood change involves sharing the benefits of increasing property values with long-time neighborhood residents. Like Bates and McDermott, she talks about the importance of involving neighborhood residents in decisions and giving them control of land-use decisions so that neighborhood amenities and services meet the needs of a range of income groups and promote economic diversity.

The second section addresses equity planning in the regional context. Chris Benner and Manuel Pastor make the case that a more regional approach to equity panning is needed. In their chapter, "Can We Talk?" they argue that the metropolitan region with its growing income inequality and absence of governmental structures opens up a new space for civic interconnections, governance, and redistribution. The metro level has recently become an area of focus for proponents of equity planning—this is where fundamental land-use patterns are set, where economic clusters are forged, and where they see the greatest potential for redistribution that is the goal of equity-oriented planning. Yet, in many parts of the country, regions are politically fragmented, and that makes it very difficult to effectuate regional change. Their approach centers on creating epistemic communities of shared learning and practice that reach across regions, places, and time frames.

Drawing on a transit-oriented development case study of regional equity planning set in the inner suburban communities of Ferguson and Pagedale, just north of St. Louis, Missouri, Todd Swanstrom stresses the importance of civic engagement in improving the land use surrounding a light-rail station. He argues that in low-income, fragmented suburbs, equity planning must come from outside government to improve the lives of suburban poor. In addition to redistributing resources, equity planners in suburbs may need to invent new institutional and civic structures for delivering those resources to those who need them the most.

The four chapters in the third section of the book discuss matters of social and economic equity in the national policy context; specifically, in the areas of transportation, workforce development, housing, and planning for an aging population. Using concrete examples from the field of transportation planning, Joe Grengs effectively argues for replacing the dominant mobility-based policy framework with an accessibility framework. This relatively new paradigm changes the current focus of transportation planning from speed and mobility to improvements that help people, especially the disadvantaged, more easily and more quickly reach the destinations they need for jobs, health care, and other social needs. Grengs urges planners to actively seek to redress past injustices and to evaluate transportation improvements within a much wider context of equitable land use and social needs than is current practice. He argues that because social equity analysis in transportation planning is mandated by law, the use of accessibility-based metrics can be used to address not only the *costs* but also who *benefits* from proposed transportation improvements.

Robert Giloth's chapter on workforce and economic development also focuses on improving access for underserved populations—in this case access to good jobs. He makes the case for more equitable workforce objectives that include neighborhood economic development, human capital investment, and manufacturing retention. His chapter traces the trajectory of institutionalizing greater access to employment opportunities from the New Deal through the civil rights movement to plant-closing legislation and includes the early focus of CDCs on job creation, economic self-help, and independence. He criticizes the current mainstream practice of subsidizing real-estate development deals and hoping for some trickling down. Instead, he recommends a new paradigm focusing on rigorous sector analysis, demand-driven workforce training, and strategies focused on long-term, anchor-based civic collaborations. He examines six promising workforce strategies with explicit attention to their scaling potential, sector partnerships, and collective impact.

Patrick Costigan describes why HUD's new Rental Assistance Demonstration (RAD) program aimed at rehabilitating 180,000 dilapidated low-income public housing units was successful. Led quietly by a committed HUD Secretary and a group of skilled planners, RAD removed a number of regulatory restraints, attracted new private sector resources, and outflanked the divisive scrum of hearings, testimony, and Capitol Hill lobbying that usually accompanies such programs. This chapter makes clear the enormous potential impact of a smart, engaged, and caring federal government while not shying away from the political realities of implementing policy change at the federal level.

In the final chapter in this section, Deborah Howe details how unprepared we are for the rapidly growing aging population. She recognizes the scale and importance of this looming issue and provides specific innovative guidelines to help equity planners create complete environments supportive of the elderly. New guidelines include zoning, housing modification, signage, and architectural changes that would make it more possible for the elderly to age in place, if that is their preference. While aging has not traditionally been considered as an equity planning issue, this chapter argues that planners have an obligation to provide more and better choices for people as they age. Howe strongly makes this case and presents several examples of cities and regions that are doing so, including Portland, Oregon, which has made concerted efforts to frame aging as an equity issue.

The final section of the book looks to the future, with suggestions for teaching equity planning along with new tools for the practicing planners. It discusses the probable future of equity planning in an era where planners at all levels are being viewed with increasing skepticism and the values espoused and practiced by equity planners are increasingly sidelined. Yet, city and regional planning continues to attract both bright young students and midcareer professionals who are interested in social equity issues and committed to making the cities of the world more just and sustainable. As Ken Reardon and John Forester point out, these items are best taught through two devices: first, through the concentration of what experts in the field have said and done, and second, through participatory action research projects, where students have an opportunity to work closely with inspired community leaders dedicated to resident-led urban revitalization. Lessons are offered in how to do both most effectively.

Michelle Thompson and Brittany Arceneaux offer a case study of one such participatory planning tool—public participation geographic information services (PPGIS)—and include examples of how and where it has been used most effectively. As a tool for employing "big data" and facilitating neighborhood-level data collection, PPGIS can support community visioning and serve as a neighborhood engagement tool. When used effectively, these "citizen science" tools can give residents a stronger voice in decisions impacting their neighborhoods. Using examples from their own experience, the authors describe ways in which planners working for municipal or university partners can effectively guide this process by providing the necessary training, resources, data, and expertise to residents and/or community groups.

In the final chapter, Norman Krumholz and Kathryn Wertheim Hexter argue that the future of equity planning appears to be bright. The concept of sustainability is now widely accepted by most planning practitioners and students, who are increasingly concerned about the deterioration of the environment, air and water pollution, and rising sea levels. Sustainability is buttressed by "the three Es"— environment, economics, and equity—and urban planners, because of their historical commitment to social change and improving the quality of city life, have a professional responsibility to be a more powerful voice for equity in decision making. Current concerns about income inequality also provide support for a stronger turn toward equity. Finally, taking the long view, an increasingly diverse population offers the hope for more liberal policies in general and more support for equity planning in particular. These generally optimistic forecasts may be temporarily stalled by the election of Donald Trump, his conservative cabinet appointments, and conservative Republican majorities in both houses of Congress. But equity planners can employ a broad range of policies, programs, laws, and tactics, including first and foremost organizing and empowering citizens to improve the livability of their cities.

Hopefully, this volume will provide planning practitioners, students, and scholars with lessons, innovations, and tools to increase the application of equity planning in the future.

NOTES

1. The Gini coefficient is a widely used measure of income inequality. Named after the Italian statistician Corrado Gini, it aggregates the gaps between people's incomes into a single measure. If everyone in a group has the same income, the Gini coefficient is 0; if all income goes to one person, it is 1 (Beddoes 2012).

REFERENCES

Beddoes, Zanny Minton. 2012. "For Richer, for Poorer." *The Economist,* October 13. http://www.economist.com/node/21564414.

Clavel, Pierre. 1991. *Harold Washington and the Neighborhoods: Progressive City Government in Chicago 1983–1987.* New Brunswick: Rutgers University Press.

Giloth, Robert. 2007. "Investing in Equity: Targeting Economic Investment for Neighborhoods and Cities." In *Economic Development in American Cities: The Search for an Equity Agenda*, edited by Michael I.J. Bennett and Robert P. Goloth, 23–50. Albany: State University of New York.

Krumholz, Norman. 1982. "A Retrospective View of Equity Planning Cleveland 1969–1979." *Journal of the American Planning Association* 48 (2): 163–74.

Krumholz, Norman, John H. Linner, and Janice M. Cogger. 1975. "The Cleveland Policy Planning Report." *Journal of the American Institute of Planners* 41 (5): 298–304.

Mier, Robert. 1993. *Social Justice and Local Development Policy.* Newbury Park, CA: Sage.

Rawls, John. 1971. *A Theory of Justice.* New York: Belknap Press.

Teitz, Michael B., and Karen Chapple. 2013. "Planning and Poverty: An Uneasy Relationship." In *Policy, Planning, and People: Promoting Justice in Urban Development*, edited by Naomi Carmon and Susan S. Fainstein. Philadelphia: University of Pennsylvania Press.

Section 1

LOCAL EQUITY PLANNING

1

GROWTH WITHOUT DISPLACEMENT

A Test for Equity Planning in Portland

Lisa K. Bates

Portland, Oregon, is considered a pioneer of regionalism, integrated land-use and transportation planning, and sustainability as a criterion for planning policy. After four decades of land-use planning, Portland has a national and international reputation for urban livability and climate change mitigation. While these successes are laudable, in the past decade Portland's underrepresented and underserved communities have been raising a voice to demand that planners address issues of income and racial inequality. In response to and in collaboration with communities, over the past five years Portland's Bureau of Planning and Sustainability (BPS) has adopted an equity strategy with a racial justice focus.

This chapter traces the evolution of Portland's planning from the Portland Plan—the 2009 citywide strategic plan that first articulated the equity framework—to the ongoing comprehensive land-use plan that addresses equitable development without displacement. These planner-community venues are spaces of both conflict and collaboration. The city's planners and advocates alike recognize the value of this relationship, although it is sometimes challenging. Communities are building their capacity to speak the technical language of planning to demand more from city policymakers and to advocate for equity planning at the planning commission and city council. Planners are gaining the language and analytic approach to develop equity policies. Through relationships with community advocates, planners are more assured of political support for their equity work. The path from setting an equity goal to developing a comprehensive land-use plan and to beginning to implement anti-displacement policies has not been a straight or quick one. However, the learning and reflection that has happened along the way suggests that while it may not have been an optimal path, it may have been a necessary one.

The experience in Portland suggests roles and possibilities for city planners and community advocates seeking to move toward a more just city. Across the United States, cities are taking on the role of policy innovators, and increasingly, leaders recognize equity as one of the major challenges they must address. Many cities are declaring their intentions to address institutional racism and inequalities— from Seattle to Austin, Philadelphia, and Boston. This Portland case study provides lessons learned in the shift, from developing an understanding of the city government's role in perpetuating and undoing inequity to incorporating equity into the everyday and technical decisions and policymaking of city plans.

Inside, Outside, in Between

Portland's turn to address equitable development has involved inside equity planners in the mold of Krumholz (1982), work by Davidoff's (1965) outside advocacy planners, and strategization from "inside activists" (Olsson and Hyssing 2012). Equity planners working for city government are people who are working with a defined goal to benefit those who are least advantaged. Their work, according to the Krumholz model advanced in Cleveland's Policy Plan, includes conducting policy analysis and evaluation on the basis of achieving more choices for those who have few (Krumholz 1982, 172) and encourages the equity planner to be a political actor as well as a technocrat and to engage not only in the arena of the planning commission but also with elected officials. Davidoff's (1965) advocacy planning model places the broader political arena front and center, suggesting that planners work with communities to develop alternative policies and plans that they can argue for, even if the plans are against status quo interests. Advocacy planners would be outside of government, pushing for change. Along this inside-outside continuum is the concept of the "inside activist" (Olsson and Hyssing 2012), the government staffer who openly maintains ties to community advocates. This model suggests that equity work can be advanced through inside activists' brokering interactions with external groups and pushing agendas inside bureaucracies. In the Portland case, all of these models for urban planning's equity work are recognizable.

I have been involved in this work as a member of advisory bodies to the Portland Bureau of Planning and Sustainability; as a consultant researcher developing frameworks for addressing gentrification; as a member of the board of directors of an advocacy organization; as a leader in advocacy planning for the African American community; and generally as an active participant in the growing movement for housing justice in Portland. This chapter represents my own perspectives as well as reflections of colleagues from the equity and advocacy planning communities in Portland—public engagement specialists, neighborhood planners, community-based-organization policy staffers, and others who have been part of the work.

The Challenge of Gentrification as a Test for Equity Planning

In examining the evolution of Portland's equity planning, I focus on the issue of gentrification and displacement as a key instance of the real challenges of implementing an equity focus. Portland was recently named the fastest gentrifying city in America by *Governing* magazine due to its rapidly changing neighborhood housing markets and dramatic racial turnover in the core of the city (Maciag 2015). The challenge of equitable revitalization highlights several critical tensions for equity planners, both inside and outside of government.

Gentrification—defined as rapidly changing housing markets that tend to push out long-time neighborhood residents who have a low income and are often people of color—is an issue that not all agree is a problem. In Portland, the influx of higher-income residents to inner city neighborhoods can be seen as a triumph of the reputation for livability and urban amenities, brought by a planning system that limits regional growth. Neighborhoods have been revitalized, and the city has invested heavily in infrastructure and economic development in what were poor and segregated areas. However, this public investment, occurring after a long history of redlining and exclusion, has disproportionately benefited newcomers to the neighborhoods and harmed long-time residents by failing to incorporate sufficient affordable housing and opportunity for inclusion in economic growth. Portland's African American community has experienced the most severe displacement, with about one-third of the region's Black population having been displaced from their historical homes in northeast Portland in ten years (as calculated by the author). Recent urban renewal efforts have compounded a history of harmful planning—once it was segregation; now it is displacement. Planners working on neighborhood development today face intense distrust and anger about past and current practices that spur gentrification, with recent controversies erupting over new bike lanes and a high-end chain grocery store (Lubitow and Miller 2013). As the region's population grows and in-migrants display a clear preference for living in the city, communities observing the rapid changes in northeast Portland recognize that the wave of revitalization and displacement will continue to push eastward.

Attempts to address gentrification and housing displacement are faced with policy barriers and political challenges. Planners who do want to address equitable development are very limited in their tools. Oregon's land-use planning system embeds goals that include equity considerations in housing and development, other policies, and laws that limit planning responses to inequality. State planning law prohibits unnecessary barriers to housing development, so explicitly exclusionary zoning is not a significant problem. However, planners are hampered by the state's having preempted local governments from using inclusionary zoning tools to require affordable housing in new development—a restriction that was only removed in February 2017. Rent control, which is broadly defined, is prohibited, and that further limits the use of inclusionary housing regulations. These restrictions occurred at the behest of Oregon's real estate industry lobby, which remains powerful in the state legislature. Further policy shortcomings related to housing stability are found in Oregon's and Portland's weak tenant protections. Landlords may evict tenants without cause and with just thirty days' notice to vacate. Changing the context of growth to address development without displacement is also politically difficult. Real estate development interests are a strong political force in cities. Elected leaders who favor Portland's makeover as a hip, sustainable urban mecca are favorable to neighborhood changes; in 2013 the mayor (a former real estate industry lobbyist) commented that he thought gentrification was a "problem of success" and was confronted by community groups over failing to identify any downside to the revitalization of inner Portland (Law 2013).

This legal and policy context explains how the growth pressures in Portland's housing market are resulting in significant housing displacement for low- to moderate-income households, all renters, and communities of color. Planners and policymakers have been limited in what they could do and limited in their focus on the issue, until the work of the Portland Plan—a general plan that created a clear mandate to pursue equity goals, and racial equity in particular. The question of how planners will address gentrification and displacement has become a significant test for whether the equity goal can be made real for communities. The Bureau of Planning and Sustainability (BPS) recognized that its ongoing work needed to address the gentrification issue. BPS adopted several approaches, from trying to bring a technical approach to using an equity lens in development decisions, to a new advisory group system, to working with a community coalition that emerged to take the issue on. Embedding equitable development into planning frameworks has been a long process characterized by both collaboration and conflict between city planning staff and community-based equity planners.

The Equity Turn: Portland Plan Sets New Goals

The adoption of an equity goal for the city of Portland emerged from a planning process that included a collaborative capacity-building effort by city planners and community advocates. Through a planning process, an advisory group worked together to learn and guide the development of the equity goal and work plan. The result of this collaboration was a powerful commitment to equity planning and to the end of racial disparities in particular, including an acknowledgment of the role that the city's planning has played in creating inequitable development outcomes. In doing so, BPS revisited its own historical connections to Norm Krumholz's equity planning model. Ernie Bonner, the first director of planning in Portland, was a protégé of Krumholz's in Cleveland and a key player in the Cleveland Policy Plan.

As of the mid-2000s, despite its increasingly positive national and international reputation for urban planning, Portland's deep inequities were becoming unavoidably obvious. The report, *Communities of Color in Multnomah County: An Unsettling Profile* (Curry-Stevens, Cross-Hemmer, and Coalition of Communities of Color 2010), revealed deep disparities for racial and ethnic minorities in Portland, with gaps in income, education, and health outcomes that are greater than the national average. The city started a major planning process as the discussion about inequality in the region developed.. In 2009, Mayor Sam Adams launched a significant series of public events to begin work on a general plan for the city and its local, county, and regional governmental partners. The Portland Plan was led by the BPS, with planners developing the process and guiding the work of prioritizing and strategizing. The Portland Plan process was extensive—two years of participation by Technical Advisory Groups that represented a wide range of stakeholders in each topic area. The Portland Plan was not originally intended to be an equity plan. However, advocates for a new approach leveraged the opportunity of Portland's culture of extensive public participation in planning activities. This plan would ultimately adopt, as its core lens for all goals and strategies, an equity goal that calls for an end to disparities for communities of color in particular.

The Portland Plan vision is stated below:

> All Portlanders have access to a high-quality education, living wage jobs, safe neighborhoods, basic services, a healthy natural environment, efficient public transit, parks and green spaces, decent housing and healthy food. . . . The benefits of growth and change are equitably shared across our communities. No one community is overly burdened by the region's growth.

Collaborative Learning and Strategy Building

The Technical Advisory Group on Equity, Civic Engagement, and Quality of Life—colloquially known as the Equity TAG—had a unique mix of members. The Equity TAG was a collaborative space with both government staff and community representatives as members (including this author). On the community side, selected representatives had both grounded knowledge of the concerns, experiences, and needs of underrepresented communities and expertise in policies and processes that could address those needs. The government's representatives included those working in civil rights and civic engagement and were prepared to bring deep institutional knowledge of the city and its practices. Jointly, the committee conducted research on best practices, investigating most thoroughly the Seattle Race and Social Justice Initiative as the basis for the equity work in the Portland Plan. Through a group learning process, the committee was able to come to an important agreement on a definition for the concept of institutionalized inequities. The group adopted a local foundation's statement of "systemic policies and practices that, even if they have the appearance of fairness, may, in effect, serve to marginalize some and perpetuate disparities" (NWHF n.d.).

Through this process, the TAG built a new expectation of who was responsible for equity work in the Portland Plan. Rather than the Equity TAG being siloed to address all aspects of disparities, separately from "mainstream" goals, each advisory group would be responsible for addressing critical inequities within its purview. For instance, the economic development group was directed to integrate issues of poverty and community development into its policies and strategies, and the environmental sustainability group, to incorporate environmental justice issues. Equity TAG members from the community side repeatedly exhorted city staff to "do the work"—in other words, to build relationships with experts from relevant communities and to learn about what an equity focus would mean in their policy arena. Planners were being called on to deepen their knowledge and skills to develop policies that would reach the least advantaged Portlanders. Discontinuing the practice that "equity people" would handle all policy and programs that addressed income, racial, and other disparities was a major effort of the Equity TAG.

Upon reflection, Equity TAG members identified three main elements of the Equity TAG's success. First, the TAG group was a space of learning as well as critique and debate. For community representatives, it was an important shift that city staffers understood their presence not only as more than just "giving voice" but also as bringing expertise. In one difficult session, I exclaimed, "this is not a bunch of people you pulled off the Number 4 bus!"—meaning that the community representatives were all experienced and knowledgeable policy and program staff from established organizations, and their knowledge needed to be treated as equally valid to government policy and program staffers' knowledge and not just as part of a general public participation exercise. With TAG members getting onto equal footing in the process of co-creating the equity strategy, we met once a week or more to talk about policy, strategy, and communications. The TAG process of the Portland Plan lasted for well over a year and often involved reiterating and rehashing the goals and strategies.

Second, through the lengthy TAG process, relationships were formed between city staff and community organization staff. Some of the planners working at BPS were emerging as "inside activists"—reliable sources of information and technical assistance for outside advocates. These planners from BPS and related infrastructure bureaus also formed the core of staff who were sharing knowledge and the equity perspective with other planning staff, creating trainings, and trying to build capacity within their planning teams to take up the equity goal. Seeing those staff members take the risk of pushing equity within their institutions built more trust with community members. With frequent contact and relationship building, there emerged a recognition that while city staff and community organizations each face different opportunities and constraints, everyone wanted to do better for the city. The group developed, as one TAG member put it, "a sense of mutual trust that there is a will to do better and a commitment to learning how."

Finally, the community advocates on the Equity TAG were also well placed to continue their advocacy in political venues. Community representatives came from major organizations with ongoing policy campaigns. One member noted that the community organizations who were represented were not putting all their eggs in the basket of the Portland Plan equity advisory group. Community-based organizations were continually hosting public forums, advocating with elected officials, and pushing in the local media for more attention to the need for government to adopt equity goals. This advocacy kept the issue of racial justice alive, not buried in a "technical advisory group" that was not very visible to the public.

Transitioning the Equity Work from Plan Goal to Everyday Practice

As equity planning work transitioned into the routine of city government activities, it became clear that changing institutional practices would be more difficult. The equity work was being widely discussed and celebrated as the city, county, and metro regional governments began to make commitments to equity. These jurisdictions moved to create offices and staff positions to work on equity policy—included "equity lens" budget procedures—and joined the Governing for Racial Equity (GRE) consortium—even hosting the GRE conference in Portland. The city created an Office of Equity and Human Rights to provide the kind of technical support to city bureaus that the Equity TAG did to the planning advisory committees. Setting clear goals was a necessary first step. There were still significant issues of implementation to address. The equity goal directed all bureaus to incorporate equity issues into resource allocation decisions, into program design and evaluation, and into service delivery, within a context of truly inclusive public engagement and a partnership between community and the city. In short, it meant changing the institutions of government in fairly fundamental ways, from the technical work of data analysis to policy alternative generation and asset management strategies. "Doing equity" was in the hands of city staff who were charged with changing their institutional practices in tangible ways—while facing high expectations from community members who had participated in advocating for the equity work. As it turned out, while getting elected officials and bureau directors to commit to the equity goal of dismantling institutionalized racism was tough, it was the incorporation of this goal into the routine practices of policymaking and implementation that was more difficult. Addressing gentrification and displacement in the city was an early, major test of the commitment to equity planning.

The Comp Plan: A Test, an Opportunity, a Miss

Soon after the city adopted the racial equity strategy, BPS had to gear up for another major planning process. The bureau was moving the state-mandated long-range comprehensive land-use plan and the associated zoning code updates. The comprehensive plan (colloquially known as the comp plan) is a land-use plan that governs development for twenty-five years, and its process began in earnest in 2013. This process offered another opportunity to implement the equity goal and lay the groundwork for more inclusive growth and development. As the comp plan started, Portland was experiencing a housing boom. Rental vacancy rates were extremely low, and there was a visible increase in homelessness in the central city. Community organizations were protesting urban renewal activities that were adding more fuel to an already hot market. The Portland Plan had recognized gentrification and displacement as major community concerns. Goals in the plan provided new focus on balancing neighborhood revitalization with the ability of residents to stay in place—recognizing that "healthy, connected neighborhoods" were not achieved if they excluded people. Furthermore, the plan's language acknowledged that gentrification was creating distrust of local government:

Portland Plan: Gentrification and displacement, whether the result of large infrastructure investments or the cumulative effect of smaller investments, have disrupted communities and resulted in serious questions about the motivations behind government investments in Portland. Today's challenge is to figure out how to provide all Portlanders with quality of life and other improvements and programs without the negative consequences of gentrification and displacement, all while improving trust and confidence in local government. (City of Portland, n.d.)

Addressing gentrification and creating a comprehensive plan that addressed housing affordability and community displacement became a moment of opportunity for planners to genuinely address an equity challenge with the traditional tools of planning policy.

Traditional comprehensive land-use plans have been recognized as a development framework that codifies and maintains segregation and inequality. They are highly technical documents that are guided by legal requirements that are often very obscure for nonplanners. In 1968, the Chicago Urban League evaluated the equity dimensions of that city's comp plan, concluding that "one of its major functions in helping to eradicate racism would be to make a start at unraveling the racial mysteries of urban planning" (Berry and Stafford 1968). The equity planning movement insists that all of the dimensions of land-use and transportation planning covered in a traditional comp plan are part of the planning scope for the least advantaged; this is in direct conflict with other powerful messages that planning can't or shouldn't do anything to stop gentrification. Actors in real estate and economic development prefer a status quo of limited involvement in restraining their redevelopment plans, unless it is to assist with public investments in infrastructure. Organized neighborhood participation often has NIMBY (Not in My Backyard) attitudes toward affordable housing. Planners who want to address equity issues in neighborhood change face these political issues on top of the challenges of addressing affordable housing and community preservation through the specific tools of land use.

Indeed, in the first major draft of Portland's comp plan, the BPS planners didn't manage to incorporate an equity component with respect to gentrification. With a new participation process and little focus on the equity frameworks of the Portland Plan or the Fair Housing Act, policies for housing, neighborhood character, and new development were developed without sufficient attention to racial justice. The draft comp plan reflected a business-as-usual model for market-led development, with no particular attention to the outcomes of housing displacement or evidence that equity impact assessments had been considered. The equity goal was referenced, but it seemed as if it would not be made real. How did this concept, so recently adopted, get lost? A series of decisions about how to implement the work on housing and neighborhood change led to disappointment for the community.

Research Fails to Provide a Foundation

An early step in this work included fleshing out the concepts described in the Portland Plan. The city contracted with me to develop research on assessing gentrification in Portland's neighborhoods and to propose a framework for addressing the potential for public investments to cause community displacement. As a former TAG co-chair who has experience of a learning collaborative, my focus was on bringing staff in BPS and other city bureaus to a shared understanding of what gentrification is and recommending cross-bureau coordination to avoid unintended consequences of policy. The report also provided vignettes of displacement experiences to describe the city's role in either fomenting or mitigating the potential harms to underserved communities when neighborhoods change rapidly. I argued that the issue of gentrification was a critical challenge for equity, and that planners needed to understand it as highly contentious—taking careful attention of the politics involving real estate interests, racial tensions, and the historical practices of the city's own redevelopment agency. I presented the concept of equitable development as a framework that must include both affordable housing and economic opportunities in neighborhood planning, particularly when we recognize a neighborhood that has been historically underserved. This work was not apolitical—it frames planners as agents with real responsibility for addressing gentrification. However, planning managers ultimately requested that this report remain a technical report that only suggested questions about prioritizing resources; it did not conclude with recommendations for the bureau to take with respect to policy.

While the study at first received fairly substantial interest in the local press and its methodology continues to be utilized by researchers and policymakers in other cities, its ultimate impact in Portland was limited. While it was certainly discussed and distributed, there was limited engagement by bureau staff in the gentrification study and policy tool-kit development. I completed the study working closely with two planners and an intern, ending with a review and discussion with the chief planner. As a new mayor had come into office, priorities turned elsewhere. Internal equity champions among planners were focused on a Climate Action Plan that was also being developed at BPS. Mayor Charlie Hales, while nominally continuing the equity goals of his predecessor, prioritized police relations and "Black male achievement" as equity issues and did not view urban planning as a key arena for addressing inequitable outcomes in the city. The mayor did not convene the recommended cross-bureau working group to assess how each department contributed to gentrification and to coordinate actions to stem displacement. Indeed, he continued the Portland Development Commission's investment practices that led to increased community conflict. Finally, community groups who had been engaged with the Equity TAG viewed my work as a technical report without clear recommendations and did not pick it up as an advocacy framework. While community advocates protested individual projects—often very vocally—there was little push for an overarching policy framework to address displacement due to growth and development. Without a strong drive to implement overarching anti-gentrification policies, development in the city continued at a rapid pace without including equity provisions like community benefits agreements. Subsidized development in urban renewal areas that did not carry affordable housing requirements, workforce agreements, or other mitigation resources went forward.

New Participation Model Leaves a Vacuum

The comp plan provided a venue to engage with a broader set of planners and to build policy with a legal status under Oregon land-use planning law. The advisory process assembled Policy Expert Groups (PEGs) analogous to the Portland Plan's TAGs, which included staff from planning and other bureaus along with community advocates. These kinds of policy venues, while important for setting the framework for equitable development in Portland, proved more difficult for integrating equity through a collaborative process. The PEG structure proved to be less amenable to foregrounding equity, and community advocates and their planning allies were much less successful in embedding affordable housing and anti-displacement policies in the draft comprehensive plan.

The PEG advisories were differently organized than the single-topic TAGs. The PEGs did not correspond directly to individual policy topics, but were organized around cross-cutting themes, such as Centers and Corridors, Networks, and Health and Environment. There was no specific venue for housing and community development, and gentrification was taken up by several PEGs at different times in the process. While we might have discussed gentrification or affordable housing at any time during the advisory process, those issues were often overshadowed by the other components of the required plan elements.

While the structure of the PEGs in hindsight created difficulty for addressing equitable growth and development, the PEG process was meant to learn from the Equity TAG. The planning managers wanted to build on the Equity TAG experience; it was important to integrate the equity discussion throughout all their work, making every PEG responsible for addressing equity within its purview. Rather than having a separate Equity PEG to provide oversight, the city staff and community representatives who were known as equity advocates were distributed throughout the PEGs to bring equity perspectives to each work group. The result was a dilution of the equity voice. The equity planning leaders in each group were numerically small compared to the twenty-five to thirty member PEG makeup, and the leaders did not have a venue for easily comparing across PEGs. While the BPS was relatively enthusiastic in adopting the equity goal, most staff planners had not been part of the Equity TAG's relationship building and did not learn about how government could address equity. There was limited support from staff for directing the PEG discussions to consider equity and race at the center of the discussions.

At first, community equity advocates who had built relationships during the Portland Plan tried to convene on the side, but it was challenging to take time away from their regular work. After a multiyear process for the Portland Plan, continuing to be involved in the comprehensive plan was draining nonprofit capacity, and advocates could not be certain about the results in an unfamiliar policy system. As the comp plan work went deeper into land-use regulation and zoning, many of the Equity TAG members found themselves out of their depths in this rather esoteric policy system. Community-based organization representatives who had ably served on the Equity TAG were not versed in the specifics of Oregon land-use law and zoning code development. The technical and legal matters of Oregon land-use law and code writing were opaque to many who had been able to contribute effectively in the broader strategic plan conversation—we went from having a conversation about transit dependent immigrant communities' mobility needs to looking at multiple versions of results from the Land Use, Transportation, and Air Quality model LUTRAQ; and from talking about root shock and community displacement to buildable lands inventories. Indeed, as the comp plan process wore on, many community-based advocates questioned whether this was a useful vehicle for making change in the city, compared to engaging in the work of other bureaus making investments in the present day. For instance, African American-representing organizations doubted what a future-oriented plan could do to address the already occurring housing displacement and chose to put most of their attention into resource allocations from the Housing Bureau, which directly subsidizes affordable housing.

In contrast, community representatives from the official Neighborhood Association (NA) system have had extensive land-use expertise. Planning bureau staff had the responsibility to respond to the NA community representatives on the PEGs who did not have equity in mind, because the NAs are an officially recognized part of Portland's government. As PEG meetings were open to the public, many residents brought their concerns to meetings. The tone of these meetings was very different from the cooperative learning venue of the Equity TAG. The PEGs for Centers and Corridors and for Residential Compatibility were most involved with discussions on housing—the former on larger scale, multifamily development, and the latter on infill and single-family housing neighborhoods. These meetings were often attended by residents expressing NIMBY (Not in My Backyard) sentiments about new multifamily apartment buildings and rental housing. For these more affluent homeowners, "preserving community character" meant architecture and urban design, not communities of color or displacement prevention. Residents were staking out positions on development, and meetings were more about debating than developing a shared analysis. For low-income and people-of-color advocates, it was difficult to engage communities in attending these meetings due to lack of understanding about the land-use plan.

It is perhaps no surprise then that the draft comprehensive plan did not address housing affordability in the context of displacement and neighborhood change in a very direct way; it also did not strongly link to fair housing, the framework proposed by my study of gentrification and displacement in Portland, or affordable housing plans of the Portland Housing Bureau. The draft was not void of equity issues, but its policy statements and goals were not as focused as the Portland Plan had been. The BPS had made many adaptations to its practices and process in the course of the land-use plan advisory period, but the question of whether it was adapting to deeply embed equity into its bread-and-butter planning work remained open. Internally and in its "expert groups," equity seemed to be getting lost as one among many values. For the community advocates who had worked with planners, the land-use plan remained mystifying, and their advocacy was refocusing on other issues where policy concepts and processes were more legible.

Responding to the Plan Draft: An Opportunity for a Do-Over

As the Portland economy returned to full swing, it became increasingly clear that real estate market pressures were becoming intense in many areas of the city. Gentrification and housing affordability and stability generally became the focus of many community-based organizations, but it wasn't clearly stated in the comprehensive land-use plan draft that was released by BPS. One community organization, Living Cully, produced its own "Not in Cully" advocacy plan to address potential gentrification in Portland's most multicultural neighborhood. Living Cully put together comments on the comprehensive plan draft but had difficulty gaining traction on it as a target. Other community-of-color serving organizations were not engaging with the comp plan.

However, the issue of housing affordability began to be raised as a reason to expand Portland's Urban Growth Boundary, triggering the attention of 1000 Friends of Oregon. The state's land-use advocacy organization, 1000 Friends has been a long-time advocate for more effective planning for affordable housing that is necessary in a system of regional growth controls. They hired an organizer to help build a coalition of community organizations around the issue of housing displacement and provided the legal and policy expertise to bolster proposals. This engagement brought focus to the work of community-based organizations that were fighting redevelopment in their individual neighborhoods, turning to the comp plan as a way to create legal frameworks for equitable development. The coalition, ADPDX (Anti-Displacement Portland), works an inside-outside strategy to develop stronger policy in the comprehensive plan and to build a larger social movement to boost equity planning with political support.

Rebooting Equity Planning through Advocacy

Seizing the opportunity of the public plan draft review period and playing on the history of equity planning at BPS, the ADPDX coalition took on the comp plan to substantially revise the city's approach to population growth and housing development. Their inside-outside game includes elements of equity planning and advocacy planning, with support by inside activists. ADPDX coalition leaders are working intensively with planners and are creating visible moments of advocacy for key decision points in the plan. ADPDX organizations have been able to put their goals into the terms of a land-use plan with the technical assistance of 1000 Friends' staff attorneys, who have extensive experience with Oregon land-use law. ADPDX leaders' and 1000 Friends' attorneys worked with staff planners to redraft major sections of the plan, reiterating questions of legality and of the appropriate boundaries of a comprehensive plan in Oregon. ADPDX has successfully advocated for the plan to take a more aspirational tone in its policy justifications, including more of the vision language from the Portland Plan. The plan had contained clear statements about inclusion and equity in neighborhoods and ensured that the least advantaged communities did not bear burdens without enjoying the benefits of revitalization. Their wins can be attributed to their inside work to bolster equity planning implementation at BPS and to outside advocacy in the political arenas of decisions about the land-use plan. ADPDX has become a successful advocacy planning example, where the community brought its own plan to the table and negotiated its inclusion into official planning documents.

Working Inside to Build Equity

In some ways, the ad hoc working groups that have emerged between ADPDX leaders and city staff are similar to the Equity TAG. ADPDX participants bring policy ideas and practices from other cities; planners try to be transparent about the potential for these strategies in the Portland context and share information about relevant projects outside of the comp plan. There is mutual learning and trust building when staff make information available and the coalition is transparent about their advocacy, and the expertise on both sides is respected. This format of collaboration does include debate and pushback from both sides, but in a tone that is very different from the PEG process—it is oriented toward problem solving, even when there is disagreement about the role of planning regulation in requiring development to address community benefits and burdens. One key strategic decision that helped build the coalition and clarify the equity planning issues was to reframe the discussion from gentrification to displacement. While gentrification is a serious issue in the city, there are many neighborhoods of poor people, renters, and communities of color that are not "hot markets" but simply are underserved by public goods. Of course, these communities are still very vulnerable to housing displacement due to the shortage of affordable units, lack of tenant protections, and unstable employment in a difficult economy. By focusing on displacement and not only gentrification, ADPDX has built a coalition that includes organizations from nongentrifying neighborhoods who were opposed to the gentrification framework on grounds that their low-income neighborhoods would not receive attention. That was a real political challenge for planners who cared about low-income people and communities of color, as equity advocacy seemed to point to two very different kinds of policies and resource allocations. The ADPDX coalition organizer worked to strengthen this cross-racial, multineighborhood alliance around issues of housing instability and displacement. With a lens on displacement, the coalition was able to flourish and the city planners were and are better able to reconcile the common issues of a stable affordable housing supply as the city grows.

Planning staff who were identified as "inside activists" have been open with the coalition's citizen planners, explaining both the process and substance of their decision making on up-zoning, mixed-use zones, and how the plan and future implementation projects will relate to one another. The staff who are officially assigned to liaison with the Neighborhood Association (NA) system recognize the inequities of working with residents who are almost uniformly homeowners with the time and education to engage in the NA. They were often able to provide additional time and information to the organizations representing low-income households and people of color.

Community-based organizations representing disadvantaged and underserved populations grew in their capacity for engaging their issues through the language of planning. In these meetings, community experiences were related in order to discover the possible planning regulatory structures that could address them. The ADPDX organizer has a professional master's degree in urban and regional planning and has served as a sort of interpreter from the everyday language of advocates to the jargon of land use. ADPDX organizations brought policy ideas they were learning about from allies in other cities, and 1000 Friends' attorneys helped to create the Oregon-specific legal language that could implement them. This aspect of the work looked like the classic advocacy planning model—outsiders bringing in policy alternatives with the analysis and legal work to back them up and proposing these plans as substitutes for the existing draft.

Indeed, the six months of renegotiation over the comp plan draft was a space of advocacy that sometimes verged on being antagonistic. I describe this space as a tough collaboration with critical friends. Staff planners sat for many hours with ADPDX member representatives and both city and 1000 Friends' attorneys, hashing out acceptable compromises for this document. These sessions debated questions of how to define "community benefits," how to determine what demands could be considered binding policies as compared to "aspirations," and precisely what the city's obligations are under fair housing law. Finally, the inside work of equity planning was happening in policy development.

Outside Advocacy Persists

At the same time, ADPDX is also deploying an outside strategy of visible advocacy. All of the community's desired changes did not occur through the process of revising policies with planning staff. The coalition was aware that the mayor put little priority on addressing displacement and gentrification and that the Planning and Sustainability Commission (PSC) had heard little about the issue. The coalition strategized to bring attention to the work in order to bolster planners' revisions and seek additional policies. ADPDX targeted individual planning commissioners who are allies on equity, asking them to introduce amendments to the plan when they felt the staff's versions were unsatisfactory. The coalition organizations brought community members to PSC hearings and wore hot pink and party hats to celebrate when those amendments were passed by the commission. As the commission approved the final ADPDX additions to the plan, ADPDX members unveiled a cake and held a public celebration. These events garnered media attention, and housing affordability became the hot topic of the plan.

The activities of ADPDX to build a social movement about housing and displacement have resulted in planning policy changes; however, they have also been met with mixed reactions by planners. After planning staff worked with the coalition on changing the plan policies' language, some were surprised and bothered that coalition members also publicly advocated at the commission. The continued calls to do more could feel like a rebuke after working together to revise policy language, even when staff continued to meet with ADPDX after their internal deadlines for the revised plan. Staff planners also questioned the addition of some specific provisions—particularly those involving extractions from developers such as community benefits agreements—that push at the boundaries of planning law and might be difficult to implement. ADPDX organizers view their public actions as building more political support for planners to do equity work by creating pressure on the elected officials who ultimately determine the direction of the bureau. They argue that planners haven't focused enough on equity goal implementation because they are being diverted to other priorities by the mayor's desire to respond to other constituencies on neighborhood issues, so they need to target his commission and elected officials on city council. They are pressuring planners, but also providing them political support and cover for their equity work. Planners do not necessarily feel this as support.

Finally, an Equity Plan: What Mattered?

The Portland comprehensive plan, as adopted in 2016, contains many of the proposals of the Anti-Displacement coalition. The comp plan policies relating to displacement, housing, and neighborhood development are now significantly stronger for implementing the equity goal. Policies include several areas of work. First, the public participation requirements are deepened to commit to "meaningful participation" by communities most likely to be negatively impacted by development pressures. This targeting of engagement aims to ensure that processes like the Equity TAG get embedded into policymaking so that equity remains at the forefront of new work. Second, the plan states that major investments and development changes require impact assessments on the most vulnerable communities—people of color, low-income households, and renters—that go beyond environmental and traffic studies to describe economic and social impacts for these specific groups. These impact assessments will determine appropriate mitigation efforts to be made by developers or the city.

The ADPDX coalition advocacy has pushed the plan dimensions beyond what planning staff initially felt was appropriate for a land-use plan, by pointing to the expansiveness of Oregon's planning requirements and by arguing that the plan needs to provide a foundation for a long period of time. For example, the proposed plan policies now include statements that the city will pursue regulatory solutions to inclusionary housing at such time as they are permitted by state law, in order to be prepared for changes in statute. By working together with staff planners, the fair housing experts in the coalition have been able to provide education on how fair housing law relates to land-use and infrastructure planning, requiring additional equity analysis and resource allocations that "affirmatively further" desegregation and access to opportunity.

This set of policies reinforces the planners' responsibility of doing technical analysis of equity impacts and allows planners to develop a wider range of programmatic responses to new development code changes and infrastructure investments. These responses include the city's creating community benefits agreements or acting to support community organizations that are pursuing CBAs with private market actors. The broader concept of impact assessment also recognizes that "neighborhood character" is more than historic architecture; it also includes community cohesion, history, and culture for those communities that have experienced segregation and discrimination. Additionally, this new version of the plan prepares Portland to develop and implement policies such as inclusionary zoning and rent control that are preempted by state law. Having an affirmative statement of pursuit of these remedies created a foundation for planners to move quickly with Portland's Housing Bureau to build an industrial zoning policy as soon as the state allowed. ADPDX coalition leaders are continuing to meet with city planners on issues of community benefits agreements, mixed-use zoning, and incentives for affordable housing; they are also advocating for broader changes to the city's housing related policies, such as the end to no-cause evictions.

Through what was like an externally imposed working advisory group between ADPDX and staff planners, both community organizations' and city planners' capacity and technical knowledge to do equity planning has been increased. With the comp plan as guidance, city planners are directed to continue to ask the question of equity through a legally recognized document, which goes beyond the Portland Plan's goal. Krumholz's lesson that planners must always analyze who benefits and who is burdened and must always assess how to provide the greatest opportunity for those who have the least is embedded into the comp plan for housing and neighborhood development issues. Planning bureau staff started to institutionalize this practice in a difficult process—of not just rewriting the plan draft but really rethinking its foundation as an equity document—while under time pressure to complete and adopt the plan and under political pressure from ADPDX. While the path to an equity comprehensive plan was not a smooth or a straight one, it was a trek with significant learning along the way.

The Equity Goal Matters

Obviously, setting equity goals isn't sufficient in and of itself—even when they are announced with great fanfare and political support. Indeed, the Portland experience with equity planning suggests that an external goal announcement that is not built up through the work of planners can even impede the institutional change needed to implement equity plans. During Krumholz's time in Cleveland, staff planners who were already engaged in equity and civil rights built up equity planning work around their technical expertise and values, creating a simply stated goal that encompassed the work to which they had already committed. Planners then disseminated this work into other departments and built organically on opportunities that emerged in policymaking. In Portland, the comprehensive plan process rolled out in a business-as-usual way, with advisory groups that did not reflect the new equity orientation and limited technical assistance for using an equity lens in the work. Community equity advocates realized that political lip service to equity was not the same as real political support for implementing equity goals when real contention over neighborhoods and development was at stake.

Having the equity goal was a critical first step. However, to really do the equity work in an area, there needs to be a constituency that is holding planners accountable and pushing the elected officials to enact new programs and policies. As the city of Portland has already adopted a very clear goal of equity with a lens of racial justice, the coalition was able to present their ideas as emerging from an established consensus. The equity goals and language of the Portland Plan could be repeated as a promise made, with a reminder that the "north star" was racial justice.

It has been important to the equity planning work in Portland for planners not only to recognize that the city's planning has not always supported equitable outcomes but also to commit to the goals of equity and racial justice. There remain challenges with consistently implementing the policy development and analysis practices that center equity questions, and community advocates continue to remind planners of their responsibilities in this area. The leadership in the planning bureau recognizes the need to insist that the equity work gets done internally and also to build the technical knowledge of existing staff, while ensuring that new hires are committed to and knowledgeable about equity planning. New projects implementing aspects of the comp plan, such as new transit line planning and infill housing zoning codes, have equity tasks as key components of the work plans.

Advocacy Planning Matters

Community representatives spent enormous amounts of time in advisory groups and working with planners. However, these processes have not always resulted in strong equity planning work. This mix of inside and outside activities is resulting in a plan development that does more than pay lip service to equity goals; the plan development starts to establish them further into policies. The Anti-Displacement Portland coalition strategized to ensure that inside, collaborative work was bolstered and furthered by outside activism and movement building. Responding to Krumholz's 1982 retrospective on the challenges of Cleveland's plan, Davidoff (1982) suggested that politics be engaged by a coalition that is cross-racial and engages multiple housing equity stakeholders—fair housing, tenants' rights, and neighborhood community development advocates. This coalition is precisely what ADPDX has developed. Through the advocacy work, new communities are connected to the policy systems and language of planning and seeing it as a viable venue for getting equity impacts. This increased engagement from usually underrepresented communities in urban planning is pushing the BPS to develop work that really responds to the most critical issues for underserved communities, rather than one that responds just to the typical growth machine actors and boosters. The coalition is building a much-needed reply to the strong real estate industry lobby that has already so seriously curtailed the ability of planners to make housing policies. It was critical that a mainstream planning advocacy organization like 1000 Friends—best known for its work on farmland and forest protection—stepped up in recognition of affordable housing as a fundamental issue of land-use planning. Realizing that inequity threatens all the region's goals for compact development and climate change mitigation, 1000 Friends brought resources and technical assistance and extended its political influence to a social justice cause. Its involvement amplified the work and built the policy advocacy capacity of smaller, community-based organizations.

The visible public advocacy by grassroots activists connected with equity policy leaders counters the city's more entrenched interests in real estate development. The outside pressure for equity is important for overcoming political inertia. Recognizing that advocates' public displays and actions are part of a productive political process may take time for planners who believe they are already working on equity. City staff have to come to realize that the advocacy was not distracting from the comp plan but was calling attention to how important it is as a policy framework. Staff planners in leadership roles came to the eventual realization that having an outside group calling for and celebrating equity policies provided them with political backing for their work implementing the equity goal. Again, referring to Portland's history was important for accepting this—after all, Portland is the city whose neighborhood activists stopped a freeway in 1974 as part of its grassroots-supported push for planning. That much-celebrated action was crucial to the livability of the city today—and ADPDX advocates argue that their loud calls for equity in 2016 will be viewed as equally important in the future. ADPDX and other community advocacy coalitions continue to keep alive the issues of growth without displacement and racial justice in a redeveloping city. The city's leaders know that there are organizations ready to bring publicity and strong outside advocacy to questions of housing and neighborhood policy. The rise of anti-displacement activism is a visible counterpoint to the lobbying and issue framing of real estate interests. With continual reference to the commitments of the city to "make equity real," community advocates will try to ensure that equity planning is the standard operating procedure in Portland, regardless of national-level politics.

Next Moves for Equity Planning: Cities Lead the Way

As planners who take a long-range view, we know that we are building our cities and regions not only for this moment, but for the long term. Although we are trying to remedy past decisions that led to sprawl, segregation, and unequal investments in communities, we also must address acute problems of housing needs and make sure that our long-term development moves toward greater equity. The case of Portland's evolution toward equity planning from a broad goal to the specifics of a comp plan provides lessons about the challenges and opportunities for building internal and external capacity to address urban growth. Portland's major issues are addressing uneven distributions of costs and benefits from population and economic growth, and the policy details of its comprehensive plan are particularly useful for similar cities. The work of ADPDX and planners to craft a land-use framework that tackles displacement and community cohesion provides ideas for how to bring equity into this arena of planning policy. It also points to methods for discovering "what's the downside" to a booming city by engaging more effectively with external advocates. These process lessons about how to collaborate to learn and shift practices are valuable for planners in a much broader set of urban contexts. Whether the equity challenges arise from growth or decline, planners can develop the processes for those with inside and outside expertise to have the tough collaboration dialogue from which emerges better work.

Municipal planners have to bring the equity goal into all of their routine work of analysis and policy formulation. Equity planning has to become an everyday practice that is always asking who benefits and who is burdened. This work requires forming new habits of inquiry; developing and maintaining data about race, class, and other important factors; and seriously weighting equity outcomes as part of policy formulation and evaluation. Planners also need to be attuned to the advocates representing historically underserved and underrepresented groups so they are aware of persistent and emerging issues. Planning agency staff have to be prepared to translate the sometimes arcane language and process of land use into everyday terms and explain the on-the-ground consequences of plans and regulations.

At the same time, it will be important for cities to institutionalize equity work as standard practice, without as much attention from advocacy groups. These communities of low-income renters, people of color, and immigrants face increasing pressure from the retrenchment of federal funds supporting poor people's needs, intense scrutiny from immigration officials, and other instability brought on by the current political climate. An important way to ensure that these issues are live in planning and policy discussions is to build diverse staffs of planners with a broad range of experiences and identities. City staff who have professional ties to community-based organizations can flag problem areas and provide input from the advocacy perspective. A savvy planning director would seek out staff who can play these roles and value a staff that represents the full range of community experiences. While planners from all backgrounds have a role in equity planning, the lived experience and knowledge of outside organization perspectives of the insider activist staff planner should be viewed as an especial asset. Having an overarching equity goal set from the top is an important feature in supporting a culture of openness that questions dominant paradigms from inside and outside a department; having staff who can forward the case on their own is also important for embedding equity into the technical work of planning.

Addressing the long history of inequality in our cities and regions remains a critical issue for planning, just as it was in Cleveland in 1974. As more urban centers become hot markets with new residents, planners will need to understand how a just city is threatened by gentrification. Taking on the fundamental questions of racial justice and housing and community displacement will require multiple strategies for change and persistence in the face of our past and present contexts. In order to maintain cities as the places where policy innovation can lead to social change, city planners need to continue to build their knowledge, technical capabilities, and political skills.

REFERENCES

Bates, Lisa K. 2013. *Gentrification and Displacement Study: Implementing an Equitable Inclusive Development Strategy in the Context of Gentrification.* Urban Studies and Planning Faculty Publications and Presentations, Paper 83, Portland State University, Portland, OR. http://works.bepress.com/lisa_bates/2.

Berry, Edwin C., and Walter W. Stafford. 1968. *The Racial Aspects of Urban Planning: Critique on the Comprehensive Plan of the City of Chicago.* Chicago Urban League Research Report, Chicago, IL.

City of Portland. 2012. *The Portland Plan,* April, http://www.portlandonline.com /PortlandPlan/index.cfm?c=56527.

Curry-Stevens, A., A. Cross-Hemmer, and Coalition of Communities of Color. 2010. *Communities of Color in Multnomah County: An Unsettling Profile.* Portland, OR: Portland State University.

Davidoff, P. 1965. "Advocacy and Pluralism in Planning," *Journal of the American Institute of Planners* 31 (4): 331–38.

——. 1982. "Comment on 'A Retrospective View of Equity Planning: Cleveland, 1969– 1979,'" *Journal of the American Planning Association* 48 (2): 179–80.

Krumholz, N. 1982. "A Retrospective View of Equity Planning," *Journal of the American Planning Association* 48 (2): 37–41.

Krumholz, N., J.M. Cogger, and J.H. Linner. 1975. "The Cleveland Policy Planning Report," *Journal of the American Institute of Planners* 41 (5): 37–41.

Krumholz, N., and J. Forester. 1990. *Making Equity Planning Work: Leadership in the Public Sector.* Philadelphia: Temple University Press.

Law, Steve. 2013. "Mayor's mind on development," *Portland Tribune,* August 15, http:// portlandtribune.com/pt/9-news/159162-mayors-mind-on-development.

Lubitow, A., and T.R. Miller. 2013. "Contesting Sustainability: Bikes, Race, and Politics in Portlandia," *Environmental Justice* 6 (4): 121–26.

Maciag, Mike. 2015. "Gentrification in America Report," *Governing,* February, http:// www.governing.com/gov-data/census/gentrification-in-cities-governing-report .html.

Northwest Health Foundation (NWHF). n.d. "Our Commitment to Equity." https://www .northwesthealth.org/about/equity/.

Olsson, Jan, and Erik Hysing. 2012. "Theorizing Inside Activism: Understanding Policy-making and Policy Change from Below," *Planning Theory & Practice* 13 (2): 257–73.

Partnership for Racial Equity. n.d. *Racial Equity Strategy Guide.* Portland: Urban League of Portland. https://ulpdx.org/wp-content/uploads/2012/02/RACIAL-EQUITY -STRATEGY-GUIDE-FINAL.pdf.

Portland Housing Bureau. n.d. "Change in African American Population in N/NE Neighborhood Housing Strategy Area 1970–2010," https://www.portlandoregon.gov /phb/65672.

2

THE EVOLUTION OF THE COMMUNITY DEVELOPMENT INDUSTRY

A Practitioner's Perspective

Mark McDermott

The evolution of the affordable housing and neighborhood development industry in Cleveland intertwine over a span of three decades with my own career. This story could be told by any one of dozens of other housing and community development professionals that worked in Cleveland following the principles of equity planning: to provide more choices for those who have few, as set out in the Cleveland Planning Commission's *Cleveland Policy Planning Report* (1975).

In his introduction, Norman Krumholz posits the importance of equity planning activity outside of official planning agencies, including at neighborhood-based community development organizations. This chapter describes such activity as it took place in Cleveland. More specifically, it describes the convergence of the broader social justice movement of the period and the work of Cleveland's equity planners. The work described called forth new iterations and forms of equity planning by both formal and informal institutions. Often, it was the nonprofit community-based organizations described, not official planning agencies, who provided the leadership, the blocking, and the tackling needed to keep the field open to equity principles.

Four key actors played a foundational role in having Cleveland's planning and community development industries make a shift to greater equity for the poor. Cleveland Mayor Carl B. Stokes set the stage by bringing an overall progressive agenda to the city. Norm Krumholz's planning staff then brought what could be possible into focus through its pronouncement of equity planning. The Catholic Commission on Community Action under the Greater Cleveland Diocese enabled the professionalization of community organizing in Cleveland by developing a pipeline of candidates and training and funding them. Finally, local foundations adopted the work as important to the future of the city and provided reliable, multiyear funding.

Thus, the Cleveland of this period provided a rich environment for experimentation with the principles of the 1975 *Cleveland Policy Planning Report* and the implementation of policies and practices built on these principles. It was a time when individual careers in planning, housing, and community development evolved in conjunction with the growth and evolution of the field.

In 1980, when I began my career, neither the HOME Program nor the Low-Income Housing Tax Credit (LIHTC) existed. There were few community development corporations (CDCs). The cadre of skilled nonprofit development professionals was small and mostly self-taught. It was a time for big ideas, incredible entrepreneurism, and future building.

This chapter covers five phases of this CDC work and my career in Cleveland:

1. Strong community organizing (1980–1984);
2. New systems capacity and resources (1984–1988);
3. Growth of the affordable housing industry (1988–1998);
4. Maturing of systems and resources (1998–2008);
5. Toward an integrated agenda (2008–Present).

Over the course of this story I describe the five key lessons I've learned by looking at real and measurable outcomes over the past thirty-five years.

1. An engaged, dual focus on place and people can overcome any particular politics. Focusing on only one of these factors leads to limited results that often set back particular equity agendas.
2. Policy that results in change always results from some type of community organizing—sometimes through conflict, sometimes through collaboration, usually through some combination of the two.
3. Money always matters in achieving change, and how and where it flows is sometimes more important than how much flows.
4. Racism and poverty are intimately intertwined—one cannot legitimately deal with one without dealing with the other.
5. Affordable housing, while a real estate product and now an industry, is an effective platform that enables low-income residents to bring about positive change in their own lives.

Strong Community Organizing, 1980–1984

Cleveland in 1980 was a confusing time for community organizing. George V. Voinovich, a moderate Republican, had just replaced Dennis J. Kucinich as mayor of Cleveland. Kucinich was a self-styled urban populist who garnered support from many progressives; he also alienated much of Cleveland's corporate leadership, which has been well documented (Swanstrom 1985). Yet Kucinich also alienated the growing community organizing movement in Cleveland. His cabinet often refused to meet with neighborhood leaders, and this conflict lead to the mayor banning the leading neighborhood organizations from city hall. Mayor Voinovich, on the other hand, was more conservative and certainly more tied to the corporate community, yet his administration had a strong commitment to the neighborhoods and was generally supportive of neighborhood initiatives.

It was against this background that in 1980, fresh out of college, I was hired as a community organizer by a neighborhood-based community organization. At that time there were eight strong neighborhood-based community organizations in Cleveland, supported by the Catholic Commission on Community Action of the Catholic Diocese of Cleveland (Cunningham 2007, Yin 1998). The commission provided hiring assistance, training, back office support, and a level of political cover. In addition, the organizations were all members of the National People's Action (NPA) of Chicago. As a national membership organization, the NPA was able to provide both training and networking that helped community organizing in Cleveland reach a high level of effectiveness in both tactics and community engagement. Locally, a citywide network of Cleveland's community organizations brought staff and community leadership together from across the city, creating a racially diverse coalition that fought together on a range of neighborhood disinvestment, city service, and poverty issues unlike any time since.

Specifically, they focused on three issues: bank redlining, strategic and equitable expenditure of city resources, and the formation of Cleveland's initial CDCs. The confrontational strategies of Saul Alinsky were used extensively, and their efforts have had lasting impact on Cleveland neighborhoods.

The issue of mortgage and lending redlining by financial institutions across the country is well documented. It was no different in Cleveland than in other older, lower-income, and racially changing cities. At a time when almost all lending institutions were local, it was very common for entire urban neighborhoods to be excluded by implicit policy and explicit practice. With Congress's passage of the Community Reinvestment Act (CRA) in 1979, and the related Home Mortgage Disclosure Act (HMDA) in 1975, community activists were provided with effective tools to confront local redlining. All of the community organizations in the city participated in the newly formed community reinvestment coalition; this coalition quickly became the premier citywide issue coalition while creating the deepest and most enduring outcomes. The coalition combined a variety of strategies over five years, including filing CRA challenges with the Federal Reserve Bank; holding community meetings with banks to create consumer, housing, and commercial investment plans; and, when necessary, disrupting annual shareholder meetings with signs, whistles, and chants. The results were mostly positive and truly set the stage for the investments in CDC-sponsored projects that would take place over the next thirty years. Several banks established their own community development divisions or set up their own CDCs, which exist to this day. And the city of Cleveland adopted one of the first community reinvestment policies in the country, using the leverage of municipal investments to force each bank to set a full range of housing, consumer, and commercial investment goals for Cleveland neighborhoods. The cooperative nature of bank and CDC relationships of the past thirty years has only been possible because of the success of this earlier coalition organizing.

Another long-term organizing success resulted from a similar coalition that focused on the strategic and equitable expenditure of Cleveland's Community Development Block Grant (CDBG) funds. In the early 1980s, the city used its CDBG funds in an unfocused way, primarily for a wide variety of improvements including sidewalks and street repair, while ignoring the new, more community-based CDCs with a stronger housing focus. The citywide coalition pressured the Voinovich administration to expand its investments in affordable housing specifically and neighborhoods in general, by analyzing prior year investments, holding coalition-sponsored meetings in each neighborhood, taking over public hearings, and marching on city hall. This organizing resulted in the adoption of a more strategic and equitable decision-making process by the administration and city council, increased investments in affordable housing, and increased block grant funding for CDCs. Again, it is due to this organizing work of thirty years ago that Cleveland has led the country in support for progressive CDCs, which continues to the present day.

The third long-term outcome for the organizers was the formation of more progressive, community-based, housing-focused CDCs. Prior to the 1980s, there existed a set of what were called local development corporations (LDCs). These organizations were funded by the city, focused on neighborhood commercial development, and had limited engagement in the community. More concerning, very few of these LDCs were located in the predominantly African American neighborhoods of the city's east side. The LDCs lost out when the community-based organizations sponsored or formed another competing set of CDCs—funded by foundations, focused on housing development, intimately engaged with the community, and active in all of Cleveland's neighborhoods, both black and white. These included the Bank on Buckeye, Broadway Area Housing Coalition, Near West Housing Corporation, and several others. These were the groups that partnered with the city, banks, and foundations to create a new affordable housing industry in Cleveland, and they were soon to form the Cleveland Housing Network (CHN), changing the trajectory of many of Cleveland's neighborhoods.

One final historical note on community organizing in Cleveland. As documented in other publications, the era of strong advocacy-based and community-based organizing in Cleveland ended by the mid-1980s. These advocacy-based organizations maintained confrontational tactics as they expanded their agendas to include issues that had additional corporate targets: the banks, utilities, and energy companies. This direction eventually led to the substantial defunding of these organizations by local foundations, a move which fairly quickly led to the demise of most of the organizations. But most of these advocacy organizations spun off CDCs whose development agendas did not include social change, and these CDCs have survived to the present.

New Systems Capacity and Resources, 1984–1988

In 1984 I left community organizing and joined the staff at the Center for Neighborhood Development (CND) at the Levin College of Urban Affairs at Cleveland State University (Simon 2009). Originally funded by two local foundations, CND was set up to provide technical assistance and training to the nascent CDCs and to put them on a sustainable path. Over the next few decades, CND would offer a sterling example of the possibilities of effective neighborhood outreach for a university-based, technical assistance organization.

This period in Cleveland was really about proving the case for CDCs. The city, banks, and foundations were asking questions about the long-term viability of CDCs, the potential impact of investment in CDCs, and whether CDCs in Cleveland could translate meaningful engagement with community residents into meaningful improvements. CND helped provide several outcomes that were crucial to assuring the various funders that the CDCs were well worth their confidence and support.

For one, CND and its partners developed basic training sessions on real estate development, weatherization, and creative financing before such trainings were common in the industry. This training and technical assistance was instrumental in building the expertise of CDC staff, evolving in sophistication as the development models and financing became more complex. CND also provided technical assistance to newer citywide coalitions that succeeded the neighborhood organizing coalitions, including neighborhood safety, weatherization, and development of strategies for dealing with the CRA. These new coalitions used a more collaborative model; yet, when it seemed appropriate, coalition members were not shy to threaten or actually use confrontational approaches based on past successes. This coalition activity resulted in finding new allies and gaining substantial new resources at both the state and city levels. State money flowed for home weatherization programs, and new foundation and city funding was made available for housing development through CDCs.

It was during this period that CHN was founded with the support of CND, the Famicos Foundation, and the Enterprise Foundation (Krumholz 1997, McQuarrie and Krumholz 2011). (The Enterprise Foundation later changed its name to Enterprise Community Partners; it is referred to as Enterprise in this chapter.) The founding organizations of CHN wanted to build on Famicos's small-scale but successful lease-purchase program for low-income buyers. The Famicos model relied solely on CDBG financing to rehabilitate vacant properties and lease them to poor families, while Famicos retained ownership of all properties. CHN believed it could improve the Famicos model and bring it to scale.

It can reasonably be argued that CHN might not have been formed and certainly would have looked very different if not for the capacity that had been developed at the other neighborhood-based CDCs and their interest in expanding the Famicos financial model. The fact is that five other CDCs from across town—the other founding members of CHN—had strong staff expertise and engaged local boards. A strong network between them enabled those CDCs to stand on par with Famicos when expressing their goal to have an equal and participatory role in forming CHN. Most of the executive directors of the five CDCs had in fact been community organizers from across the city, and the informal network they created was a direct outgrowth of the earlier community organizing coalition. The story of CHN's creation embodied the trust that had developed among very different communities and helped to launch this next phase of improving Cleveland's neighborhoods. In fact, trust is a vital component of the entire neighborhood development story in Cleveland. CHN's board structure, which to this day has representatives of all the affiliated CDCs, also helped build trust and cooperation.

CND also provided support to some of these early CDCs as they developed radically new financing models for affordable housing. For example, Near West Housing Corporation and Union Miles Development Corporation both piloted an unproven approach to bring private equity based on accelerated depreciation tax incentives into multifamily deals. This was prior to the establishment of the

LIHTC. This same tool was eventually used by CHN to finance its first two lease-purchase rehab deals. This new ability to leverage the CDBG funds enabled CHN to create more units and spread those units across the six different neighborhoods. This financing tool, along with CHN's equitable board structure, encouraged and at times even forced CDCs from across the city to work together rather than compete, thus making CHN a key player in the development of affordable housing in Cleveland.

CHN's success has been remarkable. By 2015, CHN was a membership organization with twenty-three CDCs working in partnership to develop affordable housing with an emphasis on homeownership for the poor. It had built over two thousand such homes. It may be best known for its innovative use of the LIHTC to redevelop Cleveland's deteriorated inner-city neighborhoods. Its scattered-site lease-purchase program is the oldest and largest in the country. CHN is effectively Cleveland's affordable housing provider outside of the local housing authority (Cuyahoga Metropolitan Housing Authority, or CMHA).

The third important outcome of this period was the formation of Neighborhood Progress, Inc. (NPI) as Cleveland's community development intermediary. (NPI is now known as Cleveland Neighborhood Progress, but NPI is used in this chapter.) NPI was formed principally by the Cleveland Foundation and the George Gund Foundation with the participation of Cleveland Tomorrow, a private civic organization made up of chief executive officers of the largest companies in the Cleveland area. It was formed primarily to standardize and coordinate funding of the city's developing CDCs. No other outcome of this period has had longer term or deeper impact on the CDC industry in Cleveland. NPI now coordinates four different streams of private funding from the Gund, Cleveland, Mandel, and Enterprise Foundations. These four philanthropies have funded Cleveland's CDCs via NPI for two decades, an extraordinarily long-term indication of confidence.

The close relationship between NPI and Enterprise is particularly noteworthy. Since Enterprise entered the Cleveland market, NPI has been its primary partner. Enterprise has found that NPI keeps its work grounded and serves as an effective local community development intermediary by providing strategic funding, technical assistance, and thought leadership. Enterprise has passed millions of dollars of Housing and Urban Development (HUD) Section IV capacity-building dollars to NPI because they believe the investment is strategic and effective.

CND also provided support to the CDCs and CHN as they influenced the final structure of NPI. CND staff served as a bridge between the creators of NPI and the CDCs, many of whom were distrustful of the agenda NPI was created to serve. NPI would certainly have been formed without CND's work; the foundations and the corporate sector were clear on this, but the structure may not have explicitly included CDC representation. There was also a concern on the part of neighborhood advocates that NPI was simply co-opting the CDCs to support a foundation/corporate agenda. CND helped to work through those concerns due to the trust and respect CND's staff enjoyed from all parties.

Growth of the Affordable Housing Industry: CHN and Cleveland's CDCs, 1988–1998

In 1988 I joined CHN to start up a multifamily development initiative. As Cleveland's housing stock is predominately made up of single- and two-family homes, CHN had focused its efforts to increase the supply of affordable housing on redeveloping single homes using the lease-purchase model. CHN's leadership saw the need to test the feasibility of expanding this model to the city's multifamily sector. They acquired and rehabilitated ten such properties under two LIHTC deals over two years, aggregating them across multiple neighborhoods. However, because of the weak rental market at the time and the difficulty in managing these properties in the city's historic neighborhoods, they called the experiment to an end and shifted their focus back to single-family homes.

In 1990, CHN's first director moved to city hall to become Mayor Michael White's director of community development, and I took over as CHN's executive director. Over the next eight years CHN built on its solid track record. The successful use of the (then) new LIHTCs and the growing strength of its member CDCs allowed us to become the leading affordable housing organization in the region. In our first ten years we went from an annual production of twenty-five to over two hundred units, from fifteen to fifty staff, and from six to fifteen affiliated member CDCs.

CHN was overwhelmingly successful because it paid close attention to production, partnerships, and funders. Our partnership with the city of Cleveland was strong because we could be counted on to acquire vacant properties in virtually all city wards, rehabilitate them, and lease them to responsible tenants. This pleased both the administration and city council, so funding from the city was steady. The state housing finance agency worked to prove the LIHTC program a success. They knew they could count on CHN to produce units on time and on budget and that resulted in consistent annual credit allocations. Foundation support was consistent because of CHN's ability to focus on the real estate and on improving the neighborhoods and the lives of the residents.

CHN's member CDCs also valued our partnership and the value created through the rehab program. This was evidenced by the growth in the number of member CDCs during this period—almost every CDC in town wanted to be a CHN member.

The CHN-CDC partnerships were not without problems on both sides. The primary CDC roles were property selection and property management in their neighborhoods. However, CHN reserved the right to decline properties for acquisition due to design shortcomings or budget limitations. Issues also arose related to the challenging nature of scattered-site rental property management. Together, CHN and the CDCs learned a very important lesson—property management was a business, and if the CDCs were not collecting rents and controlling expenses, they could not operate the units. Some CDCs internalized this basic rule better than others. One problem inherent to CHN's structure was that the CDCs were voting members and held a seat on CHN's board of trustees; yet, CHN might need to enforce penalties or cancel property management contracts with the same CDCs. It was a difficult but manageable balancing act.

CHN also provided measurable value for the community. Vacant homes were transformed into visible assets and opportunities for affordable homeownership. We supported the development of contractors from the community. Almost all were small, proprietor-owned businesses, and at any point in time probably half of the contractors used by CHN were minority-owned businesses.

During this time CHN developed the Homeward program, an acquisition-rehab program resulting in the direct sale of homes to home buyers. The addition of this program enabled CHN to bring both lease-purchase rental and for-sale products to neighborhoods. This allowed the CDCs to be strategic in building neighborhood real estate markets while increasing values, increasing minority homeownership, and more effectively targeting substantially all the vacant homes on a given street.

CHN also provided community value as it partnered with newer CDCs with limited experience in real estate development and risk management. CHN provided the capital for its lease-purchase and Homeward programs so that the CDC did not need to take on debt; CHN retained ownership, so all risk ultimately resided at the CHN level. This enabled newer CDCs to learn the real estate development business in a safe environment. It was not long before many of these CDCs were doing their own LIHTC deals while still participating in CHN's programs. CHN was not the only driver for this growth; NPI was also funding and supporting these CDCs, but without CHN the pace of growth would have been much slower.

One last note on CHN: the tension of the dual nature of the business—serving low-income residents and running a real estate business with a real bottom line—

played itself out within CHN's staff and board and in the CDC partnerships. Some CHN staff focused on helping poor residents, while others made sure that the bottom line was healthy and fees were earned. Some staff and trustees thought the organization should operate only the lease-purchase program and not start up the Homeward program, because they believed the Homeward program to be helping the "middle class," as opposed to the poor; others believed that we needed to promote more homeownership and build up property values. Some member CDCs wanted only to operate the Homeward program in their neighborhood while others believed that each CDC ought to be serving both low-income renters and home buyers. In this case it was CHN's membership structure and the nature of the board of trustees that forced us to work together in solving these internal policy issues; it wasn't realized at the time, but both programs brought significant positive impact to the community.

By the end of this period, in the late 1990s, Cleveland had one of the most productive nonprofit housing sectors in the nation. I would argue this was due to four factors:

1. The strength of CHN and the CDCs due to the dynamics summarized above;
2. The ongoing commitment of the foundation community and NPI to fund the CDCs;
3. Cleveland Mayor White's focus on housing production as a key to the future of the city's neighborhoods, and the ability of his administration to effectively deliver resources; and
4. The resources brought to Cleveland by national intermediaries, Enterprise, and the Local Initiative Support Corporation (LISC).

Maturing of Systems and Resources, 1998–2008

In 1998 I left CHN to join Enterprise as the director of the Cleveland office and later became its regional director. Enterprise is a national nonprofit organization founded in 1982. It relies on contributions from individual donors, corporations, and the federal government to help rebuild low-income communities. From 1982 to 2015 it raised and invested more than $18.6 billion in loans, grants, and equity to build or renovate about 340,000 homes in partnership with nonprofits across the country. Before turning to the Enterprise program, and why and how it added value to the local scene, let's look at some other important factors impacting the movement during this period.

By the mid-1990s the LIHTC had become the major source of funding for affordable housing production in the country. It had proven itself as a tool around which to build other financing and gained the confidence of investors, essentially becoming a reliable commodity. In Cleveland, local investors (through Cleveland Tomorrow) became less important as Enterprise and LISC were able to draw on their national funds. Any loss in flexibility offered by local funds was offset by the reliability of national funds. With Enterprise doing the fund-raising work nationally, local community developers were freed up to do the deals and work with residents.

This maturing of the system was also reflected in the formalization of the tax-credit allocation process at the Ohio Housing Finance Agency (OHFA). Credits became easier to use, and the equity became an essential way to finance deals; therefore demand increased and competition grew. OHFA and HFAs across the country responded to these factors by making the process more formal, with clear competitive criteria. The decentralized administration of this tax-credit program to the states was and continues to be an asset of the program. The state HFAs are far more responsive to local needs and conditions than Washington, DC, could ever be. Each HFA is required to have a Qualified Action Plan to govern its allocation of credits to local organizations. When the local community is well organized, as the Cleveland community development organizations have been, it can truly influence the prioritization of strategies for credit allocation. A good example of this is OHFA's establishment of a set-aside of credits for permanent supportive housing that serves the Housing First program described below.

As the availability of LIHTC increased, for-profit developers began to enter into this segment of the affordable housing market. In Cleveland this entry of for-profits was viewed with caution by nonprofit community developers. The production capacity of the for-profits sometimes exceeded that of the nonprofits, but their connection and commitment to the community was often lacking. It became clear, however, that some in both developer camps were able to combine being effective along with being engaged as they produced housing developments that brought benefit to the community and to residents.

At the same time, it's important to point out that some Cleveland nonprofits also lacked the necessary expertise. NPI, Enterprise, and LISC helped to establish a set of organizational and performance standards and provided technical assistance to the nonprofits in meeting and exceeding these standards. Despite this assistance, there are still some low-performing CDCs.

While this is certainly not unique to Cleveland, the city does have a unique system for funding CDCs that in some cases exacerbated this problem. As CDCs became a proven and successful vehicle for community development, each Cleveland councilperson wanted one to serve their ward. In some cases, these new

CDCs were neither effective nor accountable to the community at large. Over time, councilpersons controlled the allocation of an increasing share of the city's CDBG funds. Some CDCs stayed in business long after their ineffective business practices would have brought them to an end if it were not for the ongoing support of councilperson CDBG funds.

In Cleveland, about two-thirds of the city's CDBG funding is divided among the city's seventeen ward-based councilpersons. Each is allocated about $450,000 a year of CDBG funds to use for "neighborhood improvement." Neighborhood improvement plans must ultimately be approved by the city's department of community development, which ensures that they comply with HUD rules and regulations. When it works well, this system of allocating funding places decisions about neighborhood improvement closer to residents, who elect their councilperson. Indeed, there are more examples of positive and long-lasting outcomes than negative, but it would be disingenuous not to point out this phenomenon in the Cleveland community development industry and to note that it can also have dysfunctional aspects.

Problems notwithstanding, on the whole, Cleveland's CDC movement has matured to become an efficient, sophisticated "industry" that is known throughout the country for its ability to provide quality, affordable housing for thousands of the city's low-income residents. By 2008, however, Cleveland, even more so than the rest of the nation, was in the midst of the foreclosure crisis and recession. The city that had been known for equity planning and its pioneering community development organizations became known as the epicenter of the foreclosure crisis. Even though homeowners and renters living in CDC-assisted housing fared much better than most, many neighborhoods were decimated. The CDCs quickly realized that providing quality affordable housing and a path to homeownership was no longer enough.

Toward an Integrated Agenda, 2008–Present

Enterprise, in partnership with funders, government, and other nonprofits, took a lead role to develop a broader, more integrated agenda that addressed issues rooted in poverty and race and created solutions with lasting value for the full community in Cleveland. The following three examples demonstrate how this agenda was implemented.

The first example is the Enterprise-led Housing First Initiative (Feran 2014). As in all major American cities, in Cleveland the number of people experiencing homelessness rose dramatically after the dismemberment of the mental health services and institutions begun under President Reagan. In 2002, Enterprise, in partnership with the Cleveland/Cuyahoga County Office of Homeless Services and the Sisters of Charity Foundation, brought the Housing First model to greater Cleveland. At the time, Housing First was a proven but radical solution to chronic homelessness. Housing First prioritized stable permanent housing as the solution for persons who suffered mental health and/or addiction challenges while experiencing long-term homelessness. Enterprise worked quickly to bring together the best local implementation partners—EDEN, Inc.; FrontLine Service; and CHN. By 2015, thirteen years later, the initiative has met with such success—achieving a 78 percent decrease in chronic homelessness—that we now envision the possibility of ending chronic homelessness in Cuyahoga County by 2020.

Housing First works because of at least four key factors. The first was the creation of an implementation coalition that called for three lead organizations to do what they do best and trust that their partners would also perform. These organizations have a track record of using foundation and public resources effectively. The second factor was the building of a learning environment among the partners and funders—one that was based on outcomes and measurement. Third, the issue of chronic homelessness was defined as an issue that could be solved in an appeal to the hearts and minds of those in power. Fourth, political champions in city, county, and state government that truly wanted to solve the social problem were identified. The last two factors combined to prove that, while many in power choose to ignore issues of race and poverty, there are approaches that can bring the attention and resources needed to solve complex problems.

The second Enterprise-led example is the Cuyahoga Earned Income Tax Credit (EITC) Coalition begun in 2005 to encourage more widespread use of the federal tax credit that provides a much-needed income boost to Cleveland's working families. (Marr et al. 2015, Cuyahoga EITC Coalition n.d.). This initiative includes a coalition of over twenty partners and funders who deliver free tax preparation at sites across the county, bringing in refunds in 2015 that totaled over $18 million. About one-third of the more than thirteen thousand annual consumers served are working families who claim the EITC and receive an average credit of $1,500. They also save a typical annual tax-preparation fee of $300. The national numbers show that the EITC is one of the most effective federal antipoverty tools. In Cuyahoga County, 20 percent of eligible families were not claiming the tax credit. The EITC Coalition has been successful in focusing resources for people experiencing poverty because, as with Housing First, it has a results-focused set of partners and successfully combines a focus on positive social/economic outcomes.

The third example is the Enterprise-led Green Communities Initiative. Begun over ten years ago at the national level, Green Communities seeks to bring the benefits of green, healthy housing to residents of affordable housing. Green housing arose from the environmental movement and for years was an option only for those who lived in market rate developments and had upper- to middle-class incomes. Enterprise decided that more and more housing ought to be built to reduce carbon emissions, save energy, and benefit our environment, but we also asked the question, "Don't people with lower incomes deserve to benefit from lower heating bills and healthier environments?" Green Communities did just this. In less than a decade the separation between affordable housing and green housing was bridged in hundreds of states and localities around the country. This was the case both in the city of Cleveland and at the state level in Ohio. In Cleveland, Mayor Frank Jackson declared that, beginning in 2005, all new housing was to be built to meet Enterprise's Green Communities criteria. The OHFA did the same relative to all new LIHTC-financed housing. In both cases bold policymakers saw the dual benefit to the environment and to low-income residents and took action. The results have been impressive. Building to a strong green standard is now the norm in both cases; developers assume it's how things are done, and thousands of lower-income residents enjoy the same benefits as do more wealthy renters and homeowners across the state.

These are just three of many examples of how Enterprise has brought resources coupled with thought leadership, in Cleveland and across the country, to affordable housing and solutions for residents of low-income communities. The end result is increased opportunity for residents.

Closing Observations

Replicating the successes that I've outlined—increasing the strength of community organizing, producing new resources and policies, building housing and community development delivery systems, or integrating opportunity as our leading indicator—all fall back on the lessons described at the beginning of this chapter. Keep the following front and center—focus on people and place, keep community organizing central, influence how and where the money flows, realize that poverty and racism are always intertwined—and always keep affordable housing a leading strategy.

Several other closing thoughts seem appropriate thirty-five years after the start of this work, particularly in light of the results of the 2016 election.

Racial equity matters. Equity planning needs to prioritize racial equity first and addressing poverty second. The same is true for partnerships among nonprofits, foundations, and local government. As this chapter illustrates, advocates are most effective when they form coalitions and are able to use data to demonstrate that programs work. People of color still face a distinct disadvantage; their initial access to the ladder of opportunity begins at a lower rung than their white counterparts. To talk about providing opportunity without acknowledging this disadvantage is choosing ignorance. Good planning and the most effective programs will fail if they are based on ignorance or, worse yet, denial of racial inequity.

Housing affordability matters. We have accomplished much but we are falling further behind. Thousands of new and preserved affordable housing units have made a real difference in the lives of low-income residents. Making housing affordable and reducing costs from 50 percent to 30 percent of a family's income puts real dollars back in their pocket to pay for basic needs and to help move that family ahead. We also know that housing stability, made possible by keeping housing costs affordable, makes a difference in a family's health, education, and income. But wages have declined or remained flat, and we've lost more affordable housing than we've gained to either abandonment or rising values and market-based rents. We need to partner with policymakers to show the value of stable, affordable housing and shift from defense to offense in making the case for more resources.

Data matters. Research informs policy, and a focus on data and impact measurement only strengthens our case. Whether this focus is on racial disparities in health, education, and income, or on the best structure for access to opportunity so that a family's income stability and status actually changes over time, we can make the case. Data is our friend but it's not cheap. Funders are increasingly requesting impact measurement, but they need to pay for it. The new "pay for success" model is a good start, but it cannot be the only way. We cannot let people of color and low-income families suffer even longer by delaying programs and policies because the data cost curve is deemed to be too expensive.

People and places matter. The challenge of focusing on both place and opportunity is a difficult one. Federal and state policy currently promotes building new affordable housing and moving voucher holders out to "high opportunity" areas. Let's do that. Let's work with the residents and stakeholders in those areas to create a compassionate environment to embrace low-income people. But funding is scarce, and we cannot abandon the vast majority of low-income families who are predominately people of color to the high-poverty and high-crime areas that are the result of public and corporate disinvestment if there is no access to these programs. We know how to do this place-based work, we know what works to improve low-income neighborhoods, and we know how to implement programs that address both people and places. What's missing are sufficient resources—public and private—and political will. Oftentimes the simplest answer is the truth.

Lastly, planning and community development in America could easily become irrelevant in the near future, at least for a time. We might not have imagined this possibility until recently. If federal funding for health care, housing, and community development is slashed, and if the resulting pressure on states and local governments pushes our disinvested communities even more to the fringe of policy priorities, then what do we do? In fact, we have learned a lot about how planners and practitioners can jointly manage community development work with equitable outcomes. The history of the last thirty-five years in Cleveland has taught us that it's a matter of focus, coalition building, truth-telling, and political will.

REFERENCES

Cleveland City Planning Commission. 1975. *Cleveland Policy Planning Report.* Cleveland: City Planning Commission.

Cunningham, Randy. 2007. *Democratizing Cleveland: The Rise and Fall of Community Organizing in Cleveland, Ohio 1975–1985.* Cleveland: Arambala Press.

Cuyahoga Earned Income Tax Credit (EITC), The. n.d. Cuyahoga County, Ohio (web site). https://www.refundohio.org.

Feran, T. 2014. "Housing First Opens Newest Apartments in Work to End Homelessness," *Plain Dealer,* September 16.

Krumholz, N. 1997. "The Provision of Affordable Housing in Cleveland." In *Affordable Housing and Urban Redevelopment in the United States,* edited by Willem van Vliet. Thousand Oaks: Sage.

Marr, C., Chye-Ching Huang, Arloc Sherman, and Brandon DuBot. 2015. "EITC and Tax Credit Promote Work, Reduce Poverty, and Support Children's Development, Research Finds," *Center of Budget and Policy Priorities,* October 1.

McDermott, M. 2004. "National Intermediaries and Local Community Development Corporation Networks: A View from Cleveland," *Journal of Urban Affairs* 26 (2): 171–76.

McQuarrie, M., and Norman Krumholz. 2011. "Institutionalized Social Skill and the Rise of Mediating Organizations in Urban Governance: The Case of the Cleveland Housing Network," *Housing Policy Debate* 21 (3): 421–42.

Simon, Mary, E. 2003. *Celebrating 25 Years.* Cleveland: The Maxine Goodman Levin College of Urban Affairs, Cleveland State University.

Swanstrom, T. 1985. *The Crisis of Growth Politics: Cleveland, Kucinich, and the Challenge of Urban Populism.* Philadelphia: Temple University Press.

Yin, J. 1998. "The Community Development Industry System: A Case Study of Politics and Institutions in Cleveland, 1967–1997," *Journal of Urban Affairs* 20 (2): 137–57.

3

ECONOMIC DIVERSITY IN LOW-STATUS COMMUNITIES

Majora Carter

Inequality is linked closely to poverty. I see it everywhere I work in the United States, abroad, and in my hometown of the South Bronx, New York City. In those places where we *concentrate poverty*, we also *exacerbate inequality*.

Concentrated poverty in the United States is increasing. Often well-intentioned policies and programs meant to help people, have had the effect of segregating people by race and income. Subsidized low-income housing sounds like a good thing—serving a need. "Community centers" and "health clinics" sound pretty good too. However, too often affordable housing and social services are concentrated in low-status communities that already suffer from widespread unemployment and associated health, education, and criminal justice-related problems. Putting *more* people who are under these stressors on top of the ones that already exist is not really helping—regardless of how effectively services are delivered or how good the housing.

There are neighborhoods like the South Bronx in every city around the world; low-status[1] communities where good intentions have come and gone like the tide for decades—producing less than expected results, on both sides. I use the term "low-status" intentionally to describe places that embody inequality in a world where "equality" is, more or less, an agreed-upon universal goal. The language we use to describe places matters.

Generally, when we use terms such as "poor," "underserved," or "low-income" to describe communities, we really mean non-white. "Urban" is often used in the same way, but that is slowly changing as "urbanization" has come to mean "it's safe for white people to move back into cities." However, not all people of color are poor or urban, and not all white people are affluent. The ghetto, the reservation, and the formerly booming coal mining town may look different from the outside, but they are in the same boat by most measures, and they are all *"low-status."*

These communities are the places where the schools are worse, the air is dirtier, the parks and trees are fewer and less well-maintained, and the health statistics are not good; it is where elected officials readily acknowledge these disparities but are not held accountable when they do little to effectively address them. *Low-status communities are places where inequality is assumed*—by those living inside and those living outside of that community.

The elected officials in these communities are just as safe in their seats as those in more affluent communities—and maybe even more so. Low-status communities often internalize their low status, and very often reflexively settle for "less than" as a result.

Brain Drain

Coming from a low-status, American, inner-city ghetto like I do, people are surprised when I tell them I still live in the South Bronx. The assumption is that these are *not communities* in which people *choose* to live. So I often get, *"You could live anywhere, but you CHOOSE to stay. How noble!"*—which, I suppose, is a compliment.

I believe I conduct my work with integrity, but ultimately, I believe in the promise of America, especially in low-status communities, and I work toward the goal of creating more wealth among people who are not supported to achieve their personal potential as much as others may be. At one time, all I could think of was how to get out of the South Bronx. But today, the South Bronx is no longer a stain; it's a badge of honor for me. I believe that where I'm from helps me to see the world. Today when I say I'm from the South Bronx, I stand up straight.

Every community, no matter how many problems it may have, produces success stories. It's part of an American tradition—smart, hard-working individuals are portrayed as "making it out" of the "bad" neighborhood and into a "good" one. Too often, these people are encouraged to leave in order to succeed. What is rarely considered is that when successful individuals leave, they take with them their income-generating potential, the capacity for local reinvestment, and their day-to-day example of what success can look like. All are priceless to a low-status community.

Many of these low-status communities were once much more economically diverse. For Black communities, the successes of the civil rights movement created unintended consequences. Now, I understand that "the good old days" were not always all that *good* in many respects. But during the time of legalized segregation, while many Black communities may have been racially segregated, they were, at least, economically diverse.

It was not uncommon for a Black doctor to live within close proximity to a Black janitor, and maybe some Black steel workers. Whether they had a drinking problem or were great musicians, their successes and their failings were shared in ways that everyone could see, feel, and move through during different parts of their own lives. It provided a strong sense of social cohesion. People who lived there knew that they were in the mess of American apartheid *together*.

Those communities also provided a sense of aspiration; for example, the daughter of a janitor could see that there was such a thing as a Black doctor and realize that there was more to life than just what her own father did for a living.

But the unintended consequences of the civil rights victories eroded those communities. People who could afford to move from racially segregated areas usually did. If you look at these communities as though they were corporations, you could note that they all had a talent retention problem—one of the costliest challenges to businesses of any size.

Those communities lost their success models, their top talent, their income generators, and oftentimes the likeliest leaders of any community. Low-status communities are always recovering from those losses and now experience social isolation within concentrated poverty.

There must be a market for the kind of economically diverse community that can help propel people. . . .

. . . and there is.

Managing Neighborhood Change (Self-gentrification[2])

This chapter tells a different story of neighborhood change; one that leverages economic diversity and dissipates the negative effects of concentrated poverty. It will not be easy, and many will see it as "gentrification." But I believe neighborhoods need to change. They have always changed, and "preserving" them in place becomes counterproductive in low-status communities and makes the goal of equality even more elusive.

It is through my own personal journey growing up in the South Bronx, becoming successful, moving away, and then moving back that I have come to this conclusion. In that way, this chapter is my story. But it is not my story alone. There are success stories in every low-status community; priceless, creative, hard-working people who choose to stay or to return. Far from gentrifying these communities, we are making them more vibrant and diverse. The neighborhood amenities and services we demand appeal to a range of income groups. We build on the strengths of existing residents, providing them with a greater choice and opportunity and encouraging other middle- and low-income residents to stay and invest in the neighborhood and attract new residents to live and invest.

In my work in the South Bronx, I have found the following approaches to managing neighborhood change can improve neighborhoods AND promote a more economically diverse, equitable community:

1. Develop neighborhood amenities and services that appeal to a range of income groups and promote economic diversity. Build on the strengths of existing residents, providing them with greater choice and opportunity; encourage current middle- and low-income residents to stay and invest in the neighborhood; and attract new residents to live and invest.
2. Reclaim neighborhood control of land use.
3. Promote environmental equality.
4. Offer financial equity through long-term land leases and other mechanisms to existing local landowners so they can remain and benefit from increasing real estate values like other Americans.

Develop Amenities to Serve As Talent Retention

Strategies for *self-gentrification* can be encouraged by looking pragmatically at the underlying forces propelling successful people out of low-status neighborhoods and minimizing the resulting reinvestment gap over time—a gap which is so often filled a decade or two later by white people and labeled simply as "gentrification."

Since returning to the South Bronx in the late 1990s, I have learned a lot from addressing problems indirectly through economic development ventures that taught me how money circulates (formally and informally) and its ongoing implications for how neighborhoods get developed. These lessons are timely, given the renewed interest in cities.

We live in an urban age. For the first time in history, the majority of the world's population lives in cities. This renewed interest in cities presents a challenge and an opportunity to change neighborhoods. The challenge is that the renewed interest in cities has stemmed the tide of white flight to suburbs, and now a flood of new dollars is coming to a community near you—sooner or later. The current low-income inhabitants fear being displaced by wealthier newcomers.

The opportunity lies in planning and managing this transition in a way that benefits existing residents while attracting new residents. How are we preparing? What's not working? What is? Where can we influence economic developments for talent retention *and* attraction to mitigate the shock or make best use of the inevitable changes to come? How do we respectfully introduce that question to all the people who can benefit from a constructive conversation along those lines?

First, ask the community. My team and various squads of college and high school interns have conducted roughly four hundred surveys over the past two years. Based on this and anecdotal data of people currently living or working in the Hunts Point section of the South Bronx (see Figure 3.1), people overwhelmingly want to see their community become more economically and educationally diverse; they want a community that offers a mix of stores and services and, instead of community centers, they want commercially viable "third spaces" where people can gather. They want to live in neighborhoods with a culture of health and vibrancy instead of medication centers treating lifestyle-related maladies.

At the same time, certain types of activity and the people who perform them ought to be "displaced"—ask anyone living in a drug-infested community if they like the crime that it generates.

Property values should increase, to the benefit of local landowners.

Wealth should be generated by more people than those who are currently able to take advantage of the opportunities before us. The scale of developments that can affect these goals should be large—because the generational scale of the problem we have all helped to create is so large.

How did I come to think this way?

Growing Up

"When I grow up, I'm going to need to be a graduate of a "name college."

That was my mantra at the age of seven. It was my way of saying that a highly competitive and recognized college was the only kind worth going to for an inner-city ghetto kid. I knew I had a chance to "get out"—get out of my neighborhood, that is, through education.

I was the youngest of ten kids, and many of us were still young enough to live at home and sit down to dinner together. We were frequently joined by friends and neighbors from far and wide. Our home was a happy sanctuary to me and to many others.

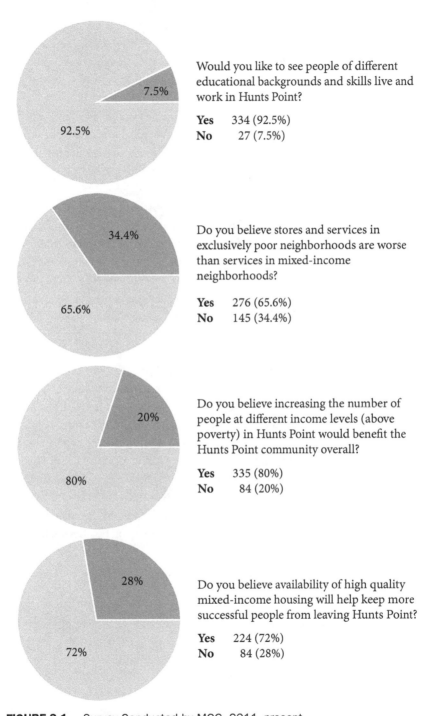

FIGURE 3.1. Survey Conducted by MCG, 2011–present.

I wasn't blind to the problems with my community. I had seen it on the news since I was very young, as I watched it nightly with my father. I somehow felt sheltered from it, as if *our* neighborhood was safe and there was this *other* neighborhood out there that didn't have people like my parents in it to protect and love the place or the people within it.

When I was seven, things changed. At the beginning of the summer, I watched two buildings on the corners of my block burn. My neighbor Pito went up and down the fire escape to get people in their pajamas and bare feet out of the buildings. *Where were the firemen? Where was the truck? Someone must have pulled the fire alarm . . . was it broken too?*

At the end of the that summer, my beautiful big brother Lenny, who wrote me letters in such a lyrical handwriting from Vietnam over two separate combat tours came home and into the drug wars. He was killed at the age of twenty-three. Shot above the left eye and—we hope—dying instantly, without suffering, in the South Bronx, 1973.

From the late 1960s to the early 1980s, it was well documented that some landlords paid to have their buildings torched, because the economics of the times made it more profitable to collect insurance money rather than trying to reinvest in their buildings.

I learned later that a combination of factors led to the South Bronx's breakdown in terms of social, environmental, or economic security over the ensuing decades. Discriminatory and destructive financial practices by the banking industry, degrading practices and policies regarding highway construction, the insertion of noxious infrastructure development along race and class lines, the erosion of quality education, no clean and safe public parks, a lack of positive economic development—all had negative impacts on residents of the South Bronx and similar inner-city American communities. Not only did such policies and practices degrade the quality of life in these neighborhoods but they also degraded the equity and wealth that people had invested in homes and businesses, truncating any hope for future prosperity.

Brain Drain

By the time I was in third grade, I was keenly aware of people moving out of the neighborhood and how class often played a role in it. On the first day of school after my brother was killed, I sat next to a girl named Judith.

Anyone could easily tell the really poor kids from the kids with money at our school. Kids like me? Our moms had saved up to buy one, or maybe two, new outfits to celebrate the new school year, whereas the more well-to-do kids had a whole month's worth of new clothes. Judith was always one of the best-dressed kids in school.

As we sat down in our assigned seats, Judith announced that she was not going to be there long. Her parents were going to move her out of the neighborhood. Within a few weeks, she was gone.

Kids that had parents like Judith's—young and with good jobs—could afford to take them from the neighborhood. Kids like me—"smart" but with poor parents—were told in spoken and unspoken terms to measure success by how far we could get away from the neighborhood. We were told that we would grow up and *be somebody*.

Of course, I wanted to get the hell out of there. No one would blame me. I was one of the smart ones, and it was to be expected. Crime, the schools, and a general sense that nothing good stays in a neighborhood like the one that you were born and raised in—even though there was a sense of community—told you to leave.

We were the epitome of Brain Drain.

The South Bronx meant pimp, pusher, or prostitute to most of America at the time. It was a stain, and I believed it, too. Like most "smart" kids, I used education as my escape. My eighth-grade teachers tutored some of their students, including me, to help us pass the entrance exam for New York City's specialized high schools. I got into the Bronx High School of Science and then on to Wesleyan University. No, not Yale, but still in Connecticut and my first choice!

At college, I was so embarrassed by my neighborhood, I would change the subject when asked where I was from.

A Reluctant Return and an Introduction to Environmental Equality

After college I didn't immediately return to the South Bronx. But then I entered graduate school and I had to come back home—I was almost thirty and could only afford to live in my parent's spare bedroom. It was a huge defeat for me.

It took a long time for me to believe the South Bronx was anything but a stain.

It changed for me when I met Steven Sapp, a cofounder of the Point Community Development Corporation (Point CDC)—an arts and youth development organization located down the street from my parent's home. They were a shining light for me. Bronx-born artists like the world-renowned modern dancer and choreographer Arthur Aviles and the jazz flutist Dave Valentin came home to perform there. The place was filled with artists and those that loved them. Soon, I started working at the Point as a volunteer and then later joined the staff part-time (but really worked more than full-time) doing arts-related community development projects such as codirecting the first international South Bronx Film and Video Festival and public arts projects. I was in heaven.

In the midst of the small Bronx Arts renaissance I was experiencing, we discovered that the city and state of New York were planning to build yet another, even larger waste facility here. Most folks that lived in the neighborhood seemed resigned about it. Neighbors would say things like, *well, it's a poor community, that's what happens in places like this.*

The education I received and the distance that I had made me realize that these things were happening to my community *because* it was a poor community of color and thus politically vulnerable—what I would now define as *Low-Status.*

I was disgusted, mostly with myself for being blind to a historic situation that caused people like me to hate ourselves and the communities we come from. I knew that all the arts in the world weren't going to save us from the city and state's massive waste management plans. It was a malignant vision of economic development that would add more insult to our injuries.

It propelled me to act. It moved my spirit in a way that I wasn't familiar with, and it changed my beliefs—the way I felt about myself and my community. I didn't define myself as an "organizer"; I simply cared about my community. I wanted something better.

I wasn't an "organizer." But I was creative and knew that, in a community where people felt demoralized about the plans to build more waste-handling capacity, informing folks that there was yet *another* awful thing coming wasn't going to move them. My challenge was: how can we inspire many to *act*, and what should that action look like ideally as well as practically?

Sometimes we would go into tenement buildings and stand on a floor and knock on all the doors until someone came out, and then we would share details related to this issue. People would nod and smile and thank us for our work, but invariably we would not see most of them again at any of the community meetings.

We started to host cool, public art events like a *garbage parade* in which we would dress up in various garbage-themed outfits and dance around the street. Once a crowd gathered, we would tell them what was going on. But deep down, I knew that telling people only about the environmental impacts was not going to motivate them because the place *was* ugly—it was the "concrete jungle."

So we took another tack. If concerns for the environment were not enough to move people, perhaps concerns for their children's health would motivate them. We directly connected kids' asthma attacks to the poor air quality from the diesel trucks driving through the neighborhood and explained that the new waste facilities meant even more of the same. This propelled people to act and demonstrate against the facility and that ultimately became part of a more sustainable waste management plan.

We fought the waste facility successfully; but in so doing, I realized it was as important to work *for* something as it is to fight against something.

Reclaiming Neighborhood Control of Land Use

We began to shift the power over land-use decisions from private interests and city hall to residents in the community—a community that people had long been resigned to being a repository for the region's waste. We needed to provide evidence that the residents mattered. A significant victory in this regard was the creation of the Hunts Point Riverside Park in 2000.

The seeds for the park were planted thanks to a small grant program to restore threatened rivers in urban areas. The grant was administered by the New York City Parks Department through a program of the U.S. Forest Service.

While I was working with the Point CDC as director of special projects, Jenny Hoffner of the NYC Parks Department repeatedly encouraged me to apply for the grant for the Bronx River. I certainly knew of the Bronx River—I had seen it on the subway map. However, it did not occur to me that anyone could or would want to visit it.

The river was only visible from a subway or a car crossing the bridge into Soundview, the next neighborhood over. Its shores were lined by industry. The river was threatened and seemed beyond repair.

One morning, when I was out jogging with my big crazy dog named Xena, she pulled me into what I thought was just another dump along Edgewater Road. As we picked our way through decades' worth of debris, tires, old beds, oil drums, molding, nasty carpeting, and weeds growing over my head, there suddenly appeared before me the Bronx River.

The dump was actually a Robert Moses[3] (the "Master Builder")–era bridge project that was never built. It was a canvas where we could paint the image of what we knew our community could be. At least, that's how I saw it. Others, I knew, would take some convincing.

Standing on the shores of the river and looking out, I forgot all the trash that lay behind me. I saw the early morning light glinting off the fifty-foot expanse of water before me as if little golden birds were alighting on the water for my amusement. On the other side was Soundview Park, which, at that time, was mostly undeveloped. Its grassy shores sloped gently down into the tidal water. There were real birds, too; although I didn't know it at the time, there were cormorants and egrets. There was a quiet there that I didn't know could exist in my neighborhood.

I finally understood why Jenny kept bugging me. She suspected that I would see value in restoring the river once I found it. I quickly realized that this little bit of forgotten nature could be just what our community needed. I ran back home and started working on the proposal for the seed grant to transform that dump into a park. It felt good to be dancing on Robert Moses's grave.

Soon the Point CDC began to organize the community to dream up a park. We started with community cleanups. But, even with the promise of a free lunch, only a few people attended. (People were pretty demoralized; I don't think people believed it could happen). However, I was there *every* time—someone had to be, to prove to a skeptical community that consistent and caring presence could happen here.

It was an extra burden of responsibility for sure, but it turned out to be one of the most valuable learning experiences of my life—and it was echoed in one of my favorite quotes from Seth Godin, author and entrepreneur, who said it is better to *"delight a few, as opposed to sooth[ing] the masses."*[4]

Some corporate neighbors and civic organizations contributed in-kind donations. A local concrete company donated concrete blocks that we painted in bright colors and used as our only seating options. The NYC Department of Transportation built a swirly but ADA-compliant asphalt path. Bronx-based community groups such as Rocking the Boat arrived with a brilliant, on-water environmental education program, and the Point CDC offered canoe rides. ConEd (the local utility) used their heavy equipment to pull out huge quantities of debris that would have taken my tiny band of volunteers decades to do. The New York Restoration Project brought Bette Midler to our little park and with her, some much needed attention—our little site got into *People* magazine!

We developed dynamic public-private partnerships that made that little park, even in its "beta" version, something that the community could feel hopeful about. We worked with the city on the shared goals of creating parks and waterfront access in a community that, according to the planning department, had the lowest parks-to-people ratio in all of New York City at that time (we had less than 20 percent of the NYC Planning Department's recommendation of 2.5 acres per thousand people). Simultaneously we worked *against* the city and state's shortsighted plans of disproportionately discriminating against low-income communities of color with regard to the siting of waste facilities.

This was possible in part because I took a different, more creative approach than the more traditional "activists" I saw around me. I smiled; shook hands; engaged in thoughtful, well-prepared exchanges; and was willing to listen to what others wanted. In short, I made sure the human beings on the other side of the table knew that I saw them as people first and what they represented second.

We were ultimately successful in the development of the park and in guiding the city to develop a more sustainable solid-waste management plan. It took seven years of nurturing the community for the residents to believe that our little, abandoned, dumped-on street was an asset. Coupled with the city's eventual $3.2 million investment, we now have the Hunts Point Riverside Park—a park that was awarded the national Rudy Bruner Award for Excellence in Urban Design. I was married there on October 7, 2006; the day started off rainy and cold but the sun came out for the celebration.

Promote Environmental Equality

Building on the success of the Hunts Point Riverside Park, we turned our attention to environmental equality, a community-specific economic development plan that explicitly linked the revitalization of neighborhood environmental conditions; sustainable economic opportunities and jobs; improved public health outcomes; and social stability. About this time, I decided to go into private practice as an urban revitalization consultant and real estate developer.

Underlying this approach is the goal of greater equality.[5] Historically, every time the social order was disrupted to achieve greater equality, economic prosperity followed, whether it was the American Revolution, the abolition of slavery, women's suffrage, the civil rights movement, or even the development of the Internet. None of these social upheavals have been models of equality itself. For example, the freedoms achieved through the American Revolution did not apply to slaves. But the very idea of freedom made it possible for future generations to accomplish more.

So, what does environmental equality look like? This is what it looks like: you don't have to move out of your neighborhood to live in a better one, because *everyone* has equal access to clean air, water, and soil: an environment that supports an excellent quality of life. The approach combines concrete development skills with reliable partners to implement high-performing, outcomes-oriented projects.

Yet, despite the very real benefits to low-status communities, investors, philanthropy, and grassroots groups alike have been hesitant to embark on community-specific economic development plans. Too often, job training programs are not linked to market research or demand. Programs are judged only on the number of graduates, and not whether their graduates find employment. And many funders—public and private—seem more comfortable supporting ineffective programs that are run by traditional social justice or nonprofit organizations (what I call the social justice /nonprofit industrial complex) than they are funding programs or enterprises that are promising but are run by nontraditional developers.

As America reurbanizes, there will be increasing opportunities to use real estate development to affect people at all levels of influence, income, and vulnerability.

Whether this development has a positive or a negative impact on low-status communities will depend on how well we engage all communities with the gospel of environmental equality right now—during these pivotal years of geographic transition from sprawl to density and everything in between.

Using development to promote greater environmental equality is a challenging undertaking. But nothing simple is ever easy. People will say there is not enough money, or that it is being spent on the wrong things; that there are too many externalities, or insufficient community education—and all of them are correct in some way.

What if community development *solutions* were based on the same principles used in nearly every successful commercial product launch? In other words— identify and develop a market that is demanding what you have to offer. A product won't sell unless there is a market that wants it. It does not make any difference how good the product's creator thinks it is. It's that simple.

This process, social entrepreneurship, has six steps:

- Identify market and/or policy need (i.e., who wants this thing?).
- Design an attractive solution.
- Obtain an "angel" investment (it could be money but could also be influence used on behalf of your project).
- Launch the beta version of your project.
- Learn from projects and refine. (Watch how people use the beta version and how they respond to it and make changes.)
- Reiterate and expand.

One of the things I noticed after I moved into private practice for urban revitalization strategy consulting was that around the country there were only two kinds of real estate development affecting the ubiquitous low-status community in America: gentrification and poverty-level economic maintenance.

In the typical *"gentrification"* model, real estate developers are attracted to a poor neighborhood for a combination of reasons, sometimes aided by a new transit station or some other investment of public dollars. Then come new businesses, better apartments, cafés, parks, and other amenities that current residents feel are not for them. Rents go up, and eventually the poor people are displaced.

The second development type is *poverty-level economic maintenance*—a term we coined that involves the attraction of businesses that meet the perceived "needs" of only the poor people in those communities. You'll find the kind of seedy places that people would leave the neighborhood to avoid, if given a choice. Instead of affordable options for healthy food, you'll find many fast food joints. Instead of banks or credit unions that help people build their financial literacy and equity, you'll find things like Rent-A-Centers, check-cashing stores, pawn shops, and pay-day loan spots. Instead of housing that is attractive to a mix of incomes, you'll find a preponderance of very highly subsidized affordable housing or low-quality market rate housing that is affordable to people with very low incomes.

All of these factors combine to concentrate poverty and exacerbate the issues associated with poverty: low educational attainment, high crime, poor health outcomes, high unemployment, and higher incarceration rates. In other words, poverty-level economic maintenance.

We wanted to be more creative about real estate development in low-status communities. All I could think was, *there must be a market for the kind of economically diverse community that meets the needs and desires of a diverse group of people with a range of incomes.*

The third way is self-gentrification. Could low-status communities *self-gentrify for their own benefit?* People in low-status communities want to live healthy, productive, and happy lives just as much as those living in exclusively affluent ones.

American Urbanization . . . *Do-Over!*

The redevelopment of the Spofford Juvenile Detention Center offered an opportunity to demonstrate, at scale, a model for mixed-income housing and mixed-use commercial development with the power to transform a chronically underperforming community. The center, like the dumps and waste treatment facilities, was another long-time neighborhood "stain." Opened in the 1950s on a five-acre site in the South Bronx, it housed more than one thousand young people at its height. The facility was closed in 2011 due in large part to the efforts of children's rights and prison reform advocates.

There is a market for economically diverse communities that meet the needs and desires of a diverse group of people. . . .

I was excited about the possibility of redeveloping the site and immediately started to identify potential allies and partners who were interested in the kind of transformational real estate development that our city desperately needed in low-status communities to help move this ball down the field. First, in 2011, I contacted Mathew Wambua, Commissioner for NYC Department of Housing Preservation and Development. Once that meeting was set, I assembled a team that included Perkins + Will, an architecture firm that donated its services to help create a conceptual design for the future of Spofford—one that could be used in our meeting with Commissioner Wambua, which was held in Perkins + Will's beautiful offices.

Together, we proposed a different type of housing for low-status communities that captured the imagination of Commissioner Wambua and his team. However, the site was under the jurisdiction of the NYC Administration for Children's Services (ACS). ACS's primary concern was that any plan needed to include a meaningful amount of "supportive housing," such as housing for youth aging out of foster care or for grandparents raising grandchildren.

A multi-agency task force was created to assess the redevelopment potential for the site. However, at the same time, Mayor Bloomberg's administration was drawing to a close. This was the first change of mayoral administrations in twelve years, and there was not enough time for a project of this scale to progress to the next stage.

We spent the next several years working to keep the possibility of redeveloping the site in the public eye and on the city's mind. First, we raised awareness through an international design competition in partnership with the architecture, engineering, and construction design software company Autodesk. The award-winning entries were showcased at the StartUp Box #South Bronx, an incubator and tech education facility in Hunts Point that we started and located on the community's main commercial street. One of the attendees was Yusef Salaam, one of the alleged "Central Park Five"—the young men that were infamously and wrongfully accused of brutally assaulting and raping a female jogger in Central Park back in 1990.

The Central Park Five had recently been awarded a multimillion-dollar settlement from the city of New York due to the wrongful conviction and the years of unjust imprisonment. Yusef, who had spent some of his formative years inside of Spofford as an inmate, looked at the designs produced for the competition and mused that it was time for Spofford to be no more.

The de Blasio administration put Spofford back on the radar in late 2014, releasing a Request for Expressions of Interest (RFEI, as opposed to an RFP—request for proposals). The RFEI included much of the specific language and concepts from the original plan. Despite the three-year hiatus, it included the concept for strategic mixed-income housing *and* mixed-use commercial development.

Urban housing affordability is a growing concern in the midst of America's reurbanization boom. Many well-meaning people look at a poor neighborhood and assume that the people living there "need" the cheapest available housing, where the *quality* of housing is subordinate to *affordability*. In terms of talent retention in these areas, however, quality-of-life issues and quality of housing for "middle-income" people are a higher priority, in my opinion.

We have all seen the effects of concentrated poverty, and they are not good. The challenge was to build housing that would be affordable to moderate-income residents of Hunts Point. For example, a married couple comprised of a school teacher and a traffic cop can earn roughly 130 percent of the area median income. That's not wealthy, but the type of stabilizing influence their day-to-day presence can add to a community suffering from high unemployment, low educational attainment, and a paucity of role models is crucial to its recovery. Yet, in today's real estate market, it is perhaps the most difficult type of housing to develop.

The RFEI was an open call for new ideas and included the goals we had outlined and the methods we had defined—economic diversity, brain-drain reduction, and progressive business development—to meet people where they are today with an eye on how far they can go tomorrow. People would no longer have to leave the South Bronx to have neighborhood amenities and services that people in higher-status neighborhoods enjoyed (see Figure 3.2).

Several teams competed to develop the five-acre site that is close to mass transit nodes as well as Manhattan. Our proposal, called Hunts Point Heights, included a strong, experienced, diverse team—a majority being minority- and women-owned and -led firms. We proposed mixed-income housing and mixed-use commercial development that could transform a chronically underperforming community

FIGURE 3.2. Former Spofford Juvenile Detention Center as proposed by BRP companies, Direct Invest Development LLC, Habitat for Humanity New York City, L + M Development Partners, Majora Carter Group LLC, Perkins Eastman and Settlement Housing Fund, Inc. Rendering courtesy of Perkins Eastman.

from being considered a tax burden into one filled with taxpayers. We built in roughly 10 percent low-income home ownership as a real means of achieving the neighborhood stability people desired.

The spirit and tone of the RFEI *indicated* a shift in NYC's perspective on the future of the South Bronx. When the RFEI was released, we were confident that whether or not we won, it signaled a change in thinking both within and outside the community about what can, should, or could be done to capture the trend of American reurbanization for the benefit of low-status communities across the country.

Sadly, in our opinion, the property was ultimately awarded to an all-white, male-led development team that proposed a fairly typical low-income housing project. It would not have any positive impact on retaining talent born and raised in the community. Instead, it included yet another *community center* and yet another health clinic designed to cater to a chronically unhealthy population. In their model, a school teacher married to a traffic cop make too much money to qualify for these apartments.

Still, I am optimistic that the work we have done in the South Bronx is shifting the collective narrative from the status quo of low expectations to a new course. Changing course will take time. There are many people and organizations who benefit greatly from the status quo, and the new course does require more creativity and patient capital in the in the short term. However, it cannot possibly be any worse than the long-term, negative consequences of gentrification or poverty-level economic maintenance.

Keep local landowners in the deal. Offer equity to existing local land owners so they can stay in the deal and benefit from increasing real estate value.

One of the goals for any new development in low-status communities should be to find ways to help existing minority property owners who have a long-term investment in the area realize some of the economic benefits. Although they are often "invisible," low-status communities have many people who are not "rich" but who own land or buildings and have worked hard to be stable, productive, and mortgage-paying participants in the economy. They have invested in their neighborhoods when no one else did.

As millennials and aging baby boomers lead the reurbanization wave, they are creating greater demand for developments that combine mixed-income housing and commercial development. Many of these projects are springing up in formerly low-status communities.

However, it is important to look at who is capturing the financial benefits of these development projects in neighborhoods previously considered to be too high risk for traditional investment. For the most part, the beneficiaries are established, large-scale developers, exacerbating the growing wealth gap between white Americans and all other minorities.

Existing minority and lower-income landowners who may want to reinvest in their communities typically do not have access to the same streams of capital available to bigger developers. This prevents them from realizing the full development potential of their properties. Furthermore, large developers are not incentivized to include these smaller landowners in their deals, leading to the small landowners cashing out early without the longer-term wealth-building opportunities that would come from owning a share of the development. This is a critical weak spot in any strategy aimed at the longer-term economic health of minority and poor white communities. Many of these local landowners have held and maintained their property through the rough years and then sell their property too quickly and for too little money relative to the future economic potential that their land assets now represent.

In this case a more equitable development option would require that two things be put in place: wealth and inclusion. Local landowners need a way to retain *skin in the game; for them wealth equals land.*

Many lower-income people don't have much wealth to speak of—and less and less so each day as predatory mortgage companies strip whatever equity has been built up through years of homeownership. The typical development process in low-status communities has a similar effect. Long-time owners liquidate their land assets in the face of reurbanization land grabs. They may realize a one-time cash profit, but that is small compared to the longer-term wealth creation potential of that land after it is developed, and the market evolves around it. Cashing out also denies future generations the opportunity to benefit from that land. Helping low-income landowners stay in real estate development deals will affect a small number of people, but the outcomes are enduring. Future generations can attend college, stay out of jail, start new businesses, live longer, and prosper.

There are two ways to accomplish this in low-status communities like the South Bronx: land leases and land trusts. Although long-term land leases are fairly common in New York City downtown office and apartment buildings, we were not able to find examples of their use in low-status communities. For example, the New York and New Jersey Port Authority owns the World Trade Center land; however, Silverstein Properties developed the site through a land lease. Both the Port Authority and Silverstein Properties had a say in how the new World Trade Center site was redeveloped, and both recoup revenues from the economic activity the site generates. This type of ownership is also found in other rural and urban contexts, but very rarely (if ever) among low-income property owners—many of whom purchased urban real estate in the 1970s to 1990s but are unable to develop it to maximum effect today.

Development *will* happen in "transitioning" or gentrifying neighborhoods. Keeping local landowners in the deals that will inevitably proceed and educating them on the benefits of economically diverse community development will help support them to be knowledgeable codevelopers in their own communities. This approach will not only incentivize local landowners from cashing out too fast and early but also it will enable them to benefit from future economic activity on the site—whatever that may be. It's not a guarantee that the resulting development will be more sensitive to the needs of current residents—but it is a guarantee that a minority landowner, who would have been cashed out of the game just as soon as it was starting, would be in it long term by using an instrument that is easily recognized and accepted by a broad range of financial and development institutions.

The land-trust option offers more control (most often by those from outside the community) over the type and affordability in any future development, but it is a longer process, requiring more upfront capital from often-fickle sources like philanthropy. Furthermore, the individual landowner does not directly benefit on the long-term wealth creation side. For these reasons, this is not where I am going to personally spend my time and energy. I think individuals should make profits, create wealth, and have options over how the land is developed.

The success of incorporating land-lease deals into new development depends on how well we attract, connect, and support real estate developers to do what they do best: finance and build. To incentivize real estate developers, it would be necessary to create a fund that can loan at below-market rates for deals that incorporate this land-lease approach. Educating and convincing landowners is actually more difficult, since these types of deals are not prevalent. Some property acquisition costs are greatly reduced, or come off the table altogether, allowing more cash to go into higher quality construction.

But whether the resulting project is one that everyone applauds or not, the land-lease prevents asset liquidation without inhibiting profitable development. Once the land assets are liquidated, it fuels America's widening wealth gap.

The land-lease approach will not directly solve problems of poverty for many people, but it will positively benefit a small number of local property owners—an important leverage point toward reversing the yawning wealth gap here. They in turn can serve as socioeconomic influencers, benefiting the community. Furthermore, the subsidy required is relatively low, especially compared to the long-term benefits of responsibly financed land ownership for educational attainment, health, incarceration, and income potential.

These strategies are drawn from my own firsthand observations of best practices in cities around the word. But no matter how good the practices, any successful development project depends on ongoing community input.

In addition to conducting community surveys as noted above, we have found that the most effective vehicles for community input are advisory boards. One of the most important lessons I have learned is "Don't assume you know the community because they will tell you themselves if you are interested in listening. . . ."

To ensure community investment and to minimize the opposition one can expect to nearly everything new (no matter how good it may be), it is important to maintain an open ear to evolving community needs. These advisory boards meet for biweekly, lightly catered forums to build trust among members who don't often get together in one place. They are structured to encourage and to allow for critical exchanges regarding projects or issues that each member is welcomed to bring to the board. They provide a safe venue to express opinions and build projects while avoiding organizational funding pressures of other agendas.

Advisory boards in this context collect real concerns from the broader community and generate fresh ideas and perspectives by bringing together disparate voices within a geographic area. They are comprised of local landowners, business owners, residents, and informal networks of local influencers. These are not the same people who generally work at, lead, or serve on the boards of established nongovernmental organizations—these people are too busy, or are not attracted to a "justice" message, or don't feel their interests are being met in a way that respects their goals of real prosperity in place.

The value of these boards comes in listening to people, finding the mutual self-interest and synergies, and keeping an open mind. Struggling small business people, moms and dads, beat cops and firefighters, pastors, retirees, students, and others who are motivated every day to improve their own communities have a lot to say, often in unpredictable and unorthodox ways, about community needs.

We have learned that this is a better measure of the potential demand than more traditional market studies. Often we will launch a beta version of a project, learn from how people react to it, refine it, reiterate it, and expand it.

The end result may look different from place to place and evolve over time, but when you market from a position of mutual self-interest, your chances of effective and ongoing engagement improve dramatically, and you can leverage any resources that might otherwise meet the typical dead ends that hinder corporate social responsibility and philanthropic sectors in all markets.

An Insider and an Outsider

I am different than many of my peers in the urban and building design worlds (I have no degrees, just experience), and I have had life experiences that set me apart from most of the people in the community where I was raised and continue to live, work, and invest.

My experiences in both worlds frequently come together in ways that challenge my abilities but give me so much hope for how America's low-status communities can be effectively developed in a more equitable way. Building communities that embrace environmental equality and economic diversity will have positive outcomes for existing residents in ways that none of us can predict but in ways all of us will benefit from. These are underutilized tools in planning today. But this is the best time in urban American history to invest in these communities.

I believe you don't have to move out of your neighborhood to live in a better one. This chapter outlines some of the ways that I am attempting to make that a reality. My solutions are not perfect, not guaranteed, and not even accepted in some circles, but the cost of doing nothing is too high.

NOTES

1. The term "low-status" was used by danah boyd on a panel at a *Fast Company* magazine salon on April 29, 2015, and in her book *It's Complicated: The Social Lives of Networked Teens* (New Haven: Yale *University* Press, 2014) on how video gaming has influenced culture. She could have used any of the other terms I mentioned above, but instead she used "low-status" to illustrate the equality gap in society, without explicitly implicating racism, classism, or geography.

2. Dr. Ronald Carter, former president of Johnson C. Smith University, an historically Black college in Charlotte, North Carolina, used the phrase "self-gentrification" to me in September 2016 when describing how he ensured that the development the university was doing would benefit both the low-income community nearby, as well as the campus.

3. Robert Moses held numerous powerful positions in New York state and local government in the first half of the twentieth century. Often referred to as the "Master Builder," he is credited with building numerous roads, bridges, and other major infrastructure projects (including Shea Stadium and the UN) that transformed the New York landscape. He is also widely criticized for his callous disregard for neighborhoods and widespread "slum" clearance.

4. Seth Godin, "Take this simple marketing quiz," June 27, 2012, http://sethgodin .typepad.com/seths_blog/2012/06/take-this-simple-marketing-quiz.html.

5. By equality I mean many of the same things that equity planners mean when they use the term equity.

Section 2

REGIONAL EQUITY PLANNING

4

CAN WE TALK?

Conversation, Collaboration, and Conflict for a Just Metro

Chris Benner and Manuel Pastor

In recent years, planners and community activists interested in broad issues of equity have shifted their attention to the metro level (Dreier, Swanstrom, and Mollenkopf 2013; Fox and Treuhaft 2005; Orfield and Luce Jr. 2010; Soja 2010). At least one of the initial impulses to move in this direction was the sense that the metropolitan region is where fundamental land-use patterns are set, where the driving clusters of the economy are forged, and where possibilities for redistribution and equity-oriented planning may be most fruitful. The argument for redistribution at a metro level has been bolstered by an emerging body of evidence that suggests that higher levels of inequality and social fragmentation diminish the potential for regional economic growth, thereby setting the stage for incorporating unusual allies into a conversation about metro futures (Benner and Pastor 2015a; Eberts, Erickcek, and Kleinhenz 2006). More broadly, the rubric of regional thinking provided a framework that at least rhetorically placed equity as a concern equal to that of the economy and the environment.

That new conversation was appealing in a world in which so many efforts to restructure opportunity had been stifled by right-wing politics—and the metro level was especially ripe because it is an arena in which the very fuzziness of jurisdictions and absence of governmental structures open up a new space for civic interconnection, knowledge creation, and governance. On the other hand, the very fuzziness of jurisdictional authority means that the metro region is also a level where tools for change can be in short supply. Transportation decisions may be at least somewhat regional, partly because of federal requirements, but the actual land-use decisions that locate housing close to or far from transit are done at the city level. Economic clusters are indeed metropolitan in character, but workforce development systems are frequently constrained to certain cities, and incentive packages used to lure business are also linked to jurisdictions. The overall pattern and affordability of housing is clearly regional but the very landscape is set by suburban jurisdictions using different density standards, while policies like inclusionary zoning are city level in their character.

The emergence of Donald Trump's presidency and the politics behind it has given us new appreciation for the importance and value of the regional equity frame. This is true for at least two key reasons. First is simply that under a Trump administration, the federal government has become a hostile force against equity in nearly all its forms, thus strengthening the need for work at a local, regional, and state scale in the years ahead. Second, on perhaps a more important level, many regions have been able to overcome the kinds of racial, ideological, and class divides that are so dominant in our national politics today. As such, they can offer lessons not just for equity planning, but for our national political environment as well.

So with this new pressing imperative, what's an equity planner to do? Is there really a new possibility for a "just metro," or is this just a new place or geographic level to talk about a "just city"? What are the metropolitan strategies and policies that can bring about change; what does it take in terms of organizing for power; and how does that intersect with conversation processes designed to build consensus? Is this really a call for more collaboration—and isn't conflict necessary to ensure that the issues of low-income and disenfranchised communities stay on the table? And what does all this imply for urban planners who may need to alter their practices to take a more metropolitan approach to equity planning and equity conversations?

These questions have preoccupied us for years—and not just as academics. We both started our journeys to metropolitan thinking from a very activist frame. One of us (Pastor) came of political age doing multiracial coalition-building both before and after the Los Angeles civil unrest while another (Benner) came to early professional practice as the research director for Working Partnerships USA, a labor-linked think-and-do tank in San Jose. This blend of activism and academics does not make us unusual among equity planners; our own observation is that equity planners tend not to be simply dispassionate technical experts who advocate for fairness—many, if not most, try to work directly with disadvantaged populations to help ensure their voices are heard in the planning process. What may set us off in this very collegial and forward-looking crowd is that we have been among those building the regional equity airplane even as we flew—that is, constructing the theory and empirics even as we embraced what looked like a promising venue for analysis and action.

The regional promise was glimpsed mostly because of frustration and a sense that we needed to catch up to the times. In the Los Angeles case, it was clear that the old focus on the neighborhood just wasn't working—after all, community development had been detached from a booming downtown, and, in the infamous 1992 civil unrest, local neighbors had been willing to burn down their own environs when police brutality struck a match to the kindling of poverty. Seeing this, organizers and their allies needed to scale up to something bigger—and from the ashes of this unrest emerged groups like the Los Angeles Alliance for a New Economy, Strategic Concepts in Organizing and Policy Education (SCOPE), and many others who sought to devise new tools like community benefits agreements and also target inequities in regional transportation (Saito 2012). In San Jose, the very nature of the labor-community model undergirding Working Partnerships USA involved understanding the metropolitan economy to better wield power on behalf of working people; this was particularly called for because there was a need to respond to the "new regionalism" that uncritically celebrated Silicon Valley without understanding its underbelly of exclusion and rising inequality (Benner 2002, Dean and Reynolds 2009).

Thus, in this chapter, we will focus on issues of process and in particular the role of conversations about the metropolitan future. We specifically want to sketch further our emerging notion of "diverse and dynamic epistemic communities"—knowledge communities in which data is generated, shared, and used to connect actors across sectors, races, ideologies, and interests in a region and forge a sense of common destiny. As we suggest below, there is not just one way to do this; we specifically suggest that the stewards of these processes can be planners, the business/civic elite, or social movement actors. We also stress that forging a metropolitan community or conversation is not without conflict; as Lester and Reckhow (2013) note, progress on equity generally emerges from more confrontational "skirmishes," particularly because justice advocates and disadvantaged communities frequently arrive with less power and so have less leverage in any such conversation. Whether through principled conflict or more collaborative processes, building diverse knowledge communities rooted in a commitment to reason and ongoing dialogue can play a critical role in creating more equitable regions.

We elaborate these ideas below as follows. We begin by discussing epistemic communities—how we discovered them, why we think they're important, and how we think they work at the metro level. We then discuss the ways in which such communities can facilitate shifts in the scale and scope of equity planning; who it is that can be the stewards of such conversations; and what skills and strategies equity planners might need in order to help build and strengthen such communities. We conclude by discussing how this all relates to improvements in planning practice and to the contemporary political scene.

Talking About the Region. . . .

Researchers generally like to start with hypotheses that can be neatly tested in the field—or, better yet, on our computers in comfortable office settings. Our discovery of the importance of talk did not follow this path. Rather, we tried in a series of research articles and a book called *Just Growth* (2012) to first ask which metropolitan regions were achieving better performance on *both* job growth and income gaps and then to discover from exploratory data analysis and site visits what was driving the superior outcomes. We expected to find that structural factors mattered—and we did. There were beneficial and stabilizing effects, for example, from having a strong public sector and a minority middle class big enough to influence the economy and politics. But we also discovered in subsequent research—much like the study done by researchers at the International Monetary Fund (Berg, Ostry, and Zettelmeyer 2012)—that initial income inequality was the single largest and most statistically significant dragging factor on sustained economic growth (Benner and Pastor 2015a). It wasn't just this income difference that seemed to impact performance. Other measures that seemed to capture social distance (such as the degree of residential segregation; the diffusion of metropolitan power; and, as mentioned in our most recent book, even the extent of political spatial sorting) also played a role in limiting growth sustainability (Benner and Pastor 2015c). Something about growing apart seemed to get in the way of growing together.

And so off we went to look at those metros that were getting it right; some metros that were getting it wrong; and some metros that were either on the upswing or seemed to have lost a former advantage.[1] The results of this latest research were published in a book called *Equity, Growth, and Community: What the Nation Can Learn from America's Metropolitan Regions.*[2] In all, over the course of these two books, we have looked at seventeen metros, with many more coming into our view by virtue of other visits and projects. In each region, we interviewed a wide array of actors, with our questions to informants focused on their experiences in collaborating within the region, both within their broad societal sector (business, government, labor, community, philanthropy), and across sectors. We specifically probed for how people dealt with conflict by trying to understand major stakeholders in regional disputes, the values and priorities held by those different actors, how tensions between different constituencies was handled, and the extent to which diverse perspectives are incorporated (deliberately or informally) into formal governance structures and processes. We also reviewed a wide range of secondary material on each region, including academic work, reports, and media coverage.

We did note that formal "ties that bind," particularly city-county consolidation and integrated metropolitan government structures, tended to cement a sense of common destiny that helped actors find common solutions. But we also discovered an amorphous set of regional cultures, social norms, and practices that seemed to set the stage for coming together—and, borrowing from some literature originally rooted in international policy conflict and cooperation (another sphere in which jurisdictional authority is not generally clear and so new implicit rules must be forged), we called these cultures, norms and practices "epistemic communities" (Haas 1992).

Formally, epistemic communities have been defined as like-minded networks of professionals whose authoritative claim to consensual knowledge provides them with a unique source of power in decision-making processes (Adler and Haas 1992, Haas 1992). As suggested above, though the concept has older roots in studies of scientific communities (Holzner 1968, Holzner and Marx 1979), it gained considerable attention in the early 1990s in the context of international policy development, particularly in situations with high degrees of uncertainty and unclear jurisdictions. The process of creating knowledge together, especially in a series of repeated interactions over extended periods of time, can help participants develop a common language and cognitive frames that allow them to communicate effectively. Epistemic communities build up trust between actors through the process of knowledge creation and sharing, leading to decisions that can produce better—if not optimal—outcomes. Think of it as a solution to collective action problems: when the invisible hand of the market won't do the trick, the very visible act of sharing knowledge can point the way.

In our research, we certainly didn't find people proudly declaring that they were part of an epistemic community—in fact, most observers think the term is clumsy till they try it on and find that our thicker description, offered below, is exactly what they're doing. But we did find a "Seattle Process"—a set of norms about talking out problems in the Seattle metro area that helped to produce a $15 minimum wage, a firm commitment to affordable housing, and set of county-level indicators to track progress on racial equity that is nearly unrivaled in the country. We did find an Envision Utah, a planning process that has settled tough planning conflicts in the Salt Lake City area, including steering transit availability to lower-income areas. We did find a transformed San Antonio—from a place riven by racial conflict over political representation and public infrastructure to an electorate that passed a sales tax on itself to support pre-K for less-advantaged children—with some of the strongest advocacy coming from a chamber of commerce that once angered activists by trying to pitch San Antonio as a low-wage paradise.

These did have the elements of epistemic communities, as written in the literature, but with several different characteristics that we think are critical. First, the traditional definition of epistemic communities involves a collection of experts—a group that is unlikely to be very diverse and indeed bonds over its professional similarities; in our case, the hallmark of a successful epistemic or knowledge community was its ability to be diverse and thus acknowledge different knowledge and ways of knowing. Second, the traditional definition of epistemic communities assumes that it is convened to solve a single problem and then disband when that is over; in our use of the concept, one key feature is that such a community is dynamic and can shift to other challenges as they arise. This is why we have labeled these collaborations "diverse and dynamic" epistemic communities.

Third, and perhaps most importantly, the traditional definition of epistemic communities seems to build on a rationalistic view of actors in which preferences are set and norms agreed to before coming together; the conversation is then about finding solutions based on a common commitment to data and the greater good. In our conception, the process itself is key because it actually shifts preferences, establishes norms, and creates identity (Akerlof and Kranton 2010). Indeed, it is crucial that members of such knowledge communities include not just the "usual suspects" of urban growth coalitions, but a broader constellation of community interests and perspectives.

While we try to concretize this a bit more below, the key point is that creating a diverse regional consciousness about the problems of poverty and its impacts on growth tends to help focus attention on these critical issues; interjurisdictional ties can help (because suburbs, for example, that can be annexed realize rather quickly that they cannot escape the drag on regional growth from high levels of poverty in the urban core); and all this can be pushed along by intentional leadership programs, collaborative planning processes, and other strategies for creating new conversations about metropolitan futures.

A New Scale and Scope

So what does all this mean for equity planners? Urban planning is typically understood as a combination of technical and political processes concerned with improving the welfare of people and their communities specifically by creating better places. The focus of urban planning, therefore, has historically been on the policies and practices that shape the use of land and the design of the urban environment, including air, water, and the infrastructure passing into and out of urban areas such as transportation, communications, and distribution networks.

Of course, it's not just physical infrastructure; planners—and especially equity planners—also sometimes pay significant attention to the social interactions and decision-making processes that shape the physical characteristics of places, including helping design institutions and procedures that bring diverse constituencies together. Given the importance of local authorities in shaping places, the vast majority of city planning practice has been focused on cities and the neighborhoods within them.

As our urban areas have grown far beyond the boundaries of individual cities, however, the scale and scope of activities that are important for being effective have expanded, often to the metro or regional level. Unfortunately, this is a new sort of "final frontier"—one where there is limited governmental authority. In the absence of true regional governments, advocacy planners today have to be more comfortable navigating the complex terrain of regional *governance*. Achieving progress at the regional scale is not simply a matter of convincing a planning commission to adopt a particular plan, or getting a majority of elected officials in city council to pass a policy; more often it requires mobilizing a wide constituency, and convincing stakeholders to endorse change through a combination of methods, including research and data (to understand), advocacy (to convince), and political pressure (to force). It also means a greater appreciation for the interactions between local, regional, state, federal, and even global governance than was the case in the past and the ability to work across multiple types of organizations, including private sector, nonprofit, foundation, labor, and advocacy organizations. But rather than the interest-group-based, winner-take-all politics of conventional political structures, regional governance can resemble more the "deliberate democracy" of conversation and consensus building described by Iris Young (Young 2000).

What does this look like in practice? In Raleigh-Durham, the importance of a governance rather than government approach to regional equity is in part deeply rooted in the "Triple-Helix" model of public, private, and university collaboration that has become the backbone of the region's impressive growth. But it is also rooted in the work of the North Carolina Justice Center, a leading progressive research and advocacy organization that is widely recognized as the "go-to" organization for information and analysis on economic, social, and political justice in the region. In essence, it serves as a common information source for those concerned in the region about social and economic justice; perhaps surprisingly in most regions we've studied, there is no single common source for this kind of information, suggesting one role equity planners can help to play.

Meanwhile, in Sacramento, regional governance processes have revolved more around regional "blueprint planning" processes, which link land-use and transportation planning. These processes were not only important in getting cities, businesses, and community organizations throughout the region to work more closely together; they were also an important model for statewide climate change legislation designed to promote denser urban development. This state legislation, in turn, then provided a new tool that affordable housing and community development advocates throughout the state were able to use, along with environmental allies, to promote more equitable allocation of transportation and development dollars in regional planning. This link from region to state and back to region means that, to be effective, advocates and equity planners had to be able to navigate comfortably between hearings with elected officials in the state capital; coalition-building strategy sessions with local community leaders throughout the Central Valley; data-analysis and scenario planning assemblies with regional technical planners; and project development meetings with city council members and private sector developers. In this case as well, a regional data center with information on equity issues—UC Davis's Center for Regional Change—played a useful role in filling out the picture in a way that brought issues of inclusion into the mix.

It's not just the navigation between levels and jurisdictions that is important. Working at the expanded scale of a region also requires an expanded scope of topics with which equity planning has to engage. In the past, most equity planning work focused on the terrain of traditional planning departments—housing, land use, neighborhood development, community economic development, urban transit systems, and the like. Equity planners working at a regional scale today also work in these areas but are just as likely to also be engaged in struggles over workforce development initiatives, early childhood education, regional goods movement patterns, cluster-based economic development strategies, and even energy efficiency and climate mitigation policies. This requires the ability to incorporate insights from a wide range of areas of expertise and to navigate an even broader range of interests.

In Salt Lake City, for example, Envision Utah's recent long-range planning initiative—looking out to 2050—engaged in eleven issues of concern in the region: water, agriculture, energy, education, recreation, air quality, housing and cost of living, jobs and the economy, transportation and communities, public lands, and disaster resilience. As of March 2017, more than 54,000 residents had expressed their preference in these areas in an online survey (Envision Utah n.d.). In Oklahoma City, through multiple rounds of investments through the Metropolitan Area Projects initiative, specific projects have included many typical capital improvement and economic development projects (such as a baseball stadium, convention center renovations, improvements at the state fairgrounds, an urban canal entertainment district, a new public library, and a near-complete rebuilding of a music performance hall) and also major environmental projects (including transforming the North Canadian River into a series of river-lakes, with associated recreational facilities including a whitewater rafting and kayak center), major educational projects (more than $700 million for technology and capital improvements in schools throughout the region), and the creation of four new senior health and wellness centers with associated active living programs. Kansas City's Mid-America Regional Council has programs on everything from early childhood education and Head Start to services for the aging, along with public health and health care, emergency services, and economic development programs that included for many years an international trade division.

What all these cases show is a willingness of metropolitan planners to go beyond the usual silos. Moving an equity agenda in that context requires also moving beyond the scale and scope of traditional planning efforts. Because this sort of bridging puts planners at the intersection of both jurisdictions and issues, detailed ongoing conversations among diverse constituencies are necessary to forge understanding and make progress. The development of data and a shared knowledge base can be helpful to go beyond "politics as usual."

Regional Stewards and Social Movements

The notion of a "regional steward" was developed with the creation of the Alliance for Regional Stewardship in May 2000. "Regional stewards," the founding document argued, "are integrators who cross boundaries of jurisdiction, sector, and discipline to address complex regional issues such as sprawl, equity, education, and economic development" (Henton and Alliance for Regional Stewardship 2000, 3). Despite its own largely elite-driven approach, the Alliance's commitment to making connections among an innovative economy, livable communities, social inclusion, and a collaborative style of governance is a useful framing, and this approach can be recognized in a much broader set of actors.

Indeed, our research suggests that, while processes creating diverse and dynamic epistemic communities might be linked to planning departments or agencies, they could just as easily happen in a range of structures and processes completely outside of formal urban planning. Importantly, such knowledge communities are not just collaborative forums; in fact, conflictual skirmishes can also both play an important role in building knowledge communities, as in San Antonio where the constant organizing of Communities Organized for Public Service (COPS)—an affiliate of the Industrial Areas Foundation organizing network—helped to change the political terrain and generate more civic concerns about disadvantaged communities.

Indeed, there is also arguably a stronger role for community organizing and expanded social movements in regional equity planning than in equitable city efforts, given the often greater challenges in shifting entrenched power interests at a regional scale than within a single city. In our own case studies, regions that did not have experiences of strong social movements were able to achieve inclusive growth for some period of time but struggled in the face of more fundamental economic transformations. Grand Rapids and Charlotte, for example, are both places where a business elite with a strong sense of regional stewardship was successful in the 1980s and 1990s in leading broadly inclusive efforts to develop and restructure their regions. But as leadership aged and the economic and demographic changes in these regions became more diverse and complex, inequality increased with few organized voices to speak for marginalized populations.

Without a tradition of strong community organizing or influence of marginalized voices in regional decision making, inequality tends to increase or go unaddressed. Yet it is also important that the conflict inherent in political struggles contribute to a sense of common regional destiny, rather than reinforce antagonistic zero-sum frameworks—a shift that seems to require repeated interactions and extended communication over time. Overall, this suggests that an expanded notion of the stewards of regional equity and an expanded role for social movements are an important part of creating the kinds of diverse and dynamic epistemic communities that can lead to more equitable metros.

In some contexts, traditional planning agencies remain important regional stewards. In Sacramento, for example, cross-sector communication processes were driven primarily by the public sector through the efforts of the Sacramento Area Council of Governments (SACOG). Through a participatory process of developing long-range regional plans, SACOG helped a wide range of constituencies understand the importance of integrating land-use and transportation planning to ensure quality of life in the region. Initiated in the early 2000s, this "Blueprint Process" was prominent in the region's efforts to recover from economic shocks of the 1990s, and it also revealed some underlying yet commonly held values around resource conservation and sustainability, helping bridge gaps among otherwise uncommon allies.

In other contexts, traditional planning bodies are minor players, and the bridge building is led by other organizations. In Salt Lake City, for example, with its broadly held conservative and antigovernment sentiments, a very similar participatory process of long-range regional planning was led not by a regional government planning body but rather by the small nonprofit organization called Envision Utah. Despite different origins, the process of information sharing across diverse constituencies and the generation of broadly shared goals for regional development patterns informed by like values across diverse constituencies was quite similar to Sacramento. Here, the inclusion of diverse constituencies in regional planning processes was also facilitated by certain characteristics of the Mormon Church, entirely outside of formal planning processes. The lay clergy structure of the church, which brings large numbers of business and political leaders in their role as local bishops directly into the church's large social welfare programs, helps build systemic ties between elite-leadership and social work activities. The widespread international missionary experience of young Mormons has contributed to a remarkably open and welcoming tone around immigrant integration for such a conservative state.

In Oklahoma City, it was the chamber of commerce who played an important role in bringing diverse constituencies together. The Metropolitan Areas Projects (MAPS) initiatives brought together a range of different interests, including across partisan lines, as the Republican mayor and chamber of commerce were the leading advocates for the increased taxes required to pursue the MAPS project. The requirement that voters either approve all or none of the related projects associated with the tax increases required residents to understand a diversity of interests in the region. In Fresno, it was the philanthropic sector and community organizations which have been critically important in bringing together different constituencies in recent years; funding from the California Endowment in their Building Healthy Communities initiative was critical in supporting the participation of community organizations in a broad consultative process to create a new general plan in 2012 that was attempting to counter decades of largely unrestricted (and sometimes developer-corrupted) urban sprawl (Benner and Pastor 2015b). So, regional equity planning efforts are emerging from a wide variety of regional actors, which are only sometimes directly linked with formal planning processes.

The example of Fresno, however, highlights another key point from our research on the ability of regional planning processes to achieve regional equity: social movements are important for addressing inequities but they seem to work best in contexts where conflict doesn't lead to the demonization of opponents but rather helps build a sense of common destiny among constituencies with competing interests and values. Fresno is a place where social movements were quite strong in the 1970s, building on the significant United Farm Workers' history in the region. But in subsequent decades, the region has been unable to shift away from an economy rooted in low-wage labor, largely unrestricted urban sprawl, and lax environmental regulations that combined have produced a region with the second highest percentage of concentrated poverty and some of the worst air pollution in the country (Berube 2006). The absence of collaboration in the region, environmental justice and community activists told us, has led them to believe that their most promising path forward is through adversarial lawsuits rather than collaborative policy development. While there are hopeful signs—including a new commitment to promoting downtown revitalization and a 2017 collaborative process to secure cap-and-trade revenues to invest in promotion of both downtown and surrounding low-income neighborhoods—as long as conflict in Fresno remains in a zero-sum and antagonistic framework, it is hard to see how the region will substantially shift from current development paths.

San Antonio provides a striking contrast. Here, in the 1970s and 1980s, the level of antagonism between activists and regional business leadership was also striking. As suggested above, COPS (an affiliate of the Saul Alinsky-founded Industrial Areas Foundation) was pursuing strategies to disrupt business to try to gain new investments in poor communities. The relationship between the organizers and business was so strained that Tom Frost, the head of a major local bank that was a COPS's target, was distributing copies of Alinsky's *Rules for Radicals* to his business colleagues in an effort to help them be better prepared to confront their adversaries. Yet this all too familiar antagonistic culture shifted over time to a more collaborative approach in which Tom Frost eventually became chair of a major COPS-initiated workforce development initiative called Project QUEST. Today, the chatter is all about how well different sectors collaborate (enough to get rewarded a Promise Neighborhood, a Choice Neighborhood, a Promise Zone, and a Sustainable Communities Initiative from the federal government). In 2012, a majority of residents voted to pass a sales tax increase that will steer additional resources to pre-K education for the least advantaged kids—with the support not only of a progressive mayor and community groups but also the chamber of commerce.

Why have key stakeholders in San Antonio been able to find ways to collaborate in the midst of conflict over competing interests and values? We believe organizing was a critical component of the story that helped to surface issues of equity and inclusion. But in contrast to Fresno, regional stakeholders were able to not let conflict get in the way of continued engagement. Over time—and facilitated through the deliberate efforts of a few key bridge-building individuals—this continued engagement evolved to a growing sense of common destiny and the broad culture and social norms of collaboration that characterize the region today. It was the repeated interactions, and a commitment on both sides to maintain a dialogue, that enabled San Antonio to move beyond unproductive conflict.

Skills and Strategies for Knowledge Building

If we are right that diverse and dynamic epistemic communities can be valuable in underpinning processes of creating a just metro, planners may need to develop new skills or at least brush up and modify the skills they have. This calls for a dramatically expanded understanding of urban futures. Not only do planners have to understand the spatial and institutional aspects of land-use planning and infrastructure development, but as we've mentioned, they may also be called on to engage in a wide range of other issues, including workforce development, early childhood education, school integration, public health, energy policy, climate change, labor relations, policing and the criminal justice system, air and water quality, to name just a few. All of these emerged in our interviews as important dimensions of achieving sustainable equity processes in different regions.

But what seems to be valuable in many regions was not just the diversity of knowledge bases, but the collective nature of that knowledge development—and the planner's potential role in guiding that process. Perhaps the most obvious example of shared knowledge development in our case studies was in Salt Lake City, with the work of Envision Utah. Here, the explicit goal of their efforts was not to develop a detailed general plan for how the region should develop but rather to help identify the key values shared by a broad swath of Salt Lake City's population and translate that into more specific goals designed to guide regional development. The seven goals that emerged from this process—improving air quality, promoting housing options, creating transportation choices, encouraging water conservation, preserving critical lands, supporting efficient infrastructure, and exploring community development—are not particularly surprising or transformative in themselves.

What is critical is that these goals did not come from professional planners but instead emerged from a broad consultative, knowledge-generation process that included more than two thousand people in fifty public workshops and more than seventeen thousand responses to Internet and newspaper surveys. This process helped ensure that priorities for development in the region were rooted in the lived experiences and values of diverse communities and were broadly shared by leaders throughout the region. These public participation and distillation skills are critical to a new generation of planners and helped underpin future rounds of regional planning processes.

But perhaps as important as the knowledge-base planners' need to effectively engage in these conversations is the skill in framing issues and discussions. As we have learned from the work of George Lakoff and others, the way issues are framed makes a significant difference in how people understand the world and how they act (Bolman and Deal 2013, Lakoff 2004, Lakoff and Johnson 2008). We are most definitely not experts on cognitive linguistics, but we were struck in our case studies by the different ways people framed issues of conflict and collaboration in their work in the region. In more equitable regions, issues were framed around a respect for difference and a sense of a common future together; in more unequal regions, the frame was more about immediate interests and frustrations about lack of influence or impact.

Again, Salt Lake City provides an illustrative (and perhaps surprising) example of the more positive framing. In many parts of the United States, undocumented immigrants are viewed as an unwelcome alien invasion, and the strength of that aversion to immigrants was a key part of Trump's electoral victory. One might expect that to be the case in Utah, one of the country's politically reddest and, until recently, demographically whitest states. However, Utah has formally allowed undocumented immigrants to have legal driving privileges since 1999, and undocumented students have been able to pay in-state tuition at state universities since 2002. In the words of one Mexican immigrant, "I've lived in California. I've lived in Las Vegas. No place is like this. Here, they don't think just because we don't have papers we aren't human beings" (Riley 2006). Partly because of the Mormon faith, partly because of the stress on family, and partly because of an appreciation of markets and hard work, the rapidly growing immigrant population is seen as part of the overall fabric of the state—and that framing has had a real impact on policy.

This inclusionary framing stands in stark contrast to places like Fresno, where a number of respondents suggested that the problems are too large and the public too divided to actually work through solutions. Many in that region think that progress on equity can only be made by "standing up" to entrenched interests. That may well be, but "entrenched" also means "not going away." Eventually, conflict will need to shift to collaboration, as occurred in San Antonio, if there is to be significant impact on actual economic and social outcomes. While this might initially sound like a "collaborative leadership" approach (Chrislip and Larson 1994; Henton and Melville 1997; Innes and Rongerude 2005, 56; Kanter 1994), we prefer to think of it as "principled conflict." From this perspective, conflict includes a commitment to the idea that struggles should be waged with integrity and that it is possible to directly address real conflicts in goals, objectives, and values with opposing actors in a way that also recognizes the need to sustain long-term relationships, despite the parties' differences. This implies the need for a particular type of strategy—an approach that is able to both effectively represent particular values and interests *and* is also able to dialogue with opposing interests and "unusual allies" in the search for common ground and shared destiny.

Finally, there is a very concrete skill and resource that planners can develop and contribute: data that focuses on equity. We are not naïve; we know that facts do not always win the day. But it's also the case that creating data sets that illustrate disparities and provide guidelines for remedies can be crucial, particularly when advocates are fighting to make sure their concerns are addressed as effectively as the concerns of those more focused on data-rich arenas like the economy and the environment. We noted in both the Raleigh and Sacramento cases how data provision from an equity perspective helped move along the dialogue; this was also the case in San Antonio where a data effort launched by then-Mayor Henry Cisneros helped keep disparities in the limelight. We have contributed to several efforts that have tried to create such tools: the Regional Opportunity Index (n.d.) that addressed integrated community opportunity throughout California; the National Equity Atlas (n.d.) which was developed in collaboration with PolicyLink; and an environmental justice screening method that was the precursor to CalEnviroScreen, a tool being using to target cap-and-trade proceeds for investment in less advantaged communities (Sadd et al. 2011). All have created platforms for discussion, policy, and organizing.

Implications for Equity Planning

In the face of rising inequality, growing social separation, entrenched political partisanship, and fragmented media, American policymaking often seems impossibly polarized. Yet even as the nation seems stuck in perpetual conflict in terms of facing our critical challenges, many metropolitan regions have found a more sustainable consensus on the direction their businesses, workers, and residents should work for, together. These better performing regions are often characterized by structural factors that facilitate coming together—such as shared jurisdictions, a stronger underlying economic base, or a sizeable minority middle class pushing for both growth and justice. But they are often also characterized by more subtle factors that seem to help explain their more successful outcomes: diverse constituencies weaving a sense of common regional destiny; ongoing dialogue and engagement despite differences that help to manage conflict in productive ways; and a commitment to data and reason rather than just opinions and ideology driving decision-making processes. Such efforts stand in stark contrast to less successful regions, where fragmented communities, zero-sum conflicts, and ideologically entrenched positions seem to undermine regions' ability to successfully address the challenges of our rapidly changing demographic and economic circumstances.

We are not Pollyannaish about these efforts; they will not lift up issues of equity in the absence of strong social movements pushing progressive agendas. Even if such movements manage to get equity issues on the agenda, urban America is facing a strong headwind from the Trump presidency—successes at the regional level may be stymied by reactionary policies from DC. State governments can also be a barrier; already, some states such as Missouri, Alabama, Texas, and Arizona have pursued "preemption" strategies to prevent key cities anchoring metros to raise local minimum wages (Rivlin-Nadler 2016). Metro-level efforts are not a substitute for national- or state-level strategies—but they can be a base for making change, and they are a level on which deep social divisions can be at least potentially bridged.

Because of this, equity planners should expand their tool-kit and organizing skills. Certainly, planning must grow its scale and scope, paying greater attention to regional- rather than city-level processes; considering issues beyond the land-use and built environments issues that dominant planning; and addressing not just physical infrastructure but also the social infrastructure that can underpin regional knowledge sharing. This also requires expanding the sense of who is considered to be an important regional leader and working to expand these leaders' role in regional planning processes. And, of course, we need the data and ideas that can actually move the needle—so research and policy development remain key.

But we want to strongly suggest, as Yochai Benkler (2011, 117) argues in his path-breaking volume, *The Penguin and the Leviathan*, that

> [t]alk is not cheap; through it we can come to define our preferences, goals, and desires in a situation; begin to build mutual empathy; negotiate what norms are appropriate and what course of action is fair; and begin to build trust and understand one another.

Conversation, in short, can help to change hearts and minds in ways that encourage collaboration rather than zero-sum competition. And this, in fact, may be one of the central things that planners can do: stop assuming that interests and preference are immutable and instead engage metropolitan and urban residents in ways that cause them to cease "othering" actors and communities and instead find uncommon common ground (Blackwell et al. 2010, Powell 2012). If they could help do that—and then bubble that up to a nation wracked by toxic inequality, social distance, and epistemic polarization—then that would be a healthy step forward for the nation as a whole.

NOTES

1. In our most recent effort, we selected the cases by examining the change in economic growth and social equity in four time periods: 1980s, 1990s, 2000s, and the entire

thirty-year period (1980–2010). The indicators we used to measure economic growth were the change in employment and the change in earnings per job while the indicators we used to measure equity were the change in the percent living below poverty and the change in the ratio of household income for those at the eightieth percentile of the distribution relative to those at the twentieth percentile. To measure where the region stood at the end-point of our time frame, we used median household income, and to measure equity, we used the Gini coefficient.

2. This book, *Equity, Growth, and Community: What the Nation Can Learn from America's Metro Areas* (Berkeley: California University Press, 2015) is available for free download at the University of California Press open access imprint: http://www.luminosoa.org/site/books/10.1525/luminos.6/.

REFERENCES

Akerlof, G. A., and R. Kranton. 2010. *Identity Economics: How Our Identities Shape Our Work, Wages, and Well-Being.* Princeton: Princeton University Press.

Benkler, Y. 2011. *The Penguin and the Leviathan: How Cooperation Triumphs over Self-Interest.* New York: Crown Business.

Benner, C. 2002. *Work in the New Economy: Flexible Labor Markets in Silicon Valley.* Malden: Blackwell.

Benner, C., and M. Pastor. 2012. *Just Growth: Inclusion and Prosperity in America's Metropolitan Regions.* New York: Routledge.

——. 2015a. "Brother, can you spare some time? Sustaining prosperity and social inclusion in America's metropolitan regions," *Urban Studies* 52 (7): 1339–56, https://doi.org/10.1177/0042098014549127.

——. 2015b. "Collaboration, Conflict and Community-Building at the Regional Scale: Implications for Advocacy Planning," *Journal of Planning Education and Research* 35 (3): 307–22.

——. 2015c. *Equity, Growth, and Community: What the Nation Can Learn from America's Metro Areas.* Berkeley: University of California Press.

Berg, A., J. D. Ostry, and J. Zettelmeyer. 2012. "What makes growth sustained?" *Journal of Development Economics* 98 (2): 149–66, https://doi.org/10.1016/j.jdevec0.2011.08.002.

Berube, A. 2006. *Confronting Concentrated Poverty in Fresno.* Washington, DC: Brookings Institution. http://www.brookings.edu/~/media/Files/rc/speeches/2006/0906metropolitanpolicy_berube/20060906_fresno.pdf.

Blackwell, A. G., S. Kwoh, M. Pastor, and American Assembly. 2010. *Uncommon Common Ground: Race and America's Future.* New York: W.W. Norton.

Bolman, L. G., and T. E. Deal. 2013. *Reframing Organizations: Artistry, Choice, and Leadership.* 1st ed. San Francisco: Jossey-Bass.

Chrislip, D., and C. Larson. 1994. *Collaborative Leadership.* San Francisco: Jossey-Bass.

Dean, A. B., and D. B. Reynolds. 2009. *A New New Deal: How Regional Activism Will Reshape the American Labor Movement.* Ithaca: ILR Press.

Dreier, P., T. Swanstrom, and J. H. Mollenkopf. 2013. *Place Matters: Metropolitics for the Twenty-First Century.* 2nd ed.; rev. ed. Lawrence: University Press of Kansas.

Eberts, R., G. Erickcek, and J. Kleinhenz. 2006. *Dashboard Indicators for the Northeast Ohio Economy: Prepared for the Fund for Our Economic Future.* Cleveland: Federal Reserve Bank of Cleveland.

Envision Utah. n.d. Website. Accessed March 2015. http://envisionutah.net (now http://www.envisionutah.org).

Fox, R., and S. Treuhaft. 2005. *Shared Prosperity, Stronger Regions: An Agenda for Rebuilding America's Older Core Cities.* Oakland: PolicyLink.

Haas, P. M. 1992. "Introduction: Epistemic Communities and International Policy Coordination," *International Organization* 46 (1): 1–35, https://doi.org/10.1017/S0020818300001442.

Henton, D. C., and Alliance for Regional Stewardship. 2000. *Regional Stewardship: A Commitment to Place.* Palo Alto: The Alliance for Regional Stewardship. http://www.regionalstewardship.org/Documents/Monograph1.pdf.

Henton, D., and J. Melville. 1997. *Grassroots Leaders for a New Economy: How Civic Entrepreneurs Are Building Prosperous Communities.* San Francisco: Jossey-Bass.

Holzner, B. 1968. *Reality construction in Society.* Cambridge: Schenkman.

Holzner, B., and J. Marx. 1979. *Knowledge Affiliation: The Knowledge System in Society.* Boston: Allyn and Bacon.

Innes, J. E., and J. Rongerude. 2005. *Collaborative Regional Initiatives: Civic Entrepreneurs Work to Fill the Governance Gap.* San Francisco: The James Irvine Foundation. http://folio.iupui.edu/handle/10244/46.

Kanter, R. M. 1994. "Collaborative Advantage: The Art of Alliances," *Harvard Business Review* 72 (4): 96–108.

Lakoff, G. 2004. *Don't Think of an Elephant! Know Your Values and Frame the Debate: The Essential Guide for Progressives.* White River Junction, VT: Chelsea Green.

Lakoff, G., and M. Johnson. 2008. *Metaphors We Live By.* Chicago: University of Chicago Press.

Lester, T. W., and S. Reckhow. 2013. "Network governance and regional equity: Shared agendas or problematic partners?" *Planning Theory* 12 (2): 115–38. https://doi.org/10.1177/1473095212455189

National Equity Atlas. n.d. Website. http://nationalequityatlas.org.

Orfield, M., and T. F. Luce Jr. 2010. *Region: Planning the Future of the Twin Cities.* Minneapolis: University of Minnesota Press.

Powell, John A. 2012. *Racing to Justice: Transforming Our Conceptions of Self and Other to Build an Inclusive Society.* Bloomington: Indiana University Press.

Regional Opportunity Index. n.d. Website. University of California, Davis. http://interact.regionalchange.ucdavis.edu/roi/.

Riley, M. 2006. "Utah's embrace: no documents, no problem," *Denver Post,* April 1. Accessed June 26, 2014. http://www.denverpost.com/search/ci_3663998.

Rivlin-Nadler, M. 2016. "Preemption Bills: A New Conservative Tool to Block Minimum Wage Increases," *New Republic,* February 29. Accessed April 3, 2017. https://newrepublic.com/article/130783/preemption-bills-new-conservative-tool-block-minimum-wage-increases.

Sadd, J., M. Pastor, R. Morello-Frosch, J. Scoggins, and B. M. Jesdale. 2011. "Playing It Safe: Assessing Cumulative Impact and Social Vulnerability through an Environmental Justice Screening Method in the South Coast Air Basin, California," *International Journal of Environmental Research and Public Health* 8 (5), 1441–59, https://doi.org/10.3390/ijerph8051441.

Saito, L. T. 2012. "How Low-Income Residents Can Benefit from Urban Development: The LA Live Community Benefits Agreement," *City & Community* 11 (2), 129–50, https://doi.org/10.1111/j.1540–6040.2012.01399.x.

Soja, E. W. 2010. *Seeking Spatial Justice.* Minneapolis: University of Minnesota Press.

Young, I. M. 2000. *Inclusion and Democracy.* New York: Oxford University Press.

5

EQUITY PLANNING IN A FRAGMENTED SUBURBAN SETTING

The Case of St. Louis

Todd Swanstrom

Equity planning emerged out of the urban turmoil and community organizing of the 1960s and 1970s. Between 1964 and 1968, cities exploded with civil unrest. Appointed by President Johnson to look into the causes of the riots, the Kerner Commission pointed to deplorable conditions in the black ghetto and famously proclaimed: "White institutions created it, white institutions maintain it, and white society condones it" (Kerner Commission 1968, 2). White flight from central cities to the suburbs, the Kerner Commission argued, was a principal cause of urban ghettos: "[C]entral cities are becoming more heavily Negro while the suburban fringes around them remain almost entirely white" (Kerner Commission 1968, 13).

In 1969, one year after the Kerner Commission issued its report, Carl Stokes became the first African American mayor of an American city with a population of over one hundred thousand.[1] He appointed a relative unknown, Norm Krumholz, as Planning Director. Gathering around him a talented coterie of progressive planners, Krumholz developed the principles of what has come to be known as equity planning. The unspoken premise of equity planning is that city governments and planning commissions can take meaningful action to improve the lives of the urban poor and disadvantaged minorities.

Recent turmoil in the small suburb of Ferguson, Missouri, following the shooting of Michael Brown on August 9, 2014, is a clear sign that the geography of disadvantage has shifted from cities to suburbs. While cities still contain a disproportionate share of poor and minorities, almost all central cities are experiencing an influx of young, educated professionals who are revitalizing neighborhoods around the urban core. Increasingly, poor people, people of color, and immigrants are settling in suburbs, not central cities. Instead of one city government and school district, they face a fragmented institutional landscape of smaller (and often weaker) municipalities and school districts. Many live in unincorporated parts of metropolitan areas, where planning and land-use authority is in the hands of a distant county government. The built environment in suburbs is different from central cities, and the challenges that marginalized populations face are also different. The practice of equity planning must adapt to the new landscape of suburban poverty.

I hope to accomplish three tasks in this chapter: (1) synthesize the literature on the growth of low-income and minority populations in suburbs; (2) identify the different challenges facing equity planners in suburbs versus central cities; and (3) draw lessons for equity planners from a case study of equity planning in the inner-ring suburbs of St. Louis. In many ways, I argue, the challenges of poverty and social exclusion are greater in suburbs than in central cities. In addition to redistributing resources, equity planners in suburbs need to invent new institutional and civic structures for delivering those resources to those who need them the most.

The Shifting Geography of Disadvantage

The "Great Divorce" of the city of St. Louis from St. Louis County froze the city boundaries in 1875. With the city unable to annex new territory, the St. Louis metropolitan area has become an extreme case of suburbanization. According to 2014 population estimates, St. Louis City contains only 11.3 percent of metropolitan area population, ranking it forty-third out of the fifty largest metros on this dimension. St. Louis is also one of the most institutionally fragmented in the nation, ranking third in both the number of local governments and the number of school districts per one hundred thousand population (East-West Gateway Council of Governments 2015, 113). The research is clear: other things being equal, the greater the fragmentation across municipalities and school districts, the higher the level of racial and economic segregation (Weiher 1991, Heikkil 1996, Bischoff 2008, Rothwell and Massey 2010). If it is true that you can understand a phenomenon best by examining its most extreme manifestation, then examining the St. Louis case should be able to shed light on the special challenges of suburban poverty.

During the founding period of equity planning, suburban poverty was rare, and equity planners focused almost exclusively on central cities. After reviewing the 1970 census, Krumholz and his staff noted that 98 percent of the suburban growth in the 1960s was white; blacks represented only 4.5 percent of the suburban population (Krumholz and Forester 1990, 17). Reflecting on this reality, in 1970, President Nixon's Secretary of Housing and Urban Development (HUD) George Romney described suburbs as a "high-income white noose" around the black inner city.[2]

After 1970, however, black suburbanization accelerated rapidly. By 1990, 37 percent of the black population of the largest metros lived in the suburbs; by 2010 a majority of African Americans (51 percent) lived in suburbs (Johnson 2014; citing Frey 2001 and Orfield and Luce 2012).[3] With race and class tightly connected, the suburbanization of poverty has followed closely on the heels of black suburbanization. Between 2000 and 2010 the poor population in the suburbs of the largest one hundred metros increased by over half (53 percent), more than doubling the rate of increase in central cities (23 percent). By 2010, 55 percent of the poor population in the largest metros lived in suburbs (Kneebone and Berube 2013, 17–18). Not only are more poor people living in suburbs, they also are increasingly living in areas of concentrated poverty. Although concentrated poverty is more prevalent in cities than in suburbs, it is increasing rapidly in the suburbs. According to the American Community Survey, from 2006 to 2010, 29 percent of the suburban poor lived in areas with poverty rates exceeding 20 percent (Kneebone and Berube 2013, 31).

St. Louis is on the leading edge of these trends. Compared to other metropolitan areas, more poor and minority households live outside the central city in the St. Louis metropolitan area. According to the 2010 census, only 30 percent of those in the metro area who identify as "black only" live in the city of St. Louis. As Figure 5.1 shows, many more poor people now live in suburban St. Louis County than in the city of St. Louis. (The city of St. Louis is its own separate county.) Bernadette Hanlon reports that in 2000 "[a]lmost half the Midwest's high-poverty inner-ring suburbs were located in St. Louis" (Hanlon 2012, 75).

Older, inner-ring suburbs are not uniformly poor. The suburbanization of black and poor households in St. Louis has followed Homer Hoyt's sectoral model of neighborhood change. According to Hoyt, households do not move out in uniform concentric circles as originally hypothesized by the Chicago School of Human Ecology. Instead, different economic groups migrate outward along transportation corridors in what looks more like pie slices than concentric circles; once established in one sector, high-rent (and low rent) neighborhoods "tend to move out in that sector to the periphery of the city" (Hoyt 1939, 119). Historically, black households in St. Louis migrated north and west out of the urban core.

Figure 5.2 shows the spread of concentrated poverty from St. Louis City into suburban St. Louis County. Concentrated poverty is spreading northwest out of

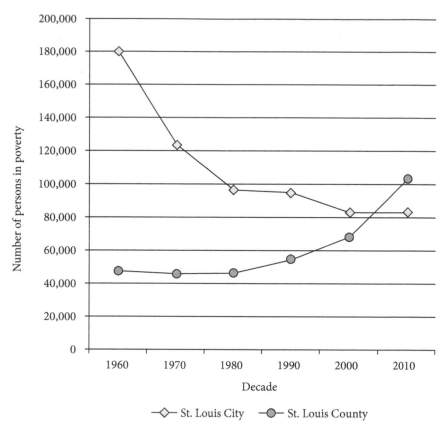

FIGURE 5.1. Persons in Poverty, St. Louis City and St. Louis County, by Decade, 1960–2010. Source: 1960–2000 Decennial Census, 2008–2012 ACS 5-Year Estimates.

the city of St. Louis into the suburbs in St. Louis County that were built under the pressure of the housing shortage after World War II to about 1965. Postwar suburbs tend to have modest homes with homogeneous architecture and often few attractive retail areas. By contrast, prewar suburbs directly west of the city of St. Louis, such as Clayton and Kirkwood, tend to have larger homes with more distinctive architecture, as well as pedestrian-friendly retail centers.

Black suburbs are basically an extension of the segregated black communities in North St. Louis City. The historical pattern of segregation was enforced by "a tangle of private practices and public policies" that largely restricted black families to neighborhoods north of the infamous "Delmar divide" in St. Louis (Gordon 2008, 83; Rothstein 2014).[4] These included racially restrictive covenants attached to deeds, the refusal of the federal government to insure mortgages in black

FIGURE 5.2.   High-Poverty Areas (20% or more residents living below the poverty level), St. Louis City and County, 2000 and 2010. Source: U.S. 2010 Decennial Census, American Community Survey 2008–2012 5-Year Estimates. Map courtesy of Jenny Connelly-Bowen.

neighborhoods, and racial discrimination by homeowners and landlords. In 1948, in a case that originated in St. Louis (*Shelley v. Kraemer 334 U.S. 1*), the U.S. Supreme Court struck down the judicial enforcement of restrictive covenants that had prevented many white homeowners from selling to blacks. In 1968 the Fair Housing Act outlawed discrimination in purchasing and renting housing, and in 1977 the passage of the Community Reinvestment Act provided a mechanism for communities to challenge redlining by federally regulated banks. Today, racial segregation is largely upheld by the inability of African American families to afford homes in more privileged parts of the region, which are walled off from the poor by high prices and exclusionary zoning laws, as well as continued racial steering. Economic segregation, which is legal, reinforces historic patterns of racial segregation.

The Challenge of Suburban Poverty

Poverty presents similar challenges for families, whether they live in a city or a suburb. The built environment of suburbs, however, presents additional challenges.

First, it drives up the cost of transportation, which can be especially burdensome for low-income families. Moreover, in both the public and nonprofit sectors institutions are generally weaker in suburbs than in central cities. The redistributive agenda of equity planning is more difficult to achieve when institutional boundaries are superimposed on historical patterns of economic and racial segregation.

Today's poor and racially segregated suburbs did not start out that way. After World War II, developers rushed to satisfy the pent-up housing demand, mass-producing smaller homes (often 800 to 1,000 square feet) in tract housing developments using a few standard floor plans. To keep costs down, these homes usually had little ornamentation or distinctive design. Typically, they were one-story bungalows, with a "picture" window marking the placement of the living room and a kitchen in back overlooking a small yard. Often the house was connected to a separate garage by a breezeway. Aided by Federal Housing Administration (FHA) and Veterans Affairs (VA) loan guarantees, the white working class flocked to the new postwar suburbs. Market demand for these modest suburban homes remained strong for decades.

As white working class families moved into the middle class, however, they yearned for larger homes with more modern amenities, such as two or more bathrooms, nine-foot ceilings, family rooms, central air conditioning, and attached garages. Developers turned to building larger homes for the middle and upper classes in the exurbs, increasing economic segregation across suburbs (Jargowsky 2002, Dwyer 2007). According to the U.S. Census Bureau, the median size of a new single-family home built in 2014 was 2,506 feet (U.S. Dept. of Commerce 2014). Exurbanization is to older suburbs what suburbanization was to central cities; it siphons off housing demand, leaving behind more obsolete housing for households further down the economic ladder. The problem has not just been that more affluent families were moving out to distant suburbs but that housing production has far outstripped household formation decade after decade—especially in weak market metros like St. Louis. Between 1990 and 2000, metropolitan areas in the bottom third of job and population growth built new housing at a rate six times the growth of population (Watson 2007). In the 1990s, St. Louis built 1.7 units of new housing for every new household in the region (Bier and Post 2006, 179). Housing overproduction leads inexorably to housing vacancy and abandonment in central cities and inner-ring suburbs.[5]

The *de facto* affordable housing policy in the United States is to subsidize the construction of new housing for affluent families on the suburban fringe, who then leave behind their old homes for those on the next rung down the economic ladder, with housing eventually filtering down to the poor. As the housing filtering chain has lengthened, increasingly, those at the bottom are moving into suburban housing. Both urban decline and urban revitalization drive poor and minority families to the suburbs: (1) as central city neighborhoods decay, many families flee to the suburbs in search of safer neighborhoods, a higher quality of life, and better performing schools; and (2) as neighborhoods gentrify, some families are forced to move to the suburbs in search of more affordable housing. The push of urban blight is much more powerful than gentrification pressures, especially in older industrial cities like St. Louis (Mallach 2015; Swanstrom, Webber, and Metzger 2017). Essentially, the relatively affordable homes in post–World War II suburbs have become the housing of last resort for low-income and minority households. According to Zillow, the median price of a home in Ferguson (the inner-ring suburb of St. Louis, where Michael Brown was shot) was $63,600 in September 2015 (Zillow 2015). Using the rough rule of thumb that families should be able to afford a home priced at 2.5 times their annual income, the median home in Ferguson would be affordable to households earning about $25,440 a year. Although these modest suburban homes are affordable, their stagnating or declining values provide little opportunity for families to accumulate equity. By contrast, primarily white upper- and middle-class households can afford to buy homes in more privileged suburbs with appreciating home values.

Attracted by the suburban lifestyle, poor and working class families have flocked to the suburbs, but in many ways the suburban lifestyle is a cruel hoax for them. The suburban lifestyle works well for middle- and upper-class families who can afford the multiple automobiles required in low-density suburbs characterized by widely separated land uses. The initial price of a home in an inner-ring suburb may be quite affordable, but this affordability ignores the operating costs of a home. The Center for Neighborhood Technology (CNT) has developed a Housing and Transportation Index. According to the conventional standard, housing is considered affordable if it consumes no more than 30 percent of income. CNT estimates that a reasonable standard for transportation affordability is 15 percent of income, so that the affordability standard for housing and transportation is 45 percent of household income. For the typical household in the St. Louis region, transportation costs are 23 percent of income, almost as high as housing costs, which are 28 percent of income. Transportation costs are generally lower in denser central cities that are better served by public transit. The typical resident of a low-income suburban neighborhood served by public transit can reach only 4 percent of jobs within a forty-five minute commute (Kneebone and Berube 2013, 60). Many suburban locations, which are "affordable" for the typical household if one counts only housing costs, become "unaffordable" when transportation costs are included.[6] Also, long commuting times undermine the ability of poor families to get ahead economically. A large study of upward mobility in counties across the country found that average commute time is one of the strongest factors affecting the odds of escaping poverty (Chetty and Hendren 2015).

With the important exception of schools, which suburban taxpayers usually generously support, suburbs invest fewer dollars in public goods and services than central cities. This works well for middle class and affluent households. The suburban lifestyle is a largely private lifestyle centered on the home and the automobile. Homes on larger lots with swimming pools and basketball hoops do not need as many public parks, pools, and recreation centers. Suburban governments were often incorporated not to provide public services but to control land use, keeping out poor and minorities by zoning out multifamily housing and requiring large lots for single-family homes.[7] In many suburbs land is zoned primarily for single-family homes with little provision for mixing in retail and commercial functions. As long as the area is thoroughly middle class or affluent, citizens feel little need for expensive public goods and services. Residents of affluent suburbs can get most of what they want on the private market, accessing dispersed locations by automobile.

As the residents of suburbs become poorer, however, they need a more active public sector to provide services for families who cannot afford to purchase them on the private market. Compared to more affluent families, low-income households have a greater need for public services such as libraries (with Internet connections), recreation centers (with youth programs), job training, English as a second language classes, and community policing. Disadvantaged suburbs suffer from a double whammy; the tax base of the community is eroding at the same time that the need for greater municipal services is increasing. Once suburban municipalities become predominantly low income, the depleted tax base becomes inadequate for even minimal services, let alone for the more robust public services needed by low-income households. As we noted earlier, suburban fragmentation increases economic segregation. A study of over five thousand suburbs found that between 1980 and 2000 the percentage of suburban residents living in poor suburbs more than doubled (Swanstrom et al. 2006).[8] According to Myron Orfield, about half of the suburban population lives in "at-risk" suburbs with high needs and low, often declining, tax bases (Orfield 2002, 33).

Instead of supporting poor people, many fiscally stressed suburban governments exploit them, pulling them further down into poverty. In an effort to raise badly needed revenues, for example, many suburban governments in St. Louis have turned to traffic fines and court fees to finance local government—with disastrous consequences for low-income residents of the area (Balko 2014, Arch City Defenders 2014, U.S. Department of Justice 2015). One inner-ring suburb of St. Louis, Pine Lawn, raised 63 percent of its general fund revenue in 2014 from traffic fines and court fees. Pine Lawn is extreme but many fiscally stressed suburbs in North St. Louis engaged in the same exploitative practices, including Ferguson (Barker 2015).[9] With low pay and inadequate training, police officers often target blacks, especially young African American men. Many low-income defendants, who cannot afford the fines, fail to appear in court. The court then issues a warrant for their arrest. In 2013 Pine Lawn, with a population of only 3,275, had 23,457 outstanding arrest warrants (Ferguson Commission 2015, 91). If motorists with outstanding arrest warrants are stopped again, the fines escalate. If they cannot pay, they are put in jail. As one report put it, "defendants are incarcerated for their poverty" (Arch City Defenders 2014). Having lost their driver's license or their freedom, many end up losing their jobs, making it even less likely that they will be able to pay their fines. Critics compare the system to debtors' prisons. According to a survey of 753 individuals appearing before municipal courts in St. Louis County, 65 percent felt their tickets were issued to raise revenues for cities rather than to promote public safety (Warren, Sandoval, and Ordower 2017, 29). The systematic exploitation of low-income, mainly minority residents of North County suburbs is a major reason why the demonstrations in Ferguson were so vehement and long lasting.

In *Crabgrass Frontier* Kenneth Jackson summed up the American suburban experience in a memorable sentence: "affluent and middle-class Americans live in suburban areas that are far from their workplaces, in homes that they own, and in the center of yards that by urban standards elsewhere are enormous" (Jackson 1985, 6). We could sum up recent trends in the suburbanization of poverty using similar language: "increasingly, poor Americans live in suburban areas that are far from their workplaces, in homes they own or rent, and in the center of yards that are by the standards of the urban poor enormous." We could also add that they are serviced by local public institutions that are, by the standards of the urban poor, exceedingly small, under-resourced, and lacking in professionalism.

The Challenge for Equity Planners

Municipal government is central to equity planning. The literature is clear about who equity planners are: "[Equity planning] . . . refers to persons working in official capacities for city governments" (Krumholz and Clavel 1994, 1). Krumholz and his band of city planners strove to move the resources of city government away from the downtown growth machine toward the community organizations that were springing up in poor and minority neighborhoods in the 1970s. "[E]quity planning developed as a government response to community organizing" (Ibid., 11).

Moving public resources toward grassroots organizations in poor neighborhoods was not easy because the elected officials and the City Planning Commission set policy, not the planners. Equity planners became skilled, however, at exploiting "institutional openings" in city government (Krumholz and Forester 1990, 211). Government did not operate in a strictly hierarchical fashion; by establishing informal relationships and using their planning skills and control over information, equity planners found that they could influence city policies and planning practices. They fed crucial information and policy ideas to grassroots organizations—but they often had to do this surreptitiously in order to maintain an image of neutrality in case elected officials challenged them. Equity planners deviated from the usual role of planners as technicians of means in order to actively pursue the end of greater equity. They justified usurping the power of democratically elected officials in favor of their equity agenda on the ground that "the existing democratic institutions are biased against the interests of those at the bottom of the social system" (Krumholz and Clavel 1994, 3).

How can equity planners operate in the suburbs, however, when municipal governments lack both the resources to plan and the high-capacity grassroots organizations to receive those resources? Compared to the 1970s, community organizing is down across the nation. However, past community organizing and federal programs like the War on Poverty helped to lay down a vigorous array of nonprofits in central cities that are generally lacking in the suburbs (Allard and Roth 2010). Compared to cities, poor suburbs have the added disadvantage of low "political-organizational endowments," encompassing such factors as "the fiscal capacity of political jurisdictions, the presence of public services such as clinics and hospitals, and the array and capacity of nonprofit organizations, which deliver many key social-welfare services" (Weir 2011, 244).[10] A 2011 study found that "suburban community foundations in the four regions studied are newer and smaller than those in core cities, despite faster growth of suburban poor populations" (Reckhow and Weir 2011, 1). Community development corporations (CDCs), nonprofit organizations devoted to revitalizing specific neighborhoods, are concentrated in cities. An association of CDCs in St. Louis, for example, has seventeen members operating in the city of St. Louis but only six in suburban St. Louis County—even though many more poor people live in the suburbs.[11]

In short, poor families have flocked to suburbs in search of a better quality of life. In many cases they ended up in communities with lower crime and higher performing schools. But as suburban poverty has risen and become more concentrated, these advantages have eroded. Moreover, the poor face additional challenges in low-density suburbs with separated land uses, including higher transportation costs and lower accessibility to needed social services. In attempting to address suburban poverty, equity planners face two daunting challenges of their own: (1) the local public sector is fragmented, under-resourced and lacking in professionalism; and (2) grassroots civic organizations are often absent or, when present, have weak organizational capacity. The case of 24:1 shows how equity planners are beginning to confront these challenges in new and creative ways.

Transit-Oriented Development in the Suburbs: The Case of 24:1

Located in the north suburbs of St. Louis County just over the city line (Figure 5.3), the Normandy School District (NSD) is highly fragmented, poor, and overwhelmingly African American. In 2010 it had a population of 35,210; 82.2 percent were African American. In 2013, the child poverty rate was 37.6 percent; in every school in the district over 96 percent of the children were eligible for free and reduced lunch.[12] Crisscrossed by twenty-four municipalities, with an average population of only 1,834, local governments in the NSD footprint are unable to achieve basic economies of scale or access professional expertise by developing a division of labor.[13] Generally lacking the institutional capacity to implement much beyond basic housekeeping services, most would fit in Myron Orfield's typology as "at-risk, segregated suburbs," with low tax capacity, high poverty, and high concentrations of minorities (Orfield 2002). Civil society is also relatively underdeveloped. A survey of local organizations conducted by 24:1 staff in 2010 found only four neighborhood organizations in the NSD footprint, including one neighborhood group, a community gardening group, and an anticrime block group (Public Policy Research Center, 2011).

The population in the NSD footprint is declining and the housing market is weak; some areas are beginning to suffer from vacancy and abandonment. In order to address the disinvestment and rising poverty in the area, which is driving the fiscal stress and police misconduct discussed earlier, the area needs strategic planning for economic and community development. Remarkably, *not a single one of the twenty-four governments in NSD has a full-time planner on staff.*[14] If equity planners are, by definition, planners who work for city governments, then there are no equity planners in large swaths of suburbia. If equity planning is going to emerge in fragmented suburban contexts, it must come from outside government.

Equity planning in NSD has been led by Beyond Housing, a high-capacity, regional nonprofit that has guided a place-based initiative in NSD since 2010. Called 24:1 ("24 Communities, 1 Vision"), it is one of the most sophisticated comprehensive community initiatives in the nation, recognized by both the White House and HUD (White House Neighborhood Revitalization Report 2011; U.S. Department of Housing and Urban Development 2012). The idea for 24:1 emerged out of a series of meetings of municipalities in 2009 to address the foreclosure

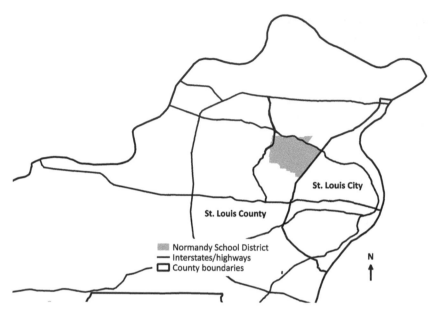

FIGURE 5.3.   Map of Normandy School District. Map courtesy of Jenny Connelly-Bowen.

crisis; a multimillion-dollar gift from an anonymous donor gave Beyond Housing the resources to staff the initiative.[15] Beyond Housing led a robust participatory planning process, involving over fifty-two meetings attended by more than five hundred people, to gather information and decide on a strategic direction. In addition to area residents, participants included NSD leaders and staff, elected leadership from area municipalities, representatives of social service agencies, and staff and faculty from the University of Missouri–St. Louis (Public Policy Research Center 2011).

Released in April 2011, the plan included forty specific strategies in eleven impact areas (For more detail on the planning process and outcome, see Swanstrom et al 2012.) Unfortunately, in 2012 NSD lost state accreditation. As a result, students could transfer to any public school in the area and NSD had to pay the tuition dollars as determined by the receiving district—over $20,000 per student in some cases. This brought NSD to the brink of bankruptcy. In order to keep NSD solvent Beyond Housing stepped in and bought seven vacant schools for $2.9 million. Since then, the number of transfers has declined and some school districts have agreed to limit the tuition charged. While it still faces fiscal challenges, NSD is no longer on the brink of bankruptcy. It has improved its student performance and recently it won provisional accreditation by the state of Missouri (Taketa 2017).

Despite working in a beleaguered school district, Beyond Housing has been able to make significant progress on its plan.[16] It now owns 422 rental units, most scattered-site single-family suburban homes, which provide quality housing for families at affordable prices. Working with twenty-five not-for-profit partners, Beyond Housing helped create 5byAge5, a collective-impact-type initiative that prepares young children for kindergarten. Every child who enters kindergarten in the NSD receives a $500 college savings account, and Beyond Housing has established individual development accounts (IDAs) that match every $1 students save with $3. Together the two programs have raised almost $1.1 million to pay for college expenses. Beyond Housing developed the first full-service grocery store and full-service bank, both of which had been missing in the community for over half a century. Pagedale Center now has a four-screen state-of-the-art movie theater, a new community health center, a branch of the St. Louis Community Credit Union, and the Red Dough Money Center, which offers an affordable alternative to predatory payday loans. Beyond Housing has formed a community land trust which owns all new development, insuring that the equity will remain in the community and under the control of the community.

One of the issues that emerged out of the 24:1 planning process was resident dissatisfaction with the light-rail station at St. Charles Rock Road in Pagedale. One of thirty-seven stations on the light-rail system in St. Louis known as MetroLink, the station has an uninviting 191-space asphalt parking lot that gets painfully hot in the summer. The area is not friendly to pedestrians. Surrounding land uses, which take little advantage of proximity to the regional rail system, included a flea market, junk yard, light industry, warehouses, and considerable vacant land. Responding to citizen complaints that something better should be done with the site, Beyond Housing decided to look into the possibility of doing transit-oriented development (TOD) at the site. TOD can be defined as development within one-quarter to one-half mile of a transit station that mixes residential, retail, office, open space, and public uses to maximize the ability of residents and employees to travel by transit, foot, bicycle, and car.

It soon became clear that TOD could have substantial benefits for residents of 24:1. If it enabled residents to reduce car usage, it could be an effective antipoverty strategy. In 2015, the annual average cost of owning and operating a vehicle was $8,698 (American Automobile Association 2015). According to a study of Minneapolis–St. Paul, moving from a transit-poor to a transit-rich neighborhood would save the average household $5,940 a year (Center for Transit-Oriented Development and Center for Neighborhood Technology 2006).[17] TOD at the St. Charles Rock Road Station could provide people with convenient and less expensive access to jobs. Research showed that 46,155 mid-level jobs were located within a half mile of a transit station in St. Louis City and County (Table 5.1).

TABLE 5.1 Living Wage Jobs within Half Mile of a Transit Station

NUMBER OF JOBS IN TRANSIT ZONES BY MONTHLY WAGE, ST. LOUIS CITY AND ST. LOUIS COUNTY

MONTHLY WAGE	ST. LOUIS CITY/COUNTY	TRANSIT ZONES*	% SHARE
Less than $1,250	207,573	30,803	15
$1,250 to $3,333	289,912	46,155	16
More than $3,333	320,107	63,721	20
TOTAL:	817,592	140,679	17

*1/2 mile buffer from transit stations.
Source: Table produced by the Public Policy Research Center, University of Missouri-St. Louis; based on data from the U.S. Census Bureau, Longitudinal Employer-Household Dynamics (LEHD), 2009.

With a monthly wage of $1,250 to $3,333, these are living wage jobs that many residents of the area would qualify for. Living in a transit-rich and more pedestrian-friendly environment can also promote healthier lifestyles, reducing obesity and cardiovascular disease (Sallis et al. 2012, MacDonald, et al. 2010).

The challenge for Beyond Housing is that TOD is rare in weak market settings, like the 24:1 area (Hess and Lombardi 2004).[18] Beyond Housing decided to fund a market and feasibility study.[19] The study confirmed that the area had a weak real estate market. According to Zillow, the median home value in the area was $73,600; no home sells for more than $120,000 (Development Strategies n.d.). With the minimum cost of constructing a new home calculated at about $150,000, no new homes will be built without subsidies. Nevertheless, the feasibility study concluded, a market existed for quality affordable housing around the transit station. The market was not young urban professionals that are the key demographic for most TOD projects. Instead, the project would mostly be attractive to working families in North County and singles or couples with more modest incomes. The project would need to be 70–75 percent affordable housing versus 20–30 percent market rate. Deep subsidies would be needed to make the project work financially. With twelve thousand to eighteen thousand trips by car per day along St. Charles Rock Road and 43,400 boardings per month at the light-rail station, the development could support twenty to thirty thousand square feet of retail.[20] Even though TOD at St. Charles Rock Road was "fraught with challenges," including environmental contamination, the feasibility study concluded that "the opportunity to create a mix of affordable and market rate housing in a walkable community is great" (Development Strategies n.d., 2).

In the fall of 2012 Beyond Housing decided to ask local residents and businesses what kind of development they wanted to see around the station.[21] A literature search determined that there was no good model of a participatory design process for planning TOD. Beyond Housing devised its own planning process, which included a steering committee composed of residents, local elected officials, experts, and other regional stakeholders, as well as a technical team made up of planners and representatives of all the agencies that had a stake in the project. Recognizing that low-income residents and renters are underrepresented in community planning processes (Silverman, Taylor, and Crawford 2008), Beyond Housing devised a range of different methods to ensure that all voices in the community would be heard. It conducted three public meetings in which 320 resident and nonresident stakeholders expressed their preferences, using keypad polling, small group discussions, and mapping exercises. Beyond Housing hired street teams from the community to distribute information (1,415 flyers and door hangers) and conduct a baseline survey of attitudes toward development around the station. Beyond Housing also erected a billboard calling for input and put up a website and phone/text line for feedback. Beyond Housing even hired a local artist who installed large wooden boxes near the MetroLink station with slots where passersby could deposit suggestions, which were then woodburned into the surface of the box. In total, over four thousand responses and ideas were received from residents and other stakeholders. In 2014, Beyond Housing won the award for the Best Civic Engagement Process from the Missouri Chapter of the American Planning Association (American Planning Association n.d.).

The equity planners and staff of Beyond Housing were taken aback when the baseline survey of ninety-seven residents and riders of MetroLink found deep opposition to the very idea of TOD. Only 7 percent of respondents wanted new housing at the site; 18 percent were opposed to any new housing. At the first community meeting 31 percent expressed opposition to new housing and if housing were built, a majority (51 percent) preferred suburban-style single-family homes. Participants said the drawings presented by Beyond Housing of multifamily housing looked like "the ghetto."

The planners went back to the drawing board. At the next public meeting, they presented information on the level of subsidy that would be necessary for different types of housing, explaining that single-family homes would require much more subsidy per unit in order to be marketable (Table 5.2). They explained that denser forms of housing would require less subsidy and by locating more housing within walking distance of the station, they would increase the likelihood of retail development. The residents got it. In a survey at the end of the planning process 76 percent reported that they viewed multifamily housing under four stories more favorably now. The same percentage reported that the meetings increased their support for TOD around the St. Charles Rock Road Station (Public Policy Research Center 2014).

Not only did the community change its views of TOD but the planners changed their plans, as well. As a result of the pushback from the community, they lessened

TABLE 5.2 Subsidy Required for Different Types of Housing

	SINGLE-FAMILY DETACHED	TOWNHOUSE WITH COMMON WALL	MULTIFAMILY 4-STORY
Number of Units	1	2	40
SF/Unit	1,500	1,000	975
Price (per Feasibility Study)	$120,000	$100,000	$750/mo
Cost Supported by Price	$120,000	$100,000	$90,000
Total Cost/Unit	$200,700	$137,400	$121,975
Surplus (Gap)	($80,700)	($37,400)	($31,975)

Source: Ken Christian, "Beyond Housing" (author's files).

the density on the site. The final plan calls for single-family housing in the form of townhouses to be phased in further from the station. TOD cannot look the same in a suburb as in a dense central city. With local zoning codes prohibiting any buildings over thirty-five feet in height, it should not be surprising that residents viewed taller buildings as jarring and out of place. In response to community input, the planners also added a banquet center, public bathrooms near the station, and more shade trees.

Since the planning process was completed in July 2013 Beyond Housing has been working to make it a reality. One barrier that needed to be surmounted was the zoning code that banned the kind of mixed-use development envisioned for the area around the station. In 2014 the city of Pagedale's Board of Alderpersons approved a Transit-Oriented Development Form-Based Code District (Cella 2014). Instead of dictating particular land uses, such as housing or retail, form-based codes direct a physical form that permits different uses to mix in the same space. Aided by an anonymous donor, Beyond Housing has purchased most of the land around the transit station, including the flea market (which has been torn down), and it is pursuing the grants and tax credits necessary to make the project a reality, including a substantial upgrade of the water and sewer systems on the site. The federal government changed the flood map for the area, presenting a further challenge that Beyond Housing is confident it can overcome.

Conclusion: The Future of Equity Planning in the Suburbs

More poor people now live in suburbs than in central cities. Equity planners need to adjust their strategies and tactics to the new suburban terrain. The suburban model of spread out single-family homes, strict separation of land uses, almost total reliance on the automobile, and smaller local governments is not well suited to the needs of poor people. Equity planners must learn how to weave vibrant nodes of urbanism into the frayed fabric of older suburbs. Equity planners need to act now to improve the lives of the suburban poor. We should not operate under the illusion, however, that substantial progress can be made at the local level without stronger suburban institutions and more supportive policies at the regional, state, and federal levels. As of this writing, Republicans control the executive branch and both houses of the legislature in the federal government and the state of Missouri. Inner-ring suburbs have always been in a kind of urban policy blind spot. Resources to help inner-ring suburbs will shrink in the immediate future. Equity planners will need to be creative in seeking new partners with foundations, as well as anchor institutions ("eds and meds").

The case of 24:1 shows what can be accomplished when a high-capacity community organization works closely with residents of disadvantaged suburbs to improve their lives. The progress did not occur overnight. Chris Krehmeyer, the charismatic president and CEO of Beyond Housing, is fond of saying, "community building happens at the speed of trust."[22] Beyond Housing has earned the trust of the 24:1 communities by working in the area for over eighteen years, demonstrating again and again that they listen to the community. Beyond Housing's motto is "Ask" (what the community wants)—"Align" (community stakeholders around solutions)—and "Act" (to implement the plan driven by the voice of the community). TOD has the potential to link low-opportunity suburbs to regional job clusters, increase disposable income by reducing household transportation costs, and bring economic development and a sense of place to disadvantaged suburbs. TOD is not easy in weak market suburban settings, nor is it well-understood by suburban residents. Equity planners need to listen to suburban residents and adjust their plans to their preferences for smaller scale development—balancing the need for walkable communities with the continued importance of the automobile. If done well, civic engagement can win acceptance for weaving urban vitality into weak market suburbs.

The case of 24:1 also shows, however, the limits of suburban equity planning led by the nonprofit sector, not government. First, the success of 24:1 is difficult to scale up because it requires a high-capacity nonprofit.[23] Beyond Housing is the highest capacity nonprofit in the St. Louis region doing place-specific community development, and it could never have accomplished what it did without the beneficence of an anonymous funder that has provided millions of dollars in flexible funding for 24:1. High-quality community-based planning is expensive. The feasibility study and civic engagement process, for example, received $65,000 of external funding. The final cost would need to include hundreds of hours of staff time not covered by outside grants. Few community-based nonprofits have that amount of resources to invest in a long planning process before a shovel is even put into the ground. Even if other community-based organizations in the St. Louis area had this kind of planning capacity, there would not be enough public funds available for the gap financing necessary to make projects like the St. Charles Rock Road TOD a reality. Because of its track record and high capacity, Beyond Housing has been able to capture a disproportionate share of public funding for community economic development. There simply is not enough public funding available for every poor inner-ring urban and suburban community to do what 24:1 has done.

Another obstacle is the fragmentation of the local public sector; this raises the costs of collective action to prohibitive levels. Beyond Housing has created a municipal government partnership (MGP) to help small municipalities in 24:1 achieve economies of scale and greater professionalism. By organizing bulk purchase of rock salt and common paving contracts, for example, municipalities have saved hundreds of thousands of dollars. MGP has now moved on to the tougher and more important challenge of coordinating economic and community development efforts across municipalities. By pooling community development block grant (CDBG) funds municipalities have improved the efficiency and impact of federal funds. But all of these collaborations require an extraordinary amount of staff time and trust building. There are 144 local elected officials in the 24:1 area who need to be committed to the partnerships (Swanstrom et al. 2012, 7). Collaboration built on trust takes time. When new officials are elected to office, trust needs to be rebuilt or the collaboration can collapse.

Equity planners need to find ways to formalize, or institutionalize, collaborations in fragmented suburbs. In Chicago, South Cook County and West Cook County have formed collaboratives representing twenty-nine municipalities that have addressed the foreclosure crisis and have put together plans for TOD. Beyond Housing helped to form the North County Police Cooperative, which now has about seventy police officers serving eight municipalities (Beyers 2018). The cooperative has implemented programs to improve relations with the community, including a Police Explorers program that gives young people a chance to learn about urban policing. In 2015, St. Louis County passed a law requiring its fifty-seven municipal police departments to meet minimal standards and achieve accreditation, and the Missouri Legislature passed Senate Bill 5 that limited the amount St. Louis County municipalities could raise from traffic fines and court fees. Courts struck down both laws as unconstitutional and, assuming appeals fail and the Trump administration's Attorney General Jeff Sessions curtails investigations of police violations of civil rights laws, municipal police departments will feel little outside pressure to reform or contract out their police functions to the county or other municipalities with accredited police departments. Ultimately, merger of small suburban municipalities would make the most sense. Beyond

Housing was able to facilitate the merger of two municipalities in Normandy—Vinita Park and Vinita Terrace—but more mergers are needed.

Poor suburbs need more supportive policies at the regional, state, and federal levels. Like many metropolitan areas, the St. Louis region has overproduced housing on the suburban fringe, leading to housing vacancy in the urban core and now in inner-ring suburbs (Bier and Post 2003). Poor suburbs occupy a kind of blind spot in federal policy. For example, even though there are more poor people in St. Louis County, the county's CDBG allocation is less than a third of the city's. First-tier suburbs need to form coalitions to lobby state and federal governments for more supportive policies. The Northeast Ohio First Suburbs Consortium (n.d.), encompassing fifteen inner-ring suburbs, describes itself on its website as "a government-led advocacy organization working to revitalize inner ring communities, and raise political awareness of the problems and inequities associated with urban sprawl and disinvestment." First-tier suburbs and central cities are both victims of policies that tilt the playing field against older parts of metropolitan areas. For decades Myron Orfield has been calling for an alliance of central cities and inner-ring suburbs to address metropolitan inequities (Orfield 1997). In 1975, such an alliance was able to enact tax-base sharing among seven counties in the Twin Cities metropolitan area.

Finally, first-tier suburbs need stronger community organizations. Equity planners have always struggled with how to balance cooperation and conflict—working together with stakeholders to implement solutions while simultaneously putting pressure on the power holders to expand resources for poor communities and change the rules of the game. Equity planners employed by city governments often worked behind the scenes to help community organizations push for more equitable urban policies. Equity planners working for nonprofits in the suburbs will need to do the same—not just to empower existing organizations but to seed new ones. What disadvantaged suburbs need most are stronger organizations for community empowerment.

NOTES

1. Richard Hatcher was elected mayor of Gary, Indiana, before Stokes, but Stokes assumed office before him.

2. The father of 2012 Republican presidential candidate Mitt Romney, Secretary George Romney wrote this in a confidential memo to his aides (quoted in Hannah-Jones 2015).

3. According to the 2014 American Community Survey, the fifty largest cities gained white population, reversing a many decades long loss of white population (Frey 2015).

4. The "Delmar Divide" was made famous by a British Broadcasting Corporation (2012) documentary which can be viewed at the URL in the references.

5. For an insightful analysis of the problem of housing overproduction, see Bier 2017.

6. The decline of affordability in suburban locations becomes clear when you compare the map of affordability in the St. Louis metro for housing only with the map for afford-

ability with housing and transportation (Center for Neighborhood Technology n.d.). CNT determines transportation costs using multidimensional regression analysis to estimate auto ownership, auto use, and transit use based on factors including the nature of the built environment. See Center for Neighborhood Technology 2015.

7. Colin Gordon (2008) reports that the city of Ferguson, whose population is now about two-thirds black, engaged in these exclusionary practices throughout most of its history.

8. Poor suburbs were defined as those whose per capita income was less than 75 percent of the per capita income for the region.

9. By way of contrast, the City of St. Louis collected only 2 percent of its revenue from traffic fines and court fees.

10. Weir cites Allard (2009) on the latter point; see also Allard and Roth 2010.

11. Community Builders Network of Metro St. Louis. Author's files; available on request. Joanna Mitchell-Brown reports that "nonprofit community development and citizen empowerment" remained almost nonexistent in the first suburbs of Cincinnati until the mid-2000s (Mitchell-Brown 2013, 185).

12. U.S. Census Bureau (2014) estimates. To qualify for free or reduced lunches families must earn less than 185 percent of the poverty level. Information on eligibility for free and reduced lunches in the NSD was obtained from the Missouri Department of Elementary and Secondary Education (2013).

13. In 2017, Vinita Terrace (population under three hundred) merged into Vinita Park (population about 1,900).

14. This fact was corroborated by Caroline Ban, manager of government affairs for Beyond Housing (personal communication).

15. Information on 24:1 is drawn largely from Swanstrom et al. 2012.

16. Updated information on Beyond Housing's accomplishments in 24:1 is from Stearn 2015.

17. Recent research shows that living near transit does reduce household transportation costs but the effect can be quite modest (Zhou and Zolnik 2013). In most metro areas it is difficult to dispense with driving completely. However, ride sharing and the spread of car rental services have made it more convenient for households to own "part" of a car—and therefore realize the savings of relying more on public transit. For a discussion of these issues, see Swanstrom 2009.

18. Examples of TOD in weak market settings are Eco Village Townhouses at Fifty-eighth Street in Cleveland; Columbia Estates in Atlanta; Steel Gardens in Charlotte, North Carolina; and Parsons Place in East St. Louis. These examples are documented in an Economics Research Associates Report commissioned by Great Rivers Greenway in St. Louis (author's files).

19. In the interest of full disclosure, I used resources from my endowed professorship at UMSL to help fund both the feasibility study and the civic engagement process.

20. An additional one to two thousand new residents would add four to eight thousand square feet to the potential for retail development (Development Strategies n.d., 66).

21. Information on the civic engagement process was obtained from an evaluation conducted by the Public Policy Research Center (2014). I also was a member of the Steering Committee and participated in one of the public meetings.

22. The quote is attributed to Tom Dewar.

23. For an argument about the need to build civic capacity to do comprehensive community initiatives, see Swanstrom 2015 and 2016.

REFERENCES

Allard, Scott. W. 2009. *Out of Reach: Place, Poverty, and the New American Welfare State.* New Haven: Yale University Press.

Allard, Scott W., and Benjamin Roth. 2010. *Strained Suburbs: The Social Service Challenges of Rising Suburban Poverty.* Washington, DC: Brookings Institution.

American Automobile Association. 2015. *Your Driving Costs 2015.* http://exchange.aaa .com/wp-content/uploads/2015/04/Your-Driving-Costs-2015.pdf.

American Planning Association, Missouri Chapter (MO APA). n.d. Missouri APA Chapter Awards (website). https://www.mo-apa.org/resources/chapter-awards.

Arch City Defenders. 2014. *Municipal Courts White Paper.* November. http://www .archcitydefenders.org/wp-content/uploads/2014/11/ArchCity-Defenders -Municipal-Courts-Whitepaper.pdf.

Balko, Radley. 2014. "How Municipalities in St. Louis County, MO., Profit From Poverty," *The Washington Post,* September 3. http://www.washingtonpost.com/news/the-watch /wp/2014/09/03/how-st-louis-county-missouri-profits-from-poverty/.

Barker, Jacob. 2015. "With Court Revenue Facing Limits, Budgets Look Tenuous in Many St. Louis County Cities," *St. Louis Post-Dispatch,* April 15.

Beyers, Christine. 2018. "Dellwood Cites Cost in Decision to Replace St. Louis County Police with North County Police Cooperative," *St. Louis Post-Dispatch,* April 11.

Bier, Thomas and Charlie. Post. 2003. *Vacating the City: An Analysis of New Homes vs. Household Growth.* Washington, DC: Brookings Institution.

Bier, Thomas. 2017. *Housing Dynamics in Southeast Ohio: Setting the Stage for Resurgence.* MSL Academic Endeavors eBooks. 4. http://engagedscholarship.csuohio.edu/msl _ae_ebooks/4.

Bischoff, Kendra. 2008. "School District Fragmentation and Racial Residential Segregation: How Do Boundaries Matter?" *Urban Affairs Review* 44 (2): 182–217.

British Broadcasting Corporation (BBC). 2012. BBC Documentary: Crossing The Delmar Divide. KPLR St. Louis, December 12. http://kplr11.com/2012/12/12/bbc -documentary-crossing-the-delmar-divide/.

Cella, Kim. 2014. "Pagedale Board of Aldermen Adopts Transit Oriented Development Form Based Zoning District around Rock Road MetroLink Station with help of CMT and others," Citizens For Modern Transit (blog), February 2, http://cmt-stl.org/pagedale -board-of-aldermen-adopts-transit-oriented-development-form-based-zoning -district-around-rock-road-metrolink-station-with-help-of-cmt-and-others/.

Center for Neighborhood Technology (CNT). n.d. "H + T Two Views of Affordability." In H&T Affordability Index (website). http://htaindex.cnt.org/compare-affordability/.

——. 2015. H + T Index Methods. March. http://htaindex.cnt.org/about/HT_Index _Methods_2013.pdf.

Center for Transit-Oriented Development and Center for Neighborhood Technology. 2006. *The Affordability Index: A New Tool for Measuring the True Affordability of Housing Choice.* January. Washington, DC: Brookings Institution Urban Markets Initiative.

Chetty, Raj, and Nathaniel Hendren. 2015. *The Impacts of Neighborhoods on Intergenerational Mobility: Childhood Exposure Effects and County-Level Estimates.* Paper, May. http://scholar.harvard.edu/files/hendren/files/nbhds_paper.pdf?m=1430722623.

Development Strategies. n.d. *A Development and Feasibility Study, Rock Road Station.* St. Louis, MO: Author's files.

Dwyer, Rachel E. 2007. "Expanding Homes and Increasing Inequalities: U.S. Housing Development and the Residential Segregation of the Affluent," *Social Problems* 54 (1): 23–46.

East-West Gateway Council of Governments. 2015. *Where We Stand.* St. Louis: Author.

Ferguson Commission. 2015. *Forward Through Ferguson: A Path Toward Racial Equity.* St. Louis, MO: Author.

Frey, William H. 2001. *Melting Pot Suburbs: A Census 2000 Study of Suburban Diversity.* June 1. Washington, DC: Brookings Institution.

———. 2015. "More Big Cities are Gaining White Population, Census Data Show," *The Avenue* (blog, Brookings Institution), October 1, http://www.brookings.edu/blogs /the-avenue/posts/2015/10/01-big-cities-white-population-frey.

Gordon, Colin. 2008. *Mapping Decline: Race and the Fate of the American City.* Philadelphia: University of Pennsylvania Press.

Hanlon, Bernadette. 2012. *Once the American Dream: Inner-Ring Suburbs of the United States.* Philadelphia: Temple University Press.

Hannah-Jones, Nikole. 2015. "Living Apart: How the Government Betrayed a Landmark Civil Rights Law," *ProPublica,* June 25, http://www.propublica.org/article/living -apart-how-the-government-betrayed-a-landmark-civil-rights-law.

Heikkil, Eric. J. 1996. "Are Municipalities Tieboutian Clubs?" *Regional Science and Urban Economics* 26 (1996): 203–26.

Hess, Daniel Baldwin, and Peter A. Lombardi. 2004. "Policy Support for and Barriers to Transit-Oriented Development in the Inner City," *Transportation Research Record: Journal of the Transportation Research Board* 1887: 26–33.

Hoyt, Homer. 1939. *The Structure and Growth of Residential Neighborhoods in American Cities.* Washington, DC: Federal Housing Administration.

Jackson, Kenneth. 1985. *Crabgrass Frontier: The Suburbanization of the United States.* New York: Oxford University Press.

Jargowsky, Paul. 2002. "Sprawl, Concentration of Poverty, and Urban Inequality." In *Urban Sprawl: Causes, Consequences, and Policy Responses,* edited by G. D. Squires. Washington, DC: Urban Institute Press.

Johnson, Kimberly. 2014. "'Black' Suburbanization: American Dream or the New Banlieue?" In *The Cities Papers,* July 23, http://citiespapers.ssrc.org/black-suburbanization -american-dream-or-the-new-banlieue/.

Kerner, Otto, et al. 1968. *Report of the National Advisory Commission on Civil Disorders.* New York: Bantam Books.

Kneebone, Elizabeth, and Alan Berube. 2013. *Confronting Suburban Poverty in America.* Washington, DC: Brookings Institution.

Krumholz, Norman, and John Forrester. 1990. *Making Equity Planning Work: Leadership in the Public Sector.* Philadelphia: Temple University Press.

Krumholz, Norman, and Pierre Clavel. 1994. *Reinventing Cities: Equity Planners Tell Their Stories.* Philadelphia: Temple University Press.

MacDonald, J. M., et al. 2010. "The Effect of Light Rail Transit on Body Mass Index and Physical Activity," *American Journal of Preventive Medicine* 39 (2): 105–12.

Mallach, Alan. 2015. "The Uncoupling of the Economic City: Increasing Spatial and Economic Polarization in American Older Industrial Cities," *Urban Affairs Review* 51 (4): 443–73.

Missouri Department of Elementary & Secondary Education. 2013. "School Finance Data and Reports: fri-2013 (Excel file)." https://mcds.dese.mo.gov/quickfacts/Pages /District-and-School-Information.aspx?RootFolder=%2Fquickfacts%2FSchool%20 Finance%20Data%20and%20Reports%2FFree%20and%20Reduced%20 Lunch%20Percentage%20by%20Building&FolderCTID=0x012000B3EF86959C3A 824680BF44E0680ED1F4&View=%7B0E813976–3BD6–4D9B-9112–5D0C54 B515E8%7D.

Mitchell-Brown, J. 2013. "First Suburbs and Nonprofit Housing: How Do Urban CDCs Develop Affordable Housing in Suburban Communities?" In *Social Justice in Diverse Suburbs: History, Politics, and Prospects,* edited by C. Niedt. Philadelphia: Temple University Press.

Northeast Ohio First Suburbs Consortium. n.d. "Consortium." http://www.firstsuburbs.org/consortium.html.

Orfield, Myron. 1997. *Metropolitics: A Regional Agenda for Community and Stability.* Washington, DC: Brookings Institution Press.

———. 2002. *American Metropolitics: The New Suburban Reality.* Washington, DC: Brookings Institution.

Orfield, Myron, and Thomas Luce. 2012. *America's Racially Diverse Suburbs: Opportunities and Challenges.* Washington, DC: Brookings Institution Press.

Public Policy Research Center (PPRC). 2011. *Year One 24:1 Evaluation Report.* St. Louis, MO: Public Policy Research Center.

———. 2014. Beyond Housing 24:1 Initiative: St. Charles MetroLink TOD Planning Process Evaluation Report. Author's Files.

Reckhow, Sarah, and Margaret Weir. 2011. *Building a Stronger Regional Safety Net: Philanthropy's Role.* Washington, DC: Brookings Institution.

Rothstein, Richard. 2014. *The Making of Ferguson: Public Policies at the Root of its Troubles.* Washington, DC: Economic Policy Institute.

Rothwell, Jonathan T. and Douglas S. Massey. 2010. "Density Zoning and Class Segregation in U.S. Metropolitan Areas," *Social Science Quarterly* 91: 1123–43.

Sallis, James, et al. 2012. "Role of Built Environments in Physical Activity, Obesity, and Cardiovascular Disease," *Circulation: Journal of the American Heart Association* 125 (5): 729–37.

Silverman, Robert Mark, Henry L. Taylor Jr., and Christopher Crawford. 2008. "The Role of Citizen Participation Action Research Principles in Main Street Revitalization," *Action Research* 6 (1): 69–93.

Stearn, Michelle. 2015. "A St. Louis Organization Goes Above and Beyond Providing Homes for Communities: An Interview with Chris Krehmeyer," Community-Wealth.org, November 30, http://community-wealth.org/content/st-louis-organization-goes-above-and-beyond-providing-homes-communities.

Swanstrom, Todd. 2009. "Breaking down Policy Silos: Transportation, Economic Development, and Health." In *Healthy, Equitable Transportation Policy Recommendations and Research,* edited by Shireen Malekafzali, 97–110. New York: PolicyLink.

———. 2015. "Capacity, Capacity, Capacity: The Challenge of Urban Policy in the Age of Obama," *Journal of Urban Affairs* 37 (1): 70–74.

———. 2016. "The Incompleteness of Comprehensive Community Revitalization," in *Urban Policy in the Time of Obama,* edited by James DeFillipis, 211–30. Minneapolis, Minnesota: University of Minnesota Press.

Swanstrom, Todd, et al. 2006. "Pulling Apart: Economic Segregation Among Suburbs and Central Cities in Major Metropolitan Areas." In *Redefining Urban and Suburban America: Evidence from Census 2000,* Vol. 3, edited by Alan Berube, Bruce Katz, and Robert E. Lang, 143–66. Washington, DC: Brookings Institution Press.

———. 2012. "Civic Capacity and School-Community Partnerships in a Fragmented Suburban Setting: The Case of 24:1," *Journal of Urban Affairs* 35 (1): 25–42.

Swanstrom, Todd, Henry S. Webber, and Molly Metzger. 2017. "Rebound Neighborhoods in Older Industrial Cities." In *Economic Mobility: Research & Ideas on Strengthening Families, Communities & the Economy,* edited by the Federal Reserve

Bank of St. Louis and the Board of Governors of the Federal Reserve System, 325–52. Washington, DC: Board of Governors of the Federal Reserve System.

Taketa, Kristen. 2017. "Normandy Schools Get Good News—and Provisional Accreditation," *St. Louis Today*, December 1.

U.S. Census Bureau. 2014. "School District Estimates for 2013: Missouri." https://www2.census.gov/programs-surveys/saipe/datasets/2013/2013-school-districts/sd13-mo.txt.

U.S. Department of Commerce. 2014. "Median and Average Square Feet of Floor Area in New Single-Family Houses Sold by Location." In *2014 Characteristics of New Housing*, 744. Washington, DC: U.S. Census Bureau.

U.S. Department of Housing and Urban Development, Office of Policy Development and Research. 2012. *Evidence Matters: Transforming Knowledge into Housing and Community Development Policy*, Winter, http://www.huduser.org/portal/periodicals/em/winter12/highlight3.html.

U.S. Department of Justice. 2015. *Investigation of the Ferguson Policy Department*. Washington, DC: Author.

Warren, Kenneth F., J. S. Onesimo Sandoval, and Henry Ordower. 2017. *Ferguson and a Dozen Others: Perceptions of Police and Municipal Court Systems in Affluent v. Non-Affluent Communities in Saint Louis County by Race*. Saint Louis University: Unpublished paper, author's files.

Watson, Tara. 2007. *New Housing, Income Inequality, and Distressed Metropolitan Areas*. Washington, DC: Urban Institute Press.

Weiher, Gregory. 1991. *The Fractured Metropolis: Political Fragmentation and Metropolitan Segregation*. Albany, NY: SUNY Press.

Weir, Margaret. 2011. "Creating Justice for the Poor in the New Metropolis." In *Justice and the American Metropolis*, edited by C. Hayward and T. Swanstrom. Minneapolis: University of Minnesota Press.

White House Neighborhood Revitalization Report. 2011. *Building Neighborhoods of Opportunity*. Accessed September 15, 2011. www.whitehouse.gov/sites/default/files/uploads/nri_report.pdf.

Zhou, Xin, and Edmund J. Zolnik. 2013. "Transit-Oriented Development and Household Transportation Costs. Household-Level Analysis." *Transportation Research Record* 2357 (10): 86–94.

Zillow. 2015. Ferguson Home Prices & Values (website). Accessed September 2015. http://www.zillow.com/ferguson-mo/home-values/.

Section 3
NATIONAL EQUITY PLANNING

6

ON THE WAY BUT NOT THERE YET

Making Accessibility the Core of Equity Planning
in Transportation

Joe Grengs

Good transportation is central to equity planning because it provides access to opportunity and promotes a wider range of choices for people who have few. Although transportation planners today are obligated to monitor progress toward social equity, thanks to recent environmental justice requirements, their actions so far have been mostly limited to merely doing no more harm in the transportation services they provide. An alternative approach for equity planners is to target transportation services to compensate for disadvantages in society as a whole. A stronger commitment to advancing social justice in transportation would place priority on serving the least advantaged first. The proper tool to help equity planners focus attention and target resources toward the people and places with the greatest need is the concept of accessibility.

It took violent and damaging urban uprisings in many of the nation's largest cities—including Los Angeles, Newark, and Detroit—in the mid-1960s to reveal how poor accessibility perpetuates social injustice. Public leaders found a range of causes for these riots, including overt institutional racism, systematic police brutality, inadequate housing, and poor schools, with consequences of particular severity for blacks in central cities (Governor's Commission on the Los Angeles Riots 1965, Kerner et al. 1968). Among the causes was an indictment of transportation policy for failing to provide adequate access to jobs and other important destinations like health-care facilities. For example, taking public transportation from south central Los Angeles to jobs at the Hughes Aircraft plant in Culver City or the General Motors factory in Panorama City was virtually impossible (Mozingo and Jennings 2015). In the summer of 1965, Watts erupted in violence, and the McCone Commission placed part of the blame on inadequate transportation. The commission argued that blacks in south central Los Angeles rose up not only against the powerlessness they felt but also against the isolation that cut them off from opportunity (Governor's Commission on the Los Angeles Riots 1965, 65): "Our investigation has brought into clear focus the fact that the inadequate and costly public transportation currently existing throughout the Los Angeles area seriously restricts the residents of the disadvantaged areas such as south central Los Angeles."

What the residents of Los Angeles and elsewhere were experiencing was a lack of accessibility. Hansen (1959, 73), in a seminal article that introduced the accessibility concept to planners, defined it as the "the potential of opportunities for interaction." This is important because the very purpose of living in cities is the access they provide to help people prosper by offering a wide range of jobs; the variety of goods provided to meet needs; the assortment of amenities and services provided to satisfy diverse tastes; and the social engagement available for interacting with other people. Accessibility is a measure of how a transportation system is meeting the needs of people in reaching the goods, services, and opportunities that help them achieve well-being and participate fully in society. Where people live has a powerful effect on their capacity to achieve a high quality of life (Dreier, Mollenkopf, and Swanstrom 2004), in part through the accessibility that a place provides.

The events of the 1960s brought urgency to the long-standing challenge for transportation planning to ensure that the costs and benefits of a transportation system are distributed among people in a way that achieves an acceptable level of fairness.[1] This task is now mandated by a series of laws and regulations that requires ongoing and active monitoring by the public agencies charged with creating the plans and programs that guide transportation provision. Despite the federal government's moves to lift up transportation equity and mitigate transportation injustice, the public officials in charge of providing transportation infrastructure and services struggle with the task of evaluating whether their decisions are in compliance with equity objectives (Deakin 2007, Karner and Niemeier 2013, Mills and Neuhauser 2000, Schweitzer and Valenzuela 2004).

Advancing the cause of social justice in transportation will surely require directing careful attention not only to uncovering and addressing unjust outcomes but also to strengthening processes that aim for a deeper engagement with the very people that environmental justice regulations are meant to protect. These steps include minimizing language barriers and actively seeking the insights of traditionally marginalized people (Deakin 2007, Pirie 1983). The focus of this chapter is to persuade equity planners both inside and outside of government agencies that they can help advance social equity goals by advocating for the replacement of the mobility-based policy framework with an accessibility framework (Levine et al. 2012, van Wee and Geurs 2011). This chapter illustrates that such a shift can improve the analytical capabilities of public agencies. These agencies are now mandated by law to monitor and detect outcomes that have disproportionately harmed transportation-disadvantaged people, such as racial minorities and low-income households, but up until now, they have lacked effective tools for doing so.[2]

Promoting a Shift in Policy from Mobility to Accessibility

A mobility-based framework for making decisions dominates transportation policy. This mobility framework defines success as easier movement, typically in the form of increasing vehicle travel speeds. In the mobility framework, faster movement is the ultimate goal that is achieved through a variety of common means, such as adding roadway capacity, mitigating congestion through travel demand management, and so forth. The problem with this dominant framework is that movement is not what people want from their transportation system. Instead, what people want is to reach destinations. They want *access*.

An accessibility framework offers a contrast to the mobility-based approach to decision making. Instead of easier movement, the goal is to increase the amount of interaction a person can achieve in the form of contact with people and places. Figure 6.1 illustrates the accessibility framework and provides five insights. First, achieving higher accessibility is the end target, as it is the core objective of transportation planning. This is consistent with the consensus of the field that transportation is a "derived demand," meaning that travelers do not consume transportation for the sake of movement but in order to reach destinations (Cheng, Bertolini, and le Clercq 2007; Meyer and Miller 2001; Wachs and Kumagai 1973). The framework therefore allows planners to directly gauge the benefits of transportation policy. Second, it demotes mobility in the hierarchy of importance, showing that mobility matters—all else being equal, speed helps reach destinations—but that it is merely one among several means to the end. Third, it shows that increasing the proximity of destinations can increase accessibility, which opens up the possibility of achieving transportation objectives through land-use planning and not just through transportation infrastructure and services. Fourth, individual characteristics such as income, availability of an automobile, the kind of neighborhood of residence, and the richness of social networks play an influential role in determining a person's ability to interact with valued destinations, aside from the transportation system and prevailing

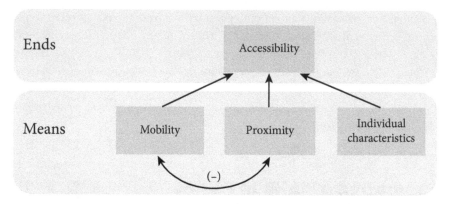

FIGURE 6.1. The Accessibility Framework: Reaching Destinations as the Policy Goal.

land-use patterns. Finally, the arrow linking mobility and proximity illustrates an essential element of this framework—in some circumstances, more mobility can actually harm accessibility. If faster travel speeds cause the mobility effect to dominate the proximity effect, accessibility can be undermined when sprawling land-use patterns spread out at a rate faster than average travel speeds (Levine et al. 2012). That mobility can be harmful is the central lesson from the accessibility framework, and sorting out the effects of mobility and proximity on accessibility is a skill that can advance social equity goals.

For a concrete example of how mobility and accessibility take shape in someone's life, consider the case of James Robertson, who came to be widely known in the Detroit metropolitan region as "The Walking Man" after a newspaper told his story of overcoming his lack of access to jobs. Robertson travels from his home in Detroit to a factory in suburban Rochester Hills, where he works as an injection molder. By car, the trip would be about twenty-three miles and take only about a half hour to drive—a high level of mobility stemming from decades of planning that placed priority on fast automobile speeds. But Robertson could not afford to buy, maintain, and insure a car, and hence he could not take advantage of this mobility. Instead, he lacked accessibility because few jobs are reachable from his Detroit neighborhood, in part because mobility-based planning fostered the spread of jobs far into the suburbs. Without a car, he instead took a bus for part of the trip and finished it with an astounding twenty-one miles of walking, each way, every day, Monday through Friday, over a ten-year period. As the *Detroit Free Press* reported, his efforts speak to the determination required to overcome the notoriously poor public transit service in a region built for cars (Laitner 2015):

Every trip is an ordeal of mental and physical toughness for this soft-spoken man with a perfect attendance record at work. And every day is a tribute to how much he cares about his job, his boss and his coworkers. Robertson's daunting walks and bus rides, in all kinds of weather, also reflect the challenges some metro Detroiters face in getting to work in a region of limited bus service, and where car ownership is priced beyond the reach of many.

Each year, Robertson walked the equivalent distance of Detroit to Los Angeles and back again. This is an investment in time and effort that would surely undermine someone's capacity to participate in other fulfilling parts of life.

Overcoming the Harms of Mobility Thinking: Making Accessibility the Core of Social Equity Analysis

The traditional mobility-based framework in transportation planning has, over several decades, promoted dispersed metropolitan spaces that principally accommodate the automobile. This framework is biased in ways that continue to harm people, including people of color and people living in poverty, who have been systematically disadvantaged by transportation policy. Placing the concept of accessibility foremost in evaluating social equity outcomes provides several advantages over mobility-based analysis.

First, as the accessibility framework of Figure 6.1 shows, sometimes improving mobility can undermine accessibility. Mobility-based metrics define success in terms of faster movement (Ewing 1995). Achieving success in providing congestion relief through added roadway capacity—a prominent public policy priority—can induce destinations to move farther apart (Transportation Research Board 1995). Travel to increasingly dispersed destinations might be accomplished at higher speeds, but the geographic spread of these destinations forces travelers to cover more distance, imposing higher costs in money and time that disproportionately fall on those with low incomes. In this way, transportation policy contributes to low-density, auto-oriented development. This form of development disproportionately harms racial minorities and low-income people who tend to live near the urban core and who have fewer resources to adapt to dispersed land-use patterns (Bullard, Torres, and Johnson 2000; Pendall 1999; Squires and Kubrin 2005).

Second, mobility-based measures such as congestion levels are attributes of infrastructure, not of people. Measuring attributes of transportation infrastructure

hides the effect on people and offers little help in understanding equity among social groups. Congestion levels, for example, have little relevance for households
without cars, yet carless people typically experience the greatest disadvantage from
the automobile-dependent cities that we have been building for decades. Accessibility metrics, by contrast, are attributes of people or places and allow for readily comparing outcomes among social groups.

Third, the mobility metrics commonly used by planners today are not clear
about whether a traveler is experiencing disadvantage or not. Commonly used
mobility metrics in equity studies include miles traveled per day, trips per day,
and minutes traveled per day (Dodson et al. 2010; Forkenbrock and Weisbrod
2001; Giuliano 2003; Johnston-Anumonwo 1995; Manaugh, Badami, and El-
Geneidy 2015). But these metrics offer little help in evaluating disadvantage.
Travelers prefer shorter travel times to longer ones. But a preference for shorter
travel time does not mean that those with longer travel times are somehow
disadvantaged. For example, women and poor people face long-standing disadvantages in transportation (Blumenberg 2004, Hess 2005, Pratt and Hanson
1988), but they typically experience much shorter travel times on average than
the general population (Pucher and Renne 2003). These shorter travel times
cannot be appropriately considered an advantage but rather result from people
having fewer choices in how they travel (Taylor and Ong 1995). When the
middle- and upper-income classes of the United States choose to trade off
longer commutes in exchange for suburban amenities, their longer travel times
cannot properly be considered a disadvantage. While mobility-based metrics in
equity evaluation are uncertain with regard to disadvantage, accessibility metrics make disadvantage readily evident: "Accessibility as a planning goal provides clear direction for policy makers. Although greater mobility may be a good
thing, greater accessibility is inherently a good thing" (Pfeffer et al. 2002, 40).
Accessibility provides a clearer basis than mobility for making decisions about
social equity.

A fourth reason for placing accessibility at the pinnacle of equity evaluation is
that mobility-based regulations sometimes push out projects that would enhance
accessibility for disadvantaged people. Mobility-based metrics influence not just
transportation projects but also interfere with land-use development projects. The
most commonly used metric of transportation performance at all levels of
government is level of service (LOS). LOS assesses the amount of delay that
motorists experience from the congestion induced by the presence of other
vehicles. Some contend that the prevalent use of LOS evaluation further encourages low-density dispersal of residences and businesses (Henderson 2011). When
planners forecast that a proposed new land-use development will degrade congestion below LOS guidelines, municipal authorities charge developers an impact

fee to bring surrounding streets up to standard, or they simply reject the development entirely. Because many urban streets in the core of a metropolis are already operating below LOS standards, and because mitigation is prohibitively expensive at higher-density locations, developers often simply shift their projects to suburban and exurban locations where traffic impacts are negligible (Dumbaugh, Tumlin, and Marshall 2014). Strictly abiding by LOS standards places limits on urban densities; most likely imposes a systematic bias against infill development; constrains the supply of affordable housing in the core of regions; and degrades overall metropolitan accessibility by interfering with people's ability to choose where to live.

When municipal authorities reject a proposed central-city grocery store because planners anticipate too much traffic on the surrounding streets, nearby residents lose a chance at better accessibility to jobs and food. When local officials turn down a real estate developer's bid to build an affordable housing project in an inner-ring suburb for fear of congested traffic, as has happened in many communities, planners will never know how many would-be residents may have gained access to the municipality's amenities and opportunities. Accessibility-enhancing projects are too valuable to be rejected by local planning authorities who rely exclusively on the narrow standards of LOS evaluation; accessibility is the tool for counteracting the harmful effects of LOS standards by accounting for the benefits side of the cost-benefit ledger.

Accessibility and the Capabilities Approach to Justice

The fifth and final point in support of the concept of accessibility is that accessibility offers more conceptual consistency with the latest philosophical debates about social justice. Theoretical views of justice have been influenced for several hundred years by the idea of utilitarianism, which argues that people achieve well-being through the goods and services they consume, and that this consumption leads to utility or happiness. Critics contend that such an approach to theorizing justice places too much emphasis on commodity consumption; they believe that it fails to sufficiently address other dimensions of well-being. Recent writers propose an alternative theory of justice that has come to be known as the "capabilities approach." This approach argues that individual well-being can be evaluated not just by the extent of goods and services that a person has command over but also by the person's capacity to convert goods and services into "capabilities" that enable a satisfying life (Nussbaum 2000, 2003; Sen 1985, 1992, 1999).

Amartya Sen's (1981) analysis of famines revealed a surprising source of starvation and illustrated how a utilitarian perspective falls short in assessing well-being. It was commonly believed that famines occur because of a decline in food production and supply. A utilitarian view would stress that a lack of commodities led to starvation. Sen's analysis challenged this conventional view by showing that famines typically occur not because of any lack of commodities—food supplies are typically plentiful during famines—but rather because some people lack the ability to purchase the food when prices shoot up. In short, this alternative perspective places emphasis on the source of starvation—not on a lack of commodities, but on a lack of *access* to the commodities. Sen's analysis showed that hunger depends not just on the availability of a good in the form of food but also, critically, on the economic and political institutions that set prices and distribute the good.

The capabilities approach offers a different and more expansive understanding of social justice than the more traditional views that have dominated social science. Instead of the traditional concern with commodities and utility, the capabilities approach focuses on the two related but distinct concepts of *functionings* and *capabilities*. A functioning is an achievement, or what a person manages to do or be. Having access to goods can enable a functioning, but a good and a functioning are not the same thing. A bike is a good that enables the functioning of mobility, in this case by moving freely to valued destinations more rapidly than by walking. But personal characteristics affect whether a person can convert this good into a functioning. For example, if one person is physically disabled and cannot ride a bike, while a second person is not, then the first person is restricted from converting the bike into the functioning of movement in ways that the second is not. Aside from such personal attributes, social and environmental characteristics can influence a person's ability to convert goods into a functioning as well (Robeyns 2005). The ability to use a bike can be hindered from a lack of sufficient income to keep it properly maintained, for example, if women are not allowed to ride bikes due to societal or cultural norms, if a neighborhood is so violent that riding a bike in certain hours is regarded by residents as unsafe, or if vehicular traffic on nearby roads is too dangerous for bikes. A utilitarian view would evaluate two people merely on the basis of their each having a bike, while the capabilities approach goes further to account for differences in the ability to convert the bike into a useful achievement.

But objectively adding up the functionings that a person accomplishes is not enough to adequately assess a person's overall well-being, because a person's quality of life is also determined in part by the opportunities that a person faces. A capability is a functioning that a person *could have* achieved—a concept with special relevance for accessibility. A functioning represents the condition of a person in terms of what one manages to do or be. The capabilities reflect the combination of functionings that a person can possibly achieve through exercising choice. Capabilities are the wide range of opportunities that contribute to having a high quality of life, and they indicate the extent of freedom of choice that a person has to achieve a set of functionings. Sen (1985) illustrates the importance of capabilities by comparing two people with identical functionings. Both experience the same functioning of starvation and the misery that comes with the lack of food. One person is hungry because poverty prevents the purchase of food. The other is fasting and is hungry as a matter of choice, perhaps due to religious beliefs. Fasting in this case is something other than just starving—it is *choosing* to starve when other options are available (Sen 1992). Although these two people may be experiencing identical misery resulting from the material lack of food, Sen argues that it would be a mistake to claim that these two experience similar levels of well-being because of the consequential difference in what they each bring by way of their freedom to choose in the matter of starvation. Quality of life involves more than material comfort. Being capable of freely choosing how to live one's life is a fundamental dimension of well-being.

Like the capabilities approach, the concept of accessibility acknowledges the intrinsic value of having the freedom and capacity to choose among a variety of options. As the distinction between fasting and starving illustrates, having a choice in one's life is a highly valued quality in and of itself (Sen 1985, 1988). To live a fulfilling and satisfying life requires engaging in freely chosen activities when one is faced with a range of valuable and feasible opportunities. Instead of utility or resources, a person's well-being should be evaluated by the functionings and capabilities that enable the exercise of choice to do or be what one values. Accessibility represents a measure of choice—as an indicator of a person's potential for seizing available opportunities. Following the equity planning movement, advancing policies that broaden the scope of choice has become a central principle in the field of urban planning (Krumholz and Clavel 1994, Krumholz and Forester 1990). Many professional planners now espouse providing "a wider range of choices for . . . residents who have few, if any, choices" (Krumholz 1982, 163)—a tenet now codified in the ethical standards of the American Institute of Certified Planners (Solin 1997). The concept of accessibility provides the needed measurement tool as the critical link between social equity and the built environment in the pursuit of expanding choices for those who have few.

The State of Practice in Transportation Equity Analysis: Notable Achievements that Remain Incomplete

Equity planners have the power of legal mandates to support their efforts in re-distributing transportation benefits to disadvantaged people. But so far, they have not yet found a way to take full advantage of this power, in part for failing to sufficiently embrace the accessibility concept.

Public agencies in the United States are now required by law to prevent discrimination in their plans and programs. Relevant laws include Title VI of the Civil Rights Act of 1964, the National Environmental Policy Act of 1969 (NEPA), and several Federal-Aid Highway Acts of the 1970s (Cairns, Greig, and Wachs 2003; Sanchez and Brenman 2007). The Clinton administration, in response to a growing environmental justice movement, issued Executive Order 12898 in 1994 and elevated attention to social equity by directing all federal agencies to develop a strategy that "identifies and addresses disproportionately high and adverse human health or environmental effects of its programs, policies, and activities on minority populations and low-income populations" (Executive Order No. 12898 of 1994).

Agencies within the U.S. Department of Transportation (DOT) adopted their own regulations for meeting these principles. For example, the Federal Transit Agency (FTA) issued specific guidance through a circular in 2007 (later amended in 2012) that provides instructions necessary to carry out Title VI regulations to ensure that the considerations expressed in the DOT's principles of environmental justice (EJ) are integrated into programs and activities (FTA 2007, 2012). Transportation agencies are required to identify and address issues related to Title VI and EJ and must ensure that their programs and policies distribute benefits widely without imposing disproportionately high burdens on any one social group. These regulations prescribe a requirement to consider impacts specifically on low-income and racial-minority groups. They direct agencies to evaluate not just the *burdens* of transportation decisions, which are typically the central concern in environmental regulation, but also the *benefits*. And the ultimate benefit of any transportation investment is improved access to opportunities, the purpose that underlies all transportation decisions.

Public agencies often find EJ requirements challenging to implement, despite the growing awareness of inequities in the transportation sector and the recent demands on governments to address them. The various laws, regulations, and internal policies that mandate ongoing equity analysis do not recommend specific methods for doing so. This lack of standardized techniques is, on the one hand, a means of providing the flexibility for planners to explore and invent the evaluation techniques that are best suited for particular circumstances. Metropolitan regions differ in their rate of growth or decline, in economic specialization, and in the problems (such as congestion and air pollution) they face, and it is sensible that methods of analysis ought to reflect these regional differences. On the other hand, because the guidelines are vague and the requirements rarely enforced, the extent and quality of analysis varies substantially among regions and commonly results in analyses that are highly incomplete (Karner 2016; Karner and Niemeier 2013; Sanchez, Stolz, and Ma 2003). Indeed, planners and decision makers have requested better technical tools for carrying out the EJ mandates (Cambridge Systematics 2002, 1).

The FTA has provided the most specific guidance on carrying out equity analysis by providing instructions for all recipients of financial assistance from the FTA; this includes state departments of transportation, metropolitan planning organizations (MPOs), and public transit agencies (FTA 2007, 2012). The FTA circulars stipulate that these agencies "should have an analytic basis in place for certifying their compliance with Title VI," including methods for identifying "locations of socioeconomic groups, including low-income and minority populations," having in place a planning process that "identifies the needs of low-income and minority populations," and having an "analytical process that identifies the benefits and burdens of metropolitan transportation system investments for different socioeconomic groups, identifying imbalances and responding to the analyses produced" (FTA 2007, chap. VI, 1). However, the circulars do not specify what methods and practices should be used.

Equity Analysis in Metropolitan Planning

Although accessibility-based evaluation has not yet been fully embraced in practice (Levine and Grengs 2011), some regional agencies have started to include accessibility metrics in carrying out equity analysis at the regional scale. The most common type of equity analysis is conducted by MPOs to certify that their regional plans are in compliance with Title VI. Several MPOs exemplify the use of accessibility metrics in equity analysis, including the Boston Region Metropolitan Planning Organization, the Metropolitan Transportation Commission of the San Francisco Bay Area, the Mid-Ohio Regional Planning Commission of Columbus, and the Southern California Association of Governments (Cambridge Systematics 2002; Manaugh, Badami, and El-Geneidy 2015; Purvis 2001). Yet even among these early adopters, recent plans reveal that accessibility metrics remain merely supplements to a mix of mobility-based metrics in their equity analyses (Boston Region Metropolitan Planning Organization 2015, Metropolitan Transportation Commission 2009, Mid-Ohio Regional Planning Commission 2012).

The guidance provided by the FTA circulars has influenced what has become a common approach for analyzing equity of regional transportation plans by MPOs, which can be summarized in three main steps (Cambridge Systematics 2002, Karner and Niemeier 2013). The first step is to identify geographic concentrations of population groups, including (at a minimum) racial-minority and low-income residents of the region. For example, a geographic concentration of low-income households might consist of contiguous groups of census tracts that exceed 40 percent of persons below the federal poverty line. The second step is to define the metrics to be used for evaluating the benefits and burdens of the regional transportation plan. The third step is to evaluate whether the distribution of the benefits and burdens are disproportionate, typically by comparing the metrics between what some refer to as a "protected population" or "EJ population" (e.g., minority or low income) to a "control population" (e.g., nonminority or non-low-income) (Steinberg 2000).

The concept of accessibility offers a way to address two main shortcomings with this approach. First, MPOs use widely divergent definitions for identifying geographic concentrations of populations, especially for "low income" (Cambridge Systematics 2002).[3] The outcome of an equity analysis is likely to be highly determined by this definition, and any equity analysis should include a sensitivity analysis to reflect the complexity of social groups (Rowangould, Karner, and London 2016). More problematic than defining the groups, however, is the approach of comparing protected populations to control populations. In the U.S. metropolis, racial minorities, people in poverty, and other vulnerable populations tend to be confined to pockets of high concentrations, although not all are. Because accessibility is an attribute of people or households—unlike mobility metrics, which are attributes of infrastructure—an accessibility-based analysis allows for overcoming the limitations of comparing geographic concentrations of populations. Instead, by attaching accessibility to people, rather than places, and then plotting out the full spectrum of all populations, a more accurate comparison can be made across full social groups regardless of whether they live at certain threshold concentrations (Grengs 2012, 2015).

The second and even more essential way of addressing shortcomings in this common approach to equity analysis is to make accessibility the fundamental metric of comparison. Even the leading MPOs continue to use a wide range of mobility-based metrics for evaluating benefits and burdens without acknowledging the central role of accessibility. Indeed, an otherwise excellent guidebook on approaches to EJ analysis provides an example of how accessibility is but one dimension of equity analysis, presenting it as though it is on par with a wide range of mobility metrics (Forkenbrock and Weisbrod 2001). Mobility-based metrics commonly used in equity analysis include trips per day, miles per day, average travel time to work, mode share distributions, congested vehicle-miles of travel, the share of population within a half mile of home, and so forth. But to consider accessibility as merely one of a set of metrics that are mobility-based is to misguidedly place on equal footing a means (mobility) and an end (accessibility).

Equity Analysis of Public Transit Service

Aside from equity analysis performed at the regional level, another common type of evaluation is required for changes in the service delivery of public transit. The FTA has done an admirable job of elevating awareness of the potential for injustice and ensuring that ongoing monitoring takes place, principally through the publication of recent circulars that are widely regarded as among the most authoritative guidelines for analyzing environmental justice outcomes (FTA 2007, 2012; Reddy, Chennadu, and Lu 2010). Transit agencies are required to maintain systemwide service standards and to perform an equity analysis of proposed changes in service or fares, including when routes or schedules are altered, or if bus lines or stops are eliminated.[4] Any finding of disparities requires corrective action. Although the guidelines are extensive, a main purpose is "to collect and analyze racial and ethnic data showing the extent to which members of minority groups are beneficiaries of programs receiving Federal financial assistance" (FTA 2012, chap. V, 1).

In summary, the standard approach to demonstrate compliance is to create maps that show the proximity of minority and low-income population groups to bus and rail stations and lines. Service levels are then evaluated on a range of metrics that include vehicle loads (e.g., passengers per vehicle), headways (the frequency of service as the time interval between vehicles arriving at a stop), on-time performance, availability of amenities (e.g., benches, shelters, trash receptacles), and service availability (e.g., whether large shares of a population live within walking distance of a transit stop). This approach suffers from a fundamental shortcoming that prevents these guidelines from being effective in advancing social equity; they say nothing about disparities in the ability to reach destinations. Because the ultimate purpose of a transit agency is to help riders reach destinations, the standard approach that has emerged from FTA guidelines is merely an indirect assessment of whether transit services are meeting the core objective of providing access to destinations.

Furthermore, the state of practice in equity analysis—including both examples of metropolitan planning and public transit service—suffers from a conceptual flaw that has the unfortunate effect of preserving the status quo and thereby perpetuating disadvantages to social groups. Equity analyses typically use as the basis of comparison a criterion of proportionality when assessing the fairness of a proposed project or a plan, and therefore fail to account for any preexisting disadvantages (Cambridge Systematics 2002; Karner and Niemeier 2013; Martens, Golub, and Robinson 2012; Steinberg 2000). If, for example, an "EJ population" is found to experience benefits and burdens from a proposed project that are approximately the same as the "control population," the project is deemed to have no disproportionate effect, and it can proceed without violating EJ provisions. This is a highly questionable approach given the long, painful history of how racial segregation and concentrated poverty have been deeply etched into the landscape of the American metropolis (Frug 1999, Goldsmith and Blakely 2010, Marcuse 1997, Wacquant 1997). For African Americans in particular, the intense and debilitating social isolation that has persisted for decades "was constructed through a series of well-defined institutional practices, private behaviors, and public policies by which whites sought to contain growing urban black populations" (Massey and Denton 1993, 10).[5] A more assertive commitment to advancing social justice in transportation would acknowledge preexisting disparities and, by taking a more explicitly normative position, would then seek to redress them.

In recognition of the severe limitations of restricting equity analysis to the proportionality criterion, equity planners ought to take a more aggressive normative stance on distributive justice. To move beyond the limitations of current equity guidelines, planners can take the position that transportation benefits ought to be provided more favorably to some groups over others to address preexisting disadvantages (Foth, Manaugh, and El-Geneidy 2013; Karner and Niemeier 2013; Martens 2012; Martens, Golub, and Robinson 2012; Murray and Davis 2001). Such a strategy would require identifying places of preexisting disadvantage and then strategically targeting investments where they can address the greatest needs. For example, the defining feature of transportation disadvantage in the typical U.S. metropolitan region is the severe difference between reaching opportunities by car or by public transit (Blumenberg and Manville 2004, Grengs 2010). Any policy that aims to address social equity in transportation must confront the conditions of people who are unable or unwilling to drive in metropolitan regions that are designed to give advantage to cars throughout the nation. Mobility metrics are not suited to identifying disadvantage. By contrast, accessibility-based evaluation tools can offer a more realistic reflection of the current distribution of transportation benefits and disadvantages and can help equity planners focus attention and target resources toward underserved people and areas.

Conclusion: Lessons for Getting to Equity Planning in Transportation with Accessibility

If planners aim to advance the goal of social equity, they should promote a fundamentally different way of thinking about transportation policy by shifting from mobility to accessibility as the primary criterion by which transportation policy is evaluated. This fundamental shift has so far not yet arrived. Although some agencies have tentatively included accessibility metrics as complements of traditional mobility metrics, none have yet fully embraced an accessibility-based perspective to guide decisions. Planners therefore do not yet have successful examples of how accessibility-focused analysis from practice can guide their work.

Public officials have, however, made notable advancements toward addressing social inequality in recent years. They have institutionalized a set of practices to ensure that planners pay attention to equity in their day-to-day work. But in contrast to the findings of many scholars, public agencies routinely find no evidence of disparities in the transportation they provide. This discrepancy is in part because planners continue to rely on the flawed framework of mobility and have not yet properly adopted the concept of accessibility.

In response to the alarming social unrest of the 1960s that awakened public officials to transportation's role in social injustice, Wachs and Kumagai (1973) took a normative stance by asserting that transportation policy ought to be directed at improving access to opportunities and thus elevating the quality of life for disadvantaged people. Decades later, equity planners of today can heed their prescient call and reinvigorate their commitment to ensuring equity in transportation by taking several steps.

First, equity planners should promote the replacement of mobility-based evaluation with accessibility-based evaluation, making the enhancement of accessibility the primary goal of policy decisions. Accessibility-based metrics address several serious shortcomings in commonly used mobility-based metrics. And because social equity analysis mandated by law is expected to address not only the *costs* but also the *benefits* of a transportation system, accessibility-based metrics gauge directly the benefit outcomes of transportation policy. An example target of such reform is the performance measures that were mandated by Congress in the federal transportation law enacted in 2012.

Second, planners should insist on avoiding the common practice of mingling the language of mobility with accessibility. When accessibility is defined properly, it subsumes mobility. Including mobility metrics in equity analysis, even when paired with accessibility metrics, reinforces the mistaken notion that mobility itself ought to be an independent goal and undermines the transformative power of the accessibility concept in equity analysis.

Third, for equity planners to overcome the built-in bias in equity analysis that perpetuates the status quo, the planners should place priority on addressing preexisting disadvantages by strategically redirecting transportation benefits to people in the greatest need. Mobility metrics are incapable of identifying need. Accessibility-based tools are essential for equity planners to target resources toward underserved people and areas because they directly assess the current distribution of transportation benefits and who experiences them.

Fourth, planners can advance transportation equity by reforming not just transportation but land-use policy as well. Making progress toward accessibility-based planning holds promise in such cases because the reform can occur at the municipal and community-based levels on a project-by-project basis. Planners should oppose the damaging effects of LOS standards that cause local authorities to reject accessibility-enhancing land-use developments. The main problem with LOS standards in evaluating the merits of a proposed land-use development is that they only count the *costs* and fail to recognize the *benefits* of land-use developments. A more legitimate approach would be to use an accessibility-based evaluation to weigh the costs against the concomitant access benefits. In this way, if local planners were to forecast the effect of a proposed development on accessibility rather than on LOS alone—requiring only one more step beyond current traffic impact analysis—they could simultaneously assess the costs (in the form of worsened nearby traffic congestion) with the benefits (in the form of people's ability to live in close proximity to jobs and important destinations).

Fifth, the tasks of equity planning—advocating for redistributive plans and policies to favor those who are disadvantaged—are increasingly carried out not by government planners but by planners from advocacy organizations, community development corporations, and other community-based organizations. The accessibility framework holds promise for constructively challenging government plans by providing a more rigorous and convincing basis for identifying and prioritizing the particular people and places that face the greatest need. However, despite the many advantages that an accessibility framework brings, several barriers have prevented the concept from making the leap from scholarship to practice. Compared to mobility-based planning, accessibility-based planning is harder to do, because it requires more data. Also, the metrics are technically more demanding to carry out, the concept is more difficult to explain to both the public and public officials alike, and the dominance of the mobility framework in current regulations makes it risky for government planners to adopt accessibility planning (Levine and Grengs 2011). Community-based equity planners can confront these barriers with steps such as developing and sharing online tools to assist with public reviews of proposed plans (Golub, Robinson, and Nee 2013) and generating data from easy-to-use online tools that promote accessibility-enhancing land-use projects at local levels of decision making (Levine, Merlin, and Grengs 2017).

Finally, equity planners are entering a turbulent era in the field of transportation. They should adopt an accessibility framework to help guide the choices they make in the face of extreme uncertainty. Driverless cars and shared-mobility services are emerging rapidly with potential for substantially altering the built environment. As of early 2017, an extremist presidential administration promises extensive new investments in infrastructure. This same administration is signaling that it will dramatically cut public transit spending, embrace public-private partnerships in delivering infrastructure, and severely weaken environmental standards. These developments will surely have implications for social justice, with the result likely causing severe harm. Equity planners do not have the option of waiting for clarity among these unknowns. The mobility of travelers is likely to change dramatically and soon. But the ability to reach destinations will remain an outcome that travelers will want from their transportation system. Accessibility provides a basis for transportation policy evaluation and reform even in the face of uncertainty. While mobility-based metrics leave uncertainty about whether social groups experience disadvantage relative to others, accessibility metrics are clear: more is better than less.

By elevating accessibility as the central consideration of equity analysis, equity planners will be positioned to take a more explicitly normative stance in their practice. Although carrying out equity analysis has become standard in the field thanks to recent, forward-thinking regulations, it remains incomplete by relying on evaluations that fail to account for any preexisting disadvantages and that preserve the status quo. The accessibility-based framework not only offers a more realistic reflection of current disadvantages than the mobility-based framework; it also provides a sound basis for identifying the people and places in greatest need. This provides equity planners with a solid foundation for going forth by taking the political action of redirecting resources to the people who are most disadvantaged by current transportation plans and policies.

Acknowledgments

Thanks to Joel Batterman for comments that helped me improve this chapter.

NOTES

1. The point was forcefully made following the urban uprisings of the 1960s through the Kerner Commission report: "What white Americans have never fully understood—but what the Negro can never forget—is that white society is deeply implicated in the

ghetto. White institutions created it, white institutions maintain it, and white society condones it" (Kerner et al. 1968, 2).

2. Technically, the requirement applies only to "major service changes" only, and a problem not addressed here is that the transit agency decides what constitutes a major change (FTA 2012).

3. To illustrate, based on reviewing the most recent equity analyses of twelve MPOs, three used the definition from the U.S. Department of Health and Human Services poverty guidelines, while nine used a definition of their own making. For instance, the Metropolitan Council of Minneapolis/St. Paul uses: "Contiguous areas where at least 40% of residents live in households with incomes below 185% of the federal poverty line." The Southeast Michigan Council of Governments in the Detroit region uses: "All households that are in the lowest income quartile."

4. Transportation equity can be evaluated across a wide range of dimensions, including exposure to negative consequences like noise and air pollution, cost, tax and subsidy incidence, and so forth. Broader overviews of conceptual issues are available elsewhere (Deka 2004, Forkenbrock and Schweitzer 1999, Hay 1993, Hodge 1995, Schweitzer and Valenzuela 2004, Taylor and Tassiello Norton 2009).

5. Transportation scholars responded with a flurry of studies seeking to better understand how transportation policy contributes to problems like poverty and social isolation (American Academy of Arts and Sciences 1968; Kain and Meyer 1968, 1970; Myers 1970; Notess 1972; Ornati 1969). The most notable of these studies came from Wachs and Kumagai (1973) in an important article that advanced several innovative improvements for transportation policy.

REFERENCES

American Academy of Arts and Sciences. 1968. *Conference on Poverty and Transportation.* Edited transcript, June 7. Brookline, MA: American Academy of Art and Sciences.

Blumenberg, Evelyn. 2004. "En-gendering Effective Planning: Spatial Mismatch, Low-Income Women, and Transportation Policy," *Journal of the American Planning Association* 70 (3): 269–81.

Blumenberg, Evelyn, and Michael Manville. 2004. "Beyond the Spatial Mismatch: Welfare Recipients and Transportation Policy," *Journal of Planning Literature* 19 (2): 182–205.

Boston Region Metropolitan Planning Organization. 2015. *Long-Range Transportation Plan of the Boston Region Metropolitan Planning Organization.* Boston, MA: Boston Region Metropolitan Planning Organization.

Bullard, Robert D., Angel O. Torres, and Glenn S. Johnson, eds. 2000. *Sprawl City: Race, Politics, and Planning in Atlanta.* Washington, DC: Island Press.

Cairns, Shannon, Jessica Greig, and Martin Wachs. 2003. *Environmental Justice and Transportation: A Citizen's Handbook.* Berkeley: University of California.

Cambridge Systematics. 2002. *Technical Methods to Support Analysis of Environmental Justice Issues.* Cambridge, MA: National Cooperative Highway Research Program.

Cheng, Jianquan, Luca Bertolini, and Frank le Clercq. 2007. "Measuring Sustainable Accessibility," *Transportation Research Record: Journal of the Transportation Research Board* 2017: 16–25.

Deakin, Elizabeth. 2007. "Equity and Environmental Justice in Sustainable Transportation: Toward a Research Agenda." In *Institutions and Sustainable Transport: Regulatory Reform in Advanced Economies*, edited by P. Rietveld and R. R. Stough, 51–69. Cheltenham, UK: Edward Elgar.

Deka, Devajyoti. 2004. "Social and Environmental Justice Issues in Urban Transportation." In *The Geography of Urban Transportation*, 3rd ed., edited by S. Hanson and G. Giuliano, 332–55. New York: Guilford Press.

Dodson, Jago et al. 2010. "Travel Behavior Patterns of Different Socially Disadvantaged Groups: Analysis of Household Travel Survey Data for a Dispersed Metropolitan Area," *Transportation Research Record: Journal of the Transportation Research Board* 2163: 24–31.

Dreier, Peter, John H. Mollenkopf, and Todd Swanstrom. 2004. *Place Matters: Metropolitics for the Twenty-first Century.* 2nd ed. Lawrence: University Press of Kansas.

Dumbaugh, Eric, Jeffrey Tumlin, and Wesley E. Marshall. 2014. "Decisions, Values, and Data: Understanding Bias in Transportation Performance Measures," *ITE Journal* (August): 20–25.

Ewing, Reid. 1995. "Measuring Transportation Performance," *Transportation Quarterly* 49 (1): 91–104.

Executive Order No. 12898 of February 11, 1994. "Federal Actions to Address Environmental Justice in Minority Populations and Low-Income Populations." https://www.gpo.gov/fdsys/pkg/WCPD-1994-02-14/pdf/WCPD-1994-02-14-Pg276.pdf.

Federal Transit Administration (FTA). 2007. "Title VI and Title VI-Dependent Guidelines for Federal Transit Administration Recipients," FTA Circular 4702.1A. Washington, DC: U.S. Department of Transportation.

———. 2012. FTA Circular 4702.1B: Title VI Requirements and Guidelines for Federal Transit Administration Recipients. Washington, DC: U.S. Department of Transportation.

Forkenbrock, David J., and Lisa A. Schweitzer. 1999. "Environmental Justice in Transportation Planning," *Journal of the American Planning Association* 65 (1): 96–111.

Forkenbrock, David J., and Glen E. Weisbrod. 2001. *Guidebook for Estimating the Social and Economic Effects of Transportation Projects.* NCHRP Report #456. Washington, DC: National Academy Press.

Foth, Nicole, Kevin Manaugh, and Ahmed M. El-Geneidy. 2013. "Towards equitable transit: examining transit accessibility and social need in Toronto, Canada, 1996–2006," *Journal of Transport Geography* 29 (May): 1–10.

Frug, Gerald E. 1999. *City Making: Building Communities without Building Walls.* Princeton: Princeton University Press.

Giuliano, Genevieve. 2003. "Travel, Location and Race/Ethnicity," *Transportation Research Part A: Policy and Practice* 37 (4): 351–72.

Goldsmith, William W., and Edward J. Blakely. 2010. *Separate Societies: Poverty and Inequality in U.S. Cities.* 2nd ed. Philadelphia: Temple University Press.

Golub, Aaron, Glenn Robinson, and Brendan Nee. 2013. "Making Accessibility Analyses Accessible: A Tool to Facilitate the Public Review of the Effects of Regional Transportation Plans on Accessibility," *Journal of Transport and Land Use* 6 (3): 17–28.

Governor's Commission on the Los Angeles Riots (the McCone Commission). 1965. *Violence in the City—An End or a Beginning?* Los Angeles: State of California.

Grengs, Joe. 2010. "Job Accessibility and the Modal Mismatch in Detroit," *Journal of Transport Geography* 18 (1): 42–54.

———. 2012. "Equity and the Social Distribution of Job Accessibility in Detroit," *Environment and Planning B: Planning and Design* 39 (5): 785–800.

———. 2015. "Nonwork Accessibility as a Social Equity Indicator," *International Journal of Sustainable Transportation* 9 (1): 1–14.

Hansen, Walter G. 1959. "How Accessibility Shapes Land Use." *Journal of the American Institute of Planners* 25 (2):73–76.

Hay, Alan. 1993. "Equity and Welfare in the Geography of Public Transport Provision," *Journal of Transport Geography* 1 (2): 95–101.

Henderson, Jason. 2011. "Level of service: the politics of reconfiguring urban streets in San Francisco, CA," *Journal of Transport Geography* 19 (6): 1138–44.

Hess, Daniel Baldwin. 2005. "Access to Employment for Adults in Poverty in the Buffalo-Niagara Region," *Urban Studies* 42 (7): 1177–1200.

Hodge, David C. 1995. "My Fair Share: Equity Issues in Urban Transportation." In *The Geography of Urban Transportation*, 2nd ed., edited by S. Hanson, 359–75. New York: Guilford Press.

Johnston-Anumonwo, Ibipo. 1995. "Racial Differences in the Commuting Behavior of Women in Buffalo, 1980–1990," *Urban Geography* 16 (1): 23–45.

Kain, John F., and John R. Meyer. 1970. "Transportation and Poverty." In *The Urban Economy*, edited by H.M. Hochman, 180–94. New York: W.W. Norton.

Kain, John F., and John R. Meyer, eds. 1968. *Interrelationships of Transportation and Poverty: Summary of Conference on Transportation and Poverty*. Discussion Paper No. 39, Program on Regional and Urban Economics. Cambridge, MA: Harvard University.

Karner, Alex. 2016. "Planning for Transportation Equity in Small Regions: Towards Meaningful Performance Assessment," *Transport Policy* 52 (November): 46–54.

Karner, Alex, and Deb Niemeier. 2013. "Civil rights guidance and equity analysis methods for regional transportation plans: a critical review of literature and practice," *Journal of Transport Geography* 33 (December): 126–34.

Kerner, Otto, et al. 1968. *Report of the National Advisory Commission on Civil Disorders*. New York: Bantam Books.

Krumholz, Norman. 1982. "A Retrospective View of Equity Planning: Cleveland 1969–1979," *Journal of the American Planning Association* 48 (2): 163–74.

Krumholz, Norman, and Pierre Clavel, eds. 1994. *Reinventing Cities: Equity Planners Tell Their Stories*. Philadelphia: Temple University Press.

Krumholz, Norman, and John Forester. 1990. *Making Equity Planning Work*. Philadelphia: Temple University Press.

Laitner, Bill. 2015. "Heart and Sole: Detroiter Walks 21 Miles in Work Commute," *Detroit Free Press*, January 31.

Levine, Jonathan, and Joe Grengs. 2011. "Getting There: Putting Accessibility Into Practice for Progressive Transportation Planning," *Progressive Planning* 189: 8–11.

Levine, Jonathan, et al. 2012. "Does Accessibility Require Density or Speed? A Comparison of Fast Versus Close in Getting Where You Want to Go in U.S. Metropolitan Regions," *Journal of the American Planning Association* 78 (2): 157–72.

Levine, Jonathan, Louis Merlin, and Joe Grengs. 2017. "Project-Level Accessibility Analysis for Land-Use Planning," *Transport Policy* 53: 107–19.

Manaugh, Kevin, Madhav G. Badami, and Ahmed M. El-Geneidy. 2015. "Integrating Social Equity into Urban Transportation Planning: A Critical Evaluation of Equity Objectives and Measures in Transportation Plans in North America," *Transport Policy* 37 (January): 167–76.

Marcuse, Peter. 1997. "The Enclave, The Citadel, and the Ghetto: What Has Changed in The Post-Fordist U.S. City," *Urban Affairs Review* 33 (2): 228–64.

Martens, Karel. 2012. "Justice in Transport as Justice in Accessibility: Applying Walzer's 'Spheres of Justice' to the Transport Sector," *Transportation* 39 (6): 1–19.

Martens, Karel, Aaron Golub, and Glenn Robinson. 2012. "A justice-theoretic approach to the distribution of transportation benefits: Implications for transportation planning practice in the United States," *Transportation Research Part A: Policy and Practice* 46 (4): 684–95.

Massey, Douglas S., and Nancy A. Denton. 1993. *American Apartheid: Segregation and the Making of the Underclass.* Cambridge: Harvard University Press.

Metropolitan Transportation Commission. 2009. *Transportation 2035 Plan for the San Francisco Bay Area: Equity Analysis Report.* Oakland, CA.

Meyer, Michael D., and Eric J. Miller. 2001. *Urban Transportation Planning: A Decision Oriented Approach.* 2nd ed. New York: McGraw-Hill.

Mid-Ohio Regional Planning Commission. 2012. "Appendix D: Environmental Justice Technical Analysis." In *2012–2035 Metropolitan Transportation Plan.* Columbus, OH: Mid-Ohio Regional Planning Commission.

Mills, G. Scott, and K. Sieglinde Neuhauser. 2000. "Quantitative Methods for Environmental Justice Assessment of Transportation," *Risk Analysis* 20 (3): 377–84.

Mozingo, Joe, and Angel Jennings. 2015. "50 Years After Watts: 'There is Still a Crisis in the Black Community,'" *Los Angeles Times*, August 13.

Murray, Alan T., and Rex Davis. 2001. "Equity in Regional Service Provision," *Journal of Regional Science* 41 (4): 577–600.

Myers, Sumner. 1970. "Personal Transportation for the Poor," *Traffic Quarterly* 24 (2): 191–206.

Notess, Charles B. 1972. "Travel in the Black Ghetto," *Highway Research Record* 403: 49–50.

Nussbaum, Martha C. 2000. *Women and Human Development: The Capabilities Approach.* New York: Cambridge University Press.

——. 2003. "Capabilities as Fundamental Entitlements: Sen and Social Justice," *Feminist Economics* 9 (2–3): 33–59.

Ornati, Oscar A. 1969. *Transportation Needs of the Poor: A Case Study of New York City.* New York: Praeger.

Pendall, Rolf. 1999. "Do Land Use Controls Cause Sprawl?" *Environment and Planning B* 26 (4): 555–71.

Pfeffer, Nancy, et al. 2002. "Environmental Justice in the Transportation Planning Process: Southern California Perspective," *Transportation Research Record: Journal of the Transportation Research Board* 1792: 36–43.

Pirie, G. H. 1983. "On Spatial Justice," *Environment and Planning A* 14 (4): 465–73.

Pratt, Geraldine, and Susan Hanson. 1988. "Gender, Class, and Space," *Environment and Planning D: Society and Space* 6: 15–35.

Pucher, John, and John L. Renne. 2003. "Socioeconomics of Urban Travel: Evidence from the 2001 NHTS," *Transportation Quarterly* 57 (3): 49–77.

Purvis, Charles. 2001. "Data and Analysis Methods for Metropolitan-Level Environmental Justice Assessment," *Transportation Research Record: Journal of the Transportation Research Board* 1756: 15–21.

Reddy, Alla, Thomas Chennadu, and Alex Lu. 2010. "Safeguarding Minority Civil Rights and Environmental Justice in Service Delivery and Reductions: Case Study of New York City Transit Authority Title VI Program," *Transportation Research Record: Journal of the Transportation Research Board* 2163: 45–56.

Robeyns, Ingrid. 2005. "The Capability Approach: A Theoretical Survey," *Journal of Human Development* 6 (1): 93–117.

Rowangould, Dana, Alex Karner, and Jonathan London. 2016. "Identifying Environmental Justice Communities for Transportation Analysis," *Transportation Research Part A: Policy and Practice* 88: 151–62.

Sanchez, Thomas W., and Marc Brenman. 2007. *The Right to Transportation: Moving to Equity.* Chicago: American Planning Association.

Sanchez, Thomas W., Rich Stolz, and Jacinta S. Ma. 2003. *Moving to Equity: Addressing Inequitable Effects of Transportation Polices on Minorities.* Cambridge: Civil Rights Project at Harvard University.

Schweitzer, Lisa, and Abel Valenzuela Jr. 2004. "Environmental Injustice and Transportation: The Claims and the Evidence," *Journal of Planning Literature* 18 (4): 383–98.

Sen, Amartya. 1981. *Poverty and famines: an essay on entitlement and deprivation.* Oxford: Clarendon Press.

——. 1985. "Well-Being, Agency and Freedom: The Dewey Lectures 1984," *Journal of Philosophy* 82 (4): 169–221.

——. 1988. "The Concept of Development." In *Handbook of Development Economics*, Vol. 1, edited by H. Chenery and T. N. Srinivasen, 10–26. London: Elsevier.

——. 1992. *Inequality Reexamined.* Cambridge: Harvard University Press.

——. 1999. *Development as Freedom.* 1st. ed. New York: Knopf.

Solin, Les. 1997. *Professional Practice Manual.* Chicago: American Planning Association.

Squires, Gregory D., and Charis E. Kubrin. 2005. "Privileged Places: Race, Uneven Development and the Geography of Opportunity in Urban America," *Urban Studies* 42 (1): 47–68.

Steinberg, Michael W. 2000. "Making sense of environmental justice," *Forum for Applied Research and Public Policy* 15 (3): 82–89.

Taylor, Brian D., and Paul M. Ong. 1995. "Spatial Mismatch or Automobile Mismatch? An Examination of Race, Residence, and Commuting in U.S. Metropolitan Areas," *Urban Studies* 32 (9): 1537–57.

Taylor, Brian D., and Alexandra Tassiello Norton. 2009. "Paying for Transportation: What's a Fair Price?" *Journal of Planning Literature* 24 (1): 22–36.

Transportation Research Board. 1995. *Expanding Metropolitan Highways: Implications for Air Quality and Energy Use.* Special Report 245. Washington, DC: National Academy Press.

van Wee, Bert, and Karst Geurs. 2011. "Discussing Equity and Social Exclusion in Accessibility Evaluations," *European Journal of Transport and Infrastructure Research* 11 (4): 350–67.

Wachs, Martin, and T. Gordon Kumagai. 1973. "Physical Accessibility as a Social Indicator," *Socio-Economic Planning Science* 7: 437–56.

Wacquant, Loïc J. D. 1997. "Three Pernicious Premises in the Study of the American Ghetto," *International Journal of Urban and Regional Research* 21 (2): 341–53.

7

THE OPPORTUNITY CHALLENGE
Jobs and Economic Development

Robert Giloth

Opportunity means many things—the chance to live in a supportive neighborhood, the ability to build wealth, or the ability to have transportation access to work and amenities—but above all opportunity is about the ability to obtain and retain jobs and build sustainable careers. Unfortunately, far too many people lack meaningful opportunities to obtain such employment. Analysis of employment in several older industrial cities, for example, suggests that these cities would need to add hundreds of thousands of jobs to match employment rates in their regional metropolitan areas (Giloth and Meier 2012). Our track record for closing employment gaps has been less than hoped, especially for black men and communities of color, and predictions about the future of work from automation suggest further erosion of equitable employment opportunities (Avent 2016).

Jobs and careers are building blocks for household economies and families, healthy neighborhoods, competitive regions, and robust civic life (Wilson 1996, Wiewel and Giloth 1996). Work is a fundamental way we organize our lives, build social networks, and create meaning for ourselves. A job and career provide economic resources, benefits, information, and well-being essential for pursuing a good life. Jobs are a foundation for equitable opportunity and citizenship.

Economic and workforce development became core features of local and regional planning during the past fifty years. Mainstream approaches focus on overall real estate and business growth, big infrastructure, downtown revitalization, tourism, and new industries like biotechnology. An alternative approach, "equity planning," is the focus of this chapter. In contrast to traditional economic and workforce development, this approach focuses on access to good jobs, manufacturing retention, neighborhood economic development, and human capital and workforce investments. Equity planning takes place in a variety of contexts and seeks to influence the types of development that are supported locally, the people who come to the table to make development decisions, the use of data about development and workforce impacts, and the people who will benefit in the short and long terms.

The chapter begins with a background discussion about how local economic and workforce strategies became a focus of equity planning during the past fifty years, and how they remain relevant in today's economic and policy context.[1] Six promising equity workforce strategies are examined with explicit attention to their scaling potential: sector partnerships, anchor institutions, workforce/economic development, collective impact, entrepreneurship, and regional equity planning. These promising strategies provide a context for describing skills and competencies that today's equity planners need for promoting equitable employment opportunities. Finally, the chapter suggests a next generation of ideas linking economic and workforce development which push the limits of current equity policies and practice.

Background

The past fifty years have seen the development of an array of innovative equity planning tools, investment strategies, and public policies that advance inclusive employment opportunities. This period is characterized by the maturation and unraveling of the New Deal coalition, economic growth and decline, the civil rights movement, urban disinvestment followed by "comeback cities," the rise of metros and regions, and the evolution from structural to individualistic policy solutions (Weir 1992, O'Conner 2002). This evolving context shaped the emergence and practice of equity planning.

The overall approach of equity advocacy and planning has been to open up labor markets and overcome occupational and industry segregation while promoting job quality and family supporting incomes. There have been many twists and turns in this advocacy, but the dual interests of open labor markets and job quality have reunited in today's advocacy movements for equitable opportunities.

Civil rights advocacy for fair employment expanded during World War II, building on previous efforts of national civil rights organizations, unions, and national coalitions. Legislative action at the state and federal levels opened up labor markets in the 1940s and produced fair employment laws which established affirmative action employment and business procurement policies in the 1960s.

This period saw the creation of equity goals, an infrastructure for implementation and accountability, and an array of local and state efforts (MacLean 2008). Full citizenship meant inclusion in employment and career opportunities.

The invention of community development corporations (CDCs) in the 1960s expanded the self-help dimension of equity advocacy. The Ford Foundation's Gray Areas Program and the federal War on Poverty spurred the growth of CDCs. CDCs represented a turn from "rights" advocacy to direct involvement in economic investments for job creation. CDCs launched enterprises, supported small and minority businesses, assembled land for industrial development, and established new financing mechanisms (Perry 1987, Sviridoff 2004).

Black political power expanded in the sixties and multiple urban civil disturbances raised awareness about lack of racial progress. The Kerner Commission identified root causes for these disturbances, high among them being the lack of jobs and income. At the same time, the election of black mayors began realigning the employment benefits of urban political machines toward new constituents (Kerner et al. 1967, Downs 1985).

The recessions of the 1970s and early 1980s and the wave of deindustrialization pushed equity planners and advocates to create stronger links between economic and workforce development. Black mayors combined civil rights, black nationalism, and a broad-based inclusion agenda (Alkalimat and Gills 1989). Community organizers inspired by the passage of the Community Reinvestment Act (CRA) of 1974 turned attention to the equity performance of local economic development investments.

A number of cities and states developed equity plans where jobs and opportunity were central—the Cleveland Policy Plan in Cleveland, *Chicago Works Together* in Chicago, *The Homegrown Economy* in St. Paul, and the *Greenhouse Compact* in Rhode Island (Giloth and Moe 1999). A particularly important planning document was the *Rational Reindustrialization* plan for Detroit; this plan called for rebuilding Detroit's economy on the basis of its existing industrial assets (Luria and Russell 1981). Likewise, the City of Chicago report, *Building on the Basics*, called for reindustrialization policies and investments that leveraged core assets of the region's steel industry (City of Chicago 1985). So-called "progressive cities" like Cleveland, Hartford (CT), Boston, Burlington (VT), Berkeley (CA), and Santa Monica (CA) experimented with new forms equity planning, linked development, and community ownership (Clavel 1986).

Progressive cities and leaders improved the connections between economic and workforce development. Strategies included the development of sector-focused or industry partnerships, policies to prevent industrial displacement, worker buyouts as plants closed, the introduction of new industries like recycling, and new community financing vehicles for business development. Equity policies and system reforms included "first source" hiring agreements, linked development for housing and employment, and industrial protection ordinances. New or adapted planning tools matured for evaluating the economic impacts of big projects and tracking the jobs and businesses created with public incentives, as well as creating local opportunities for stimulating local economic growth and labor-focused industry planning.

The period of the 1990s and 2000s saw the expansion of sector strategies and the emergence of regional equity planning. Economic growth and tight labor markets encouraged the broader application of sector-based workforce strategies, community development financing, the living wage movement, and increased public accountability of economic development incentives. Cities like Seattle and Austin developed ambitious plans to link economic and workforce development and to support municipal responses to welfare reform (Bennett and Giloth 2007). The smart growth and regional equity movement arose in the same years in reaction to the narrow equity focus on cities in terms of housing, transportation, access to jobs, economic development, and environmental quality. Regional equity strategies built on our long history of regional planning and focused attention on transforming the opportunity structures of metropolitan areas. Community leaders organized regional coalitions around economic competitiveness, affordable housing, transportation, and jobs (Henton, Melville, and Walesh 1999; Dreier, Mollenkopf, and Swanstrom 2001).

The Great Recession of 2008 provoked another round of equity-oriented workforce and economic development planning. The drivers for this innovation were massive job and wealth loss, the decline and collapse of cities like Detroit, the precipitous loss of state and local government revenues, and deepening racial and economic divides. In coordination with new federal initiatives, local planners, stakeholders, and advocates focused on both old and new sectors like manufacturing and "green" business, identified reliable sources of economic growth such as anchor institutions, developed regional sustainability planning, called for new investments in infrastructure, incubated collective impact efforts to better align cradle-to-career educational investments, and supported a new round of living wage and job quality campaigns that focused on such issues as paid and family leave and work scheduling. Debates about growing inequality and racial disparities began to focus on linking workforce and economic development. An ambitious, multifaceted example occurred in Los Angeles through a collaboration between a community/labor coalition, Los Angles Alliance for a New Economy, and city government leaders, including former mayor Anthony Villaraigosa (Meyerson 2013).

Employment discrimination persisted during this period—one in four job seekers of color experienced some form of bias, whether hiring, interviews, or wages (Fix and Turner 1999). Today's lack of equitable opportunities is evident in unconscionable incarceration rates for black men and racial wealth gaps—conditions that became national concerns after unrest in Ferguson, Baltimore, and elsewhere (Alexander 2012, Coats 2015). This lack of inclusive opportunity is starkly present in the growing numbers of youth and young adults of color who are not in school or working and are disconnected from the labor force (Annie E. Casey Foundation 2012, Lewis and Burd-Sharps 2015).

Inclusive Economic and Workforce Development

Creating economic opportunity involves a range of system changes, policies, planning frameworks, and civic organizing models that link economic and workforce developments. Will these approaches together change overall equity in cities and regions? The answer in the short run is probably not. For the longer run, however, lessons derived from designing and implementing these innovations are important contributions toward developing a more robust equity movement. These lessons, in Benner and Pastor's (2014) phrase, are part of an "epistemic community" of shared learning and practice that reaches across regions, places, and timeframes.

Inclusive economic and workforce development focuses on the building blocks of the economy, the lack of accountability for and enforcement of economic development agreements, lowering transaction costs for job-producing economic development, and setting goals for jobs and equity. Equity employment strategies address several key labor market challenges: connecting people to jobs that exist, improving job quality, providing support to students to promote credential attainment, shaping employment networks and intermediaries, and providing appropriate social and economic supports (Schrock 2014).

What are favorable contexts for advancing equity employment policies in cities and regions? There is no simple formula; equity policies are possible in weak or strong market cities and with or without progressive political leadership. What is needed, however, are heightened market, political, and community pressures to achieve more equitable access to jobs and a public policy opportunity to do business differently. That pressure might stem, for example, from a large-scale infrastructure project that requires public approvals and substantial investment. It could involve retaining or attracting a high-profile industry that is experiencing talent shortages. It could be a civic emergency that drives the need for more and better jobs. Over time, though, long-term progressive political leadership at the local and state levels is needed to sustain complementary equity employment policies; it is the critical element in achieving such policies at a large scale. In this context, federal policies can accelerate or impede equity employment policies and projects.

Sector Partnership Strategies

Sector strategies have proliferated in recent years as a leading approach for workforce development (Conway and Giloth 2014). At their origin in the 1980s, however, they were also applied to economic development planning, with old and new industries (Alexander, Giloth, and Lerner 1987; Siegel and Kwass 1996). The basic idea behind sector strategies is that there are efficiencies—and the potential to promote more equitable economic opportunities—in working with groups of companies with similar products and technologies to plan growth, workforce, physical infrastructure, and land use. Costs and risks for sector innovations are spread across firms. In the context of tight labor markets or spot workforce shortages, equity gains are possible for opening up occupations and industries if the right incentives, networking, and workforce training are provided.

Several years ago, the Metropolitan Studies Program at the Brookings Institution undertook a sectoral study of the Baltimore economy in conjunction with local stakeholders (Vey 2012). It was a version of labor-centric economic development planning. The study dug deep into the economy with secondary data and conducted multiple interviews with companies and industry leaders to answer a practical question: Are there sectors with innovative, export-driven firms that provide good wages and have jobs that only require some college? These types of jobs are attractive and accessible to young adults with fewer credentials and less work experience. Brookings went on to ask: If these firms and sectors exist, how can Baltimore grow them more intentionally to provide more job opportunities? The study produced some surprising results, identifying old and new sectors like advanced manufacturing, logistics, information technology, and biotechnology.

Growing industry sectors is more difficult than designing training programs that address present business demand for skilled workers. Those expansion strategies must examine the factors preventing growth and what impacts are likely from targeted investment strategies. Moreover, sectoral growth strategies require civic and business collaborations that focus on growing companies and jobs to achieve the win/win of economic growth and increased employment. Unfortunately, this is where the Baltimore effort fell down. There was not sufficient economic pain or opportunity to sustain new civic and business partnerships, although some productive follow-up occurred that is yielding benefits. Sector analyses and strategies must be matched with long-term civic collaboration and leadership that mobilizes resources to achieve durable equity results.

New types of sector intermediaries are emerging that combine training, economic development, social enterprise, job quality, and policy advocacy. Cooperative Home Care Associates is a long-term cooperative enterprise, now organized as a B Corp, which has sought to transform the home-health-care industry. The Restaurant Opportunity Center (ROC) uses advocacy, research, training, and running businesses to change the restaurant industry and the experience of low-wage workers. In particular, ROC has advocated against the segregation of people of color in low-paying restaurant jobs. ROC is now being replicated in several cities after starting up in New York.

Not all sector strategies, however, are successful. The green economy "bubble" of recent years demonstrates the challenge for sector strategies when they pursue wishful thinking ahead of real market opportunities. Moreover, promised infrastructure investments may or may not expand apprenticeship opportunities and careers without explicit policy attention to inclusion.

Anchor Institutions

Structural economic shifts and corporate reorganizations have transformed civic leadership and economic engines in cities and regions. In the past, urban "growth coalitions" of place-based stakeholders like banks, newspapers, utilities, and corporate headquarters rallied public and private leaders and institutions for big development projects and visions. This leadership scenario has largely disappeared because of globalization, technological change, and corporate consolidations. Starting in the 1990s, urban analysts began talking about "eds and meds" as the only institutions left with sufficient self-interest in place-based quality of life and economic growth to make a difference. Over time, the definition of "eds and meds" has expanded and we generally refer to these entities as anchor institutions (ICIC 2011, Dubb and Howard 2011).

Anchor institutions share a range of characteristics. First, they are economic engines, individually and together, that employ thousands of workers in many occupations, purchase goods and services, attract external income and resources, generate innovations, and incubate new companies that in turn produce economic benefits. Anchors generally include hospitals, health-care institutions, and universities, but a plausible case may be made for including airports, government agencies, and authorities, and even downtown commercial districts. Second, the leadership of these anchor institutions has an ongoing self-interest in investing locally—that is, the immediate environs of the anchor institutions and also more broadly in their city and region. This self-interest is a matter of economic and reputational survival; relocation is costly and a city's poor reputation costs anchors business—whether it's leased space, students, or patients. As a consequence, anchor leaders advocate for a variety of large-scale, urban development solutions. Third, many anchor institutions require public investment or regulatory relief and support on a regular basis; therefore, they are practiced at articulating the benefits they generate for the community and demonstrating their civic engagement.

Many distressed cities are now paying attention to anchor institutions. Most anchor initiatives to date have focused on revitalizing anchor districts. New initiatives are tapping the stream of economic resources and benefits produced by anchors to create more business and job opportunities for low-income members of the community. These sorts of initiatives require planning that must analyze such factors as anchors' employment turnover, purchasing regulations and standards, and the operations of human resources and purchasing departments. A recent national report argues that scaling anchor initiatives must get beyond "transactional" relationships and move to systematic, strategic partnerships of "shared interests" (Kleiman et al. 2015). The *Democracy Collaborative* has developed a dashboard of anchor benefit indicators for planning and self-assessment (Dubb, McKinley, and Howard 2013).

Cleveland has the most publicized anchor initiative supporting job and business creation. The Greater University Circle (GUC) Economic Inclusion program involves health-care and educational institutions located in University Circle. The collaboration, focused on improving the quality of life in surrounding neighborhoods, is now over a decade old. It has developed strategies aimed at increasing the anchor share of hiring from the GUC neighborhoods by linking a community-based portal for entry level jobs with job training, coaching, and a career pathway. The retention rates for employees hired through this portal are higher than for employees hired through the traditional process (Hexter et al. 2017). The Greater University Circle Initiative (GUCI) is probably best known for creating a number of worker-owned enterprises, called *Evergreen Cooperatives*, that have tapped into anchors' purchasing and building operations in food service, energy conservation, and laundering. This initiative received major support from the Cleveland Foundation—a community foundation which is arguably another form of anchor institution. Despite the positive publicity, the *Evergreen Cooperatives* have created only a modest number of jobs (Dubb and Howard 2011, Kelly and Duncan 2014).

The University of Pennsylvania has played a key role in revitalizing the surrounding area in West Philadelphia. But it wasn't until five years ago that the university joined with other nearby health and education anchors to create a job training, placement, and career advancement program called the West Philadelphia Skills Initiative that targets training and hiring for anchor institutions from surrounding zip codes. Similarly, ten health-care institutions joined together ten years ago in Baltimore and formed the Baltimore Alliance for Careers in Health-care, or BACH. One signature BACH program, paid for largely by the hospitals, hires career coaches who are experienced employees that work with entry level workers to help them plan their careers and navigate institutional obstacles and opportunities (Klein-Collins and Starr 2007).

A promising job creation strategy taps the self-interest of anchor institutions (including local and state government) to reduce energy costs by installing solar and other energy conservation technologies. Having underutilized roof space is an economic asset for pursuing energy sustainability. Improving anchor energy conservation saves operating costs and creates local construction and manufacturing jobs (Irwin et al. 2011).

Anchor strategies for improving equity are not without risk. The recent controversy at Syracuse University about the supposed tradeoffs between academic excellence and reducing inequality is a case in point (Wilson 2011).

Linked Development

Connecting low-income populations to economic development projects dates back to the 1960s and1970s and includes opening employment opportunities in the construction industry for people of color. Equity advocates began questioning the employment and civil rights impacts of local and state economic development investments, ranging from large infrastructure projects to financial incentives for individual businesses (Cleveland City Planning Commission 1975, Squires 1986).

Equity planners had several responses. The first response was evaluative analysis of the true benefits of public investments—that is, how many jobs were actually created and for whom. In many cases, job creation was more rhetoric than fact (Giloth 1992). Second, many cities established "first source" hiring programs that required companies receiving public investments to consider preferred candidates, such as job seekers referred by local employment and training providers, although there was no requirement for hiring them (Schrock 2015). Third, a few cities like Boston set up Neighborhood Jobs Trusts to allocate payments from developers of large-scale projects to support job training (Keating 1986). Finally, some cities like Chicago set overall jobs goals for all of their city development investments (Mier 1993, Giloth and Moe 1999).

Today's equity innovations build on these early efforts. Community benefits agreements (CBAs) are formalized agreements for large economic development projects that specifically identify numbers of jobs, quality of jobs, and career pathways for both construction and permanent jobs they generate (Wolf-Powers 2010, Liu and Damewood 2013). These agreements designate jobs that are targeted to low-income job seekers in geographic areas like neighborhoods or cities.

CBAs frequently identify sources of revenue from these projects to support employment and training or related supports needed to create workforce pipelines. CBAs must be based on the analysis of occupational demand, the timing in the development process when jobs will occur, and mechanisms for hiring and accountability. CBAs work for large-scale, highly visible development projects that require local approvals and investments.

Some cities institutionalized CBAs into more robust forms of first source hiring.[2] In Los Angeles, for example, with pressure and guidance from Los Angeles Alliance for a New Economy, several city agencies and authorities have adopted targeted hiring policies and ongoing data collection for accountability purposes (Liu and Damewood 2013). Organizing in Oakland led to a landmark agreement for three thousand good jobs on the reuse of a major military base (Partnership for Working Families 2015). In Baltimore, neighborhood and city job targets were set by local officials for construction and permanent hiring on the East Baltimore Revitalization Initiative with Johns Hopkins University, a $1.8 billion multiuse development (Annie E. Casey Foundation 2015).

Equity employment agreements and policies are tough to negotiate; perhaps more challenging is implementation—that is, getting contractors to adhere to agreements, organizing effective pipelines of job-ready workers, and collecting timely data for continuous improvement. A perennial problem is that projects inevitably are slower than anticipated in getting off the ground. Even when these mismatches are overcome, getting a job does not always lead to a career, especially in the construction industry in which workers move from job to job. Such challenges suggest apprenticeship programs are important for promoting long-term construction careers, but apprenticeships have been off limits for people of color for decades and disparities remain in graduation rates (Helmer and Altstadt 2013).

Few cities have followed Chicago's example of setting overall jobs targets for public investments. Turning lofty goals into numerical job targets comes with ample political risks about delivering on promises. And, despite decades of scrutiny and evaluation of public incentives, cities still feel compelled to offer public subsidies for attractive development projects and to companies without serious policies to capture the economic benefits for local residents.

Achieving linked development frequently requires long-term organizing. Unfortunately, another round of important organizing occurs during implementation when organizers have moved onto other important issues.

Collective Impact

In the past few years, the theory and practice of *collective impact* has attempted to harness civic leadership to solve these challenges. The most relevant example of collective impact for our examination of equity planning is the "cradle-to-career" education pipeline. The *Harlem Children's Zone, Promise Neighborhoods*, and the *StriveTogether* network are examples of education-focused, collective impact initiatives that are achieving results (Giloth, Hayes, and Libby 2014).

The theory of collective impact is that communities should invest together in linked educational experiences and programs to give low-income students the best shot at graduating from high school with the needed competencies and confidence to achieve postsecondary credentials and a good start in the labor market. That is, making sure children are ready for school should link to efforts to improve third grade reading; and high school algebra instruction should be linked to efforts to improve high school graduation and to help students transition to postsecondary opportunities. Using a collective impact strategy to improve educational pipelines addresses common challenges, including a lack of galvanizing goals, program proliferation, a lack of evidence about programmatic performance, poor implementation, and the inability or unwillingness to pursue continuous improvement. Collective impact demonstrates that good implementation and system building are key dimensions of equity planning and advocacy.

Can collective impact strategies advance equity strategies in the domains of workforce and economic development? The jury is out on this question (Annie E. Casey Foundation 2016). Creating an education pipeline is centered on school systems with lots of money and widespread agreement about the metrics of success for children and youth. Workforce and economic development, by comparison, are challenged by the involvement of many systems, the lack of agreed-upon metrics, and the preeminent role of the private marketplace as generator of economic activity and jobs. Workforce systems are frequently more focused on their own survival than achieving breakthrough outcomes (Giloth 2004). And the evidence about the success of local job creation strategies is less developed, plagued by uncertainty about how to align strategies with targeted populations. However, collective impact strategies are being used to inform community benefits agreements and to target hiring efforts for populations like disconnected youth.

Two current collective impact campaigns are organizing civic stakeholders with a focus on expanding economic opportunity. In Cincinnati, the Partnership for Competitive Workforce has established a metric of regional "gainful employment" that is used to close the employment gap for low-income, low-skilled job seekers. In the San Francisco Bay Area, Rise Together is a poverty alleviation campaign led by the United Way of the Bay Area that seeks to cut in half the poverty rate in five counties by 2020 by adopting a handful of promising programs and policies at a wide scale (Annie E. Casey Foundation 2016).

Coalitions and collaborations have organized for decades around important equity issues like housing reinvestment, fair employment, and policy strategies that directly link growth and opportunity. What is new and promising today is the emphasis these efforts place on shared data and measurement, the building of integrated data systems, and communitywide continuous improvement to achieve bold results. On the other hand, collective impact collaborations are often seen as elite, top-down initiatives with little community input, especially from communities of color. Some communities like Portland, Oregon, are directly addressing this issue by formalizing partnerships to increase diversity (Giloth, Hayes, and Libby 2014).

Collective impact is a buzz phrase that speaks to the need for aligning resources and contributions to achieve powerful results. Too often initiatives are renaming what they do to take advantage of the new-sounding approach.

The Entrepreneurship Sector

It has long been held that small businesses are the heart of our economy, creating jobs and generating innovation (Schramm 2006). Minority firms, in particular, are a source of jobs for workers of color (Bates 1993) and represent a fast-growing segment of small businesses. At the same time, small businesses fail with some frequency in their first few years, and minority businesses are hampered by lack of access to credit and capital (Klein 2016). Equity planners have had a hard time supporting conventional entrepreneurship and often prefer worker co-ops, minority firms, or public enterprises.

Entrepreneurship is evolving, with the growth of incubators, accelerators, maker spaces, crowd-sourced funding, B Corps, socially responsible businesses, social enterprises, and the technology-based, shared economy. We have had decades of mixed experience with microenterprise and self-employment, and today it is seen primarily as a tool for income enhancement rather than a pathway to business success. For many, such as new immigrants, young parents, or the formerly incarcerated, who often face barriers to employment, starting a business is easier than obtaining employment. Youth and young adults, meanwhile, are melding culture and business as they create start-ups—a necessity for some, given the high rate of youth unemployment.

What is an equity approach to entrepreneurialism (Chapple and Giloth 2011)? I have already highlighted several related equity innovations that include business or entrepreneurial efforts. First, community benefits agreements and economic inclusion policies frequently identify goals for contracting with minority- and women-owned businesses and sometimes address specific barriers facing these firms, such as challenges obtaining insurance or financing. There is no reason that economic inclusion for entrepreneurship cannot be built into other forms of community development, commercial revitalization, and public purchasing. Second, anchor institutions have frequently targeted local and minority enterprises in their purchasing and/or place-making investments. The Evergreen Cooperatives in Cleveland is an example of anchor institutions supporting small business development.

Another dimension of entrepreneurship is social enterprise—double-bottom-line businesses started by nonprofits that provide social benefits like jobs; if the business breaks even or makes a profit, that can be reinvested in the mission-driven work. Nonprofits have had mixed experience with social enterprise over the years, discovering that their core competencies are not always in running businesses. Nonprofit supporters have also learned that individual start-ups are more at risk than a cohort of enterprises supported by a network of investors and technical assistance providers (Javits 2011).

Three success stories demonstrate the potential of social enterprises for providing job opportunities for those left out of labor markets. Cooperative Home Care Associates in the South Bronx employs two thousand home-care workers and invests in their skill building, work schedules, career development, and training as co-op owners (PHI 2010). Goodwill Industries has the largest social enterprise in the United States, focusing on used goods and generating $4.3 billion in revenue from two thousand and eight hundred retail outlets. Goodwill hired nineteen hundred thousand workers in 2013 and supports a large proportion of its mission activities from its enterprises (Rodriguez 2013). The third example is the Roberts Enterprise Development Fund (REDF), started in the Bay Area but now spreading throughout California with an eye on national expansion. REDF is a supportive investor that enhances the capacity of social enterprises to achieve double-bottom-line goals related to employment (Javits 2011).

Enterprise development has great potential to attract impact or social investors from the philanthropic community and beyond. These enterprises promise financial returns and social benefits and could potentially attract significant investments. To do this will require building a supportive investment and technical assistance infrastructure for new and growing enterprises.

Questions about how to grow local economies are answered not only by plans but also by entrepreneurial discovery. There are many ways to build entrepreneurial cultures in cities and regions with a particular emphasis on including low-income communities. A useful tool is mapping the "entrepreneurial ecosystem" in regions. Broader conceptions for socially engaged enterprises have been talked about as a "third sector" (Gunn 2004; Williamson, Imbroscio, and Alperovitz 2014). In years to come, equity planning for entrepreneurship and jobs will likely become more significant.

Starting new businesses is as much about failure as success. There are ways to increase the probability of success but the risks are still present. This is true for individual enterprises as well as for co-op or social enterprises.

Regional Equity Planning

While regional planning has been underway since the 1920s, including a focus on equity in regional planning began only in the 1960s and has received only intermittent attention. Today, after several decades of experimentation and research, equity goals are a fundamental part of regional planning, along with the promotion of environmental sustainability and economic competitiveness (Chapple 2015).

Attention to regional equity in the 1970s addressed the segregation effects of rapid suburbanization in land use, housing, and labor markets and the role of public and private sector actions in creating racially divided metropolitan areas (Downs 1975). A few valiant efforts sought to promote and stabilize inner-ring racially integrated communities like Oak Park, Illinois; promote open housing regulations and practices; and support new-town planning schemes that sought to relocate black communities to the suburbs. A few other metropolitan areas chose regional government as a way to overcome intractable financial and development challenges. By the close of the 1970s, housing agencies and advocates launched mobility initiatives in Chicago, spurred by the Supreme Court's Gautreaux desegregation rulings (Polikoff 2007).

By the late 1990s, conventional as well as equity planners embraced the regional paradigm. Suburban populations and economies had come to dominate metro regions with inner-ring suburbs facing the same challenges as traditional cities. At the same time, another round of housing mobility experiments launched, and political economists began to argue that tolerant, equitable regions were more prosperous. Just as importantly, the fields of equity planning and community development abandoned a sole focus on neighborhood and city development as too limiting and adopted regional equity strategies that attacked the constraints on regional "opportunity structures," whether transportation, business location, infrastructure investment, or open housing.

The past decade has seen an array of regional equity strategies, ranging from community organizing, development around light rail lines, the use of inclusionary regional housing, and efforts to expand school choice and promote desegregation. The U.S. Department of Housing and Urban Development's Sustainable Communities program awarded 143 regions resources to develop equity plans and pilot projects in coordination with a wide array of stakeholders. Planning in Denver and the Twin Cities, in particular, have advanced the practice of transit-oriented development to shape regional opportunities (Marsh 2014).

One of the most ambitious efforts to reshape a regional economy for prosperity and equity purposes is the ten-year old Fund for Our Economic Future in Northeast Ohio. It not only has helped shaped a vision for the future Cleveland economy but has also established new institutional mechanisms to direct investment in incubating companies and sectors. It is now working more explicitly on developing workforce pipelines (Katz and Bradley 2013).

In the wake of civil unrest in Ferguson, New York City, and Baltimore, research has underscored the importance of regional equity disparities and opportunities. Long-term research confirmed that children in low-income families who moved to the suburbs not only achieved mental health and educational gains but they also experienced significant income gains as young adults (Chetty and Hendren 2015; Chetty, Hendren, and Katz 2015). Access to safe, mixed-income neighborhoods can translate into opportunity.

In 2010, suburban poverty exceeded urban poverty in many metropolitan areas, and after a dip in the late 1990s, concentrated poverty is again on the rise. Job growth remains high in the suburbs while transportation access to these jobs is limited, and there is a shortage of affordable, worker housing nearby. The regional equity challenge for economic opportunity remains—and it is daunting.

Conclusions and New Directions

Over the past fifty years we have seen the growth and evolution of equity employment and economic development practices at the local and regional levels. Much has been learned and accomplished, even as overall economic and racial progress has stalled in many communities (Sharkey 2013). The Great Recession and slow recovery brought into focus an estimated twenty-five million long-term unemployed persons—people who had given up looking for work or had settled for part-time jobs. In many inner-city neighborhoods of color, life and opportunity is characterized by a permanent economic recession, jobless recovery, and the effects of mass incarceration (Coats 2015). Moreover, even with rapid growth and wealth creation over the past decades, income and wealth inequality has increased for many groups and communities. To make matters worse, discussions about the technological change and the future of work call into question whether employment as an equity goal is plausible for decades ahead (Thompson 2015).

The planning skills required to advance these six equity innovations are not new or foreign to planning schools. What may be a stretch for many planners is understanding in more depth human capital and business development. In a broader sense, more attention will have to be paid to civic organizing and partnership building; planners will need to feel comfortable with inside/outside strategies and the conflict that goes with the pursuit of equity goals. The advent of big data and advances in data visualization and access promise the potential for more engaged and informed citizen planning. Equity planners have a key role to play.

I conclude this chapter by highlighting several equity-oriented employment and economic development strategies for the future. Equity planners will need to free up their imaginations about a new generation of equity ideas while, at the same time, implementing today's equity innovations. This kind of planning sensibility recalls the visionary and sometimes utopian elements of planning in the past century. The current political and policy context encourages this type of local and state experimentation.

- *New forms of work*—Private and public job creation is insufficient now and likely in the future for closing employment gaps and disparities. We need to invent or reinvent other forms of engaged work that combine contribution and benefit, new forms of household economics, or community service, for example.
- *Organizing a social sector*—The outlines of a robust social or "third" sector exist now—including social enterprises, socially responsible firms, and nonprofits—that could, if better organized, provide an on-ramp for many individuals and communities excluded from the labor market.
- *A new social contract*—A major public and private policy question is whether we as a country will recognize the long-term limits of the private labor market and put in place a new generation of income and work supports that allows for such innovations as shared work.
- *New forms of community building*—What will communities look like when we redefine work and the social contract? Will new communities be designed to provide meaningful work, enterprise opportunities, and cooperative mechanisms for reducing the cost of living?

A piecemeal approach to advancing robust equity goals is not enough. Rather, we need to work on two fronts simultaneously, scaling today's practical equity strategies while planting the seeds for new ideas and designs that take account of future trends. To be sure, advancing this inclusive opportunity agenda will require a new civil rights movement with a renewed focus on the importance of jobs and careers as a foundation for full citizenship. Today's political conversations are certainly about jobs, but equity, job quality and work supports are unfortunately not central to the current federal agenda.

NOTES

1. I use the term equity planning broadly to include a range of advocacy, planning, development, and policy activities by grassroots, civic, and public sector actors guided by principles of social and racial justice. A recent review of planning and social justice makes little mention of employment and jobs (Manning Thomas 2012).

2. Included with formal first hiring policies are CBAs, apprenticeship utilization standards, project labor agreements, and other economic inclusion policies.

REFERENCES

Alexander, M. 2012. *The New Jim Crow: Mass Incarceration in the Age of Colorblindness.* New York: The New Press.

Alexander, S., R. Giloth, and J. Lerner. 1987. "Chicago's Industry Task Forces," *Economic Development Quarterly* 1 (4): 352–57.

Alkalimat, A., and D. Gills. 1989. *Harold Washington and the Crisis of Black Power in Chicago.* Chicago: Twenty-first Century Books.

Annie E. Casey Foundation. 2012. *Youth and Work.* Baltimore, MD: Author.

———. 2015. *Expanding Economic Opportunity: Lessons from the East Baltimore Revitalization Initiative.* Baltimore, MD: Author.

———. 2016. *Collective Impact in Workforce Development: A Working Paper.* March. Baltimore, MD: Author.

Avent, R. 2016. *The Wealth of Humans: Work, Power and Status in the Twenty-first Century.* New York: St. Martin's Press.

Bates, Tim. 1993. *Banking on Black Enterprise.* Washington, DC: Joint Center for Political and Economic Studies.

Benner, C., and M. Pastor. 2014. "Knowing Together, Growing Together: Epistemic Communities and Equitable Growth." In *Connecting People to Work,* edited by M. Conway and R. Giloth. New York: The American Assembly, Columbia University.

Bennett, M., and R. Giloth, eds. 2007. *Economic Development in American Cities.* Albany: State University of New York Press.

Chapple, K. 2015. *Planning Sustainable Regions: Towards More Equitable Development.* New York: Routledge Press.

Chapple, K., and R. Giloth, eds. 2011. *Big Ideas for Job Creation. A Policy Brief Highlighting Job Creating Initiatives.* Baltimore, MD: The Annie E. Casey Foundation.

Chetty, R., and N. Hendren. 2015. *The Impacts of Neighborhoods on Intergenerational Mobility.* Working Paper, April. Harvard University and the National Bureau of Economic Research.

Chetty, R., N. Hendren, and L. Katz. 2015. *The Effects of Exposure to Better Neighborhoods on Children: New Evidence from Moving to Opportunity.* Harvard University and the National Bureau of Economic Research.

City of Chicago. 1985. *Building on the Basics: The Final Report of the Mayor's Task for on Steel and Southeast Chicago.* Chicago: City of Chicago, Department of Economic Development.

Clavel, P. 1986. *The Progressive City.* New Brunswick, NJ: Rutgers University Press.

Cleveland City Planning Commission. 1975. *Cleveland Policy Planning Report.* Vol. 1. Cleveland: Author.

Coats, T. 2015. "The Black Family in the Age of Mass Incarceration," *The Atlantic,* October, http://www.theatlantic.com/magazine/archive/2015/10/the-black-family-in-the-age-of-mass-incarceration/403246/.

Conway, M., and R. Giloth, eds. 2014. *Connecting People to Work: Workforce Intermediaries and Sector Strategies.* New York: The American Assembly, Columbia University.

Downs, A. 1975. *Opening up the Suburbs*. New Haven, CT: Yale University Press.

——. 1985. "Conclusion." In *New Urban Reality*, edited by P.E. Peterson. Washington, DC: The Brookings Institution.

Dreier, P., J. Mollenkopf, and T. Swanstrom. 2001. *Place Matters: Metropolitics for the Twenty-first Century*. Lawrence: University of Kansas Press.

Dubb, S., and T. Howard. 2011. "Leveraging Anchor Institutions for Local Jobs and Wealth Building." In *Big Ideas for Job Creation*, edited by K. Chapple and R. Giloth. Baltimore, MD: The Annie E. Casey Foundation. http://community-wealth.org/sites /clone.community-wealth.org/files/downloads/paper-dubb-howard.pdf.

Dubb, S., S. McKinley, and T. Howard. 2013. *The Anchor Dashboard: Aligning Institutional Practices to Meet Low-income Opportunity Needs*. College Park, MD: The Democracy Collaborative.

Fix, M., and M.A. Turner, eds. 1999. *Report Card on Discrimination in America: The Role of Testing*. Washington, DC: The Urban Institute.

Giloth, R. 1992. "Stalking Local Economic Development Benefits," *Economic Development Quarterly* 6 (1): 80–90.

——, ed. 2004. *Workforce Development Politics: Civic Capacity and Performance*. Philadelphia, PA: Temple University Press.

Giloth, R., G. Hayes, and K. Libby. 2014. *Laying the Groundwork for Collective Impact*. Baltimore, MD: The Annie E. Casey Foundation.

Giloth, R., and J. Meier. 2012. "Human Capital in Legacy Cities." In *Rebuilding America's Legacy Cities: New Directions for the Industrial Heartland*, edited by A. Mallach. New York: The American Assembly, Columbia University.

Giloth, R., and K. Moe. 1999. "Jobs, Equity, and the Mayoral Administration of Harold Washington in Chicago (1983–1987)," *Policy Study Studies Journal* 27 (1): 129–46.

Gunn, C. 2004. *Third-sector Development: Making up for the Market*. Ithaca: Cornell University Press.

Helmer, M., and D. Alstadt. 2013. *Apprenticeships: Completion and Cancellation in the Building Trades*. Washington, DC: Aspen Institute, Workforce Strategy Initiative.

Henton, D., J. Melville, and K. Walesh. 1997. *Grassroots Leaders for a New Economy*. San Francisco: Jossey-Bass.

Hexter, Kathryn W., Candi Clouse, Nick Downer, and Liam Robinson. 2017. *Greater University Circle Initiative: Year 6 Evaluation Report*. Urban Publications 5-2017. Cleveland: Levin College of Urban Affairs.

Holland, B. 2014. *A Toolkit for the Workforce Development Planner*. Washington, DC: American Planning Association.

Initiative for a Competitive Inner City (ICIC). 2011. *Anchor Institutions and Urban Economic Development*. Boston: Author.

Irwin, J., S. Rhodes-Conway, S. White, and J. Rogers. 2011. "Retrofitting Institutions." In *Big Ideas for Job Creation*, edited by K. Chapple and R. Giloth. Baltimore, MD: The Annie E. Casey Foundation.

Javits, C. 2011. "Social Enterprise." In *Big Ideas for Job Creation*, edited by K. Chapple and R. Giloth. Baltimore, MD: The Annie E. Casey Foundation. http://redf.org /wordpress/wp-content/uploads/2013/10/REDF-Carla-Javits-Big-Ideas-for-Job -Creation-Paper-2011-.pdf.

Katz, B., and J. Bradley. 2013. *The Metropolitan Revolution*. Washington, DC: The Brookings Institution.

Keating, W. D. 1986. "Linking Downtown Development to Broader Community Goals: An Analysis of Linkage Policy in Three Cities," *Journal of the American Planning Association* 52 (1): 133–41.

Kelly, M., and V. Duncan. 2014. *A New Anchor Mission for a New Century*. Takoma Park, MD: The Democracy Collaborative.

Kerner, Otto, et al. 1968. *Report of the National Advisory Commission on Civil Disorders*. New York: Bantam Books.

Kleiman, N., L. Getsinger, N. Pindus, and E. Poethig. 2015. *Striking a (Local) Grand Bargain: How Cities and Anchor Institutions Can Work Together to Drive Growth and Prosperity*. Washington, DC: The National Resource Network.

Klein, J. 2016. *Business Ownership and the Racial Wealth Gap: Expanding the Growth of Minority Firms*. Washington, DC: The Aspen Institute.

Klein-Collins, R., and R. Starr. 2007. *Advancing in Health and Health Careers—Rung by Rung*. Boston: Jobs for the Future.

Lewis, K., and S. Burd-Sharps. 2015. *Zeroing in on Place and Race: Youth Disconnection in America's Cities*. Washington, DC: Measure of America, Social Science Research Council.

Liu, K., and R. Damewood. 2013. *Local Hiring and First Source Hiring Policies: A National Review of Policies and Identification of Best Practices*. Pittsburgh, PA: Regional Housing Legal Services. http://rhls.org/wp-content/uploads/First-Source-Hiring -Overview-RHLS.pdf.

Luria, D., and J. Russell. 1981. *Rational Reindustrialization: An Economic Development Agenda for Detroit*. Detroit, MI: Widgetripper Press.

MacLean, N. 2008. *Freedom Is Not Enough: The Opening up of the American Workplace*. Cambridge: Harvard University Press.

Manning Thomas, J. 2012. "Social Justice as Responsible Practice: Influence of Race, Ethnicity and the Civil Rights Era." In *Planning Ideas That Matter*, edited by B. Sanyal, L. Vale, L., and C. Rosan. Cambridge, MA: MIT PRESS.

Marsh, D. 2014. "The Sustainable Communities Initiative: Collective Impact in Practice," *Community Investments* 26 (1): 30–36.

Meyerson, H. 2013. "The Los Angeles Alliance for a New Economy: A New Model for American Liberalism," *American Prospect*, August 13, http://rhls.org/wp-content /uploads/First-Source-Hiring-Overview-RHLS.pdf.

Mier, R. 1993. *Social Justice and Local Development Policy*. Newbury Park, CA: Sage Publications.

O'Conner, A. 2002. *Poverty Knowledge: Social Science, Social Policy, and the Poor in Twentieth Century History*. Princeton, NJ: Princeton University Press.

Paraprofessional Health Initiative (PHI). 2010. *Best Practices: Cooperative Home Care Associates*. http://community-wealth.org/sites/clone.community-wealth.org/files /downloads/paper-dubb-howard.pdf.

Partnership for Working Families. 2015. *Paving the Path to Opportunity: How Revive Oakland Invented a New Model for Inclusive Economic Development*. Oakland, CA: Author.

Perry, S. 1987. *Communities on the Way: Rebuilding Local Economies in the United States and Canada*. Albany, NY: State University of New York Press.

Polikoff, A. 2007. *Waiting for Gautreaux: A Story of Segregation, Housing, and the Black Ghetto*. Evanston, IL: Northwestern University Press.

Rodriguez, G. 2013. "The Most Important Social Enterprise in 2013?" *Forbes*, March 28, http://www.forbes.com/sites/giovannirodriguez/2013/03/28/the-most-important -social-enterprise-in-2013/.

Schramm, C. J. 2006. *The Entrepreneurial Imperative*. New York: Collins.

Schrock, G. 2014. "Connecting People and Place Prosperity: Workforce Development and Urban Planning in Scholarship and Practice," *Journal of Planning Literature* 29 (3): 257–71, doi: 10.1177/0885412214538834.

Schrock, G. 2015. "Remains of the Progressive City? First Source Hiring in Portland and Chicago," *Urban Affairs Review* 51 (5): 644–75.

Sharkey, P. 2013. *Stuck in Place: Urban Neighborhoods and the End of Progress toward Racial Equality*. Chicago, IL: University of Chicago Press.

Siegel, B., and P. Kwass. 1996. *Jobs and the Poor: Publicly Initiated Sectoral Strategies*. Washington, DC: Aspen Institute.

Squires, G. 1986. *Industrial Revenue Bonds: Equal Opportunity in Chicago's IRB Program*. Chicago: Illinois Advisory Committee to the U.S. Commission on Civil Rights.

Sviridoff, M., ed. 2004. *Inventing Community Renewal: The Trials and Errors that Shaped the Modern Community Development Corporation*. New York: New School University, Milano Graduate School.

Thompson, D. 2015. "Technology Will Soon Erase Millions of Jobs. Could That Be a Good Thing?" *The Atlantic* 316 (1): 51–61.

Vey, J. 2012. *Building from Strength: Creating Opportunity in Greater Baltimore's Next Economy*. Washington, DC: Metropolitan Policy Program, The Brookings Institution.

Weir, M. 1992. *Politics and Jobs: The Boundaries of Employment Policy in the United States*. Princeton, NJ: Princeton University Press.

Wiewel, W., and R. Giloth. 1996. "Equity Development in Chicago: Robert Mier's Ideas and Practice," *Economic Development Quarterly* 10 (3): 204–16.

Williamson, T., D. Imbroscio, and G. Alperovitz. 2014. *Making a Place for Community: Local Democracy in a Global Era*. New York: Routledge.

Wilson, R. 2011. "Syracuse's Slide," *The Chronicle of Higher Education,* October 2, http://chronicle.com/article/Syracuses-Slide/129238/.

Wilson, W.J. 1996. *When Work Disappears*. New York: Alfred E. Knopf.

Wolf-Powers, L. 2010. "Community Benefits Agreements and Local Government," *Journal of the American Planning Association* 76 (2): 141–59.

8

EQUITY POLICY AND PRACTICE AT THE FEDERAL LEVEL

HUD's Rental Assistance Demonstration

Patrick Costigan

When Shaun Donovan became President Obama's initial Secretary of the Department of Housing and Urban Development in 2009, he immediately committed himself to overhauling the nation's failing public housing system. As the new administration dealt with the unyielding recession triggered by the collapse of the single-family housing market, the new HUD secretary faced a crisis-dominated agenda from day one. Righting the long-in-the-making decline of public housing was not his biggest problem.

Yet Donovan put this at the top of his agenda for any number of good reasons. His previous experience gave him considerable perspective on public housing's litany of problems—its regrettable history of racially discriminatory practices in isolating it to undesirable areas and skimping on its construction and upkeep; the fact that housing authorities struggled with unpredictable and less-than-needed funding from Congress in doing their jobs; and the sense that most of Congress had lost interest in doing anything about it. Mostly he knew that the residents of public housing bore the brunt of this lost support, enduring poorly maintained apartments and having to scramble to find other options when their housing became unlivable. Given his earlier roles, he was well aware that HUD's other forms of housing assistance were oversubscribed and afforded little in the way of alternative help, and that the private market offered virtually no housing for the elderly, disabled, or the chronically underemployed and poor who compromised the vast majority of public housing residents (Center on Budget and Policy Priorities 2017). At the same time, it was confounding to Donovan that so much public housing was demolished each year due to deteriorating conditions when the need for it was so great. Waiting lists for public housing apartments soared into the millions at agencies across the country. At the New York City Housing Authority alone, with which he was quite familiar, the waiting list exceeded 257,000 households (NYCHA 2017). Donovan saw public housing as a failing system that most egregiously failed the residents who were truly dependent upon it. They had virtually no other housing choices and no effective power to change it.

To Donovan's way of thinking, not doing something to fundamentally address these inequities was not a choice. What he did and how he shaped the Rental Assistance Demonstration by responding to them from the outset of his tenure at HUD can arguably be seen as a classic equity policy approach—a notable and perhaps encouraging message that it could be (still) undertaken at the federal level.

Federal Equity Agenda?

Overhauling the federally directed public housing system might seem a long-odds bet at best for even the most seasoned equity-minded leader. Public housing is a large, unwieldy federal program with many masters across Congress, within HUD—which oversees public housing management through nearly sixty field offices—along with the 3,100 state-chartered but locally constituted housing authorities that administer it. Unsurprisingly, accountability is too often diffused and effects circular-pointing in face of problems.

Similar to most federal systems, public housing is looked after by a contingent of established stakeholders whose roles have largely been defined by the need to petition Congress annually for funding and to help agencies comply with a complex maze of federal statutes and regulations. Public housing's low-income residents are largely codependent upon these stakeholders, including a diminishing number of congressional supporters, to bolster their voices and advocate for their interests.

All of this works to reinforce a protective, status quo bubble around how public housing works at the federal level. When reforms are needed—even when grounded in socially progressive goals—the bubble favors incremental steps over deeper, structural change; this is further constrained by the realities of a four- or even eight-year term of a presidential administration.

The meld of these challenges in taking on a federal system may partly explain why most social equity policies and practice—and nearly all of the literature, including this book, *Advancing Equity Planning Now*—have tended to address specific issues and actions at the local and regional levels more than at the massively complex federal level.

Nonetheless, matters of social and economic equity have worked their way onto the national stage and succeeded as social and political movements and economic threats pushed them forward. As Norman Krumholz's introduction to this book points out, the beginnings of equity planning efforts at the national level can be seen in the turn of twentieth century Progressive-Era urban reforms that influenced some of President Roosevelt's New Deal antidotes to the Great Depression in the late 1930s. As the civil rights movement gained momentum in the late 1950s and early 1960s, equity-minded federal officials seized on opportunities to advance more equitable public education, housing, and community development policies in programs under the banner of the Johnson administration's War on Poverty. Decades later, HUD Secretary Henry Cisneros in the Clinton administration directed several billion dollars into replacing some of the nation's most troubled public housing under the HOPE VI program. At the right time, with compelling circumstances and with committed and determined leaders and supporting actors, it has been possible to advance progressive, equity-oriented policies and new programs on the national agenda.

Whether by instinct or by lessons learned along the way or both, when Secretary Donovan and his HUD colleagues in the Obama administration set out to transform public housing, they somehow followed nearly all of the equity-oriented planning principles and strategies. They also struggled with the practice lessons that Krumholz and others had in waging equity planning and practices in local and regional battles. Donovan and his team were able to accomplish the following.

- They *analyzed* the long-worn inequities of the public system—the declining funding, poorly located and racially segregated properties, inferior-quality living conditions, poor management, and dwindling support in Congress—and contrasted them to the funding, conditions, and support of all other forms of affordable housing and how the larger housing system worked more generally. They concluded that pursuing piecemeal reforms would only produce the same inequitable results.
- In response, they *seized an opportunity* and offered a *non-status quo vision for change* that was more basic than radical, calling for public housing to be made to work comparably to other forms of affordable housing so that its residents could enjoy benefits similar to those offered to residents of assisted housing.
- Secretary Donovan assembled a HUD team that *drew on outside help* to help guide the change process, particularly in persuading both internal and external stakeholders that there was a better option than just continuing to press Congress for more funding into the same poorly performing system.
- Beyond a new approach, Donovan pushed his staff to make new housing options available to public housing residents as part of the changes being

sought—essentially insisting that *"more choices be offered to those who have few."*

- And when they initially stumbled, the secretary and his key staff quickly responded to warranted criticism, *made needed course corrections*, and ultimately *persisted in mobilizing diverse constituencies* in both passing needed legislation and then implementing a major, new approach to public housing with broad support.

Within a few years, this approach would culminate in HUD's Rental Assistance Demonstration, or what has now simply become known as "RAD." Five years after being given initial approval by Congress, a long-time affordable housing practitioner marveled that, "In just a few years, RAD has achieved results nobody... thought possible. Allowed to grow, it will finish revolutionizing and revitalizing an inventory and a system that many had quietly given up for dead" (Smith 2017, 6–7).

It is too soon to tell if RAD will be allowed to grow into something that can truly resuscitate public housing as an enduring form of affordable housing for the future. It is equally premature and perhaps an unreasonable expectation in any event to look to RAD as a major new strategy for achieving housing equity in the United States. Its aims, and perhaps its smart focus, were much less grandiose. In an era of rapidly declining federal support for conventional public housing, Secretary Donovan and his HUD team sought to enable public housing to function like other well-established forms of affordable housing in order to turn around its decline. It was hoped that RAD would improve the quality of public housing and offer residents additional choices beyond what the conventional public housing system has been able to offer them in recent decades. Whether in fact it delivers will be a reasonable test of RAD's promise.

Regardless of its ultimate potential, how RAD became a promising new federal initiative seems worthy of review. It surely offers insights for practitioners on the process and realities of advancing equity objectives through the thicket of federal policy, Congress, and a bureaucracy like HUD. And it seems to show that tried-and-true equity planning principles, strategies, and lessons applied in other settings can be made to work even on the national stage.

Broken System

When Donovan took over HUD in 2009, public housing funding had been substantially decreasing for nearly a decade. He proved unable to stem this trend in his initial years as secretary. According to the Center on Budget and Policy Priorities, in the period from 2000 to 2014, the annual funding that Congress provided to the nation's 3,100 housing authorities to meet operating and capital needs lost a quarter of its inflation-adjusted value (Fischer 2014). The long-term funding cuts for making necessary improvements to the then–1.2 million unit stock of public housing over roughly the same period was particularly debilitating: federally provided public housing capital funds had decreased over 50 percent (Rice 2016). By 2011 these reductions led to a reported accumulated capital funding backlog that exceeded $26 billion across the inventory (Abt Associates Inc. 2010).

When basic repairs are deferred too long, housing authorities are perversely forced to demolish nearly irreplaceable stock while thousands of families remain on public housing waiting lists. Until just recently, HUD routinely approved and ultimately paid for the demolition of well over 10,000 units of public housing across the country each year. Just in the last two decades over 300,000 units, or more than a fifth the total public housing stock, had been torn down or disposed of as another form of housing (Collinson, Gould Ellen, and Ludwig 2015). Compounding this, when a household must be relocated from public housing due to demolition, it is usually awarded a more costly publicly subsidized voucher to secure housing elsewhere (PHADA n.d.), including initial moving and relocation expenses. Beyond calculable costs to HUD are the less apparent disruptions to thousands of families that are uprooted from their homes each year: children are forced to abruptly change schools; seniors are displaced from their established communities and supports with which they are familiar; and working adults have to rearrange their commutes.

Prior to becoming HUD secretary, Donovan was the director of the Department of Housing Preservation and Development in New York City for five years under Mayor Michael Bloomberg. Earlier on he had served as deputy assistant secretary for Multifamily Housing in the Clinton administration. In both positions, Donovan was responsible for administering assisted rental housing programs—but not public housing. Yet each of these roles enabled him to see public housing's chronic issues and political fate—a marked contrast to the assisted multifamily housing that he administered.

He came away from these experiences convinced that the best way to assure public housing's long-term availability to those who depended on it was to find a way to enable public housing to function more like the better-performing assisted multifamily housing with which he was familiar. He had concluded that multifamily housing was generally newer, in better shape, and not as dense or as concentrated in undesirable locations as was public housing. Little of it was demolished each year. It received better and more stable funding from Congress than did public housing. And perhaps most tellingly, it enjoyed a formidable political constituency tied to the larger housing sector that comprised a substantial component of the overall economy.

Many long-time affordable housing policy analysts, including Donovan, thought the discrepancy between the conditions and political realities of public and multifamily assisted housing were largely due to the relatively limited capacity and messaging of the traditional public housing constituency. Comprised mostly of staff, board members, and residents of agencies, public housing industry associations, and organizations that advocated for an array of issues affecting low-income people, public housing's primary constituency was no match for the firepower of other stakeholders petitioning the Transportation, Housing, and Urban Development (THUD) appropriations subcommittee each year—particularly the transportation industry or even that of the broader housing sector—the mortgage bankers, other lenders and investors, home builders, developers, legal and accounting firms, and other deep-pocketed actors.

Compounding this, public housing advocates tended to repeat the same message about the need for more public funding year after year. This seemed to make it harder for Congress to hear that message in an era when "public-private partnerships" were more the norm. Whereas other affordable housing interests pointed to their ability to leverage limited public funds with tax credits, excise and density bonus fees, transit-oriented development set-asides, philanthropic funds, and other diverse sources in preserving and producing more affordable housing, public housing advocates continued to demand more federal formula dollars to flow to public housing agencies. Fairly or unfairly, when so much of the public housing inventory appeared poorly managed, their requests seemed to be throwing good money after bad with little or no political upside. One message pointed to innovative ways that nonprofit and for-profit developers could produce additional housing in which it was easy to see growing families—and therefore more-inclined voters. The other message reinforced the perception of complete dependence on public funds of public agencies struggling to meet the needs of very poor households and fragile individuals and—unfortunately—fewer active voters.

Different Fixes

By the time he arrived at HUD a second time, now as secretary, Donovan was already persuaded that the anachronistic public housing system—especially its near total dependence on public funding—needed to be changed. Along with many other affordable housing analysts, he believed that it should be converted to something similar to the long-term Section 8 project-based contracts that underpinned the comparatively better-functioning multifamily assisted-housing system. This strategy ran flat against the prevailing notion among most advocates that what public housing really needed was more public funding and that Congress should and could be persuaded to provide it.

However, Donovan and many of his new senior HUD team read the downward trend line in public housing appropriations in recent years (especially for much needed capital improvement funds) not only as an indication of a failing funding strategy but also as evidence that Congress was losing confidence in the public housing system more broadly. Many members routinely saw public housing in their own districts and heard more about its poor conditions and management across the country from their colleagues and the media. Others picked up on the narrative of poorly run public housing for political or ideological reasons. In reaction, more and more members became increasingly reluctant to go out on a limb for additional funding for public housing, with fewer and fewer defenders among their colleagues.

At the outset of the new administration and in face of the continuing recession and the still-fragile housing market, this debate lingered. Nearly all affordable housing interests—including public housing advocates—expected that the new secretary, in face of this recession, would finally do something to help public and assisted rental housing in the years ahead. And they were prepared to support him in doing whatever he could.

Opportunity and Action

At the outset of the Obama administration, for the first time in decades, a new HUD secretary had a large, consequential role in dealing with a spiraling national crisis—one that owed mostly to the collapse of the single-family home ownership market. Immediately, Secretary Donovan was called on to direct Federal Housing Administration (FHA) resources to help home owners, which mostly benefited more affluent Americans and helped ease the pressure of large financial institutions that were increasingly seen as having triggered the housing crisis. This and other actions the secretary undertook in conjunction with the Treasury Department to help the larger housing sector fortuitously created an opening to also bolster rental housing—including public housing. Secretary Donovan, urged on by affordable housing stakeholders, made the most of the opportunity.

Early on, Donovan began to seamlessly press the case for supporting affordable rental housing along with housing reforms. Smartly and out of basic conviction, he and other affordable housing advocates argued that investing in rental housing, particularly as growing numbers of households that had lost homes to foreclosure were now increasing pressure on the rental market, was both a fair and equitable action and a reasonable policy response to the needs of the larger housing sector.

Secretary Donovan proved quite able at knitting these themes together. In nearly every forum or setting where he had a chance to do so, he made the pitch for supporting rental housing in the stimulus legislation that the new administration was preparing for Congress as a matter of basic equity for lower-income citizens who were also very much hurt by the recession. Along with the advocates, he argued that making needed repairs to the public and multifamily assisted-housing inventories was an ideal "shovel-ready" stimulus measure. With a strong push from affordable housing stakeholders, the new secretary delivered.

In the Obama Administration's large economic recovery package rolled out in 2009, Secretary Donovan managed to direct billions to ready-to-go public and assisted housing renovation projects, including $4 billion into public housing and another $2 billion for the assisted-housing inventory that were central to HUD's primary mission. Beyond this one-time injection of additional capital funds, Donovan also found a way in the administration's first two annual budgets to increase public housing funding each year by over $425 million above the amount offered in the last year of the Bush Administration. (CLPHA 2013, 1)

Policy Challenges

Paradoxically, Donovan began his effort to transform public housing by pumping as much additional public funding as possible into the current system—a system he considered broken and too dependent upon public resources. He did this because he had a chance to do so and because it modestly improved HUD's budget baseline for rental housing (which had been cut in the previous administration) going forward. He may have also done this, wittingly or not, to show the limits of what could be done to prop up the current public housing system just as he was drafting a plan to transform it.

Along with promoting the stimulus bill and shoring up FHA in his first months as secretary, Donovan had also assembled an experienced senior team within HUD and charged it with "transforming rental assistance" for public housing to function more like multifamily assisted housing. This was a formidable task, especially when the secretary directed his team to include a limited number of multifamily housing programs, since they lacked a viable subsidy renewal option in the effort. Taking on both of these charges would require devising a painstakingly comprehensive policy initiative in the ways of Washington, which generally is more suited to incremental policy steps.

The first challenge that the HUD team had to figure out was how to jettison public housing's antiquated funding structure while retaining and converting committed resources into a workable form of Section 8 project-based contracts. This involved reworking how Congress annually provided public housing funds to HUD in large buckets of operating, capital, and administrative funds, from which HUD then allocated to agencies according to mechanistic formulas. Housing authorities received the formula funds at the entity or enterprise level and were left to direct them to maintaining their properties and running their operations as they thought best.

Yet agencies could neither predict the level of funding they would get in the annual appropriations process nor know at what point in a fiscal year that they would receive it. As appropriations levels for public housing tended to decrease more than increase from year to year, each new budget cycle posed an "appropriations risk" as to the actual amount an agency would receive. Even more complicating, when the annual appropriations process was delayed or purposively forestalled through temporary "continuing resolutions" that constrained next year's funding to current-year levels—or worse, the threat or actual shutdown of government—agencies sometimes would not learn the actual amount of funding they would receive from HUD until the middle or even near the end of the current fiscal year.

While the enterprise-funding method offered housing authorities some measure of flexibility in applying funds, the chronic unpredictably of the appropriations process forced HUD to provide less-than-needed or a pro-rated amount of funds to housing authorities most years. When forced to make do with varied "pro-rations" from year to year, agencies could not properly plan, let alone commit, any funding to needed near- or longer-term capital repairs, major redevelopment projects, administrative needs, or any type of future expenditures common to most businesses. More than a few properties in an agency's portfolio would have to defer needed capital repairs for later attention. If the repairs failed to happen, many of these properties were triaged—vacancies were not filled and units (and then eventually entire buildings) were boarded up and left to stand; these inevitably became blighting influences on the surrounding community. Eventually the properties would be demolished. Ultimately, when properties were subjected to a triage cycle, too many residents would have to bear the burden of temporary relocations and/or permanent displacement from their homes and neighborhoods.

Although inadequate federal funding underlies public housing's problems, in a cruel irony, housing authorities are usually left to shoulder the blame. The enterprise-funding method makes it relatively painless for Congress when facing budget constraints to reduce funding to the large, amorphous buckets instead of having to directly cut funds for the identifiable homes of families, children, and the elderly. And when the funding flows through HUD and onward to agencies according to mechanistic formulas, it's harder for local communities to see Congress's responsibility, let alone hold their representatives accountable for the conditions or fates of individual properties. From the vantage point of residents, local officials, the media, and, conveniently, Capitol Hill itself, it mostly seems that housing authorities cannot properly maintain or manage their properties. In a "catch-22," agencies are consistently underfunded yet are still held accountable to HUD and Congress through a maze of compliance and reporting requirements in which the poor conditions of their properties negatively impact their funding formulas—and lead to reduced entity funding in subsequent years.

The next complicating constraint that the HUD team had to grapple with was supplanting the statutory requirement of placing a problematic federal encumbrance on local housing authority property when public funds were allocated to it. The decades-old "declaration of trust" (DoT), or long-term superior lien placed on public housing land and improvements, discouraged private or even other public sources from lending to public housing as they would have to accept lien subordinate to the DoT. So little or no such financing had been available to housing authorities. Originally conceived as a means to protect the public investment in public properties, the DoT actually worked to undermine it. Unable to access conventional capital markets in the way that all other forms residential real estate were able to, agencies were mostly left to depend on less-than-sufficient federal funding to maintain their properties as best they could.

By the time Donovan became HUD secretary in 2009, the cumulative impact of all of these issues had become overwhelming to most agencies. Nearly all housing authorities had enormous backlogs of needed capital repairs to their properties. The director of the city of Baltimore's housing authority estimated that it would take nearly two hundred years to aggregate annually allocated capital funds from Washington in order to fully address an estimated $800 million in improvements needed across the agency's 11,000-unit inventory (HABC n.d.) To help quantify the extent of this problem across the public housing inventory, Secretary Donovan directed HUD to commission an independent assessment of the accumulated backlog of capital repairs across public housing nationwide. When completed a few years later, the extent of needed improvements was shown to exceed $26 billion and was estimated to grow by $3.6 billion a year (Abt Associates Inc. 2010). Unfortunately, that estimate appears to be bearing out. The New York City Housing Authority recently reported its capital backlog alone to exceed $17 billion (NYCHA 2015).

As if unraveling these constraints and reassembling them more in the mold of established Section 8 project-based programs were not challenging enough, Secretary Donovan tasked his HUD team with a further policy objective in remaking public housing. Donovan came to HUD with a strong belief that public-housing residents were effectively trapped in public housing with no other real housing options. He and many housing advocates thought that residents might be better served by the ability to vote with their feet, potentially nudging housing authorities to improve management of their properties where they could, and ideally for Congress to better see its responsibility where they couldn't.

Convinced that this was the right and politically smart thing to do, the secretary directed his HUD team to include a new "choice and mobility" option for public housing residents in the design of the transformation initiative. This would enable them to claim a Housing Choice Voucher or "mobile" voucher to seek other available housing after a limited tenure. Although this was not currently a feature of the long-established multifamily Section 8 project-based program, it was an option under the more recently enacted Project-Based Voucher program operated by housing authorities. While an equitable and seemingly reasonable gesture, extending the mobility option to public housing residents as part of the reforms to be made would prove to freight them with greater complexity and challenges down the road.

Crafting Legislation

Although the work to be done was daunting, Secretary Donovan and the team he assembled at HUD to remake public housing believed, if overconfidently, that the time was right to promote comprehensive rather than incremental reforms. They began work in 2009 on framing a broad set of policies and detailed legislation under the rubric of "transforming rental assistance" (TRA). A senior adviser for rental assistance was detailed to lead the transformation effort out of the secretary's office. Dozens of new political appointees and senior career staff were convened into highly focused working groups to plan through various TRA components.

While its primary focus was on transforming public housing, the TRA framework also sought to address other complementary affordable housing objectives. Contract extensions for a number of older Section 8-like multifamily programs with terminating subsidies were tacked on. An effort to "streamline" over a dozen variations of Section 8-based contracts that had evolved over the years was conceptualized. Needed administrative reforms to housing vouchers that had been stalled in pending legislation on Capitol Hill were also taken up. The long-standing HOPE VI program, which had provided large capital grants to tear down and rebuild the most-deteriorated public housing and which then came under a fair measure of criticism, was extensively reworked as the Choice Neighborhoods Initiative and taken under the TRA umbrella.

Early on, HUD focused less on engaging affordable housing's broad constituency in the details of what it was crafting than it did on how to graft needed challenges to current statutes and regulations governing the public and assisted housing. Much of the major policy development work was presumed to have already been considered and endorsed by key stakeholders in the run-up to change in administrations. Beyond similar recommendations made in the 2002 Millennial Housing Commission report (Millennial Housing Commission 2002), in a 2008 public-housing summit convened by the well-regarded Council of Large Public Housing Authorities (CLPHA), shifting conventional public housing from the unpredictable Section 9 form of funding to the more reliable long-term contracts afforded by the Section 8 multifamily assisted-housing platform was a top priority conveyed to the incoming Obama administration (CLPHA 2009).

HUD worked intently in the latter half of 2009 on turning what it thought to be already-endorsed policies into needed legislation, with much of the real work going on behind closed doors. Along the way HUD periodically briefed and sought input from a range of stakeholders—housing authorities and owners of other affordable housing and their industry groups; residents and their policy advocates; financing sources; legal counsel and technical advisers; and housing developers and managers—on what it was devising. Yet more than a few stakeholders would later remark that it seemed these briefings were mostly to solicit their support on matters that had already been decided.

Within a year, HUD formally introduced its comprehensive blueprint for transforming public housing and selected multifamily assisted-housing programs. Framed as the "Preservation, Enhancement, and Transformation of Rental Assistance" (PETRA), this fifty-seven-page blueprint made good on the secretary's pledge to transform how public housing worked while offering its residents new housing options in three basic ways.

- *Conversion of Assistance.* PETRA called for combining and then converting public-housing operating and capital funds that were annually provided to housing authorities at the enterprise level into a new form of Section 8 operating subsidy, obligated to individual properties' fifteen- to twenty-year contract periods. The long-term contracts eliminated the appropriations risk to unpredictable operating and capital funding. The new contracts were renewable and coupled with low-income housing use restrictions throughout their duration, which supplanted the need for the antiquated DoT-encumbering public housing properties that lenders found unworkable. Taken together, these changes would enable housing authorities to access additional private capital to manage and improve their housing much in the way that other forms of affordable housing did.

- *Resident Choice and Mobility.* PETRA granted residents, after a limited tenure in any converted public housing unit, the right to claim a mobile Housing Choice Voucher (HCV) to secure privately owned, managed housing of their choosing. Now as matter of right, a family or elderly or disabled public-housing residents would have the ability to move elsewhere with a subsidized voucher. To facilitate voucher sharing and help reduce redundant administrative costs, smaller housing authorities were encouraged to enter into regional consortia.
- *Transfer of Assistance.* As another new way to afford residents better housing options, PETRA allowed housing authorities to transfer the subsidy stream from a poorly functioning property to another development in good condition or to one that would be constructed to replace it. While preserving the inventory of "hard units," transferring assistance in this way would enable agencies to build or locate public housing in better locations, including within new mixed-income developments favored in many communities, potentially offering residents access to improved education, transportation, or employment options.

Beyond public housing reforms, PETRA's scope also included an ambitious effort to streamline HUD's many forms of multifamily Section 8 project-based contracts; it also extended new contract authority to assisted-housing programs whose subsidies were terminating—the so-called multifamily "orphans." Owners and managers of these properties, along with resident advocates, would now also have an interest in PETRA and presumably join the traditional public housing constituency in supporting it on Capitol Hill.

After introducing PETRA to stakeholders, HUD featured the new rental assistance initiative as the centerpiece of its fiscal year 2011 budget request to Congress. In a proposed first phase of the initiative, $350 million in new funding was requested to back key elements of the plan, which was projected to extend to about 300,000 public and assisted-housing units. The bulk of the new monies was for needed "incremental" funding to augment deficient public-housing funding levels prior to converting them to long-term Section 8 contracts. Approximately $50 million was sought to increase the number of HCVs to be made available to housing authorities to support the new "choice-mobility" component. Another $10 million was earmarked for technical assistance, resident education, and evaluation.

To spread the word about PETRA, from late 2009 through 2010 HUD conducted dozens of regional briefings and roundtables—and even an Internet-based comment process—to get input from stakeholders. HUD also made several presentations to industry association meetings in Washington. As PETRA laid out highly detailed public-housing reforms and a fix for multiple forms of multifamily Section 8 contracts that most did not consider broken, it got considerable input and suggestions from housing authorities and affordable housing practitioners along the way.

Most stakeholders generally understood the need to fix how public housing was funded and to offer its residents better and additional housing options. Many seasoned housing practitioners offered initial support. Despite taking issue with some of its more prescriptive provisions, CLPHA (the respected public housing industry association) played an early leadership role in backing PETRA. Others, including affordable housing developers, lenders, management groups, and resident advocates followed suit in offering modestly qualified support. In considering PETRA, most seemed inclined to give the new HUD secretary the benefit of the doubt and the space to try to achieve something beyond incremental reforms.

Mounting Questions and Opposition

Nonetheless, the initial support offered to HUD began to give way as PETRA's many detailed prescriptions were shared more broadly and reviewed more closely. Plus, whenever a federal agency proposes to increase its year-over-year budget, the level of scrutiny about who might benefit and who might lose under a potential offset intensifies. Inevitably, varied HUD stakeholders began to raise multiple issues, many of which proved to be at cross-purposes and difficult to reconcile.

Some housing authorities were anxious that their autonomy and some of their administrative funding could possibly be lost under PETRA's comprehensive changes, particularly as regional consolidation was encouraged in the plan. Others questioned the fairness of some public housing residents now being able to claim a new "choice-mobility" voucher ahead of others on the very long waiting lists for HCVs. More were concerned about PETRA's ambitious push to move nearly one-third of the public housing inventory from its unique Section 9 funding method to Section 8 contracts in an initial phase of converting assistance. It seemed a bit too much too quickly.

Many owners and managers of multifamily assisted-housing resisted the provision to adopt the newly proposed, streamlined form of Section 8 "project-based contract" when seeking to renew rental assistance, which varied from the long-used Project-Based Rental Assistance (PBRA) contract that they were comfortable using. Others were concerned about now having to include converted public housing properties in "their" well-established line item for PBRA in the federal budget, potentially making it a bigger target for budget cutting by Congress down the road.

Some residents, their tenant councils, and more of their advocates worried about residents being displaced as public housing was converted and rehabilitated under the less familiar multifamily housing system that, up to now, had been operated by for-profit and nonprofit owners and managers. Despite PETRA's guarantees otherwise, similar promises had been made and broken under HOPE VI and a few earlier HUD programs. They were also concerned that resident rights and processes under public housing might be different under the Section 8 requirements, especially the provision providing annual funding for tenant councils.

More than a few members of Congress who had tirelessly fought for increasing public housing funding over the years—including then-Chairman Barney Frank of the House Financial Services Committee—thought that introducing private mortgage debt into public housing risked the prospect of default and foreclosure; this would possibly subject public assets to private taking and ownership. Despite the limited historical record of foreclosure under the Section 8 program and PETRA's proposal for HUD to purchase and maintain foreclosed properties, Chairman Frank pointedly grilled Secretary Donovan over the mortgage-lending elements of PETRA in a hearing on HUD's FY 2011 budget. Congressional appropriations staff and budget analysts were likewise concerned about the PETRA provision to permanently add $300 million to HUD's annual budget for incremental Section 8 funding needed to set public housing subsidies comparable to Fair Market Rent levels in higher-cost markets.

In face of these and other concerns, by the summer of 2010, HUD found itself increasingly on the defensive about what PETRA would and wouldn't do. One explanatory document widely circulated by HUD during this period was titled "PETRA Myths and Facts" (U.S. HUD 2010). Perhaps more tellingly, in the best form of Washington's peculiar humor, critics and even HUD loyalists began to suggest that the TRA acronym actually stood for "Terrorizing Rental Assistance," and PETRA to mean "People for the Ethical Treatment of Rental Assistance."

Even within Secretary Donovan's senior HUD team there was growing disagreement about the scope of PETRA, differing strategies for cultivating stakeholder and Hill support, and who would be responsible for what going forward. Conventional public housing was under the domain of the Office of Public and Indian Housing. But PETRA would convert its subsidy stream—and budget authority—to the Office of Multifamily Housing under the responsibility of the FHA commissioner.

As debate about PETRA mounted in mid-2010, and with a highly detailed HUD-drafted bill already in hand, Secretary Donovan had difficulty in recruiting congressional sponsors for needed authorizing legislation for PETRA. Nonetheless,

Representative Keith Ellison, a progressive Democrat from Minnesota who had been long involved in affordable housing and social equity issues, thought that PETRA could help preserve public housing stock and offer its residents some promising new choices that they otherwise might not get. He agreed to work with HUD in making changes to some of the more confusing and controversial elements of the PETRA concept.

Adding his own legislative imprimatur, PETRA was recast as the "Rental Housing Revitalization Act of 2010" (RHRA) and introduced by Representative Ellison in the House in November. Despite Mr. Ellison's sponsorship, most critics and even many supporters were not satisfied that much had changed in RHRA when compared to what HUD had detailed in its original proposal. Regrettably, Mr. Ellison's bill only seemed to intensify less-veiled criticisms that HUD had faced with PETRA. Toward the end of 2010, the political support for PETRA and the companion RHRA legislation were seriously foundering, perhaps because it had not been effectively cultivated in the first place.

Step Back and Redirection

One attribute of an equity-minded leader observed by Krumholz and others is the ability in the face of criticism from key constituencies to recognize when a basic strategy is not working, and then to step back and make necessary changes. Another is to seek help from outside actors in correcting one's course. And perhaps the most essential characteristic is for a leader to be persistent in working through and around obstacles, be they self-made or occurring out of resistance to change. Along with a few people in his inner circle, Secretary Donovan revealed each of these instincts, as PETRA-RHRA failed to take hold and needed to be reworked.

By the winter of 2010, a new senior adviser with a fair measure of experience in both the public- and assisted-housing worlds and a good understanding of how Capitol Hill worked was brought into the secretary's office to help redirect the TRA strategy. The secretary's charge to his new adviser reaffirmed his determination to deliver what he set out to do nearly two years earlier, only with a reflective flexibility. He affirmed PETRA's main goals but was open on how to best achieve them. He realized that both external stakeholders and Congress needed to be more purposively involved in revising the approach. He was also willing to reorganize HUD's internal TRA team and to make himself available whenever needed. Mostly, he was determined that a revamped initiative get approval from Congress within its FY 2012 legislative calendar (Donovan and Costigan 2011).

With the secretary's redirection, the new adviser and a revamped group of senior HUD staff working on TRA began to reframe PETRA-RHRA with greater external input and help. Dozens of quiet conversations were conducted with well-respected affordable housing leaders, resident advocates, and congressional staff to review just how things had unraveled with HUD's initial efforts and to assess their willingness to work with HUD in making needed changes to PETRA. Their input underscored a few themes about HUD's efforts to date.

- *Laudatory Goals, Overreaching Design.* Nearly all were supportive of PETRA's main goals of transforming public housing's funding system to preserve and improve it while offering its residents better housing choices. Yet most felt that PETRA had overreached in attempting to craft a "master stroke" policy that included periphery reforms such as creating a new form of Section 8 contract or pushing housing authorities to form regional consortia.
- *Poor Process.* Although nearly all offering feedback had participated in one or more of HUD's dozens of briefings or input sessions, most felt that HUD had skipped over more customary give-and-take deliberations with important constituencies common to other policy reforms. Many thought that PETRA was more of an overly detailed legislative proposal presented to them mostly for perfunctory input and endorsement rather than a collaborative reform effort.
- *Hill Missteps.* While echoing much of the critical feedback that they had heard directly from stakeholders, staff to HUD's authorizing and appropriations committees took umbrage at not having been properly involved in drafting the needed legislation, especially when PETRA-RHRA posed a hefty $300 million annual increase in HUD's funding.

If discouraged about what the feedback implied about his leadership of the process to date, Secretary Donovan was not defensive about it. He actually seemed to anticipate or share most of it. He readily endorsed the recommendations made by his new TRA advisers on what needed to be done to turn things around. This included some politically delicate steps.

One was to immediately ask Representative Ellison to not reintroduce his RHRA bill in the new session of Congress. It was thought that the bill had become too big of a distraction to keep in play. It was greatly appreciated that Mr. Ellison had gone out on a political limb for Secretary Donovan in introducing RHRA amid some controversy. Nonetheless, when the secretary asked him to hold his legislation for the time being, the congressman proved surprisingly amenable and could not have been more gracious—and apparently politically astute—in agreeing to do so.

Another was that, although PETRA-RHRA was no longer active legislation, it remained a central part of HUD's budget that had been drafted several months earlier, It was also to be included in the administration's official FY 2012 budget request that was to be presented shortly to Congress. It had to be maintained as a placeholder for something else to be reworked to mollify reasonable critics, including many on the Hill. Nearly overnight, HUD struck the PETRA budget language in favor of a reduced $200 million request for a vaguely defined "demonstration of HUD's proposed Transforming Rental Assistance initiative" (U.S. HUD 2011). With its revised budget language, HUD adroitly announced that it was backing away from the details of PETRA-RHRA and yet intended to persist in in its efforts.

Next, the TRA team began to signal in various forums and meetings HUD's intention to drop some of PETRA-RHRA's more controversial provisions in favor of some of the alternatives offered in recent feedback sessions. It would rely on established forms of Section 8 project-based contracts rather propose a new form of project-based assistance; housing authorities would not be prodded to form regional consortia; no initial participation targets needed to be set (rather, agencies would simply be encouraged to test converting assistance for as many properties as they thought best); a more workable approach to maintaining public ownership and control of public housing assets in the unlikely event of foreclosure would be devised; further efforts would be made to reinforce how tenant rights, processes, and tenant council funding would be maintained in the conversion process; and the demonstration would be limited to public housing properties and a defined set of multifamily properties lacking contract renewal authority and not "streamlined" to a dozen or so other multifamily properties.

Inside of HUD, the original broadly representative but unwieldy TRA team was winnowed and reorganized as a more focused "TRA-RAD Steering Committee" that regularly met with Secretary Donovan to discuss issues and review progress. HUD also began to insinuate the acronym for a "rental assistance demonstration"—or RAD—in its communications. In suggesting something new but simple, "RAD" became a half-clever way for HUD to say that it intended to focus on the basics in way that was very different from PETRA-RHRA.

Redux RAD

To back its new words with new deeds, HUD moved quickly to repair PETRA-RHRA's Achilles' heel—the failure to genuinely engage important stakeholders and Congress early enough—in working through the concepts and many complexities of the public housing changes it envisioned. HUD enlisted fourteen

Washington-based organizations that were representative of national public housing and multifamily leadership associations, resident advocacy groups, policy centers, affordable housing counsel, and intermediaries to join a working group in devising a new rental assistance demonstration. Participants included those who had been modestly supportive of PETRA-RHRA, along with those who criticized it most loudly—many of whom were mistrustful of the motives of one another as well as HUD over the PETRA process to date. Self-anointed as the "RAD stakeholders' working group," HUD's representatives pointedly agreed to facilitate the group rather than try to direct it.

The newly convened RAD working group met regularly in the spring of 2011. It agreed to come up with a framework for a new rental assistance demonstration that could pass muster with their respective constituencies and be considered by Congress within its 2011 legislative calendar. Underscoring that PETRA-RHRA's problems owed more to process than substance, the group readily endorsed what had been HUD's basic policy goals all along: that the deteriorating public housing inventory needed to be preserved; that converting public housing subsidies to long-term, Section 8 project-based contracts to leverage private capital would be the best way to offset declines in public funding; and that residents of public housing deserved additional housing choices and greater mobility.

While a few issues weren't readily resolved and required more back and forth negotiation, within a few months of intensive and good-faith discussions, the RAD working group agreed on the main components to be recommended back to Secretary Donovan and to Congress for a "new" rental assistance demonstration—which the group also referred to simply as "RAD." Many of the components drew from and improved on what had been offered in PETRA-RHRA, while others posed significant differences that were thought to be more politically expedient or more sensible. They included:

- *Scope:* Enabled public housing and a limited set of the so-called multifamily "orphans" most at risk of being of being lost from the assisted-housing inventory—known as the Rent Supplement (Rent Supp), Rental Assistance Program (RAP), and Section 8 Moderate Rehabilitation Programs (Mod Rehab)—to convert their current forms of subsidy to project-based Section 8 contracts. HUD's earlier ambition to streamline over a dozen multifamily assisted-housing programs into a new form of project-based contract was scrapped.
- *Choice of Contract Assistance:* Housing authorities and owners of eligible multifamily properties would be offered the option to convert assistance to either the well-established forms of project-based Section 8 assistance.

- *Choice and Mobility:* Public-housing residents could request a Housing Choice Voucher after limited tenures in converted housing to find other available housing options. Also, subsidy contracts could be transferred from poorly functioning properties to existing or newly constructed properties in neighborhoods with better amenities.
- *Voucher Commitments:* As required under the existing PBV program, residents could request choice-mobility vouchers from an agency's current voucher pool after one year of tenure for properties that had converted assistance. In a new measure, if a property was converted under the Section 8 PBRA option, residents would be required to maintain two years of tenure before being eligible for a choice-mobility voucher from a sponsoring agency. Housing authorities were granted limited exemptions from these requirements if they proved overly burdensome.
- *Voluntary:* Housing authorities would neither be encouraged to consolidate into regional consortia nor meet ambitious conversion targets; instead, participation for both housing authorities and owners of the eligible assisted-housing properties was to be completely voluntary.
- *Permanent Affordability:* RAD-converted Section 8 contracts for public housing would be mandatorily renewed by HUD so long as the housing authority performed satisfactorily over the initial fifteen- or twenty-year contract term. Companion use restrictions would be placed on converted housing that would be "long-term and renewable" and run co-terminus with the new Section 8 contracts, which exceeded the initial thirty-year use agreement for public housing.
- *Foreclosure Protections:* In the unlikely event of foreclosure on a public housing property by a private lender, RAD would require that the property be disposed of first to another public entity and, only if that proved unworkable, then alternatively to a qualified nonprofit or for-profit entity.
- *One-for-One Preservation:* While PETRA allowed for the reduction of public housing inventory under certain circumstances, RAD affirmed that units needing to be demolished be replaced on a one-for-one basis; aside from temporary relocation needed to accommodate renovations, residents could not be involuntary displaced from their housing.
- *Resident Rights, Processes and Funding:* Funding would still be made available to duly recognized tenant councils in the conversion process, and more familiar terminology about resident rights and processes would be included in newly issued Section 8 contracts.

- *Funding:* The $200 million placeholder HUD had requested in its FY 2012 budget proposal for the now well-defined rental assistance demonstration was endorsed as a reasonable starting point in seeking funding from Congress.

With agreement on the basic components to a new demonstration, HUD and the RAD working group turned to codifying what they had agreed to into possible legislative language. Many of the stakeholders had significant experience in drafting legislation and regulations, and a few had worked for HUD previously. In a back-and-forth with HUD, the authorizing language ultimately adopted by the group was refined and finalized by the stakeholders themselves. In contrast to the fifty-six-plus pages of legislative language that HUD had drafted for PETRA on its own, the working group had distilled possible authorizing language for RAD into a little over a half-dozen pages.

With Secretary Donovan's ready support, the working group participants quickly garnered endorsements from the broader constituencies in which they were involved for proceeding with the new demonstration. Remarkably, despite the din over the PETRA-RHRA legislation introduced just months earlier, the new rental assistance demonstration bill crafted by multiple hands had garnered a chorus of support. Now it could be offered to Congress for consideration—along with strong stakeholder endorsement.

Courting Congress

In as much as HUD had re-engaged critical stakeholders, it also worked to overcome its earlier missteps on the Hill in shepherding RAD. Here, too, Secretary Donovan and his new HUD TRA-RAD team proved more adept in cultivating Congress's support the second time around. This time they were more attentive to the complexities of how a good idea actually becomes law in Congress.

The redesigned demonstration required statutory authority along with actual appropriations of any authorized funding, both of which required the blessings of selected members of Congress. Getting support for both is a delicate dance of courting majority staff and members of HUD's congressional committees in both the House and Senate while not neglecting their minority counterparts. The 2010 mid-term elections had shifted majority control of the House of Representatives from Democrats to Republicans. In any legislative scenario, it would be essential for HUD to work closely with the Republican majority of the House Financial Services Committee in cultivating support for RAD, especially with its then-new chairman, Representative Spencer Bachus of Alabama.

While continuing to work with Representative Ellison and attempting to court Democratic members of the Financial Services Committee who had been critical of PETRA-RHRA, Secretary Donovan and his team established a trusted, working relationship with Chairman Bachus and his staff that proved quite helpful. To hasten the introduction of needed authorizing legislation for the new demonstration, Mr. Bachus officially requested that HUD draft prospective authorizing legislation to be taken up by the Financial Services Committee. In an ironic twist, HUD was once again providing to Congress legislation for its rental assistance initiative. This time, however, Congress requested that it do so, and the RAD working group helped HUD detail the requested language.

With the new RAD proposal under review by a Financial Services subcommittee, ideally it could then be introduced as freestanding authorizing legislation, or its language could be attached to other germane housing legislation moving in the House. Plus, the authorizers' review served as a necessary legislative stamp for a parallel, fallback appropriations strategy. If the conventional authorizing path failed, HUD would have the procedural clearance from its authorizers to turn to its appropriations committees to make the demonstration into law in their annual funding bill.

In the spring of 2011 it seemed unlikely that Congress would take up RAD through a standard authorizing process. By then, housing-oriented stimulus and economic recovery bills had effected a fatigue on Capitol Hill about additional housing legislation. Unfortunate partisan bickering about the growing federal deficit and the role of government in stabilizing the economy had also overtaken the earlier bipartisanship in combatting the recession. HUD quietly began to position RAD for possible inclusion in the FY 2012 THUD appropriations bill, which Hill staff were beginning to mark up for consideration by the end of the federal fiscal year on September 30.

However, the central issue that had dogged PETRA-RHRA earlier remained an obstacle with RAD. A sizeable differential remained between what housing authorities received in annual appropriations (funding that could then be converted to long-term Section 8 contracts) and established "Fair Market Rents," or FMRs, provided under standard Section 8 contracts and offered to multifamily assisted-housing properties. Theoretically, this differential would have to eliminated or reduced to motivate housing authorities to participate in the new demonstration, which was the reason for the $200 million in "incremental" subsidies that HUD had proposed in its FY 2012 budget request. Although this was a significant decrease from the $300 million that HUD had sought for same purpose for PETRA-RHRA, it was still an amount that appropriations staff balked at, given the constraints on the federal budget as the recession lingered in 2011.

After a few months of quiet back-and-forth with appropriations staff, HUD's negotiators were persuaded that Congress could not offer any additional funding to HUD's budget for RAD or much of anything else in the FY 2012 funding cycle. Anticipating this, HUD had thoroughly assessed the prospect of launching the rental assistance initiative without any incremental funding. According to its analysis, potentially as many as 400,000 or more public housing units could be preserved and improved, even on a cost-neutral basis, as their current public housing subsidies (when converted to Section 8 contracts) would be at or exceed the established FMRs in their market areas. Although additional incremental rent subsidies would likely be needed to reach the remaining two-thirds of the inventory, HUD believed that the demonstration could be started without additional subsidy on a current- or no-additional cost basis.

Indicative of its now-good-faith working relationship with stakeholders, Secretary Donovan convened the RAD working group in his office and sought their input about proceeding with the demonstration on a cost-neutral basis. Underscoring the value of having reset RAD in a collaborative fashion, the stakeholders' group unanimously urged the secretary to launch RAD without additional funding. All agreed that it was better to start with available resources and see how they might be used more effectively than to tilt at congressional appropriators for the initial amount of funding that was unlikely to be forthcoming.

RAD Approved, Implemented, and Extended

Agreeing to a "no-additional cost" approach, HUD and Hill staff nimbly deployed an infrequent legislative maneuver to have RAD included in the final markup of the Transportation, Housing and Urban Development appropriations bill. Republican leaders of the House Financial Services Committee offered their authorizing stamp, enabling its consideration by House appropriators. HUD simultaneously worked closely with the Democratically controlled Senate's authorizing and appropriations committees to put forward RAD appropriations language. House appropriators, where Republicans constituted the majority, then agreed to the language. A highly unusual deal was struck in both chambers—one controlled by Republicans and the other by Democrats—by both authorizing and appropriations committees to take RAD into a moving appropriations bill.

After nearly three years of effort, in a divided Congress and less than a year from when Representative Ellison's RHRA bill had to be withdrawn, RAD was passed as part of the FY 2012 appropriations bill approved by the 112th Congress in November 2011—in nearly the same language as it had been proposed and drafted by the RAD stakeholders group at the request of Congress. However,

Congress limited RAD in one significant way that was not proposed in the language offered by HUD and the RAD working group. Owing to PETRA-RHRA concerns that converting public housing subsidies to Section 8 contracts might quickly become all-encompassing without some form of evaluation, some Democratic members sought to underscore the "demonstration" in RAD. They limited the number of public housing units that could convert assistance under RAD over a three-year time period to 60,000 units nationwide, or approximately five percent of the total public housing inventory, and included an evaluation requirement to assess if and how RAD's design would work in practice.

While passing federal legislation of any sort is a good test of support for a new policy in Washington in these times, carefully implementing it to be practicable and quickly taken up is all the more crucial for its near-term success. After its halting start with PETRA-RHRA, HUD wisely continued to regularly engage the RAD working group while soliciting a wider range of input from diverse stakeholders and congressional staff as it drafted the notice to implement the demonstration. In working through the initial notice details, it looked to other HUD programs for workable practices or improvements; for example, how to incorporate some of RAD's new requirements into existing PBV and PBRA contract forms.

Within four months of being authorized by Congress, HUD published the initial RAD notice to begin the program, which, beyond its quick publication, was cited for it practice-oriented tone of flexibility and responsiveness that came to be associated with RAD's implementation (Smith 2015). The application process was structured as a two-step initial review and approval process both to set a low barrier to participation and to afford agencies a reasonable amount of time to bring forward completed plans for final approval. After a statutorily defined ninety-day period to encourage to housing authorities of varying sizes across geographies to apply, HUD issued a revised notice to relax the previously required requirements in favor of a first-come, first-served application and approval process. It also introduced new flexibilities for larger housing authorities that it had previously held back so as not to disadvantage smaller and medium-sized housing authorities lacking the capacity of their larger counterparts.

In rolling out RAD, HUD conducted scores of trainings and application consultations around the country, devoting as many resources as it could to help housing authorities, their partners, and residents use the new program. It introduced needed financing, development, and transactional partners to housing authorities seeking help with their RAD projects. It offered on-demand technical assistance effort comprised of experienced internal staff and capable practitioners. It also sought help from tenant and advocacy organizations to work with public housing residents in understanding RAD's changes, processes, requirements, and benefits and in how to best to engage with their home housing authorities that were participating in the new program.

Many if not all of these customer-oriented steps paid off. Just a year after being approved by Congress, HUD had received applications from public housing authorities seeking to convert assistance under RAD in excess of 180,000 units—along with additional applications to convert assistance for thousands of units under the eligible multifamily legacy programs. Within another year, Congress responded to this level of demand and raised the cap on public housing units from 60,000 units to 185,000 units, while extending the application period for public housing and suspending it entirely for the multifamily legacy programs. In April 2017, Congress once again increased RAD's public housing cap by an additional 40,000 units, bringing RAD's total authority to 225,000 units. And in the recently passed omnibus appropriations bill for fiscal year 2018, the public housing cap for RAD was increased to 455,000 units, or now just over 40 percent of the inventory.

RAD So Far

In the six-plus years since it was first approved by Congress, RAD has already demonstrated proof of concept, as evidenced in a congressional required initial evaluation (Econometrica, Inc. 2016). RAD has also more than passed the primary tests set by Secretary Donovan and his HUD team—it has generated additional and more dependable funding to public housing authorities for improving and preserving their housing inventories, and it seems to be on the way to offering its residents not only better housing but also additional choices than are available under the conventional public housing system.

Through the end of 2017, nearly 115,000 units of public and assisted housing have been converted to long-term Section 8 project-based contracts, including 88,000 public housing units. More than $5 billion in construction improvements (U.S. HUD 2018) were underway at the public housing developments—or about $60,000 per unit on average—flowing mostly from new private sector debt and equity investments that had been inaccessible to housing authorities previously. This constitutes a remarkable leverage ratio of approximately $19 of private capital for every $1 HUD provided (U.S. HUD 2017a, 1). If this rate of leverage continues across the entire 455,000 units of public housing conversions authorized by Congress, over $27 billion could be generated for needed public housing improvements. This would entirely cover the earlier-estimated $26 billion backlog of public housing in just a handful of years, all without any additional outlays to the current level of public housing funding. Plus, just the RAD-converted public housing that is currently under construction has already generated an estimated 94,700 direct and indirect jobs across the country (U.S. HUD 2018, 1).

What's more, RAD is making good use of available, typically underutilized public and private financing resources. Nearly three in ten RAD projects are tapping 4 percent Low-Income Housing Tax Credits and companion tax-exempt bond financing that are not fully used each year in nearly every state. Plus, 13 percent of projects financed through 2017 are relying on FHA-insured mortgages, which, prior to RAD's introduction, were hardly ever used in financing public housing developments (U.S. HUD 2017c, 3). Equally encouraging, despite not being able to convert subsidies at full FMR levels in most cases, RAD is being successfully applied in some of the country's most expensive housing markets, including San Francisco and Santa Barbara (CA), Portland (OR), Chicago, Boston, Cambridge (MA), New York City, Washington, DC, and Atlanta.

Underscoring that RAD is able to drive public housing preservation in an extremely high-cost area, the office of Mayor Ed Lee declared in September 2015, with then-HUD Secretary Julian Castro and House Democratic Leader Nancy Pelosi in attendance, that "RAD is an historic program that will allow San Francisco to leverage approximately $700 million in investor equity, $300 million in debt financing, and between $50 and $100 million in City funding for the rehabilitation of over 3,475 public housing units." Leader Pelosi added, "With the RAD initiative . . . we are unleashing new resources, protecting tenants' rights, and preserving a strong voice for our families in the housing policy decisions that affect their communities" (City of San Francisco, Office of the Mayor 2015).

Unseen in these results is something perhaps even more encouraging. Beyond initial improvements made under RAD, long-term renewable Section 8 contracts require (and for the first time give agencies) the resources to properly maintain and budget for long-term replacement reserves. With RAD contracts in place, they can now plan to recapitalize and upgrade their properties when needed. Fewer properties will likely suffer from year-to-year neglect owing to limited availability of Public Housing Capital Funds and accumulated capital repair backlogs, which would ultimately be lost to demolition. Already, RAD is reported to be slowing the amount of public housing that is demolished from over 10,000 units per year now down to less than 8,000 units annually (U.S. HUD 2017b).

Perhaps most importantly, the demonstration is just now progressing to the point where residents can begin to potentially claim the a RAD "choice-mobility" voucher after one or two years of tenure, which would enable them to move from housing converted under RAD to other available options of their choosing. At this writing, it is too early to assess if and how public housing residents might choose to exercise it. But their right to do so has been firmly established.

At the same time, housing authorities are beginning to embrace RAD's new "transfer of assistance" provision, which enables them to provide better public housing options for current residents in other locations. Current data show that over one hundred RAD conversions of assistance involved construction of new units to replace badly deteriorated properties or the transfer of assistance "to lower-poverty neighborhoods, with greater access to jobs, quality schools, and transportation" (U.S. HUD 2017a, 1).

While only a few dozen transfer of assistance projects have been completed to date, and resident reactions so far are only anecdotal, this new RAD feature may prove to be the hallmark of Secretary Donovan's determination to offer more equitable choices to public housing residents. The appreciable value of this new choice is perhaps best captured in the words of a long-time resident of a now-demolished public housing project in DeKalb County, Georgia, who described her experience in moving to new replacement housing in a less-dense, more amenity-rich part of the community that was completed under the new transfer of assistance provision:

> I was not excited about the move at first because I really didn't want to move. I raised my children there and it was home to me . . . I had not moved in a very long time and didn't know what to expect. When the [housing authority] staff took me to see the place where I live now I thought I had died and gone to heaven . . . I love, love, love my new home. I feel safe and comfortable in my new surroundings. They have so much stuff to do here and I am in walking distance to food, shopping, and the bus, if I need it. I can't wait to start my garden. (U.S. HUD n.d.)

RAD as Federal Equity Policy and Practice

While RAD seems to have taken hold in practice, the work is by no means done. RAD's current authority to convert 225,000 public housing units reaches to approximately two-fifths of the total public housing inventory and now extends to an additional 180,000-plus units of assisted multifamily housing potentially at risk of losing subsidies with the recent increase of authority granted to this inventory in the FY 2018 appropriations act. What's more, RAD is not yet a fully approved HUD program duly authorized by the Senate Banking and House Financial Services committees; its initial and subsequent authorities were extended through appropriations rather than authorizing processes. And despite evidence to the contrary, a few Democratic members of the consequential House Financial Services Committee—particularly its ranking member, Representative Maxine Waters of California—remain concerned that RAD could somehow effect the loss of public housing stock rather than help preserve it.

Nonetheless, the demonstration—launched by Secretary Donovan and then ably carried forward by Secretary Castro and dedicated HUD career staff, along with hundreds of housing authorities and dozens of stakeholder groups and a few of their exceptional leaders—has made a persuasive case for being made a permanent program. Following the Obama administration's efforts in its waning annual budget requests, the new Trump administration also called for making RAD permanent in an official administration request in its initial two budget submission to Congress. And more compellingly, Senate Transportation, Housing and Urban Development Chairwoman Susan Collins of Maine, one of RAD's earliest champions in the Senate, sought to make RAD a permanent option in the Senate's version of the HUD appropriation bill for FY 2018.

RAD's future fate may owe itself to how well Secretary Donovan and his HUD colleagues applied and rooted basic equity planning principles and practices— the same practices that Krumholz and other equity practitioners used in making lasting change at the local and regional levels in their times.

Secretary Donovan and his team seemed to have followed many of those principles in their efforts. The secretary led with a clear vision for moving public housing to the Section 8 platform with a belief that doing so would enable public housing authorities to access private capital and produce better results for their residents than could be done under the conventional system. While the sweep of the policy he proposed was not without controversy, he recognized and seized a rare opportunity to take bold action afforded by other housing policy changes that needed to be made in response to the historic recession gripping the country at the onset of the Obama administration. The impact on residents of the continuous loss of housing stock and the declining conditions of what remained helped make the case that a policy change to a more proven approach was warranted. While they stumbled initially with the TRA-PETRA legislation, HUD made the needed course corrections and persisted and delivered RAD in a more collaborative process.

Donovan's payoff has already delivered nearly three times as much investment as Congress was able to provide in capital funding to the *entire* 1.1 million units remaining in the public housing system in the FY 2017 budget (NH&RA 2017, 1). Considered another way, it would have taken participating housing authorities forty-six years to accumulate the same amount of funding under the conventional public housing system that RAD has already generated in a matter of few years to make critical improvements to their properties (U.S. HUD 2017a, 1). Even more encouragingly, public housing residents now have two more housing choices than they did previously. As RAD further unfolds, they will increasingly be able to live in other communities, perhaps making it easier to secure a new job or attend a different school.

Possibilities for a More Equitable National Housing Policy

Hopefully, RAD will be allowed to build on its initial promise in the years ahead. Despite the antigovernment rhetoric, austerity policies, and ideological bent of the unfolding Trump presidency, there are indications that the new HUD team is mindful of these prospects.

In his written testimony to the Senate Banking Committee as part of his confirmation process, then-HUD Secretary-designate Dr. Ben Carson stated that "I have been very encouraged by early results from the last administration's efforts in the Rental Assistance Demonstration program. I believe in building upon what works no matter whose idea it was. I look forward to working with Congress to expand this worthy program" (U.S. Senate n.d.). Once he took the helm at HUD, Secretary Carson has pointed to RAD as example of a new kind of public-private partnership with proven potential (Fitze 2017). Plus, there are some reports that the secretary and his new HUD team are working to establish a dedicated process within HUD to expedite viable public-private partnerships, including RAD.

Assuming that RAD continues to evolve in the current administration and beyond, it offers a few additional lessons for equity planners and practitioners in promoting more equitable federal housing policies going forward. Unsurprisingly, they, too, are not dissimilar from some of the lessons that Krumholz and others observed in their local and regional work. Perhaps they can be guideposts well into the future.

First is the difficulty of pulling back on a policy that generates momentum in early implementation. Although it took nearly three years to win initial statutory approval, once approved, RAD quickly produced the promised results—in the amount of additional investment in the public housing stock and the pace of improvements underway—especially when compared to the usual pace of typical federal program implementation. This was the result of a patient, inclusive policy development process. The process prepared HUD to move quickly to implementation once the program was approved. HUD then offered a well-designed, flexible application and initial review and approval process for interested housing authorities, which it actually marketed. It relied considerably on external stakeholders involved in devising RAD for support. All of this enabled RAD to quickly gain traction in its initial implementation and will perhaps help it "stick" in continuing practice.

Assessing the department's efforts to design and launch RAD, a long-time affordable housing policy analyst pointed to RAD as a model "for stealth reformers seeking to make constructive change in our otherwise sclerotic government." He then went on to outline ten reasons for RAD's early success in a column entitled, "Why RAD Worked," which future initiatives might consider modeling. Among the reasons cited:

> *RAD was voluntary:* No housing authority is compelled to participate . . . it lets the enterprising and optimistic discreetly separate themselves from the larger observant herd. *HUD wanted RAD to work:* As a small demonstration, RAD could be and was staffed by a few HUD specialists, including some drawn into federal service explicitly for this purpose . . . [who] could and did create practical, encouraging guidance. . . . *RAD offered low-cost, low-risk intake:* Knowing that RAD was being greeted skeptically, the program designers wrote the rules for easy entry and no-risk exploration . . . this combination encouraged the curious and disarmed the fearful. . . . *As a demonstration, RAD could evolve quickly . . .* RAD was governed by HUD administrative notices; these in turn were informed by early adopters' suggestions. . . . Learning by doing is speedy; rule-writing by practitioners who are domain experts beats hollow the clanking machinery of full-blown program rollout. . . . *Liberated RAD properties could attract new resources:* Not only is legacy public housing encumbered by anachronistic regulatory chains, it is precluded from tapping . . . allocated LIHTC, volume-cap bonds, HOME and CDBG and state/local trust funds. Shedding the legacy public housing covenant made these RAD properties . . . eligible for new money. (Smith 2015, 20–21)

Second, RAD proved to be smart national policy that (eventually) realized considerable stakeholder support—and bipartisan appeal. In having little choice but to adopt a cost-neutral approach to launch the demonstration and then intentionally attempting to match RAD to less-used public resources such as tax-exempt bonds, 4-percent LIHTCs, and FHA insurance, HUD worked hard to have RAD make better use of existing, limited public resources. It then offered as much flexibility as it could in the subsidy-conversion process, partly in acknowledgement of its inability to augment those subsidies. Conversion of assistance under RAD also reduced the regulatory burden for public housing authorities, compared with the traditional public-housing operating and capital funds. Regardless of politics, it seems most policymakers can generally agree to reduce regulation and use already allocated public funds to help leverage substantial private sector participation.

Third, as part of finding a way to appeal to Congress a second time, HUD built a constituency for RAD that has served it well. As one congressional staff person succinctly stated about the delicacy of the annual funding process, "it's hard to make appropriations policy if there's too much noise outside the room." Furthermore, the HUD team that shepherded RAD through the legislative process was careful to build trusted working relationships with key congressional staff in order to facilitate their efforts inside the room. Little legislation of any stripe can get passed without minding these practices.

It was also not lost on Secretary Donovan and his colleagues that an expanded, more politically capable constituency than that which typically supported public housing would be crucial in expanding RAD beyond its initial authority—and the fate of public housing more generally. As HUD designed RAD, it engaged lenders, investors, developers, attorneys, tax accountants, construction services, and other potential transactional partners in thinking through how RAD could best put into practice. Their engagement—and subsequent involvement in the now hundreds of RAD projects with housing authorities across the country—has added their voices to the RAD constituency that has already worked to expand RAD on three occasions to date.

What's more, many of these actors have been long involved in supporting and defending Section 8 project-based subsidies, LIHTCs, and other resources integral to the success of multifamily assisted housing. Secretary Donovan clearly understood that their clout was a distinguishing factor in why project-based Section 8 assistance consistently fared better in annual appropriations battles than did public housing subsidies. As an ancient African proverb underscores, when elephants fight, it is the grass that suffers. Now that many more able actors are involved in RAD projects that rely on continued, steady annual appropriations to maintain the viability of long-term project-based contracts, it is more than likely that their stewardship of the Section 8 project-based programs will grow on Capitol Hill.

Evidence of this can already be seen in the affordable housing industry's concerted response to the Trump administration's initial HUD budgets. To no one's surprise, drastic cuts were proposed to both the public housing Capital Fund and Operating Fund levels integral to converting assistance under RAD *and* project-based Section 8 subsidies critical to honoring long-term multifamily housing contractual obligations in the administration's initial budget submissions. Yet both the FY 2017 and FY 2018 appropriations bills passed by congress repudiated these cuts and actually increased funding for each of these programs.

A fourth lesson for future equity-oriented policy initiatives from the RAD experience might be that there is little value returned to the public sector in dutifully insisting on the primacy of a pure public funding model when the evidence of its limitations and detrimental impacts become so clear. This is not to further the trope that private financing is always a more efficient and better approach than public investment can be. Rather, it is simply to acknowledge that when a long-standing public policy or approach fails to produce needed results, equity planners and practitioners should seek and advocate for better policies and approaches.

Secretary Donovan and other advocates for RAD recognized that much of public housing's failings owed to fact that its funding model was anachronistic and not aligned to the way that all other forms of assisted housing have been financed and performed for the last thirty-plus years. Continuing to wish only for increased public funding as the best means to turn around public housing's plight in face of its chronic challenges—many of them political in nature—is wishful thinking at best and arguably naïve in failing to comprehend political reality at worst.

Finally, the RAD team at HUD has been more than attentive to the true test of any equity-oriented policy that can and should endure. It worked assiduously in shaping RAD's legislative framework and detailing its initial and subsequent revisions to implementing notices, and it continues to maintain a strong vigilance in RAD's implementation, to see that all of the parties participating in RAD respect its original purpose—to provide public housing residents better outcomes than the conventional public housing system has been able to do. So far, those efforts seem to have helped RAD pass this consequential test. Tens of thousands of residents have had their homes improved. Most seem impressed with the results. Some have even planted new gardens. Regardless of the setting, assuring that those with few choices truly benefit and are afforded more options than before seems to remain the north star of equity planning and practice into future.

REFERENCES

Abt Associates Inc. 2010. *Capital Needs in Public Housing.* Revised Final Report, November 24. https://portal.hud.gov/hudportal/documents/huddoc?id=PH_Capital_Needs.pdf.
Center on Budget and Policy Priorities. 2017. *Public Housing.* Policy Basics, November 15. https://www.cbpp.org/sites/default/files/atoms/files/policybasics-housing.pdf.
City of San Francisco, Office of the Mayor. 2015. "Mayor Lee Celebrates Milestone in U.S. Department of Housing & Urban Development Partnership to Re-Envision, Revitalize & Rebuild City's Public Housing," press release, October 14.
Collinson, R., I. Gould Ellen, and J. Ludwig. 2015. *Low-Income Housing Policy.* National Bureau of Economic Research Working Paper No. 21701, April. http://www.nber.org/papers/w21071.
Council of Large Public Housing Authorities (CLPHA). 2009. "Future of Public Housing Framework." Web page. http://www.clpha.org/future_of_public_housing_policy_framework.
———. 2013. *Public Housing Operating and Capital Fund Pro-rations, 1.* Internal data table, FY 2001–FY 2014.

Donovan, S., and P. Costigan. 2011. Private meeting at U.S. Department of Housing and Urban Development, January 7.

Econometrica, Inc. 2016. *Evaluation of HUD's Rental Assistance Demonstration.* Interim report, September. Washington, DC: U.S. Department of Housing and Urban Development. https://portal.hud.gov/hudportal/documents/huddoc?id=RAD _InterimRpt_Final.pdf.

Fischer, Will. 2014. *Expanding Rental Assistance Demonstration Would Help Low-Income Families, Seniors, and People with Disabilities.* Washington, DC: Center on Budget and Policy Priorities, November 7. https://www.cbpp.org/sites/default/files/atoms /files/11-7-14hous.pdf.

Fitze, J. 2017. "Carson, in return to Baltimore, backs sales of public housing to private developers," *Baltimore Sun,* June 29. http://www.baltimoresun.com/news/maryland /politics/bs-md-carson-visits-baltimore-20170629-story.html.

Housing Authority of Baltimore City (HABC). n.d. "Summary of RAD Questions and HABC Response." Fact sheet, 3. http://static.baltimorehousing.org/img/events /radfactsheet68775771.pdf.

Kimura, D. 2017. "Big Cuts Proposed to HUD 2018 Budget," *Affordable Housing Finance,* May 23. http://www.housingfinance.com/policy-legislation/big-cuts-proposed-to -2018-hud-budget_o.

Millennial Housing Commission, The. 2002. *Meeting Our Nation's Housing Challenges.* Washington, DC: Author, May 30. https://govinfo.library.unt.edu/mhc/MHCReport .pdf.

National Housing & Rehabilitation Association. 2017. "Omnibus Appropriations Enacted for Remainder of FY 2017; HUD Sees Slight Increase," *Federal/Agency News,* May 3. https://www.housingonline.com/2017/05/03/congress-considers-omnibus -remainder-fy-2017-budget-hud-sees-slight-increase/.

New York City Housing Authority (NYCHA). 2015. "De Blasio administration unveils NextGeneration NYCHA." Press release, May 19. http://www1.nyc.gov/site/nycha /about/press/pr-2015/de-blasio-unveils-nextgen.page.

———. 2017. *NYCHA 2017 Fact Sheet.* April 13. https://www1.nyc.gov/assets/nycha /downloads/pdf/factsheet.pdf

Public Housing Authorities Directors Association (PHADA). n.d.. *Saving America's Public Housing.* Washington, DC: Author. https://www.phada.org/pdf/Proportionality _FINAL.pdf.

Rice, Douglas. 2016. *Chart Book: Cuts in Federal Assistance Have Exacerbated Families' Struggles to Afford Housing.* April 12. Washington, DC: Center on Budget and Policy Priorities. https://www.cbpp.org/research/housing/chart-book-cuts-in-federal -assistance-have-exacerbated-families-struggles-to-afford.

Smith, D. A. 2015. "Why RAD worked," *Tax Credit Advisor* (August): 20–21.

———. 2017. "The Guru Is In: RAD and the Preference Cascade," *Tax Credit Advisor* (April): 6–7.

U.S. Department of Housing and Urban Development (HUD). 2010. "Myths vs. Facts: Setting the Record Straight about PETRA." July 1. https://portal.hud.gov /hudportal/documents/huddoc?id=PETRAMythsvsFacts.pdf.

———. 2011. *FY 2012 Budget Summary.* Washington, DC: Author, February. https://portal .hud.gov/hudportal/documents/huddoc?id=2012BudgetFinal_03_07_Web.pdf.

———. 2017a. "$4 billion in construction achieved under RAD." May 11. https://portal .hud.gov/hudportal/documents/huddoc?id=RAD_4B_Construction.pdf.

———. 2017b. Internal meeting, May.

———. 2017c. "Rental assistance demonstration update." Internal PowerPoint presentation, April 11.

2018. "RAD Talk, January 2018."

U.S. Department of Housing and Urban Development. n.d. "DeKalb County, Georgia Using RAD to Create Diverse Communities," RAD Spotlight. https://portal.hud .gov/hudportal/documents/huddoc?id=RAD_CS_DeKalb_GA.pdf.

U.S. Senate. n.d. "Questions for Dr. Benjamin Carson, Secretary-Designate, U.S. Department of Housing and Urban Development from Senator Warren." https://www .warren.senate.gov/files/documents/Carson_QFR_Responses.pdf.

9

PLANNING FOR AGING
Addressing Issues of Equity

Deborah Howe

"Why should government be obligated to help people who are having problems that are the direct result of their own decisions?"

This question was posed by a graduate student in a 2013 planning studio focused on developing a county-level housing alternatives plan for an aging population. Twenty-five years earlier, at a community planning for aging training session, I was explaining the challenges of aging in place when a professional planner asked, "Well—why don't they move?"

Both questions pose a lack of understanding of life as it is actually lived in the built environment. These perspectives challenge efforts to change the paradigm of how and what we build to ensure that our communities can support people of all ages.

I maintain that government has an obligation to proactively plan for an aging society. One issue of equity is continuing to create built environments that present major challenges to people as they age, resulting in dangerous living and transportation situations, excessive personal and societal costs (particularly in caregiving), and isolation. Urban planners should be in the lead here. The planner's skill set and professional responsibilities position them to incorporate attention to aging in all aspects of community planning. The size of the aging population, the impact on caregivers, and the competition for limited resources between this demographic and various other social needs is setting society up for major conflict. A focus on aging will by definition put people at the center of planning.

The numbers that dimension aging in the United States are almost incomprehensible. In 2015, the U.S. population included nearly 48 million older adults.

This number will double to 88 million by midcentury, including 19 million aged eighty-five and over. There will be over 387,000 centenarians at that time, compared to 72,000 in 2015 (U.S. Census n.d.). Older adults, as a proportion of the population, has changed from one in twenty-four in 1900 to one in seven in 2013. By 2030, it will be one in five.

Improvements in health care have dramatically reduced the probability of death from infections and has increased the capacity to live with chronic conditions such as heart disease. This has resulted in longer life spans, and that means that more people are dealing with the vagaries of old age. Our physical, cognitive, and/or mental capabilities will be affected in some manner. We can expect some combination of loss of vision and hearing, stiffer joints, decline in muscle tone, loss in bone density leading to higher risk of fractures, difficulties in keeping balance, decline in an ability to think clearly and quickly, etc. The specific challenges will vary from person to person depending on genetics, environment, health care, and injury.

In 1950 a sixty-five-year-old could expect to live an additional 13.9 years. By 2010, this had increased to 19.1 to 17.7 years for males and 20.3 years for females (AOA 2014). An older adult may live with a disability for up to eight years on average and can expect to outlive their ability to drive safely by six to ten years (Foley et al. 2002). This means that at some point, we are each likely to be dependent on others for health care, transportation, and other activities of daily living.

Historically, the family supported their elders through multigenerational households. This arrangement provided for an exchange of services among the generations, reduced living costs, and the ultimate transfer of property to (generally) the eldest son. Structural economic changes allowing for more broadly based wealth accumulation, combined with longer life-spans, gave older adults the wherewithal to live independently, thereby maintaining more control of their own lives. According to Gawande (2014, 21–22), the rapidly increasing percentage of older adults living alone is "a sign of enormous progress," and there "is no better time in history to be old." He further argues that veneration of elders has "been replaced by veneration of the independent self." But the inevitability of infirmity and illness raises questions about what to do when independence cannot be sustained.

The older adult demographic includes people who range in age from sixty-five years to over 105. There is, of course, no one aging experience—it is a deeply personal process and thus every story is different. The Center for Home Care Policy and Research of the Visiting Nurse Service of New York has found two distinct aging clusters. The "fortunate majority" are thriving. They are financially secure, socially active, and relatively healthy. The "frail fraction" are struggling. This group tends to have less than a high school education, have poor health, be isolated, live in poor neighborhoods, and have inadequate financial security (Feldman et al. 2004). Since minority elders have a greater likelihood of having one or more of these characteristics than their white counterparts, they are overrepresented in the "frail fraction."

The population of older adults will continue to diversify. By 2050, 42 percent will be minorities compared to 20 percent in 2010. Among those aged eighty-five years and older in 2050, one third will be minorities compared to 15 percent in 2010 (Vincent and Velkoff 2010). The aggregate minority population in total is projected to become the majority in 2042, underscoring that the service providers and social security supporters for the nation's older adults will be predominantly non-white. The extent to which discrimination continues to limit opportunities for non-whites has long-term implications for society's capacity to support older adults.

The median income for older men was $29,327 in 2013; for women, it was $16,301 (AOA 2014). In 2009, 40 percent of older households carried a housing burden, paying more than 30 percent for housing and utilities (Federal Interagency Forum on Aging-Related Statistics 2012). The Economic Policy Institute's analysis suggests that 48 percent of older adults are economically vulnerable; this is defined as those with income that is less than two times the Supplemental Poverty Measure. This percentage increases to 58.1 percent for those aged eighty and over—52.6 percent for women, 63.5 percent for blacks, and 70.1 percent for Hispanics. "Many of America's 41 million seniors are just one bad economic shock away from significant material hardship. Most seniors live on modest retirement incomes, which are often barely adequate—and sometimes inadequate—to cover the cost of basic accessories and support a simple, yet dignified, quality of life" (Gould and Cooper 2013, 3). Proposed cuts in Medicare and Social Security will increase the number of older adults who are vulnerable.

In 2000, the U.S. Census found that 80 percent of older adults were homeowners who had lived in their home a median of twenty years. Over two thirds (68 percent) of this group had no mortgage. The median size of older adults' homes (single-family detached and mobile homes) was 1,743 square feet on a median lot size of 0.37 acres (U.S. Census 2005). Over one quarter (28 percent) of older adults live alone, rising to one half (46 percent) for women aged seventy-five and older (AOA 2014). Over half (54 percent) live in suburban communities, reflecting the dominant post–World War II housing preferences; this percentage is expected to increase in the years ahead. Nearly one in five older adults (19 percent) are located outside of metropolitan areas in rural and small communities (AOA 2014).

It should come as no surprise that older adults overwhelmingly prefer to age in place. A 2010 AARP survey, for example, revealed that 78 percent of those aged sixty-five and older want to remain in their residence as long as possible. In contrast, this preference is expressed by only 60 percent of those aged forty-five to forty-nine (Keenan 2010). The stronger desire of older respondents to age in place is logical. Moving is extremely difficult. It involves relinquishing a lifetime of memories of place and objects. Some older adults have deferred maintenance on their home; this means lower resale values and less equity that can be used for a housing alternative, assuming one is available. A move at an older age also means comprehending a new community, and that might be challenging due to changing health circumstances.

Staying in one's home can be very difficult. Most houses are not designed to accommodate people with disabilities. Barriers include internal and external stairs, doorways that are not wide enough for wheelchairs, inaccessible kitchens and bathrooms, and no bedroom on the first floor. Adaptations can be very costly, assuming they are feasible. Taxes and the costs and logistics of home maintenance can be problematic. If a home is located in an area where there are limited alternatives to the automobile, then this can present significant constraints to continued independence and lead to the risk of severe isolation.

Who will provide care for our aging population? One fifth of the baby boomers are childless; 17 percent have only one child. Sixteen percent of those eighty-five and older have no surviving children to provide care (Creamer 2012). The dependency ratio of those aged sixty-five and over compared to the number aged twenty to sixty-five (multiplied by 100) was 21 in 2010 and projected to be 36 in 2050. The corresponding child dependency ratio is likely to remain relatively stable over this time period (declining from 38 to 37) yielding a combined ratio of 59 in 2010 and 74 in 2050 (Ortman and Velkoff 2014). The stress on family members will be extraordinary. The low number of working age adults relative to older adults will have an impact on the Social Security system. Furthermore, fewer working-age adults relative to older adults are likely to result in higher wages and thus increased costs for professional care services.

As a further complication, the health-care capacity to support the unique needs of older adults is in decline. Geriatrics is a medical specialty that focuses on understanding the complex health challenges of older adults. It has a particular emphasis on managing for quality of life and maintaining function rather than aggressive care for certain medical conditions. It tends to not pay as well as other specialties. As of 2013, there were only 7,500 certified geriatricians in the United States against a current need of 17,000. There is a projected need for 30,000 by 2030 to serve the 30 percent of older adults with complicated medical situations (Olivero 2015). Comparable deficits are occurring in other medical specialties such as geriatric social workers.

It is abundantly evident that older adults are facing realities that have implications for society as a whole. Every one of us will be affected.

What we should be doing is ensuring that our communities are livable, age-friendly, and supportive of people throughout their life-span. We need communities that encourage healthy lifestyles by enabling physical activity such as walking. We need opportunities for social interaction to avoid isolation. We need alternatives to the private automobile. And we need to stop building Peter Pan housing. It is time to connect development policies and practices with real life. Real life involves aging. The solutions speak to divergent political interests in that they emphasize the enablement of continued independence and personal responsibility in a caring culture, which can achieve efficiencies in both public and personal costs. In other words, Democrats, Republicans, and Libertarians should be able to see their interests served through an aging focus. While it would be helpful to work within a federally supportive environment, there is a considerable amount that can be achieved at the local level through comprehensive planning policies touching on land use, housing, transportation, and infrastructure. It is at the local level, of course, that the activities of daily living are carried out.

A 2006 survey of 10,000 U.S. jurisdictions found that 46 percent have begun to address the needs of aging primarily through basic health and nutrition programs (N4A 2011). Few jurisdictions have undertaken a comprehensive assessment of their communities to ensure livability for all ages, and they have not developed the policies, programs, and services needed by older adults that will help maintain independence.

A review of comprehensive plans for one hundred large U.S. cities suggests limited attention to aging. According to Jordan Yin, "Issues related to aging are found to a small extent in many plans, but usually in a general and minor way (perhaps even superficial)—often in sections related to housing, social services, and transportation. There doesn't seem to be any 'big city plan' that has a full chapter on aging or has goals and policies related to aging as a 'top level' concern." He notes that Raleigh addresses fair housing, universal design, and aging in place within the housing element; Denver speaks to older adults and the importance of helping to meet their needs, including maintaining their independence through the human services element; Sacramento intentionally integrates aging issues in their housing element (Yin 2015).

So why does it seem like there is little sense of urgency? This may boil down to attitudes about aging. A Pew Research survey reveals that only 26 percent of U.S. respondents view aging as a major problem—placing the United States as the third lowest percentage out of twenty-one countries represented in the survey. Japan, South Korea, and China ranked at the top with respectively 87 percent,

79 percent, and 67 percent of respondents viewing aging as a major problem. The authors report that Americans are more confident than Europeans that they will have an adequate standard of living in old age. Furthermore, the United States is one of the few countries "where a large plurality of the public believes individuals are primarily responsible for their own well-being in old age" (Pew Research Center 2014, 7).

The Frameworks Institute conducted a systematic review of expert versus public attitudes regarding aging. Experts view aging as a normal part of biological design that is distinct from disease and decline. Older adults can remain healthy and maintain high levels of functioning. The public views aging as "a process of deterioration, dependency, reduced potential, family dispersal and digital incompetence." Aging is something to be dreaded. This negative view leads to marginalization of those "old people" or the "elderly." The public has not considered the policy implications of increased longevity and is not aware of the extent to which older Americans face discrimination and the "need to address it via legal and other systematic means" (Lindland et al. 2015, 7–8).

Urban planning as a profession has been slow to recognize the importance of an aging focus. This is a profession that is remarkably conservative, constrained by political directives, and charged with providing the physical infrastructure and processes that support the private sector. The emergence of advocacy planning as inspired by Paul Davidoff (1965) revealed the profession's blind spots. Aging is simply not on this profession's horizon, and thus there is little thought given to this marginalized population. This may be in part because planners tend to frame issues as compilations of numbers, which makes everything abstract. Aging is best understood as individual, detailed stories which reveal personal challenges and opportunities, enabling one to comprehend the importance of the human scale. The stories, however, may also reinforce the notion of individual responsibility, thus undermining the idea that the public sector has a role to play in supporting the aging process.

I would argue that the planning profession buys into the public attitudes toward aging as clarified by the Framework Institute study and revealed in the two quotes that were shared in the beginning of this chapter. Simply put, individuals are viewed as responsible for addressing the challenges associated with aging. Personal choices certainly are significant. But are planners ensuring meaningful choices? When a young couple looks for housing, will they find decent schools, parks, and transit alternatives in a walkable, affordable community? Or will they need to look to the suburbs because the cities have too many problems? What options will be available to the low-income couple? When these couples age, will it be possible for them to adapt their houses or move to a more suitable dwelling within their community? Is it their fault if alternatives do not exist?

Leadership in promoting livable communities has come from outside the planning profession. AARP has a well-developed Livable Communities program that focuses on advocacy, best practices, tool kits, policies, and education (see AARP Livable Communities n.d.). They facilitate the AARP Network of Age-Friendly Communities under the auspices of the World Health Organization. Involved jurisdictions represent over 30 million people. Partners for Livable Communities has long advocated for community planning for aging through their mission "to improve the quality of life and economic and social wellbeing of low- and moderate-income individuals and communities." Their contribution focuses on networking, research, technical assistance, and education (see Partners for Livable Communities n.d.). The National Association of Area Agencies on Aging (N4A) has spent the past decade working with Area Agencies on Aging (AAAs) to promote the concept of Livable Community for All Ages. The N4A has been involved in conducting "community aging readiness surveys," working with stakeholders to develop livable community agendas, and distributing best practices information. According to the N4A, over 70 percent of surveyed AAAs report work on developing livable communities initiatives (see N4A n.d.). The U.S. Environmental Protection Agency's Aging Initiative (2002–17) sponsored a monthly newsletter with information on aging-relevant research, funding opportunities, and conferences. The EPA was also able to provide funds to train older adults as environmental stewards to develop intergenerational environmental programs and redesign communities and the built environment in support of aging in place.

The American Planning Association is developing some capacity to support community planning for aging. The APA recently published a Planning Advisory Service report entitled *Planning Aging-Supportive Communities* (Winick and Jaffe 2015). National conferences are including an increasing number of sessions focused on aging. In July 2014, the APA board of directors approved the *Policy Guide on Aging in Community*. This is a comprehensive set of recommendations for planners to apply in any given community. It does not commit the APA to further action. Ramona Mullahey, a senior analyst with U.S. HUD, played a leadership role in securing support for the *Policy Guide*. She expresses concern that there still is a lack of urgency in the planning field about aging as an issue; it is not getting focused attention (Mullahey 2015).

Three Case Studies

There are some hopeful signs of change. We will consider the cases of Portland, Philadelphia, and the Atlanta region. These three examples reflect concerted efforts to frame aging as a community planning imperative. There is little history of comparable efforts to build on, so it has been necessary for the protagonists to be innovative and to pursue opportunities specific to their local context.

Portland, Oregon

Portland, Oregon is a locus of innovative planning. This city is well known for considering issues of equity in its land use, transit, and bicycle planning as well as efforts to accommodate regional development growth through high density development, accessory dwelling units, and zoning codes that allow for very small houses (see chapter 1 in this volume by Lisa K. Bates). In 2006, Portland was invited by the World Health Organization as one of thirty-three cities from twenty-two counties to participate in the Age-Friendly Cities Project. This work was led by Portland State University's Institute on Aging, including Margaret Neal (professor and director) and Alan DeLaTorre (research associate). It involved conducting focus group interviews of older adults, caregivers, and service providers using a WHO protocol. The topics included outdoor spaces, transportation, housing, respect and social inclusion, social participation, communication and information, civic participation, and community support and health services (Neal and DeLaTorre n.d). The WHO ultimately published (in 2007) a guide to age-friendly cities and developed the WHO Global Network, including 287 cities and communities in thirty-three countries representing a population of 113 million. In 2011, then-Mayor Sam Adams signed Portland up to participate in this network, but without any financial commitment.

Portland's WHO age-friendly report was ultimately referenced in *The Portland Plan*, a "strategic road map" adopted in 2012. Aging is addressed in a two-page section entitled "Portland is a Place for All Generations" (City of Portland 2012, 24–25). The plan calls for achieving an age-friendly community through accessible housing, community hubs, and transit streets, as well as expanding medical services and encouraging intergenerational mentoring. The city also committed to working with community partners in building on Portland's participation in the WHO Age-Friendly Cities Project and to developing an action plan on aging that would focus on implementation.

Under the leadership of the PSU Institute on Aging, the all-volunteer Age-Friendly Portland Advisory Council developed the *Action Plan for an Age-Friendly Portland*, which was approved by the city council in October 2013. The plan uses all the themes incorporated in the WHO project (calling out two additional areas: economy and community services) and is presented as an agenda for action. The plan was not vetted by the public, and it had no implementation authority, although aspects of the plan are being furthered by standing committees focused on civic engagement, employment and economy, health services, housing, and transportation.

To a certain extent, city officials may believe that the full range of livability policies that are already in place speaks to the issue of aging. One can certainly see that perspective in former Mayor Charlie Hales's interview with AARP, in which he described Portland as an age-friendly city (AARP Livable Communities 2015). But without an explicit focus on aging, certain things are missed. For example, the city's promotion of row housing on narrow lots as an affordable housing alternative ignores the fact that the resulting living space above a garage may be inaccessible to someone who cannot negotiate stairs. A universal design requirement that calls for stacked closets that could be inexpensively transformed into an elevator shaft might make this housing form more age-friendly.

The Age-Friendly Portland Advisory Council has since expanded to include Multnomah County; they had earlier prepared an intriguing plan (Multnomah County Task Force on Vital Aging 2008) that focuses on employment and civic engagement and views the increasing number of older adults as an economic asset—a source of volunteers and a highly skilled work force that has much to offer to younger generations. This plan transforms the negative image of "silver tsunami" into a positive image of "silver reservoir."

There have been concerted efforts to frame aging as an equity issue in Portland. *The Portland Plan* notes that equity exists when "everyone has access to opportunities necessary to satisfy their essential needs, advance their well-being and achieve their full potential" (City of Portland 2012, 18). This concept is explicitly connected with aging in a two-page section entitled *Portland Is a Plan for All Generations* that details an equity framework by recognizing that "Portland must become a city where access to opportunity, safe neighborhoods, safe and sound housing, healthy food, efficient public transit and parks and greenspaces are available for people of all ages and abilities" (Ibid., 24). However, aging has not been an obvious equity issue. When the city established an Office of Equity and Human Rights in 2011, the initial focus was on race and ethnicity. Advocates argued in favor of adding age, disability, and sexual orientation. They prevailed only on disability.

DeLaTorre and Neal continue to try to elevate aging as an equity issue, having published a white paper on this topic in January 2014 (DeLaTorre 2015, Neal 2015). They have become politically active in soliciting support and securing votes for the next city and county budget cycles in order to obtain the needed resources to move the aging agenda forward. Aging is competing against the need to devote government funds to address a severe homelessness crisis. In November 2015, the city council voted five to zero to allocate approximately $50,000 in funding to work on age-friendly housing issues and to support the coordination of the Portland and Multnomah County Advisory Council.

Philadelphia, PA

Philadelphia Corporation for Aging (PCA) is a nonprofit organization that has served as Philadelphia County's Area Agency on Aging for over forty years (the county is coterminous with the city boundaries). The PCA provides social, economic and health services of over 100,000 older adults and their caregivers. This AAA is distinguished by having a particularly strong research and advocacy focus. In 2008, PCA initiated the Age-Friendly Philadelphia (AFP) project under the leadership of Kate Clark, planner for policy and program development (2011). This project was directed at helping "older adults remain healthy, active, and engaged in their communities for as long as possible." PCA used EPA Aging Initiative guidelines that blended concepts of active living and Smart Growth that effect supportive physical and social environments. PCA framed their work on social capital, housing, mobility, and healthy eating. The projects focused on defining and implementing age-friendly improvements for parks, expanding housing alternatives, involving older adults in developing community gardens, and improving standards for bus shelters. PCA sponsored the development of Gen-Philly, a network of emerging leaders in their twenties and thirties who were willing to incorporate an aging perspective in their respective fields, recognizing that this could be an asset to their work (see GenPhilly n.d.).

The AFP was able to extend its reach beyond a limited number of PCA staff because they worked through existing organizations. They asserted the aging perspective at every opportunity, trusting that some momentum would be established.

The Philadelphia Department of Public Health facilitates the Get Healthy Philly program. This program brings together the public and private sectors, community organizations, and academia to improve health by addressing issues of smoking, obesity, and food access through programs, policies, and improvements to the built environment. In December 2010, the Public Health Department published *Philadelphia2035: Planning and Zoning for a Healthier City: The City's New Comprehensive Plan and Its Role in Improving Public Health*. The report highlights a range of public policies that were under consideration, such as transit-oriented developments, food access, open space, and walkability and explains how these approaches would support healthier lifestyles. It also introduces Health Impact Assessments (HIAs) that would allow planners and policy makers to evaluate initiatives against baseline health conditions and preferred outcomes. Philadelphia was noted as being one of the first major U.S. cities to standardize the use of HIAs in district plans and rezoning (City of Philadelphia Department of Public Health 2010, 32). The concept of "age-friendly neighborhoods" is limited to a single paragraph referencing relevant zoning policies (Ibid., 28) and is mentioned in reference to the notion of walkability (Ibid., 16). The aging issue is otherwise absent from this document.

While Philadelphia's comprehensive plan (adopted in June 2011) did not end up incorporating the "age-friendly" term, it does include a policy calling for a variety of housing options in support of older adults. The AFP initiative was successful in securing some very limited attention to aging issues in the comprehensive revision to the zoning code in 2012. The definition for daycare was extended to include adult daycare. The code now allows accessory dwelling units, but the actual zones have to be approved through a city council ordinance which has not happened to date. Visitability is a set of limited design features that would enable a person with a disability to visit a house. These requirements include one zero-step entrance, doorways/hallways at least thirty-two inches wide on the first floor, and an accessible half bath on the first floor. The Philadelphia zoning code requires visitability standards in at least 10 percent of the housing units in subdivisions of fifty or more houses. Such subdivisions, however, are rare.

At the district planning level (the means by which the city is applying the comprehensive plan at a more local level), the *South District Plan 2015* includes a recommendation for senior pedestrian zones to promote street-level improvements in support of locally high concentrations of older adults. This builds on an approach that has been developed by the New York City Department of Transportation, who designated twenty-five such zones where targeted improvements such as narrowed roadways, pedestrian safety islands, and increased crossing times have contributed to a 19 percent decrease in fatalities among older adults (City of Philadelphia Planning Commission 2011b, 73). The incorporation of health considerations in a district plan is facilitated by a planner who serves as the healthy communities coordinator for the Get Healthy Philly program; this position is split between the public health and planning departments.

The city's focus on aging has been dominated by service considerations. The Mayor's Commission on Aging issued a three-year strategic plan in 2011 that set goals for coordination, education, and engagement, serving as a catalyst for new solutions. Specific mention was made of transit services and walkability and supporting aging in place. This plan laid the groundwork for the city to engage in the WHO Age-Friendly Cities program. An assessment was subsequently completed by the mayor's office, and not the planning commission (Huang and Horstmann 2012).

In 2015, Philadelphia Corporation on Aging organized a workshop focused on park design that would be more inclusive of older adults. None of the city's park designers were in attendance. One of the workshop participants was Chris Dougherty, project manager with the Fairmont Conservancy, a nonprofit organization that provides support for the city's parks system. He notes that aging has been invisible in park planning efforts. He sees more innovation among nonprofit organizations and independent professionals such as landscape architects (Dougherty 2015).

What is striking about the Philadelphia case study is the extent to which only incremental changes have been achieved, despite the efforts of aging advocates to comprehensively advance an aging perspective within the city's planning framework. Aging advocates remain hopeful that a new mayoral administration committed to social justice issues will lead to more focused attention to aging (Dougherty 2015, Clark 2015, Davis 2015).

Atlanta, GA

The Atlanta Regional Commission (ARC) has embraced aging through their Lifelong Communities Initiative (see ARC Lifelong Communities 2009). The ARC serves as the designated Area Agency on Aging (AAA) and as such oversees $28 million in federal and state program funding for aging and disability services provided both directly and through partnerships with providers.

The initiative has its origins in Aging Atlanta, a partnership founded in 2001 of fifty public, private, and nonprofit organizations. The director of the initiative was hosted by ARC. Supported through development and implementation grants from the Robert Wood Johnson Foundation's Community Partnerships for Older Adults program, Aging Atlanta sought to gain a better understanding of the needs of older adults and opportunities for improving long-term care and supportive services. In 2003 they conducted forty focus group interviews involving 1,200 older adults and conducted 400 surveys. They ultimately developed a work plan that addressed increasing awareness of the needs of an aging population and improved services.

The interviews and surveys revealed a high level of concern for issues associated with "place"—affordable and accessible housing and transportation, opportunities for social interaction, perceptions of safety, etc. The AAA came to realize that their historic emphasis on collecting data that favored health measures (such as blood pressure and chronic diseases) was not accounting for the home address, which is an indicator of the built environment (Lawler 2015). This environment is a huge quality of life determinant and as such is directly connected to health outcomes.

In 2007, the ARC created the Lifelong Communities Initiative as a means of extending the lessons learned through the work of Aging Atlanta (ARC Lifelong Communities 2009). The next two years were focused on extensive outreach in the region's ten counties, engaging a broad range of perspectives including community residents, elected officials, and public and private professionals. Participants were asked to examine data about the aging population in their community and then analyze the extent to which the communities provide for housing and transportation options, healthy lifestyles, and information and access. Key areas and priorities were identified for specific communities.

In 2008, the ARC adopted the three Lifelong Communities Initiative goals as agency policy. These include (1) promoting housing and transportation options; (2) encouraging healthy lifestyles; and (3) expanding information and access. The ARC regional *Plan 2040 Framework* (adopted in 2011) does not include Lifelong Communities as a planning framework but does reference the initiative and associated goals and speaks to the importance of strategies emerging from local community partnerships. The ARC Division of Aging and Health Resources's *Live Beyond Expectations: Regional Strategic Plan July 2015–June 2020* presents Lifelong Community principles as a tactic in support of a goal to enhance housing diversity.

In 2009, the ARC partnered with Duany Plater-Zyberk and Company to run a nine-day charrette focused on developing plans for transforming five existing places into lifelong communities, including three historic train depot towns, an inner-city brownfield, and an outdated, underutilized site. Over 1,500 people participated (ARC Lifelong Communities 2009). The intent of this exercise was to generate meaningful alternatives to existing development patterns and regulations and to develop guidelines for evaluating the extent to which proposals support Lifelong Community goals. These communities have since implemented a number of the recommendations, including adoption of form-based zoning codes, walkability and roadway connectivity improvements, a new town square, a community garden and farmers' market, and a senior shuttle. The ARC continues to provide technical assistance to communities interested in incorporating Lifelong Community principles.

To provide further tangible examples of these principles, in 2014 ARC hosted a demonstration project that used "tactical urbanism" to temporarily transform two blocks of the Atlanta neighborhood of Sweet Auburn into a Lifelong Community. Volunteers from forty organizations cleaned up a vacant lot, built street furniture, installed a protected bike lane, developed new signs, and arranged for live music and celebrations of local history. Over a two-day period, over seven hundred people were able to see and experience a more livable environment for residents of all ages (ARC 2014).

There has been a great deal of external interest in the Lifelong Communities Initiative with ARC regularly fielding inquiries from small and large cities throughout the United States. According to Kathryn Lawler (2015), ARC's aging and health resources division manager, and Renee Ray (2015), ARC's AAA principal program specialist, the focus on aging has not been a hard sell with planners.

The challenge is integrating Lifelong Community principles into practice, especially with respect to infrastructure design. It is difficult to retrofit an auto-dependent, low-density landscape.

ARC has succeeded in elevating consideration of aging at the community planning level. The term "lifelong" is inclusive, thereby creating the potential for a broader constituency. The three lifelong communities' goals have been embraced as regional policy. Implementation is incremental, dependent on community-level initiatives.

The Case Studies in Review

In both Portland and Philadelphia, the aging advocates emerged from outside government. Thus, they needed to assert themselves into ongoing planning initiatives. They had some limited success—securing a statement about communities for all ages in Portland's strategic plan and some relevant but weak zoning provisions in Philadelphia. The advocacy will need to continue in order to exploit these policy openings to realize further gains. It is fortunate that the Atlanta Regional Commission also serves as the Area Agency on Aging, as this has placed the aging perspective in direct contact with regional planning efforts. The Aging Atlanta initiative was key in revealing the role of the built environment in the aging experience and thus establishing the direct connection to the traditional planning domains of land use, housing, environmental health, etc.

The relatively more effective efforts in Philadelphia and Atlanta may have been a result of more attention given to engaging stakeholders in dimensioning the locally specific challenges of aging and identifying alternatives to address these challenges. The Philadelphia Corporation on Aging advocated for a focus on aging by working through existing organizations. The Atlanta Regional Commission's use of focus group interviews, a charrette, and tactical urbanism is particularly noteworthy in fostering broad support for an aging focus among professionals and citizens at large; this led to a more robust embrace of aging at the policy level and may ensure a continuing focus even with changes in professional staff who led the effort.

Alternative Planning Frameworks

We will turn now to discussing alternative planning frameworks and policies for a community that is seriously interested in addressing the needs of an aging society.

As previously noted, there are various templates for assessing aging needs at a community level, such as the AARP Livable Communities Guide and the WHO

Age-Friendly Communities Guide. These templates carry the risk of communities conducting such an analysis in isolation and not integrating the results within other planning initiatives which would enhance opportunities for implementation. Thus Portland's strategic plan did little more than call for developing an Aging Action Plan. Philadelphia's WHO Age-Friendly Cities analysis was prepared by staff in the mayor's office; the extent to which the findings have risen to actionable initiatives is not clear.

Given the enormous challenges, an aging focus merits explicit attention in a comprehensive plan. This could take various forms. It could be covered as an element in the plan on par with other traditional components such as transportation, housing, economic development, or parks and recreation. The substance of such an element might incorporate the content of the WHO Age-Friendly Communities analysis, ensuring that this framework becomes an integral part of a community's policy guidelines.

Another alternative would be to embed an aging perspective in each of the comprehensive plan elements. This would ensure that aging is not perceived as a separate issue to consider but rather one that is already fully integrated into mainstream planning.

For some communities, the concept of Lifecycle Communities or Lifelong Communities might be a more acceptable way of addressing aging, as it avoids the appearance of pitting one generation against the next and is more inclusive. This is a viable approach as long as it includes explicit attention to the aging experience. This concept can be promoted by providing public incentives for project implementation as is done by both the Atlanta Regional Council and the Twin Cities Regional Planning Commission (see Metropolitan Council n.d.). An even stronger policy framework would move beyond incentives for private development to the requirement that public investment in infrastructure and economic development supports the development of Lifecycle Communities.

There are key provisions that would provide significant support for an aging society within functional areas of planning such as housing and transportation.

Building codes specify minimum construction requirements to protect public health and safeguard occupants. Given the aging of society, it is time to incorporate universal design requirements in building codes for all residential construction. This would reduce the barriers to continued independent living and lessen the need for expensive renovations. The cost of providing accessibility features such as wide halls and doorways, first-floor bedrooms and bathrooms, and zero-step entrances is minimal at initial construction. In contrast, one assessment of requirements for fire suppression systems revealed that the average cost of sprinklers per square foot was $1.35 (Newport Partners 2013). Protection from fire has been successfully framed as a public health concern justifying the added costs. Support for continued independence for older adults must also be recognized as a public health issue.

As an example of how quickly building code requirements can transform the housing stock, Pima County, Arizona, adopted visitability requirements for new construction, including a zero-step entrance, lever door handles, reinforced walls in a ground-floor bathroom for eventual installation of grab bars, switches at 48 inches of height or lower, and 36-inch wide hallways on the main floor. As of 2008, 15,000 new houses had been built to these standards (NCIL n.d). The Arizona Court of Appeals rejected a challenge to the regulations; the county had provided compelling evidence that the population of older adults was increasing, that approximately 41 percent of older adults have some form of disability, and that the requirements added only about $100 to the cost of construction (The Center for an Accessible Society 2003).

Communities should also allow the incorporation of accessory dwelling units (ADUs) on single family residential properties. ADUs enable the adaptation of single family structures to changing needs. The units can provide affordable rentals (with no public subsidy) and a source of income for the property owner. They can also facilitate caregiving by providing a separate dwelling on-site. ADUs represent a significant investment of the property owner, and thus jurisdictions should avoid imposing excessive restrictions such as time restrictions and requirements for familial relationships among the occupants. Demographic changes suggest that an increasing number of caregivers for older adults will be nonfamilial. Portland, Oregon, has found that ADUs are an important source of affordable housing in a very tight rental market and are actively seeking to modify requirements to encourage their construction (Law 2015). Unlike many jurisdictions, Portland does not require owner occupancy; there have been few problems associated with this policy.

Universal Design requirements and provisions for ADUs will go a long way toward enabling older adults to remain in their homes. There is much more that can be done, including providing subsidized housing for low-income older adults, programs that support housing adaptations and ongoing maintenance, property tax abatements, and services that provide support for daily life (such as grocery shopping and house cleaning). Specific needs will vary by community and should be determined through a careful assessment.

Mobility is a key aspect of how an older adult relates to the larger community and accesses services. Transportation planning needs to account for the aging of the population. Older adults will continue to rely on private automobiles due to the prevailing low-density land-use pattern that limits options for public transit. Furthermore, it is often easier to drive than take transit when one's abilities change. It could be very difficult, for example, to use the bus if it involves a long walk from home or if the bus stop offers no comfortable place to sit while waiting.

It is imperative that planners look at transportation from the perspective of the older driver, transit user, and pedestrian. Road-design standards need to address the reality that older people experience a range of changes, including reduced vision, decreased flexibility, reduced reaction time, and changes in perception. This has implications for signage, intersection design, lighting, duration of crosswalk signals, provision of pedestrian amenities, etc. The Federal Highway Administration has developed the *Handbook for Designing Roadways for the Aging Population* (Brewer, Murillo, and Pate 2014). This publication is offered as a resource to preemptively enhance safety and/or to address problems with specific crash sites. It is specifically not represented as a "new standard of required practice." This raises the question: at what point will the standards reflect the design driver and design pedestrian as being aged sixty-five and older? Given that the eighty-fifth percentile of drivers is the norm for speed and reaction standards, it would seem that the aging perspective should already be embedded in engineering standards. Local governments might consider mandating these standards within their jurisdictions.

The range of transportation alternatives will vary from community to community. They might include public transit on fixed routes, paratransit, door-to-door service, and volunteer drivers. Again, it is imperative to appreciate the actual experiences of older adults in using these services to ensure that they can be used effectively. Routes may need to be modified to serve preferred destinations; drivers may need to be trained on how to serve older people who might have vision, hearing, and/or movement restrictions. The older adult may need training on how to use transit services. Volunteer drivers may need stipends to cover their out-of-pocket costs. The community planning process can help determine what is needed in a specific community if it engages older adults and seeks to understand their experiences and the challenges they face on a daily basis.

The notion of Complete Streets (Smart Growth America n.d.) is a popular concept involving reconfiguring streets so they serve various transportation modes, including cars, buses, bicyclists, and pedestrians. This planning framework could support older adults as long as their needs are explicitly considered. Thus, it may be necessary to provide for longer walk signals and advance signs that indicate upcoming intersections. Other planning paradigms such as New Urbanism and Neotraditional Development also have the potential for incorporating an aging focus, especially in the extent to which transit alternatives, walkability, and housing diversity are supported. At the same time, it is easy to overlook key considerations. For example, the charming porches of Seaside, Florida, an exemplar of New Urbanism, can serve as barriers for those with disabilities.

While there are many other dimensions of planning that warrant a focus on aging, such as parks and recreation and community facilities, a special note should be made of the importance of a focus on economic development. The aging of society has huge implications for our economy. Some communities are seeking to capitalize on retiree's spending power by encouraging in-migration. Others, such as the previously mentioned Multnomah County, are embracing the value of older adults' continuing contributions to the workforce. Most older adults will have many years of health and vitality in which they will continue to contribute to society. Even when they are on fixed income, they will be spending money and often contributing to society in nonmonetary ways—such as family care and volunteer services. In the extent to which older adults can be recognized as contributors to the economy, the aging of society will be viewed more positively.

This review of planning frameworks within which aging can and should be embedded suggests the extent to which aging as an equity issue should be promoted by the planning profession as a whole and not just a small group of informed planners. Ultimately, consideration of aging issues needs to become the norm and not an outlier. If concepts such as visitability (and preferably universal design) become standard practice, this would then be reflected in all new construction designs. It would allow equity planners to concentrate attention on seizing opportunities to transform the existing environment to become more aging supportive. Such transformation, of course, would need to be ongoing, but the incremental opportunities such as redesigning a bus stop or repurposing a building to serve older adults adds up to a more livable environment in the long run.

Equity planners focused on aging will need to collaborate closely with equity planners who are focused on other issues, such as affordable housing or children. The notion of livable environments should embrace all needs, thus avoiding pitting one perspective against another. A combined child and elder care center, for example, can more efficiently meet multiple needs and in so doing avoid segregation, isolation, and division. The overall goal should be creating inclusive, supportive communities.

One of the challenges of promoting a focus on aging is the extent to which older adults might be missing from the planning process. Mobility limitations and health constraints can place elders and caregivers in survival mode, leaving limited opportunities for community engagement. This reality underscores the importance of equity planners promoting the aging perspective and actively soliciting input from older people to better understand their challenges. This can involve helping healthy, active, older adults anticipate and plan for their changing needs and working with caregivers to enable them to appreciate and articulate the impact of the built environment on their efforts. It can also involve soliciting the views of frail older adults by meeting them on their own turf, whether it be at a senior center, a church, or a home.

Ultimately, aging is a highly personal experience that will be shaped by individual choices. Equity planners can help ensure that there are choices, such as the opportunity to remain in one's home or access to alternative means of mobility when driving is no longer feasible. Attention does need to be given to enabling people to make informed choices; thus, education will always be an important part of planning for aging.

Conclusion

The aging of society is a remarkable time in human history that reflects the sum total of achievements in medicine, public health, and economic prosperity. At the same time, personal, daily struggles play out in built environments that favor the young, wealthy, and mobile. It is ironic that as we grow older, many of us will age into inequity, forced to live in unsupportive environments that exacerbate daily challenges and lower the quality of life. Even older adults with adequate financial resources may find their options severely limited. Many, many people will suffer needlessly.

We can choose to do nothing. In a sense, the "problem" resolves itself as people will eventually die. The more caring and ethical approach is to view aging as a lens through which we can comprehend how the built environment is experienced by individuals over time. This understanding can be translated into principles for guiding the creation of a built environment that is supportive of life as it is actually lived and thus contributes to the creation of healthy, livable, and sustainable communities that would benefit people of all ages.

The question is whether the planning profession has the courage, capacity, and willingness to embrace aging as a planning imperative. To do anything less is a disservice to humanity.

REFERENCES

AARP Livable Communities. 2015. *5 Questions for Charlie Hales.* Washington, DC: AARP. http://www.aarp.org/livable-communities/livable-in-action/info-2015/mayor-charlie-hales-portland-oregon.html.

——. n.d. Website. http://www.aarp.org/livable-communities/.

Administration on Aging (AOA). 2014. *A Profile of Older Americans: 2014.* Washington, DC: Administration on Aging. https://www.acl.gov/sites/default/files/Aging%20and%20Disability%20in%20America/2014-Profile.pdf.

The Age-Friendly Portland Advisory Council. 2013. *Action Plan for an Age-Friendly Portland.* Portland, OR: Portland State University. http://www.pdx.edu/ioa/sites/www.pdx.edu.ioa/files/Age-Friendly%20Portland%20Action%20Plan%2010-8-13_0.pdf.

American Planning Association. 2014. *Aging in Community Policy Guide.* Chicago, IL: American Planning Association. https://www.planning.org/policy/guides/adopted/agingincommunity.htm.

Atlanta Regional Commission (ARC). 2011. *Plan 2040 Framework.* Atlanta, GA: Atlanta Regional Commission. http://documents.atlantaregional.com/plan2040/docs/lu _plan2040_framework_0711.pdf.

———. 2014 *Sweet Auburn Living Beyond Expectations: Tactical Urbanism Demonstration Project Summary Report.* Atlanta, GA: Atlanta Regional Commission.

Atlanta Regional Commission (ARC) Aging and Health Resources Division 2015. *Live Beyond Expectations: Regional Strategic Plan July 2015–2020.* Atlanta, GA: Atlanta Regional Commission. https://atlantaregional.org/wp-content/uploads/2017/03/r egionallivebeyondexpectationsstrategicplan-1.pdf.

Atlanta Regional Commission (ARC) Lifelong Communities. 2009. *Lifelong Communities: A Regional Guide to Growth and Longevity.* Atlanta, GA: Atlanta Regional Commission. https://www.aarp.org/content/dam/aarp/livable-communities/learn /planning/Lifelong-Communities-A-Regional-Guide-to-Growth-and-Longevity -AARP.pdf.

———. n.d. Website. http://www.atlantaregional.com/aging-resources/lifelong-communities.

Brewer, Marcus, Debbie Murillo, and Alan Pate. 2014. *Handbook for Designing Roadways for the Aging Population.* FHWA-SA-14-015. Washington, DC: Federal Highway Administration. http://safety.fhwa.dot.gov/older_users/handbook/.

Center for an Accessible Society, The. 2003. *Nation's First "Visitability" Law Withstands Court Challenge.* San Diego, CA: The Center for an Accessible Society. http://www .accessiblesociety.org/topics/housing/pimacoruling.html.

City of Philadelphia. 2011. *The Philadelphia Code: Zoning and Planning.* Cincinnati, OH: American Legal Publishing Corporation. http://library.amlegal.com/library/pa /philadelphia.shtml.

City of Philadelphia Department of Public Health. 2010. *Philadelphia2035: Planning and Zoning for a Healthier City.* Philadelphia, PA: City of Philadelphia.

City of Philadelphia Planning Commission. 2011a. *Philadelphia2035: Citywide Vision.* Philadelphia, PA: City of Philadelphia. https://www.phila2035.org/citywide-vision.

———. 2011b. *Philadelphia2035: South District Plan.* Philadelphia, PA: City of Philadelphia.

City of Portland. 2012. *The Portland Plan.* Portland, OR: The City of Portland. http://www .portlandonline.com/portlandplan/index.cfm?c=58776.

Clark, Kate. 2015. Planner for Policy and Program Development, Philadelphia Corporation on Aging. Phone interview, September 11.

Cooper, David, and Elise Gould. 2013. *Financial Security of Elderly Americans at Risk.* Washington, DC: Economic Policy Institute. http://www.epi.org/files/2013/financial -security-elderly-americans-risk.pdf.

Creamer, Anita. 2012. "Childless boomers wonder who will handle their long-term care," *Sacramento Bee,* November 13. http://www.mcclatchydc.com/news/nation-world /national/economy/article24740179.html.

Davidoff, Paul. 1965. "Advocacy and Pluralism in Planning," *Journal of the American Institute of Planners* 31 (4): 331–38.

Davis, Keith. 2015. Healthy Communities Coordinator, Philadelphia City Planning Commission. Phone interview, September 18.

DeLaTorre, Alan. 2015. Research Associate, Institute on Aging, Portland State University. Personal interview, September 26.

DeLaTorre, Alan, and Margaret Neal. 2014. *Aging and Equity in the Greater Portland Metropolitan Region.* Portland, OR: Coalition for a Livable Future. https://pdxscholar .library.pdx.edu/aging_pub/8/.

Dougherty, Chris. 2015. Project Manager, Fairmount Park Conservancy. Phone interview, September 17.

Federal Interagency Forum on Aging-Related Statistics. 2012. *Older Americans 2012: Key Indicators of Well-Being.* Washington, DC: Federal Interagency Forum on Aging-Related Statistics. U.S. Government Printing Office. https://agingstats.gov/docs /pastreports/2012/oa2012.pdf.

Feldman, Penny, Mia Oberlink, Elisabeth Simontov, and Michal Gursen. 2004. *A Tale of Two Older Americas: Community Opportunities and Challenges. AdvantAge Initiative: 2003 National Survey of Adults Aged 65 and Older.* New York City: Center for Home Care Policy Research, Visiting Nurse Services of New York.

Foley, Daniel, Harley Heimovitz, Jack Guralnik, and Dwight Brock. 2002. "Driving Life Expectancy of Persons Aged 70 Years and Older in the United States," *American Journal of Public Health* 92 (8): 1284–89.

Gawande, Atul. 2014. *Being Mortal: Medicine and What Matters in the End.* New York: Metropolitan Books.

GenPhilly. n.d. Website. http://www.genphilly.org/.

Huang, Yuan, and Mary Horstmann. 2012 *World Health Organization: Global Age-Friendly Cities: Assessment of Philadelphia.* Philadelphia, PA: Mayor's Office of Policy Planning and Development. http://www.phila.gov/aging/Documents /Age%20Friendly%20Cities%20Assessment%202.7.13.pdf.

Keenan, Teresa. 2010. *Home and Community Preferences of the 45+ Population.* Washington, DC: AARP Research and Strategic Analysis. http://assets.aarp.org/rgcenter /general/home-community-services-10.pdf.

Law, Steve. 2015. "Code changes could boost the number of ADUs," *The Portland Tribune,* September 22. http://portlandtribune.com/pt/9-news/273749–146747-code -changes-could-boost-number-of-adus.

Lawler, Kathryn. 2015. Aging and Health Resources Division Manager, Atlanta Regional Planning Commission. Phone interview, conducted jointly with interview of R. Ray, September 24.

Lindland, Eric, Marissa Fond, Abigail Haydon, and Nathaniel Kendall-Taylor. 2015. *Gauging Aging: Mapping the Gaps Between Expert and Public Understandings of Aging in America.* Washington, DC: FrameWorks Institute. http://archstone.org/docs /resources/Guaging_Aging_mtg.pdf.

Metropolitan Council (St. Paul, MN). n.d. Website. http://www.metrocouncil.org /Communities/Services/Livable-Communities-Grants.aspx.

Mullahey, Ramona. 2015. Senior Analyst—Field Policy and Management, U.S. Department of Housing and Urban Development, Honolulu Field Office. Phone interview, August 24.

Multnomah County Task Force on Vital Aging. 2008. *Everyone Matters: A Practical Guide to Building a Community for All Ages.* Portland, OR: Multnomah County. https:// www.pdx.edu/ioa/sites/www.pdx.edu.ioa/files/VitalAging2008.pdf.

National Association of Area Agencies on Aging (N4A). 2011. *The Maturing of American: Getting Communities on Track for an Aging Population.* Washington, DC: National Association of Area Agencies on Aging. http://www.livable.org/storage/documents /reports/AIP/maturing_of_america.pdf.

——. n.d. Website. http://www.n4a.org/livablecommunities.

National Council on Independent Living (NCIL). n.d. "Is Visibility Legal?" Visibility.org. https://visitability.org/policy-strategies/is-visitability-legal/.

Neal, Margaret. 2015. Director of Institute on Aging, Professor of Community Health, Portland State University. Personal interview, August 28.

Neal, Margaret, and Alan DeLaToree. n.d. *The World Health Organization's Age-Friendly Cities Project in Portland, Oregon: Summary of Findings.* Portland, OR: Portland

State University, Institute on Aging. https://www.pdx.edu/sites/www.pdx.edu.ioa/files/ioa_who_summaryoffindings.pdf.

Newport Partners. 2013. *Home Fire Sprinkler Cost Assessment—2013 Final Report.* Quincy, MA: The Fire Protection Research Foundation. http://homefiresprinkler.org/wp-content/uploads/2016/05/HomeFireSprinklerCostAssessment2013.pdf.

Nutter, Michael A. 2011. *Mayor's Commission on Aging: Strategic Plan 2011–13.* Philadelphia: Mayor's Commission on Aging. http://www.phila.gov/aging/Documents/MCOA%20Strategic%20Plan.pdf.

Olivero, Magaly. 2015. "Doctor shortage: Who will take care of the elderly?" *US News and World Report*, April 21. http://health.usnews.com/health-news/patient-advice/articles/2015/04/21/doctor-shortage-who-will-take-care-of-the-elderly.

Ortman, Jennifer, and Victoria Velkoff. 2014. *An Aging Nation: The Older Population in the United States.* Current Population Reports P25–1140. Washington, DC: U.S. Department of Commerce, U.S. Census Bureau. http://homefiresprinkler.org/wp-content/uploads/2016/05/HomeFireSprinklerCostAssessment2013.pdf.

Partners for Livable Communities. n.d. Website. http://www.livable.org/program-areas/livable-communities-for-all-ages-a-aging-in-place/overview.

Pew Research Center. 2014. *Attitudes about Aging: A Global Perspective.* Washington, DC: Pew Research Center. http://www.pewglobal.org/2014/01/30/attitudes-about-aging-a-global-perspective/.

Philadelphia Corporation for Aging (PCA). 2011. *Laying the Foundation for an Age-Friendly Philadelphia: A Progress Report.* Philadelphia, PA: Philadelphia Corporation on Aging. http://www.pcacares.org/wp-content/uploads/2016/01/PCA_Age-Friendly_WhitePaper_web.pdf.

Ray, Renee. 2015. Principal Program Specialist, Area Agency on Aging, Atlanta Regional Planning Commission. Phone interview, conducted jointly with interview of K. Lawler, September 24.

Smart Growth America. n.d. "What Are Complete Streets?" Washington, DC: Smart Growth America. https://smartgrowthamerica.org/program/national-complete-streets-coalition/what-are-complete-streets/.

U.S. Census Bureau. 2005. *American Housing Survey for the United States: 2005.* Current Housing Reports Series H150/05. Washington, DC: U.S. Census Bureau. http://www.census.gov/prod/2006pubs/h150-05.pdf.

——. n.d. "2014 National Population Projections Tables." https://www.census.gov/data/tables/2014/demo/popproj/2014-summary-tables.html; https://www.census.gov/population/projections/data/national/2014/summarytables.html.

Vincent, Grayson, and Victoria Velkoff. 2010. *The Next Four Decades: The Older Population in the United States: 2010–2050.* Current Population Reports. P25–1138. Washington, DC: U.S. Census Bureau. https://www.census.gov/prod/2010pubs/p25-1138.pdf.

Winick, Brad, and Martin Jaffe. 2015. *Planning Aging-Supportive Communities.* PAS Report No. 579. Chicago: American Planning Association.

World Health Organization (WHO). 2007. *Global Age-Friendly Cities: A Guide.* Geneva: World Health Organization. http://apps.who.int/iris/bitstream/10665/43755/1/9789241547307_eng.pdf.

Yin, Jordan. 2015. Director of Undergraduate Programs, Levin College of Urban Affairs, Cleveland State University. E-mail correspondence with Norm Krumholz, May 19.

Section 4

LOOKING TO THE FUTURE

10

THE FUTURE OF EQUITY PLANNING EDUCATION IN THE UNITED STATES

Kenneth Reardon and John Forester

In this chapter, we address the origin and the possible future of equity planning. Working in cities characterized by inequalities and power differences along lines of class, race, gender, and more, equity planners have struggled for decades to translate lessons about political structure and organization into specific, useful practices serving ends of social justice. In so doing, equity planners have integrated concerns with the "ends" or "outcomes" of social justice with the "process" skills and interactive techniques of organizing and coalition building. They have engaged sensitively and productively with "difference" and listened critically not only to learn, to honor community history, and to respect community partners but also not least of all to get results.

In addition, we will suggest that learning to use social media will matter. Studying urban communities ethnographically via area studies will matter. Examining and rejecting racial privilege will matter. Coalition building by mediating differing interests and values will matter. Organizing and problem solving with others in participatory action research will matter. Equity planners will have to assess both the written texts of researchers as well as the lived texts of community members. They will have to learn about potential outcomes and practices, about both goals and methods, about ideals of social justice, as well as about grounded methods of paying respect and building working relationships with community partners, too.

The Origins and Precedents of Equity Planning

Deeply influenced by the civil rights movement and his Cornell planning education, Norm Krumholz assumed his position as Cleveland's Director of Planning in 1969 with a strong commitment to redistributive policies aimed at improving living conditions for the city's long-suffering African American population. He quickly assembled a talented staff that included Ernie Bonner, Janice Cogger, John Linner, Doug Wright, Susan Olson, and Joanne Lazarz—all of whom shared his commitment to working for social justice within the city and the region.

In 1974, Krumholz and his colleagues produced the landmark Cleveland Policy Plan, a document designed to achieve the following goal: "In a context of limited resources, the Cleveland City Planning Commission will give priority attention to the task of promoting a wider range of choices for those individuals and groups who have few, if any, choices." This plan, along with the Chicago Policy Plan produced by Louis Wetmore and his staff, challenged mainstream planning thought and practice by incorporating significant economic and community development proposals into planning documents that had historically focused more narrowly on physical development. In addition, these plans explicitly addressed the question of who benefited from municipal policymaking and planning.

Between 1969 and 1979 Krumholz and his staff worked with passion, persistence, and creativity with allies inside and outside of city hall to advance policies and plans aimed at expanding employment and business opportunities for low-income communities of color. Through the mayoral administrations of Carl Stokes, Ralph Perk, and Dennis Kucinich, Krumholz's planners challenged public subsidies for downtown developments that produced few jobs and little tax revenue. They questioned proposals to increase commuter rail service at the expense of local bus service while negotiating service guarantees and fare reductions for the transit dependent. They struggled to expand affordable housing and changed state law and administrative responsibilities regarding delinquent housing. They also supported land-banking projects in the city's most distressed neighborhoods and advocated cleaning up Cleveland's extensive parks.

The Cleveland equity planners focused research to highlight the distributional effects of current and proposed city policies and projects. They cultivated networks of sympathetic elected and appointed officials. They built coalitions with small business owners, corporate leaders, foundation executives, suburban influentials, and urban affairs writers. They encouraged investment in the city's rapidly expanding community development sector. In all these ways Krumholz and his staff created a significant base of nonpartisan political support inside and outside of local government for redistributive polices that represented a serious alternative to the urban renewal policies of Cleveland's Growth Machine.

Equity Planning's Influence within Planning Education

Norman Krumholz's record of accomplishment and subsequent books, articles, and lectures reflecting on his equity planning efforts in Cleveland encouraged several generations of American planning educators to feature his work in their introduction to planning and planning theory classes. This exposure, in turn, generated widespread student demand for classes offering "hands-on" experience working with public agencies and community-based organizations that advocated redistributive policies and participatory decision-making processes aimed at improving conditions within poor and working-class communities.

During the past four decades, an overwhelming majority of U.S. planning schools have established equity-planning-oriented workshops, studios, and internship programs. These efforts have prepared students for leadership positions within municipal governments and community organizations that are committed to expanding economic opportunities and enhancing the quality of life for the urban poor. Many of these field-based teaching and learning experiences were organized by prominent planning scholars, including but not limited to Rachel Bratt, Lisa Peattie, Marie Kennedy, Marcia Marker Feld, Pierre Clavel, Peter Marcuse, Ron Shiffman, Rob Mier, Dennis Keating, Al Hahn, Ed Blakely, Michael Dear, and Jackie Leavitt. Many more were affiliated with Planners for Equal Opportunity and The Planners Network. Together their projects and scholarship helped to establish equity-oriented fieldwork as an essential element of mainstream planning education.

During this period, a range of innovative and "best practices" in equity planning education have emerged from the most successful of these fieldwork efforts, some of which are included below:

- A focus on the organizing, research, planning, design, and development needs of the *poorest neighborhoods* within metropolitan regions;
- The commitment to actively engage university students and local stakeholders in the cooperative collection and analysis of the *primary data* needed to prepare high-quality and impactful plans;
- An emphasis on exposing students to the extraordinary work carried out by *long-time community activists* who have successfully designed and implemented innovative revitalization projects—projects that respond to critical community needs in the context of serious resource limitations and significant opposition from powerful local elites;

- A shift away from what William F. Whyte described as the professional-expert model of practice in favor of a *participatory action research model* of practice that involves local actors as co-investigators with university-trained professionals at every step of the planning process;
- A discipline of *ongoing critical reflection* on these cooperative community-building, problem-solving, and neighborhood revitalization planning efforts by participating community residents, students, and faculty, with the goal of improving the theory and practice of community-based planning;
- A trend toward *structuring more sustained forms of community engagement*, enabling students and faculty to acquire a deeper understanding of the complex forces that contributed to neighborhood decline as well as the always-challenging politics and management of plan implementation processes needed for their recovery; and,
- A commitment to *shared risk and mutual benefit* among community and community partners.

Reconsidering the Importance of Equity Planning

At the same time, recent trends and events have contributed to very high levels of frustration and anger among residents—especially youth—in our nation's low-income communities of color. Among these are the anemic and uneven recovery that has failed to restore the economic security of millions of poor and working-class Americans; the growing income, wealth, and power disparities that are creating further social distance between the haves and the have-nots in our society; and the rash of police-involved shooting of unarmed African American youth. As increasing numbers of African American youth have joined local and national protest movements through groups such as Black Lives Matter, leaders of many mainstream business, political, media, civic, and service organizations have either appeared indifferent to these concerns or engaged in various forms of "victim blaming," attributing the increasingly marginal economic and political position of African Americans in our society to flaws in their culture. Such responses have, in many cases, significantly deepened the alienation and anger that many African American youth feel toward mainstream institutions such as local businesses, government, universities, and, in some cases, even established civil rights organizations.

In many low-income African American communities, the level of frustration, anger, and rage has reached heights not seen since the pre-urban uprising period of the mid-1960s, when street violence erupted in dozens of America cities—among them Rochester, Newark, Detroit, and Los Angeles—prompting President Lyndon B. Johnson to appoint a national commission to investigate the causes of this violence.

An exhaustive study of existing social conditions in the African American neighborhoods of these and other American cities prompted the authors of the federally appointed National Advisory Commission on Civil Disorders (better known as the Kerner Commission) to conclude, "Our nation is moving toward two societies, one black, one white—separate and unequal." Published in 1968, this landmark report documented the pervasive nature of racial injustice in American society and called for massive new spending on education, workforce development, housing, and human service programs to expand opportunities for residents of our nation's low-income communities of color. The Kerner Commission also asked for new programs designed to promote greater racial diversity and multicultural sensitivity among the nation's overwhelmingly white police forces— especially those serving minority neighborhoods.

Sadly, available funding for these domestic social programs soon evaporated due, in large part, to the mounting costs of the Vietnam War. Decades later, on the thirtieth anniversary of the Kerner Commission Report's publication, the Eisenhower Foundation funded two studies by former U.S. Senator and Kerner Commission member Fred Harris. These reports documented how early successes in addressing high levels of concentrated poverty following the urban uprisings of the late 1960s had been undermined over time by a series of global economic shocks and misguided government policies. Senator Harris argued, "Today, thirty years after the Kerner Report, there is more poverty in America, it is deeper, blacker, and browner than before, and it is more concentrated in the cities, which have become America's poorhouses" (Harris and Curtis 2000).

Nearly twenty years following the publication of the Eisenhower Foundation-supported Millennium Report and its Locked in the Poorhouse program evaluation study that documented the pervasive and corrosive effect of unexamined racism in our society, economic and social conditions in a large number of low-income communities of color have further deteriorated. This has created "tinderbox-like" conditions that rival those of the mid- to late-1960s. The stark insight of James Baldwin, the African American novelist, echoes once again. In his book *The Fire Next Time,* Baldwin warned us of the end of the American dream in his powerful statement on American race relations: "The Negroes of this country may never be able to rise to power, but they are very well placed indeed to precipitate chaos and bring down the curtain on the American dream" (Baldwin 1963).

In our current context of increasing disparities and tensions between white and non-white Americans, Norm Krumholz's equity-oriented planning philosophy and methods can serve as a critical, nonviolent pathway to a more just and democratic urban America. It offers planners, designers, administrators, and elected officials—who seek a constructive strategy to address the consequences of white privilege—a set of values, policies, procedures, and techniques to respond to the problem of persistent and intensifying racial inequality in our cities. However, faculty seeking to prepare students to apply the lessons learned from Krumholz's equity-oriented planning experiences in Cleveland will need to consider a number of important ways that American cities have changed since 1975. Among the most important of these changes are:

- dramatic increases in racial, ethnic, and religious diversity;
- a significant rise in the percentage of new and undocumented immigrants;
- heightened levels of suspicion and tension between whites and non-white residents;
- greater skepticism regarding government's ability to effectively promote positive change;
- growing numbers and concentrations of poor families in older residential areas of the central city as well as inner-ring suburbs;
- a decline in the power of locally owned and operated businesses, including media, relative to the power of absentee-owned, multinational corporations;
- steep declines in the size, power, and influence of urban institutions with a history of advocacy on behalf of the poor (faith-based organizations, trade unions, and civil rights and citizen organizations such as the Association of Community Organizations for Reform Now [ACORN]); and
- an explosion in the power and influence of social media to shape public policy agendas on the local, state, national, and international levels of governance.

New Directions for Equity Planning Education

These and other important differences distinguish metropolitan regions of the mid-1970s—when Krumholz and his colleagues were struggling to transform Cleveland's urban policy landscape—from today's urban context. This suggests the need for a significantly new approach to the education of the next generation of equity-inspired planning. We suggest that this approach must feature several new and/or modified elements.

1. Krumholz's work in Cleveland's city hall suggests that we need a far more sophisticated attitude toward applied research in equity planning contexts. If the early twentieth-century Progressive Era had a tradition of detached experts finding solutions for a waiting and needy public, the late twentieth century overthrew that paternalistic, one-directional, expert-knows-best, engineering-based "technical assistance model." Krumholz and his chief of staff Ernie Bonner provided evidence again and again that applied research depends on a partnership between the public and experts and between experts and users. Krumholz networked with agencies and diverse coalitions, and Bonner produced technical analysis well targeted as a result—for the mayor, for other city departments, and not least of all for the press. This essential requirement of partnership implies that equity planning students must understand that their expertise needs always to be organized not independently of users but in response to them, not done "for" but done "with," not to be autonomous but to be accountable to community members or other city users.

2. This suggests that equity planning is more about partnership and cogenerated research than about hit-and-run "missionary work." This implies, in turn, that a solid *introduction to urban ethnography* must prepare future equity planners to effectively enter and establish close and respectful working relationships with long-time community residents and leaders representing cultural identity groups different from their own.

Using their ethnographic training in informal and formal interviewing and participant observation, future equity planners will be better able to acquire an insider's view of the all too often "taken-for-granted" understandings and rules that enable community members to sustain the social organization and human dynamics of their neighborhoods. Using these and other field-based research methods to gain a deeper understanding of how local communities function, future equity planners will subsequently be able to validate their newly acquired community knowledge with a small core of trusted "key informants" who can confirm, modify, or reject their preliminary understanding of community structures and dynamics, thereby laying the foundation for much more historically and contextually sensitive planning interventions. Students can be introduced to the fundamental principles, methods, and ethics of urban ethnography through lectures and seminar courses. However, mastery of these methods can only be attained through repeated practice in field settings supervised by community leaders and university faculty skilled in facilitating cooperative inquiry across the formidable divides of race, class, gender, ethnicity, and religion in cities and regions.

3. Ethnographic methods involve not just collecting information, of course, but understanding what matters, understanding hopes as well as fears, specific interests as well as deeper values. In equity planning contexts, students are challenged to understand histories of inequality and racism—histories that make "planners" objects of suspicion before they can prove themselves as the allies they might be. Ethnography must turn inward toward the university too, challenging the histories of taken-for-granted privilege and antiseptic but authoritative expertise. Privilege depends, as James Baldwin classically put it, on its not needing to be confronted every day by those who enjoy it. When whiteness is normalized, the historically constructed privileges of where one can live, study, and find work become transparent, and the focus shifts to what can be done "for" people of color. But what of that violent history of the construction of privilege?

So, our courses must explicitly address unexamined white privilege and institutional racism within the planning profession in ways that will focus needed attention on the role that racial, class, and gender-biased policies play in denying poor and working-class communities of color meaningful participation in the economic, social, political, and cultural life of metropolitan America. Rather than give serious consideration to the structural barriers to equal opportunity that limit the life chances of poor people of color, many white Americans readily embrace the so-called "culture of poverty" as an explanation for the growing achievement and quality-of-life gap separating white and black Americans. Having identified various attitudinal and behavioral patterns central to African American culture (complicating what Ruby Payne describes as "pathways out of poverty"), many white policymakers essentially advocate self-help approaches to the elimination of poverty in low-income communities of color. Ruby Payne—as well as other increasingly popular antipoverty consultants—is often hired by networks of local foundations. These foundations routinely ignore the Kerner Commission's and Millennium Report's advice to seek a meaningful solution to persistent poverty by focusing on unexamined racism and institutional bias within the majority culture rather than continuing our overwhelming focus on the so-called pathologies of African American community life.

The case is similar for the arrogant presumptions of expertise. Planning students must be familiar not only with the work of Donald Schön but also with that of the Brazilian popular educator, Paolo Freire. Schön rejected a narrow technical rationality because he knew that expertise alone would short circuit the "reflective practice" of learning in action that he had extended so powerfully from John Dewey. Freire took a still more practical approach. He criticized the "banking model" of the technical assistance ideal ("We experts have the answers, and we will deposit them into your heads!") and he proposed instead a critical dialogic model of "problem posing" and joint problem solving instead.

But, anticipating a wide swath of social and political theory, Freire did more when he tied together everyday structural conditions of inequality with our ordinary abilities to learn and talk freely about our lives. In so doing, he radicalized what Dewey had done in his prescient *The Public and Its Problems* (1927). So Freire wrote, "Any situation in which some men prevent others from engaging in the process of inquiry is one of violence" (Freire 1970, 73). Freire writes here as a planning educator—one concerned not with service delivery but with poor people's own abilities to improve their lives. Freire's criticism of "banking education" is also a devastating criticism of the hit-and-run planning consultant's report and a criticism of the use of expertise that obstructs rather than promotes joint problem-solving processes or community-based problem solving—be it via participatory action research, via organizing for resident-driven problem solving, or via community responsive public planning processes.

We know all too well the problems of technical work. It can be wonderfully done, but it can be done too late to make a difference. We know too much about reports that lay unused on shelves and about results produced for research agencies that are never translated into efforts to improve community welfare. Too often the technical operation is a success, but the patient dies. Equity planning must address how the culture and institutions of planning education risk reproducing an isolated technical rigor, even as they more subtly reproduce a selective inattention to race, legacies of institutional racism, and opportunities for new partnerships.

So in post-Katrina New Orleans, for example, a community-university partnership with ACORN (a leading national, activist, grassroots citizens organization) assured that good technical analysis gained the ear of political officials (Reardon and Forester 2016). In ambitious equity-oriented community mapping initiatives as far away as Sicily, Laura Saija and Guisy Pappalardo found that partnerships with local officials allowed innovative river mapping and community development initiatives to take hold and not to remain on paper alone (Saija, De Leo, and Forester 2017). And so we see too what Lily Song powerfully calls, in the community development contexts of Cleveland and Los Angeles, "coalitional work"—among, for example, organizers, planners, foundation staff, CDCs, city staff, and others (Song 2016)—that extend ideas of partnership, collaboration, and even participatory action research. Future equity planners can be prepared for the often-challenging work of building popular bases of citizen and institutional support for redistributional policies and plans through coursework on grassroots social movements, urban politics and governance, and theories and methods of social change and internships—including project-oriented experiential learning classes with community organizations, issue coalitions, policy institutes, elected officials, and legislative bodies actively engaged in efforts to reduce poverty and regional inequality.

The curriculum of equity planning programs must *incorporate strong area studies* components to more effectively prepare planners for practice in increasingly diverse neighborhoods, cities, and regions. Area study programs systematically introduce students to the origins, evolution, and contemporary state of significant cultural identity groups in our society; groups with whom too many planning students may have had little or no previous contact and/or knowledge. This is especially important given the frequently distorted presentation that the history, culture, and folkways of these groups often receive from traditional and social media outlets.

While planning theory emphasizes the importance of considering a community's history and culture when developing policies and plans, few planning programs challenge their professional students to acquire a deeper understanding of African American, Latino/Latina American, Asian American, and Native American communities with whom they will be working by asking them to incorporate a concentration or specialization in one of these areas into their program of study. The increasing diversity and hyper-segregation of our cities and regions, along with the current generation's lack of familiarity with the social movements of the 1960s that sought to advance the civil rights of these groups, requires us to significantly reduce this knowledge gap. In Courtney Knapp's account of equity planning and participatory action research in Chattanooga, for example, we see community-based planning efforts in partnerships with public institutions like the public library, all done in the explicit context of the racialized history of African American and Native American community struggles in the city (Knapp 2018).

Planning history and theory courses can be modified to highlight plans that base their analysis of existing conditions and vision for the future on a detailed study and analysis of the history and culture of important yet all too often marginalized identity groups. In northern Montana, for example, Salish and Kootenai tribe planners successfully challenged a state highway-widening project by demonstrating how human mobility was being enhanced at the expense of culturally significant wildlife (bison, moose, elk, foxes, and coyote). They countered the state's highway-widening plan with proposals to enhance existing mobility options for wildlife through the construction of new underpasses, causing the state to reevaluate their initial highway proposal (Reardon 2005).

Graduate planning programs can also work together to identify, collect, and share plans that propose unique solutions to common urban problems that reflect the unique cultural values, insights, and practices of marginalized identity groups. Petra Doan's work on the contribution that LBGTQ communities and queer sensitive plans have made toward stabilizing Ybor City and other parts of Tampa offers another example of how nonmajority cultural identity groups can expand the policy tools and practices of those seeking to stabilize and revitalize economically challenged neighborhoods (Doan 2015).

We must provide equity-minded planning students with *a more rigorous introduction to the ever-changing and increasingly complex nature of urban and metropolitan politics.* This is especially important given the dramatic decline in the relative power and influence of many of the traditional urban institutions, including inner-city churches, municipal unions, fraternal organizations, and the Democratic Party—groups that once provided the political base of support for planning within cities. The increasing political power of suburban and exurban cities, towns, and villages relative to central cities within many metropolitan regions provide another reason for reform-minded planners to have enhanced power analysis, community organizing, and coalition-building understanding and skills. Just as white outer suburbs threatened massive housing destruction and population displacement to put a freeway through Cleveland's African American neighborhoods, challenges of these types in urban and suburban politics were central concerns to Krumholz's staff in their equity planning efforts in Cleveland (Krumholz and Forester 1990, Sugrue 2005).

There is another reason why equity-oriented planners of tomorrow will need to have excellent political analysis and organizing skills. There have been attacks on public planning both by Tea Party leaders who have used the U.S.'s endorsement of UN Urban Agenda 21 to argue that local planning is now being influenced by sinister international forces and by Tactical Urbanism leaders who question the efficiency and effectiveness of municipally sponsored planning activities. The work of organizing partnerships and coalitions and mobilizing participation has many faces: overcoming distrust, learning in one-to-one conversations and interviews, relationship building across organizational boundaries, coalition building, finding allies and supporters, working with the press, and much, much more. What appears in planning theory as "communicative planning" in the work of Patsy Healey and Judith Innes can appear to skirt problems of power and conflict, both structurally in the settings of urban politics and in the innards of public participation and even participatory action research. Planning students must also study work assessing community organizing, social movements, and urban regime theories, as in work of Boyte (1980), Tarrow (1994), Castells (1983, 298–63), Fainstein and Fainstein (1994), and Stone (2005) (cf. Sugrue 2005, Reardon and Forester 2016). But in linking studies of collaborative planning and relationship building with those of systematic inequality and power structures we find a third strand of literature that reaches from Dewey (1927) to Alinsky (1971)—both paying explicit and critical attention to "communication"—to Davidoff (1965) to Andre Gorz (1968) to Freire (1970) to Krumholz (Krumholz and Forester 1990) to Reardon (Reardon and Forester 2016; cf. Forester 1999, Song 2016, and Knapp 2018).

Addressing the Institutions of Planning Education

All this has implications for the structure and composition of institutions for planning education. A *new commitment to student and faculty diversity by the Association of Collegiate Schools of Planning (ACSP) and its member schools* is needed to encourage more critical reflection on the origins, nature, scope, and consequences of the uneven pattern of development, hyper-segregation, and concentrated poverty increasingly characterizing our major metropolitan regions. Such reflection is less likely to occur within a homogenous community of scholars where multiple perspectives based on the differing "positionalities" of racial, ethnic, and cultural backgrounds are not present. The underrepresentation of African American, Latino/Latina American, Asian American, and Native Americans within the student bodies and teaching faculties of our graduate planning schools denies those teaching and studying at these institutions the deep historical and cultural knowledge and insights that these individuals possess of their communities—the same communities that are the focus of a significant amount of contemporary planning. The absence of individuals from underrepresented minority groups from the teams pursuing campus-sponsored urban research and planning in nonwhite communities also reduces the likelihood that local residents and leaders will contribute to such efforts, and that hard-earned distrust and distance will continue to significantly complicate the task of developing thoughtful policy and planning interventions. The absence of individuals from underrepresented minority groups from university-supported research teams also reduces the likelihood that residents and leaders of the communities being "studied" will accept their findings and recommendations, regardless of the quality of the work.

A concerted effort is needed to *encourage the discipline's major peer-reviewed journals to give greater consideration to articles that address the corrosive effect of unexamined racial, class, and gender bias and conflict on contemporary professional practice.* There has been a significant drop in the number of research articles examining issues of racial, class, and gender in our profession's major scholarly journals despite the current level of social tension and conflict evident in our cities and the growing number of manuscripts addressing these issues being submitted by our field's slowly expanding number of scholars of color. This situation has two negative impacts on the training of future equity planners. First, many younger planning scholars of color, in response to repeated rejections by mainline planning journals of their articles addressing racial, class, and gender bias in the profession, increasingly choose to publish these articles in urban affairs, public administration, social work, and area studies journals. However, when these scholars are going through their third- and/or fourth-year review as part of the tenure process, these "nonplanning" publications can be heavily discounted by many promotion and tenure committees, placing their careers at risk. Second, the profession's failure to publish articles that address the negative impact that racism and other forms of discrimination is having upon the planning efforts of low-income communities and the professionals who work with them leaves future equity-oriented planners less well prepared for the messy and often-unpredictable work of practice. A partial response to this situation would be the establishment of a high-quality journal focused on the intersection of critical race theory and planning—which members of ACSP's Planners of Color Interest Group and Planners Network have been discussing.

ACSP, in partnership with the American Planning Association (APA), could work with ACSP's Planners on Color Interest Group and APA's Planning and the Black Community and Indigenous Planning Divisions to *produce a series of books highlighting the many contributions of Native American, African American, and Latino/Latina planners and planning organizations to our communities and field.* These volumes would expand the access current and future planners have to inspired stories of community preservation, stabilization, and redevelopment based in the history, cultural, and community practices of often-overlooked cultural identity groups. These volumes could make an important contribution to equity planners' efforts to promote more diverse and democratic approaches to contemporary planning.

Not least of all, we should not underestimate the increasing importance of social media and mobile communication devices. *Equity-oriented planners seeking to design and implement highly effective strategic and/or comprehensive planning processes will need to understand and use social media, perhaps in wholly new forms of communicative planning, to promote participation in traditional citizen participation activities and to complement face-to-face processes with those that are virtual/asynchronous.* In doing so, they must consider the uneven nature of access to the Internet and the different levels of comfort and skill that various cultural identity groups have with its use.

An interesting use of social media included the collection and analysis of e-mail, Facebook, Twitter, and Instagram activity by residents participating in a Smart Cities Project, cosponsored by the city of Siracusa in Sicily, IBM, and the United Nations. This effort generated a rich set of data regarding local stakeholders' assessment of current conditions and visions for the future. It also subsequently mobilized scores of local residents to work together on a wide range of community revitalization projects in the absence of the large grant they had initially come together to pursue.

Advancing Equity Planning Pedagogy

Planning educators committed to preparing the next generation of inspired equity planners need to train their students to "listen eloquently," as Myles Horton suggested, to the hopes and aspirations of the people with whom they are working. Once they have been introduced to various critical listening and in-depth interviewing strategies developed by W. F. Whyte and others, they should be exposed to a wide range of citizen participation techniques aimed at building organizational and community consensus regarding the kinds of transformational change local stakeholders seek (Forester 2006). These skills are every bit as important for planners who are activists within the bureaucracy. They must build networks with others who have equity-serving agendas in public, private, or nonprofit organizations. Those networks are the infrastructure of equity planning—they make learning and access possible by sharing information and cultivating trusted relationships. All that establishes a basis, in turn, for ad hoc coalitions that can form as different issues arise on local planning agendas (Krumholz and Forester 1990, Reardon 1993).

Armed with a clear sense of local stakeholders' preferred development policies, plans, programs, and projects, equity planners can then be prepared to assist local leaders in identifying and recruiting traditional and nontraditional allies willing to support resident-led change. They can then be trained to support, co-design, and implement public interest-oriented projects or campaigns using a wide array of skills, strategies, and techniques; such techniques can range, for example, from social media to direct action organizing methods to encourage elected and appointed officials across the ideological spectrum to support revitalization plans promoting more balanced and sustainable forms of growth.

By studying and adapting, drawing from and refining time-tested community organizing techniques pioneered by Saul Alinsky, Fred Ross, Caesar Chavez, Wade Rathke, and others, the next generation of equity planners should be probing and contributing to their own theory building in organizational change and management. Both literatures and training related to organizing and to negotiation inform grounded practices in the face of power (Reardon and Forester 2016). Experiences of participatory action research and multistakeholder facilitative leadership can strengthen each other and contribute to the equity-oriented leadership of community-based organizations, municipal departments, regional planning agencies, and public/private partnerships engaged in implementing redistributive policies and participatory planning processes.

The growing influence of "limited government" ideas will also require the emerging generation of equity planners to be well trained in grantsmanship, grassroots fundraising, and crowdsourcing methods to secure the resources to "pilot" innovative economic and community development ideas. Not least of all, these equity planning leaders will have to be well trained in participatory approaches to program monitoring and evaluation to help local leaders refine those economic and community development ideas that may really contribute to improving the quality of life in too often overlooked, underresourced communities.

Conclusion

After nearly four decades, student and faculty interest in equity planning remains strong throughout the United States and in many parts of Europe, especially in Sicily. While the initial principles of good practice for equity planning education that emerged in the period immediately following Krumholz's work in Cleveland (as outlined in the early part of this chapter) were effective in preparing reform-minded planning students for this work in the 1980s and 1990s, American cities and regions have undergone significant changes requiring the development of refined approaches to the education and training of future generations of equity planners—a goal to which this chapter seeks to contribute.

REFERENCES

Alinsky, Saul. 1971. *Rules for Radicals: A Pragmatic Primer for Realistic Radicals.* New York: Vintage.

Baldwin, James. 1963. *The Fire Next Time.* New York: Dial Press.

Boyte, Harry C. 1980. *The Backyard Revolution.* Philadelphia, PA: Temple University Press.

Castells, Manuel. 1983. *The City and the Grassroots: A Cross Cultural Theory of Urban Social Movements.* Berkeley: The University of California Press.

Davidoff, Paul. 1965. "Advocacy and Pluralism in Planning," *Journal of the American Institute of Planners* 31 (4): 103–14.

Dewey, John. 1927. *The Public and Its Problems.* New York: Swallow Press.

Doan, P.L., ed. 2015. *Planning and LGBTQ Communities: The Need for Inclusive Queer Spaces.* London: Routledge.

Fainstein, Susan S., and Norman Fainstein. 1994. "Urban regimes and racial conflict." In *Managing Divided Cities,* edited by Seamus Dunn, 141–59. London: Keele University Press.

Forester, John. 1999. *The Deliberative Practitioner.* Cambridge: MIT Press.

Forester, John. 2006. "Policy Analysis as Critical Listening." In *Oxford Handbook of Public Policy,* edited by R. Goodin, M. Moran, M. Rein, 124–51. New York: Oxford University Press.

———. 2013. *Planning in the Face of Conflict.* Chicago: American Planning Association Press.

Freire, Paolo. 1970. *The Pedagogy of the Oppressed.* New York: Seabury.

Gorz, Andre. 1968. *Strategy for Labor.* Boston: Beacon Press.

Harris, Fred R., and Lynn A. Curtis, eds. 2000. *Locked in the Poorhouse: Cities, Race, and Poverty in the United States.* Paperback ed. Lanham: Rowman and Littlefield.

Hartman, Chester. 1975. "The Advocate Planner: From Hired Gun to Political Partisan." In *The Politics of Turmoil,* edited by R. A. Cloward and F. F. Piven. New York: Vintage.

Knapp, Courtney E. 2018. *Constructing the Dynamo of Dixie: Race, Urban Planning, and Cosmopolitanism in Chattanooga, Tennessee.* Chapel Hill: The University of North Carolina Press.

Krumholz, Norman, and J. Forester 1990. *Making Equity Planning Work: Leadership in the Public Sector.* Philadelphia: Temple University Press.

Logan, John R., and Harvey Molotch. 1987. *Urban Fortunes: The Political Economy of Place.* Berkeley: The University of California Press, 50–98.

Payne, Ruby K., Phillip E. DeVoi, and Terie Dreussi Smith. 2010. *Bridges Out of Poverty.* Moorabbin: Hawker Brownlow Education.

Reardon, Kenneth M. 1993. "Participatory Action Research from the Inside: Community Development Practice in East St. Louis," *American Sociologist* 1: 69–91.

———. 2005. "Straight A's? Evaluating the Success of Community/University Development Partnerships," *Communities and Banking, Federal Reserve Bank of Boston* 16 (3): 3–10.

Reardon, Kenneth, and J. Forester. 2016. *Rebuilding Community After Katrina: Transformative Education in the New Orleans Planning Initiative.* Philadelphia: Temple University Press.

Saija, Laura, D. De Leo, and J. Forester. 2017. "Learning from Practice: Environmental and Community Mapping as Participatory Action Research in Planning," *Planning Theory and Practice* 18 (1): 127–53.

Schön, Donald. 1983. *The Reflective Practitioner.* New York: Basic Books.

Song, Lily. 2016. "Enabling transformative agency: community-based green economic and workforce development in LA and Cleveland," *Planning Theory & Practice* 17 (2): 227–43.

Stone, C. 2005. "Looking Back to Look Forward: Reflections on Urban Regime Analysis," *Urban Affairs Review* 40 (3): 309–41.

Sugrue, Thomas. 2005. *The Origins of the Urban Crisis: Race and Inequality in Post-War Detroit.* Princeton: Princeton University Press.

Tarrow, Sidney G. 1994. *Power in Movement: Social Movement and Contentious Politics.* New York: Cambridge University Press.

11

PUBLIC PARTICIPATION GEOGRAPHIC INFORMATION SYSTEMS

A Model of Citizen Science to Promote Equitable Public Engagement

Michelle M. Thompson and Brittany N. Arceneaux

Community engagement takes many forms. In planning, community engagement is part of a multistage process of identifying and prioritizing resident concerns to shape neighborhood planning projects. Equity-based planners' use of community engagement is no exception; residents define their needs and worries that are then translated by neighborhood planners to see if, or how, these fit in the short-term or long-term comprehensive planning process. Over the past twenty years, as Norman Krumholz has pointed out, with the rise in community-based organizations (CBOs), equity planners are no longer working solely in government offices (Welle 2015). Many of these nongovernmental planners are finding that web-based technology (and technical assistance) can give residents and CBOs field-training and data collection experience that is similar to professional planners. The theory and application of developing community information data systems includes techniques to standardize, validate, and visualize community expertise in order to highlight issues and inform policy. In addition, residents can more easily obtain and integrate data sets that traditionally were withheld from the public. They also have access to crowdsourced community data. Taken together, these two sources have increased the capacity of everyday citizens to use map-based technologies. For example, citizen planners do not have to wait for or rely on "official" neighborhood plans or data, because many of those sources are now open and freely accessible on local and national government websites. Integrating the top-down data sources and comparing those with bottom-up community knowledge creates a data validation loop from the "middle out" (Ferreira 1999).

In addition to these new data streams, measurements of the community impact of projects have improved when geospatial tools are used to visualize the results. The software, which integrates municipal data sets with community data within a geospatial framework, is often referred to as a Public Participation Geographic Information System (PPGIS).

As a mapping technology, PPGIS can support community visioning and serve as a neighborhood engagement tool. Although PPGIS often requires cooperation with municipal and university partners to provide training, resources, data, and expertise to residents and/or community groups, it enables communities to visualize, quantify, and more generally bring to the forefront neighborhood issues such as blight and accessibility. Digital Interactive Visual Arts Sciences (DIVAS) for Social Justice, for instance, is using a PPGIS platform in partnership with the Centers for Disease Control and Prevention to map and record alcohol advertisements in New York City. DIVAS for Social Justice aims to bridge the digital divide by combining media literacy and cultural awareness with a better understanding of technology. Even volunteers with limited educational backgrounds can utilize mapping technology to share data in a format that anyone can understand.

PPGIS does not have a universal definition within the academic literature, nor is it constrained by a single, applied approach. PPGIS tends to be based in a partnership model. Often the models are framed using various combinations of residents, volunteers, university staff and students, and representatives of local municipalities. An emerging community of practice supports users by designing data development tools and standards for analysis and reporting. Their goal is to empower communities in new and sustainable ways and to give residents increased independence in decision making. PPGIS can be used to make attempts at equity planning more participatory and, as a result, more equitable.

The framework of PPGIS continues to evolve depending on community access to municipal data and/or technical assistance. A combination of information from the federal to state to local government, combined with neighborhood data, is critical to the ability for a PPGIS to be successful and maintained. A significant change has already emerged since the start of the Trump administration in 2017. The use of "alternative facts"—and the definition of what information is considered real or reliable—has changed. The lack of access to data sets at the federal level has reestablished a knowledge gap that cannot solely be filled by state or local governments (e.g., the U.S. Census Bureau). As a result, it may become increasingly important for decision makers to initially involve community members in the concept of data collection, sharing methodologies and expanding the conversation about how data is being analyzed and used. PPGIS outlines a planning tool that helps to loosen barriers of community participation so that residents can take ownership of the narrative being told about their communities. The basis for how data is developed (metadata) and types of exclusions or additions has created an opportunity for citizen scientists to emerge and drive the data development process into unchartered territories.

The Role of Citizen Science

PPGIS is a form of citizen science and part of a trend that has seen the role of citizen participation in science transformed over the past decade, thanks to both technological advances and expanding scientific networks. Introduced in 1989, the term *citizen science* has only recently been integrated into conversations of planning and citizen engagement (Oxford English Dictionary 2014). A citizen scientist is one who participates in the collection, analysis, or processing of data as part of a scientific inquiry on a nonprofessional basis (Haklay 2013, Silvertown 2009). As technology has become increasingly accessible, citizen science projects have grown in popularity. Projects range from Clickworkers, an environmental monitoring program at NASA, to post-disaster recovery groups that utilize satellite imagery to identify areas of devastation (Dunbar 2011). Technology has been the primary driver of the evolution of citizen science, enabling increased public participation and access (Silvertown 2009). It works as follows:

> Participants provide experimental data and facilities for researchers, raise new questions and co-create a new scientific culture. While adding value, volunteers acquire new learning and skills, and deeper understanding of the scientific work in an appealing way. As a result of this open, networked and trans-disciplinary scenario, science-society-policy interactions are improved leading to a more democratic research based on evidence-informed decision making. (European Commission 2013, 6)

This open platform facilitates new participatory relationships that transcend geographic centralization and build instead a collective global intelligence. *Public Lab*, for instance, is an environmental science community that shares methodologies for technical development and real applications for communities. They have been able to expand their network from southeast Louisiana to a global community, reaching countries such as Lebanon and Uganda (Public Lab 2015). Their participatory approach is an example of how citizen science can contribute to inclusive education, digital competences, technological skills, and a wider sense of initiative and ownership.

Although the Internet enables data collection from a completely new set of communities and by a completely new set of amateur contributors, it often results in disparities in data quality due to the varying levels of technological access and education of those contributors. As a result, recent projects place more emphasis on scientifically sound practices and measurable goals for public education. Since the practice of citizen science is built on a participatory model, it helps that science can be facilitated by (and can depend more on) technological tools such as smartphone applications. The level of participation and engagement is subject to how well citizens can overcome barriers and the ability and/or willingness of the citizen to manage responsibilities when using advanced technologies. For example, neighborhood blight information can be collected on a smartphone, but in order for this data to be updated, citizens must take ownership in managing, securing, and storing the information.

Acknowledging gaps in social inclusion will aid in developing rubrics for project development, implementation, integration, and reflection. Depending on the field, models for citizen science vary as much as the policy initiatives, community values, and neighborhood (or even global) goals. A good deal of progress in this area has been accomplished with one application of citizen science—public participation geographic information systems—with the hope that it can be used to promote the goals of equity planning.

Public Participation Geographic Information Systems, Engagement, and Empowerment

While there are numerous examples of community-based partnerships and citizen science, PPGIS offers a practical model by using bottom-up applied data management systems and mapping technology.[1] As a community engagement model, PPGIS integrates the use of mapping as an active visioning process and, in so doing, creates opportunities to empower residents (albeit with support from municipal and university partners). Ideally, PPGIS is fully adaptable to "inputs from ordinary citizens and other non-official sources" (Obermeyer 1998, 66).

PPGIS began during a time when innovations in communication, data sharing, and technology were in their infancy. The term Public Participation Geographic Information System (PPGIS) was created in 1996 at the annual conference of the National Center for Geographic Information and Analysis, "GIS and Society—The Social Implications of How People, Space, and Environment are represented in GIS" (Ghery-Butler 2009, 1–3). The definition of PPGIS has evolved along with the changes in data use, types of technology, protocols, community priorities, and partner relationships. PPGIS is defined by how information is developed, shared, and disseminated, as well as the process by which the action occurs. PPGIS is not defined by the technology that is used nor by the methods deployed to evaluate data but instead is an applied scientific model that includes public participation. For the purposes of this chapter, PPGIS is defined to include the following elements:

(1) *The uses and applications of geographic information and/or geographic information systems technology* (Tulloch 2016).

(2) *Participation by members of the public, both as individuals and grass-roots groups, and neighborhood organizations* (Ibid.).

(3) *Participation in the public processes through data collection, mapping, analysis and/or decision making* (Ibid.).

(4) *The application of academic and government practices of GIS and mapping to the local level and offers a voice for empowerment and inclusion to marginalized populations* (Ghery-Butler 2009, 1–3, Thompson 2015).

As described later in the chapter, a wide array of PPGIS tools and approaches can be used. "A full framing of PPGIS may include the most sophisticated applications; it also will need to encompass the paper map and pencil, coupled with meaningful participation that is fully cognizant of situational influences and diverse goals" (Sieber 2006, 496, 502). Organizations that implement a PPGIS need to:

(a) collect demographic, administrative, environmental, or other local-area databases,

(b) do something to the data to make it more useful locally (e.g., address matching of individual records; creating customized tables), and

(c) provide this information to local nonprofit community-based groups at low or no cost. (Sawicki and Peterman 2002, 24)

The uses of PPGIS vary, as do the roles of the actors (community, university, and municipality). The balance of engagement is based on the needs and/or talents of the partners. Traditional neighborhood planning models often rely on top-down decision making. PPGIS is more of a tool that enables broad grassroots, public participation to drive plans that normally would not fit into the "traditional" top-down model. One could imagine that, had it been available in 1975, it could have been used to promote the *Cleveland Neighborhood Improvement Plan* that Norm Krumholz helped to develop and implement. That plan "enlisted the citizens in resolving some of their own perceived problems" (Krumholz and Forester 1990, 173). Instead, Krumholz's planners asked neighborhood residents to identify the problems in their neighborhood so that they could convince the city government of the need to address those problems. This is a task for which PPGIS tools are ideally suited. They enable residents not only to identify the issues but also to give specific locations and show clusters in a visual way, and in some cases, in "real time."

However, PPGIS alone does not ensure public participation. Many of the most prevalent neighborhood planning models do not adhere to these principles. "Community mapping may derive from top-down city planning in which decisions were made for a community without their input or when a community wanted some type of public service but did not have the information to build a case" (Ghery-Butler 2009, 1–3). The movement to promote bottom-up planning, which is resident led and community based, has significantly increased community engagement and improved communication with city administrations. Open source technology has allowed for greater access to so-called small and big data, along with technology that makes it easier to integrate public and community data. However, data source identification, definition, translation, manipulation, and/or conversion have, in the past, required high levels of technical expertise and understanding. There are issues about data integrity, validity, and reliability, and many residents or CBOs do not have the fundamental knowledge or experience to conduct neighborhood data analysis. Partner organizations (government or university) can aid in the development of the data for policy or planning purposes. These "data intermediaries" (Sawicki and Peterman 2002) offer a range of services, from establishing data definitions and collection methods to providing analysis, visualization, reporting, and education. In contrast to the tradition of municipality-driven planning and city management that inhibited information, access, and education of the public, we join Bassler in arguing that:

> Local leaders need to broaden their list of responsibilities to include roles as facilitator, supporter, collaborator, and empowerer of local community members. This change requires letting go of some of the traditional reins of power and trusting that citizens can and will effectively engage in the issues. The result is a partnership that is nearly always healthy for a community. (Bassler et al. 2008, 3)

PPGIS has expanded the conversation to a more inclusive model for resident involvement. Geography and mapping technology can now play a key role in top-down, bottom-up, and in-between communication that will support communities both inside and outside an organization. In general, PPGIS provides an opportunity for communities to collect, analyze, and display data that reflects their priorities. PPGIS tools and techniques create a way to collect data related to the priorities that are community defined, taking what begins as an aspatial idea (e.g., likes/dislikes of a proposed highway development) and rendering it spatial (e.g., location of respondents in relation to the highway development site). PPGIS can serve as a forum or avenue for community engagement.

As Sieber notes:

> PPGIS provides a unique approach for engaging the public in decision making through its goal to incorporate local knowledge, integrate and contextualize complex spatial information, allow participants to dynamically interact with input, analyze alternatives, and empower individuals and groups. (Sieber 2006, 496, 502)

PPGIS has both formal and informal means to integrate marginalized populations into participatory planning. Some are direct, others indirect; interactions can be remote or virtual, on-site, or mediated in other ways. However, while the doors are open to all, some residents fail to enter, because there are barriers to PPGIS that cannot be overcome. PPGIS critics argue that it can negatively impact attempts to empower marginalized groups (Baldwin 2010). It has also been suggested that GIS can hinder community participation, or that it simultaneously empowers and marginalizes (Harris and Weiner 1998).[2] Still, the use of GIS for community empowerment has strong support and, as with any new planning tools or methods, needs more rigorous assessment to understand where it can have the most beneficial impact. As Ghose and Elwood (2003) suggested,

> [T]here is a need to follow up such work with evaluations on how community organizations actively use GIS in their daily planning activities, on what types of policy changes they are able to bring with such information empowerment and on whether the introduction of GIS within community organizations creates its own set of power relations between those who possess the new technical skills and those who do not.

Revisiting each project after the fact can help incrementally move the use of PPGIS toward being a tool that can be used by, and direct the expression of, a broader set of each community of potential users. Before turning to some examples, we first discuss a little about the importance of the "public" in PPGIS.

For the purposes of this paper, the term "public" will be synonymous with "community." We recognize that the definition of "community" remains nebulous in the field and practice of planning. When municipalities engage the public, the choice of who represents the "public" becomes intertwined with affiliated community organizations that may or may not represent all residents. These community organizations, then, end up serving as a proxy or a de facto "public." In the literature there is a "notion of public involvement [that] may seem intuitive at first and easy to understand, [but] clearly there are different biases, opportunities, and limitations to how a public is selected and incorporated into a PPGIS project depending on the frame of reference one uses" (Schlossberg and Shuford

2005, 23). For instance, when university partners engage with the public, the definition of community is typically based on a client-partner relationship.

As Kyem notes, from the partner's perspective:

> Community empowerment is a political process that entails redefinition of existing power relations between the haves and have-nots in a community. Empowerment is an investment that involves risk taking, occasional failures and disappointments, constant reviews of strategy and persistence. (Kyem 2002, 2)

However, while PPGIS provides a means to minimize top-down political influence, planners need to be cognizant of the potential adverse impacts in the short- and long-term that must be avoided in order to maximize community participation.

Municipalities and universities often need to engage the community in order to create more sustainable resident-led projects or programs. Depending on what or how technology is brought into the planning process, a community can be more or less reliant on the university or municipality. A properly implemented management process allows for equal participation and reassessment of roles and modifications of the power relationships through a feedback system. It should be the goal for the citizen planner, and any related organizations, to become independent from the university-municipal partners in order to manage their own GIS.[3]

PPGIS has aided in creating a wider array of choices that planners can use to engage the community in identifying problems and developing more equitable, community-facing solutions. The premise is that the model should have a community focus, be neighborhood-centric, and be supported with technology and tools provided by the academic community or a data intermediary using municipal data and resources. We now turn to how this can look in practice.

PPGIS in Practice

Equity planning can be an instrument of redistributive justice. Practitioners constantly face political and social barriers; forging new paths is necessary to combat questionable public and private efforts. "With careful planning cities are rebuilt and replaced; with the citizenry-led change, the same places are regenerated and reborn, combining new and old into vibrant authentic places" (Gratz 2015). Numerous examples of the use of community-led strategies that integrated PPGIS can be seen in the many projects developed by New Orleanians after Hurricane Katrina to combat urban renewal style development; residents created their own community narrative in order to guide a more equitable neighborhood recovery.

In 2012, approximately 43,755 properties were designated as "blighted" by the city of New Orleans (Editorial Board 2012). In an attempt to battle the concentration of deteriorating properties, the Landrieu administration developed an aggressive blight eradication policy where 1,598 properties—including 2,280 units—were demolished (Editorial Board 2012). A significant share of this growing stock of newly demolished vacant lots was bought by out of-state investors hoping to cash in when market values returned (Ebeling 2006). This created two challenges for residents trying to reestablish their community fabric: a vast number of overgrown, unmanaged lots and a bevy of uninhabited properties. In the Lower Ninth Ward and other neighborhoods, it was not uncommon to see blocks with more overgrown lots than houses. Market forces went seemingly unregulated, so residents had no control over the uninhabited investment property scattered throughout their neighborhood. Unfortunately, this increased the impediments to the in-migration of former residents.

In response to the traditional, top-down hazard planning models implemented after Hurricane Katrina on a citywide scale that didn't take measure of the effects at the neighborhood scale, groups of volunteers from around the country and a wide range of nonprofits developed alternative recovery strategies built on social capital and resident empowerment. In 2011 the University of New Orleans's Department of Planning and Urban Studies began to apply PPGIS practices with neighborhood associations in order to collect, map, and quantify quality-of-life challenges faced by residents. Information collected was used by communities to build task forces and prioritize areas for intervention. When a community lacked technological skills, volunteers from the university filled the gaps through education, training, and supervision of the development, management, and mapping of data. This multiyear PPGIS program worked with neighborhoods across the city—each with very different cultural identities and urban planning literacy. Each university/neighborhood partnership required a different approach and yet prioritized collecting information that was auditable and representative of community desires. The partnerships aimed to empower neighborhoods to become more strategic and sophisticated as public and private forces transformed the landscape of their neighborhoods.

Each PPGIS project was completed under a *Community-Supported,* *Community-Led,* or *Community-Sustained* model. In some cases, data compatibility (unit size), interoperability (method of integration), and definitions (metadata) increased conflicts. Some of these conflicts were how to meet the project goals, maintain data integrity, and involve and/or support the community. Residents had a difficult time obtaining the necessary data and accessing the protocols and training that are sometimes required to work with high-end technology. Outlined below are examples of the different PPGIS models used. Each example highlights the roles of the project partners and their primary contribution to the process (e.g., residents as citizen scientist, government as municipal planner, and university as trainer and technology advocate).

One *community-led* application of PPGIS was the community mapping undertaken as part of an initiative started by the Historic Faubourg Tremé Neighborhood Association's (HFTA) land-use committee. The association provides a vehicle for community members to come together to speak with one voice on issues that preserve culture, architecture, and quality of life. Located directly northwest of New Orleans's French Quarter is the Historic Faubourg Tremé neighborhood, simultaneously one of the most notable and most endangered places in the city. Considered to be the oldest African American neighborhood in the United States, Tremé has been a center of resistance both politically and socially since the earliest days of French occupation, even before it was established as a neighborhood in 1812 (Campanella 2008). However, decades of disinvestment and damage from Hurricane Katrina have left this historically low-income community vulnerable.

Community members began to organize around issues of uninhabited investment properties and opportunities to capitalize on traditionally unseen city reinvestment programs. PPGIS was used as a tool to develop a baseline understanding of recovery progress and levels of blight; it was also used to bridge the gap between residential needs and unwieldy city programs such as the code enforcement blight remediation efforts. Their goal was to implement a blight and vacant lot survey that could help the community advocate for better land-use decisions and policies. The PPGIS project was developed through a partnership with the University of New Orleans's Department of Planning and Urban Studies (UNO PLUS) and WhoData.org (a community data information system created in 2009 by Dr. Michelle Thompson of UNO PLUS). Academic planners and GIS experts worked to establish protocols for data collection and analysis while garnering community expertise in order to construct a narrative visualization.

University researchers provided the neighborhood association with tools to survey over eight hundred parcels; the community volunteers walked block by block to collect data and spent evening hours entering survey results into an integratable spreadsheet format. Community members were asked to stand in front of a property and assign a good, fair, or poor rating after reviewing evaluation guides and training in the field. Assigning a rating opened up a larger a conversation about what "blight" means in the context of their community. Within the PPGIS framework these conversations are often used (in a planning round table) as a tool to expand community literacy around injustices by tying physical examples to larger patterns and policy decisions.

University researchers integrated and consolidated the survey results to show trends (level of blight), status (in the blight remediation process), and mitigation (by the owner or city). Technical analysis skills were used to leverage city property data and link information about code enforcement violations with the community crowdsourced information. The result highlighted discrepancies between properties the community identified as blighted with the City of New Orleans's Department of Code Enforcement's blight list. Using maps, spreadsheets, and infographics, the university researchers packaged the information collected and validated by community members to be used in HFTA's advocacy efforts.

The information was initially used to prioritize nuisance properties to target when communicating with the city's code enforcement department. Oftentimes it was communities such as HFTA that faced the highest levels of blight and the lowest levels of city response. More affluent New Orleans's neighborhoods were able to recover and remediate properties at a faster rate by leveraging private funds of individual property owners. Additionally, high levels of ownership in other New Orleans's neighborhoods impeded speculative out-of-state investment, reducing the amount of disjointed negligent owners within their communities.

With over an estimated forty thousand blighted proprieties across the city, the city's office of code enforcement lacked the resources to constantly monitor a neighborhood at a block level or to ensure an equitable distribution of resources (Editorial Board 2012). Patterns of mislabeled addresses and empty lots without physical identifiers only made this monitoring responsibility more onerous. Code enforcement staff depended on unique identifiers to track properties in city databases—identifiers that were inaccessible to anyone without city records and advanced GIS technical skills. Using the *WhoData PPGIS* package maps and spreadsheets linked to city data, HFTA was able to accurately describe their targeted list of blighted properties when communicating with code enforcement staff. During these communications HFTA highlighted the high concentration of structures that were susceptible to fires and/or potential collapse and empty lots that functioned as breeding grounds for rats and mosquitoes. Using the *middle-out* spatial data summarized in maps, these conversations transitioned from ambiguous locations to conversations about at-risk properties in proximity to schools and historic resources.

These maps presented neighborhood residents with the opportunity to evaluate the neighborhood properties on their own terms. The linked data was crucial for identifying and taking action against property owners who owned numerous properties and held multiple code violations. PPGIS was used to empower residents to guide decision making and capture resources. In the case of HFTA, using a standardized methodology and visual aids, community members were able to prioritize areas of need in their communities and communicate with code enforcement staff to address properties posing health and safety risks in their communities.

Our second example is *community-focused* PPGIS and is based in the Lower Ninth Ward and Holy Cross neighborhoods of New Orleans. At the time of this project a very limited number of residents had returned to the neighborhood, so researchers from the University of New Orleans worked with two nonprofits embedded in the community to conduct outreach to existing residents and bring in volunteers from outside the community. They also worked with the regional planning commission who acted as the municipal agent to support the project. In this case, the communities needed a full array of support.

A survey was completed by the researchers with the help of volunteers and partnering organizations, including Lowernine.org (who was working with and representing the neighborhoods) and Project Homecoming (a nonprofit housing developer who was helping residents return and rebuild in the neighborhood after Hurricane Katrina). Data were provided to anyone interested in knowing the condition and occupancy of the Lower Ninth Ward and Holy Cross neighborhoods.[4] The data were also summarized in a Lower Ninth Ward profile report, along with an analysis of the neighborhood recovery. The information has been used by neighborhood groups to monitor the repopulation of the neighborhoods as well as by Senator Mary Landrieu's staff, who drew from it as part of her initiative to raise up the Lower Ninth Ward and procure funding for redevelopment projects. The mayor of New Orleans used it to help identify lots for the city to mow and maintain.

The third example illustrates the use of *community-sustained* PPGIS, where the community itself has been the project lead or has taken over after the researchers and government officials left. This model works best in communities that are present (always an issue in post-Katrina New Orleans, although not always elsewhere), educated, and dedicated to project sustainability. The City Council of New Orleans asked the Uptown Triangle Neighborhood Association what their infrastructure priorities were; they identified a lack of streetlights as an existing threat. After UNO researchers provided them with data standards, residents collected the information and used GIS to map their own data. Since the residents act as citizen scientists, the technology and expertise resides in the community. The success of this model depends on their ability to self-govern and manage a PPGIS. Residents who drive data collection now have the capacity to monitor neighborhood change, update their data set, identify and catalogue new issues, and build on the baseline analysis initially provided by the university.

The primary difference between the *community-supported, community-led,* or *community-sustained* PPGIS projects is the degree to which the community has the capacity to instigate the project (by finding the university, nongovernmental organization, or public partners it needs to enable the community to carry out its idea); the ability to bring the project to fruition; and the skills necessary to continue the project once the partners leave. Although each of these community projects requires different levels of support and skill sets, we believe the general lessons learned below can be applied to any of these project types.

Lessons Learned, Best Practices, and Limitations

While PPGIS can offer equity planners a way to share data and effectively involve residents in planning and decision making, like any community-based effort it has its drawbacks and limitations; these are primarily related to the level of citizen participation and the quality of data.

• *Sustaining citizen participation:* The ability of a project to adapt to participants' work schedules along with limitations on volunteer availability and motivation may impact the end goal. Participation in the project needs to offer some kind of benefit that outweighs the value of competing leisure activities that volunteers would otherwise be doing. In such cases, it is important for the planners to work with participants in understanding the role of data in public policy decision making and the value in collecting, analyzing, or presenting the information. Participants may not understand the importance of methodology, but planners can help them make the connection to the importance of the activity and the goal of the project. This can be done as part of the pre-project development process and the establishment of project goals with resident participants.

• *Neighborhood challenges and data standards:* Residents of areas that are distressed or have multiple challenges tend to have more limited levels of participation. Yet there is an enormous benefit to engaging volunteers who live in, or are familiar with, the area where the data are being collected. Bringing in outside volunteers creates a bifurcation in understanding the local environment and makes it difficult to calibrate perceptions of data, as opinions may differ when conducting a survey on the quality of housing and choosing a rating of "good," "fair," or "poor," for example.[5]

• *Municipal barriers to participation:* Local governments are great sources of data but they can also present barriers to citizen participation. The inability of city departments to seamlessly share data with the public, or even between departments, continues to thwart practical implementation of a citizen participation program. While many governments create online GIS viewers where public records (e.g., parcel boundaries and zoning) can be viewed, data behind those maps ought to be shared with PPGIS users, as it can provide the foundation for their participatory maps. For example, free availability of the city blight layer enabled the Tremé residents to overlay their map of neighborhood blight over the city's map for easy contrast.

While technology has increased opportunities for crowdsourced data, some municipal officials have concerns about the accuracy, validity, and utility of such data. More generally, the effectiveness of PPGIS processes can be improved by identifying the types of participants and their roles in project development, data collection, analysis, and presentation and by establishing protocols accordingly. "Notwithstanding the good intentions of PPGIS experts, the goals of many community based projects are rarely attained. This is due in part to the ad hoc nature of PPGIS organizations and the poor conditions within the communities. Currently, very little feedback . . . exists to help us gauge the full impact of PPGIS projects" (Kyem 2002, 2). Experts from academia and practice agree with Haklay and Tobón (2003, 23) that "even if the PPGIS designers believe that they have managed to create something [i.e., a useable evaluation tool] that is easy to use, only appropriate testing even using simple methods . . . will show if the design is successful in meeting users' needs or not."

Even when PPGIS projects effectively provide data as a resource for decision making, they may not go the next step in providing a platform to singularly catalyze policy change. PPGIS products are often used as a "representation of space that enables political struggle to shape political discourse" (Craig, Harris, and Weiner 2002, 8).

Conclusion

PPGIS has become a way to collaborate, integrate, and evaluate data in order to provide sustainable engagement by and for the community. The ability to garner resources for technology and training remains a priority for the future and needs to include education around data management and ethics as well. Some of the real value of a public participation GIS, or perhaps more appropriately, community-integrated PPGIS, will come if the maps and analysis that are produced can help inform planning processes and relationships rather than simply extracting patterns from large volumes of data, as one would with a conventional GIS (Craig, Harris, and Weiner 2002). It is a technology that is best used as a means to share ideas and information between and within the public, private, and nonprofit sectors.

Needless to say, PPGIS is not a universal panacea. Valid criticisms remain as to whether PPGIS serves all citizens and if the engagement it engenders is truly democratic. As a start, PPGIS removes the question as to whether data should be available to the public. New levels of accountability in public decision making are fostered as a result. Moreover, crowdsourced information that comes from use of a PPGIS project can help decision makers make better informed and more measurable choices. Locally generated data helps give voice to groups of people that are constantly overlooked and leads to improved visualization and data accuracy that can induce further justice. Data can be used to help to support and solidify equitable points of view that are commonly pushed aside in the face of stereotypes or social indifference.

It just may be possible that through empowering communities, PPGIS applications can provide a key to placing their interests and concerns—often those of less-privileged groups—on both regional and national agendas. Applying PPGIS to a range of policies within the urban planning realm should become an automatic response to patterns and changes within a community and can be used as a platform for making issues such as rising home prices visually and spatially quantifiable and therefore politically actionable.

Too often, planning is a data-driven, top-down process, but with PPGIS the ability to use data from the *middle out* is possible. Like many contributors to this volume, we believe it is imperative that communities are given the education and tools to tell their own story. Education regarding standards and protocols and the implementation of predevelopment project assessments in conjunction with municipal data standards can improve citizen participation. In this way, communities can be provided with an opportunity to offer auditable data to influence decision making that addresses their needs and concerns.

The process of community engagement must begin with redefining how data are used in policy development and analysis. Technology—whether desktop-, smartphone-, or web-based—will allow the convergence and access for resident-led projects. PPGIS can be at the heart of this empowerment, so long as we recognize the need for ongoing support from educational, civic, and municipal organizations. For the near future, this will continue to be the case. Access to the technology will make this more of a reality as new actors and applications are added.

However, PPGIS-centered projects are facing new challenges with the change in access and definitions of federal data that is now constrained or not accessible. The ability to conduct neighborhood, regional, or national comparisons on a wide range of community issues may be affected. On March 27, 2017, the White House announced the creation of the "Office of American Innovation" which has a "particular focus on technology and data" (Parker and Rucker 2017). It is hoped this new community of practice will openly and equitably share public data, participate in transforming development, and expand the possibilities for the communities they serve, leading to outcomes that are more equitable for all.

NOTES

1. The model is getting support from the U.S. federal government, who has begun to organize a "community of practice" that focuses on data standards, use, and interoperability. The effort to get federal organizations to use disparate department data and include citizen data has been ongoing since the early 1970s. In October 2015, a new "Strategy for American Innovation," including citizen science and crowdsourcing, was announced. The goal is to raise awareness of citizen science and crowdsourcing inside and outside of the federal government and to encourage more agencies and more Americans to take advantage of these approaches (Gustetic, Honey, and Shanley 2015).

2. For the purposes of this chapter, we acknowledge these limits and suggest that there is a reasonable expectation that not all community members (and their perspectives) will be captured. This chapter does not address the sociological, psychological, or physical constraints that inhibit engagement.

3. In order for PPGIS to expand beyond a concept and toward a "science," there must be a way to document the knowledge transfer and brand the policies, practice, and methods into measurable, quantifiable, and verifiable terms.

4. The data is still available at www.whodata.org.

5. Steps to create a localized set of standards should be included in the educational and training portion of any PPGIS project.

REFERENCES

Arnstein, S. 1969. "A Ladder of Citizen Participation," *Journal of the American Institute of Planners* 35 (4): 216–24.

City of Cleveland. 1975. *The Cleveland Policy Report.* Accessed August 1, 2015. http://www .worldcat.org/title/cleveland-policy-planning-report/oclc/679927701?referer =di&ht=edition.

Baldwin, B. 2010. "The Role of Geographic Information Systems in Post-Disaster Neighborhood Recovery: Lessons from Hurricanes Katrina and Rita." Master's thesis, University of New Orleans. Accessed August 1, 2015. http://scholarworks.uno.edu /cgi/viewcontent.cgi?article=2125&context=td.

Bassler, A., Kathy Brasier, Neal Fogle, and Ron Taverno. 2008. *Developing Effective Citizen Engagement: A How-To Guide for Community Leaders.* Harrisburg: The Center for Rural Pennsylvania. Accessed December 1, 2015. http://www.rural.palegislature.us /Effective_Citizen_Engagement.pdf.

Brown, G., D. Weber, and K. Bie. 2014. "Is PPGIS good enough? An empirical evaluation of the quality of PPGIS crowd-sourced spatial data for conservation planning," *Land Use Policy* 43: 228–38.

Butler, G.K. 2009. "Community Mapping in Post-Katrina New Orleans: A Comparative Analysis of Citizen Participation in The Gentilly Project and The Broadmoor Project." Thesis, University of New Orleans.

Campanella, R. 2008. *Bienville's Dilemma: A Historical Geography of New Orleans.* Lafayette: University of Louisiana at Lafayette.

Carver, S. 2001. *Participation and Geographic Information: A Position Paper.* Leeds: University of Leeds. Accessed August 1, 2015. http://www.geog.leeds.ac.uk/papers/01-3/01-3 .pdf.

Cope, M. 2012. "Public Participation GIS as a Cultural Process: Cultural Theory, Participation Preferences, and GIS-aided Decision Making among Farmers in Central Illinois." PhD diss., University of Illinois at Urbana-Champaign.

Craig, W., T. Harris, and D. Wiener, eds. 2002. *Community Participation and Geographical Information Systems.* New York: CRC Press.

Dunbar, B. 2011. "Flagship Initiatives." NASA. Accessed August 1, 2015. http://www.nasa.gov/open/plan/peo.html.

Ebeling, A. 2006. "Gambling on New Orleans," *Forbes,* June 2, http://www.forbes.com/forbes/2006/0619/092.html.

Eccles, J., C. Midgley, A. Wigfield, C. Buchanan, D. Reuman, C. Flanagan, and D. Iver. 1993 "Development during adolescence: The impact of stage-environment fit on young adolescents' experiences in schools and in families," *American Psychologist* 48 (2): 90–101.

Editorial Board. 2012. "Progress on blight in New Orleans: An editorial," *The Times-Picayune* (LA), January 3.

European Commission. 2013. *Green Paper on Citizen Science.* Accessed August 1, 2015. https://ec.europa.eu/digital-agenda/en/news/green-paper-citizen-science-europe-towards-society-empowered-citizens-and-enhanced-research-0.

Environmental Systems Research Institute. 2015. *GIS Empowers Community Engagement: Geography Can Serve as a Starting Point for Building Strong, Lasting Relationships with Communities.* Accessed August 1, 2015. http://www.esri.com/esri-news/arcnews/summer15articles/gis-empowers-community-engagement.

Ferreira, J. 1999. "Information Technologies that Change Relationships between Low-Income Communities and the Public, and Nonprofit Agencies that Serve Them." In *High Technology and Low-Income Communities: Prospects for the Positive Use of Advanced Information Technology,* edited by D. A. Schön, B. Sanyal, and W. J. Mitchell, 163–89. Cambridge: The MIT Press.

Forrester, J., and S. Cinderby. 2015. *A Guide to Using Community Mapping and Participatory-GIS.* Managing Borderlands project and funded by the Rural Economy and Land Use (RELU) programme of the Economic & Social and Natural Environment Research Councils under grant number RES24050020. Accessed October 4, 2015. http://www.iapad.org/wp-content/uploads/2015/07/Borderlands-Community-Mapping-Guide.pdf.

Ghery-Butler, K. 2009. "Community Mapping in Post-Katrina New Orleans: A Comparative Analysis of Citizen Participation in The Gentilly Project and The Broadmoor Project." Thesis, University of New Orleans.

Ghose, R., and Sarah Elwood. 2003. "Public Participation GIS and Local Political Context: Propositions and Research Directions," *URISA Journal* 15 (2): 17–24. Accessed November 1, 2015. http://dusk2.geo.orst.edu/virtual/2007/Ghose_Elwood03.pdf.

Gratz, R. 2015. *We're Still Here Ya Bastards: How the People of New Orleans Rebuilt Their City.* New York: Nation Books.

Grey, F. 2009. "Viewpoint: The Age of Citizen Cyberscience," CERN Courier, April 29. Accessed August 1, 2015. http://cerncourier.com/cws/article/cern/38718.

Gustetic, J., et al. 2014. "Designing a Citizen Science and Crowdsourcing Toolkit for the Federal Government." *White House blog,* December 2. Accessed August 1, 2015. https://www.whitehouse.gov/blog/2014/12/02/designing-citizen-science-and-crowdsourcing-toolkit-federal-government.

Gustetic, J., K. Honey, and L. Shanley. 2015. "Open Science and Innovation: Of the People, By the People, For the People," *White House blog,* September 9. Accessed November 29, 2015. https://obamawhitehouse.archives.gov/blog/2015/09/09/open-science-and-innovation-people-people-people.

Haklay, M. 2013. "Citizen Science and Volunteered Geographic Information: Overview and Typology of Participation." In *Crowdsourcing Geographic Knowledge*, edited by D. Siu, S. Elwood, and M. Goodchild, 105–24. Dordrecht: Springer.

———. 2017. "Volunteered Geographic Information: Quality Assurance." In *The International Encyclopedia of Geography: People, the Earth, Environment, and Technology*, edited by D. Richardson et al. Hoboken, NJ: John Wiley.

Haklay, M., S. Basiouka, V. Antoniou, and A. Ather. 2010. "How Many Volunteers Does It Take to Map an Area Well? The Validity of Linus' Law to Volunteered Geographic Information," *The Cartographic Journal* 47 (4): 315–22.

Haklay, M., and Carolina Tobón. 2003. *Usability Evaluation and PPGIS: Towards a user-centred design approach.* London: University College London. Accessed December 1, 2016. http://discovery.ucl.ac.uk/5241/1/5241.pdf.

Harris, T., and D. Weiner. 1998. "Empowerment, Marginalization and Community-Integrated GIS," *Cartography and Geographic Information Systems* 25 (2): 67–76.

Hoyt, L., R. Khosla, and C. Canepa. 2005 "Leaves, Pebbles, and Chalk: Building a Public Participation GIS in New Delhi, India," *Journal of Urban Technology* 12 (1): 1–19.

Integrated Resources Management Co. Ltd. 2015. *PPGIS Practical Guide.* European Union: Mare Nostrum Project. Accessed August 1, 2015. http://marenostrumproject.eu/wp-content/uploads/2014/09/Mare_Nostrum_Project_PPGIS_Practical_Guide.pdf.

Klosterman, R. 2013. "Lessons Learned About Planning," *Journal of the American Planning Association* 79 (2): 161–69.

Krumholz, N., and J. Forester. 1990. *Making Equity Planning Work: Leadership in the Public Sector.* Philadelphia: Temple University Press.

Kyem, P. A. K. 2002. "Examining the Community Empowerment Process in Public Participation GIS Applications." In *Proceedings of the First International PPGIS Conference.* New Brunswick, NJ: Rutgers University, URISA.

Laituri, M. 2003. "The Issue of Access: An Assessment Guide for Evaluating Public Participation Geographic Information Science Case Studies," *URISA Journal* 15 (2).

National Neighborhood Indicators Partnership. 2015. "About NNIP." Accessed August 1, 2015. http://www.neighborhoodindicators.org/about-nnip.

Obermeyer, N. 1998. "The Evolution of Public Participation GIS," *Cartography and Geographic Information Systems* 25 (2): 65–66.

Oxford English Dictionary. 2014. "New Words Notes June 2014," *Oxford English Dictionary.* Accessed August 1, 2015. http://public.oed.com/the-oed-today/recent-updates-to-the-oed/june-2014-update/new-words-notes-june-2014/.

Parker, Ashley, and Stephen Rucker. 2017. "Trump taps Kushner to lead a SWAT team to fix government with business ideas," *Washington Post,* March 26. Accessed April 2, 2017. https://www.washingtonpost.com/politics/trump-taps-kushner-to-lead-a-swat-team-to-fix-government-with-business-ideas/2017/03/26/9714a8b6-1254-11e7-ada0-1489b735b3a3_story.html?utm_term=.20ff56a665ef.

Phillips, T., and M. Ferguson. 2014. *An Introduction to the User's Guide for Evaluating Learning Outcomes from Citizen Science.* UG Webinar. Ithaca: Cornell Lab of Ornithology.

Public Lab. 2015. *Media documentation.* Accessed August 1, 2015. http://publiclab.org/places.

Sawicki, D., and W. Craig. 1996. "The Democratization of Data: Bridging the Gap for Community Groups," *Journal of the American Planning Association* 62 (4): 512–23.

Sawicki, D., and D. Peterman. 2002. "Surveying the extent of PPGIS practice in the United States." In *Community Participation and Geographic Information Systems*, edited by W. Craig, T. Harris, and D. Weiner, 17–37. London: Taylor and Francis.

Schlossberg, M., and E. Shuford. 2005. "Delineating 'Public' and 'Participation,'" *PPGIS/URISA Journal* 16 (2).

Sieber, R. 1997. "Computers in the grassroots: Environmentalists, Geographic Information Systems, and Public Policy." PhD diss., Rutgers University.

———. 2006. "Public Participation Geographic Information Systems: A Literature Review and Framework," *Annals of the Association of American Geographers* 96 (3): 491–507.

Silvertown, J. 2009. "A new dawn for Citizen Science." *Trends in Ecology & Evolution* 24 (9): 467–71.

Talen, E. E. 2000. "Bottom-up GIS: A new tool for individual and group expression in participatory planning," *Journal of the American Planning Association* 66 (3): 279–94.

Thompson, M. 2011. "Managing GIS: GIS Management Scholars: Applying Practice to Praxis," *ArcNews,* Spring. Accessed August 1, 2015. http://www.esri.com/news/arcnews/spring11articles/gis-management-scholars-applying-practice-to-praxis.html.

———. 2015. "Public Participation GIS and Neighborhood Recovery: Using Community Mapping for Economic Development," *International Journal of Data Mining, Modeling and Management* 7 (1).

Tulloch, David. 2016. *What PPGIS Really Needs Is . . .* New Brunswick: Cook College. https://www.researchgate.net/publication/267800366_WHAT_PPGIS_REALLY_NEEDS_IS.

Welle, J. 2015. "On Equity Planning in Cleveland, Segregation, CDCs and More—A Long Chat with Norman Krumholz, Former City Planner of Cleveland," *Scene News,* October 8. Accessed December 1, 2015. http://www.clevescene.com/scene-and-heard/archives/2015/10/08/on-equity-planning-in-cleveland-segregation-cdcs-and-more-a-long-chat-with-norman-krumholz-former-city-planner-of-cleveland.

Wiggins, A., G. Newman, R. Stevenson, and K. Crowston. 2011. *Mechanisms for Data Quality and Validation in Citizen Science.* "Computing for Citizen Science" workshop at the IEEE eScience Conference, Stockholm, Sweden.

Conclusion

THE FUTURE OF EQUITY PLANNING PRACTICE

Norman Krumholz and Kathryn Wertheim Hexter

Equity planning tries to provide more choices for those who have few
and to redistribute resources, political power, and participation toward
the lower-income, disadvantaged residents of their cities. Early equity
plans were adopted in several cities by official planning agencies. Since
that time, equity planning has expanded beyond city planning departments and commissions. Social equity is now the primary focus of
nonprofit community planning, regional planning, and other groups that
use city planning techniques and often employ planners. They include
community development corporations; public interest research groups
(PIRGs); and groups working on the environment, access to healthy
food, workforce development, and other issues. It seems clear that the
most effective contemporary planning for social equity is now taking
place within the community planning field, and the issues of sustainability, income inequality, and the diversification of our society suggest the
probable expansion of equity planning in the future.

Equity planners have a professional obligation to bring the voices of the disenfranchised and disadvantaged to the decision-making tables. Contemporary city
planners are professionals who deal with the physical form and function of cities: streets, parks, land use, and development, as well as zoning regulations of the
physical city. Equity planners plan the physical city and also deal with policies and
programs that address the social and economic conditions of city residents. In
their day-to-day practice, equity planners deliberately attempt to move resources,
political power, and political participation toward the lower-income, disadvantaged population of their cities.

The object of all planner's activities—whether consciously redistributive or
not—is the form and function of cities and regions from neighborhoods and
downtowns to transportation, from housing provision to the environment and
economic development. Virtually all of the emphasis is placed on physical development. Cities continue to demand planning services, and outstanding students

continue to be drawn to the planning profession because they want to help plan and build a more sustainable, just, and greener world. But actual planning practice in the bureaucracies of city hall, although essential, is often routine and uninspired. Planning could be much more than it is by expanding its scope and contributing to the resolution of inner-city problems like poverty, high unemployment, and poor health. This is part of the work in which equity planners are engaged; work which is making tangible contributions to the well-being of millions of human beings.

The concept of a more just society is not new to planning; it has always been there, but in recent years has been driven to the margins of the profession. Rising inequality and other well-publicized socioeconomic changes now challenge the neoliberal belief that a rising tide lifts all boats and make a powerful argument for a new emphasis on equity and justice.

This book examines the issues and modifications in urban planning practice and proposes changes that would strengthen the profession as an instrument of redistributive justice. Drawing from the real-world examples, it seeks to influence today's practicing planners as well as planning educators who are preparing the planners of the future. At the same time, it seeks to inspire future planners by demonstrating how the skills of planners to gather and synthesize relevant information and frame conclusions and recommendations have been used in cases around our country to support equitable outcomes. In these cases, planners have used their understanding of urban and regional structures and processes to address the pressing issues of our times—poverty, the deterioration of the environment and employment, the need to invest in infrastructure, and other crucially important matters. This book demonstrates how, at a time of impoverished governments, faltering economies, and federal neglect, planners have been freer to build alliances with collaborating organizations and propose their own equitable solutions, because everyone is looking for workable proposals that can make the most of resources they can tap.

Their guidelines are few but important.

Guidelines for Equity Planners

In general, equity planners are guided by a number of lessons and distilled values from their history. First, their work must be oriented toward the user; instead of basing the goals they seek on their own values, they must relate to the values and goals of the people for whom they are planning. A second lesson is related to the first: planners, no matter how wise, do not know all the answers; nor do the members of conventional boards, commissions, and councils. The breadth for whom planners and related professional bodies plan needs to be clear at the out-set. Diversity is important, and people are entitled to live any way they choose so long as that way is not destructive to them or to their fellow citizens. Planners ought to respect their goals and objectives and provide people with the opportunity, resources, and freedom to choose what they want to do.

The third lesson is that genuine democracy in America cannot be achieved without much greater economic, social, and political equality, and this requires a concentrated attack on poverty and racial segregation. Most equity planners today believe that poverty and racial segregation are among the prime causes of the urban crisis and the major problems to be solved if the quality of urban life is to be improved for all the people in our cities. The Kerner Commission Report, although out of date and superseded by numerous books and research studies, provides the most candid indictment of racism and segregation seen in such a document before or since (Kerner et al. 1968). The Commission famously told America that our country was "moving toward two societies, one black, one white—separate and unequal" and urged an end to racial discrimination. The Commission also "identified residential segregation and unequal housing and economic conditions in the inner city as significant causes of . . . social unrest," thus underscoring the report's contemporary significance. Recent events in Ferguson, Missouri, Baltimore, Chicago, Cleveland, and other cities make clear that the Commission's advice has gone largely unheeded, but America would be a different, and better, country had we taken seriously our responsibility to end racial segregation.

These three lessons have led to principles that guide equity planning today. Americans generally believe in advancing equality—at least in opportunity if not by right—as a civic value. Equity planners have incorporated that as a principle of their practice, believing that all plans and policies should be evaluated using the criterion of "who benefits, who pays." Planners should always pose the question of who are the least advantaged in any situation, and what would genuinely advance their life circumstances. Then planners should actively support those plans and policies that favor the disadvantaged as a matter of basic equity.

The fourth lesson of equity planning practice involves hope and persistence. Rather than an optimist or pessimist, the equity planner should be a "possible-ist"— realizing that all things are possible under the right circumstances. What may seem impossible today becomes tomorrow's reality. Consider that in the 1980s, in one decade alone, the Berlin Wall fell, communism collapsed, and apartheid ended. More recently, in just a matter of years, gay and lesbian adults who endured a mismatch of half-rights in forming "civil unions" when seeking a legally sanctioned bond with their partners have now been accorded the full rights of marriage. The equity planner must have faith that change in the direction of a more equitable society is possible and that their work may contribute to that change. The planner must not hesitate to suggest plans and policies that are currently impractical or politically infeasible even though that may be the case. The institutions of society change constantly, but they change very slowly, and ideas that at first seem impractical become practical when the time is ripe. When good ideas are rejected, the equity planner must pick them up and put them back on the table to advance in new and different ways. If the planner demonstrates professional competence, argues the merit of ideas, and backs up their constructive recommendations with sound data and careful analysis, these suggestions may be adopted. More importantly, the equity planner knows that a steady diet of cynicism and self-doubt can be spiritually corrosive and politically enervating.

Advancing Equity Planning

A number of cities have adopted an equity planning approach in their planning and development activities. In the 1970s, Cleveland (under Mayor Carl B. Stokes) pioneered equity planning practice. In the 1980s, Chicago (under Mayor Harold Washington) did the same. Other cities—some with minority mayors as in Cleveland and Chicago, and others with white mayors like Boston, Denver, Hartford, Jersey City, Berkeley, and Santa Monica—also adopted an equity-oriented approach to planning that included pressing for fair-share regional low-income housing schemes, increased accessibility to public transit for those without cars, rent control, broadened citizen participation, and other programs designed to aid lower-income residents. Liberal mayors are more likely to provide equity planners with essential support, but progressive planning ideas have also been implemented under more conservative political leadership (Krumholz and Clavel 1994).

More and more planners seem to be turning to equity-oriented planning, both at the official level and especially at the community level. Moreover, because of the events and changes in legislation and technology over the past fifty years, the future seems to hold promise of much more equity planning at all levels—developments that have radically changed government and planning practice. The 1960s empowered the civil rights movement through the 1964 Civil Rights Act, the 1965 Voting Rights Act, and the 1968 Housing Act. The rights of citizens who would be directly affected by certain actions began to be protected and written into laws mandating citizen participation. The environmental legislation of the 1970s focused attention on protecting the natural environment and gave power to citizens to protect their quality of life (Rees 1995). The 1980s introduced concepts of environmental justice and sustainability, coupling the social objective of equity along with environmental and economic concerns. Smart Growth and the New Urbanism of the 1990s integrated design into concepts of livability (Duany, Plater-Zyberk, and Speck 2000).

In 1991, Congress passed the Intermodal Surface Transportation Efficiency Act (ISTEA), which implemented dramatic changes. The law gave metropolitan regions great flexibility in how they spend transportation dollars while also mandating more transparency and accountability. It established stronger rules for public participation and required consideration of social issues, thus providing an opening to transportation decision making. President Clinton's Executive Order 12898 (1994) also ordered that federal agencies not adversely impact minority or low-income communities. The first decade of the new millennium saw the rise in values associated with community health, food systems, and designs to encourage physical activity (Dill 2009, Kaufman 2004). In the 1970s and 1980s, the Internet was a novelty, and social media and "big data" were unknown. Within this expanding landscape, an equity planner could easily reconcile professional practice with the championing of their ideals, so long as the planner can be seen as speaking for the community.

These changes are being absorbed and adopted by traditional planning agencies, but they are also the primary focus of new nonprofit community planning groups that are multiplying rapidly. These groups represent urban planning activity outside the formal planning organizations of the city and state. Changes in laws over the past fifty years have given status and importance to nonprofit groups formerly excluded from the development process; these changes have enabled them to challenge development proposals and work on their own projects (Teitz 2014). Other nonprofits have emerged, including community development corporations (CDCs), green groups concerned with the environment, groups focused on access to healthy food, PIRGs, groups working on workforce and employment issues, comprehensive community initiatives, and others. Influenced early on by the pioneering support of the Ford Foundation for various initiatives tied to the War on Poverty in the 1960s and 1970s, they have been strengthened by HUD's HOPE VI and Sustainable Communities program, and these programs have awarded 143 regions with the resources to create equity plans. Also significant is the work of national intermediaries like the John D. and Catherine T. MacArthur Foundation, the Annie E. Casey Foundation, Local Initiative Support Corporation, and Enterprise Community Partners. Most of these organizations follow basic equity planning practices in their work, including extensive data collection and analysis. Most have planners on their staffs and reflect a new consciousness of social equity by creating new opportunities for equity planning.

The chapters in this book demonstrate that it is possible for planners to practice equity planning across disciplines and at all levels. The work ranges from rebuilding more equitable neighborhoods to reinvigorating federal programs and policies to serve the goals of equity and inclusion. In the following section, we summarize how these lessons have been applied and identify the strategies that have been successfully employed to increase choices for those who have few.

Applying Lessons and Strategies
Local

The first section of the book offers lessons from local planners who are working outside of city hall and have been strong advocates for more equitable cities, neighborhoods, and communities. Lisa Bates, an academic, describes the struggle to include equity concerns related to affordable housing in Portland, Oregon's comprehensive land-use plan. Mark McDermott, a community developer, chronicles how equity planning principles and strategies shaped the community development sector in Cleveland. Majora Carter, an urban activist, tells her story of working in her home neighborhood of the South Bronx in New York through a dual focus on environmental equality and economic diversity.

Although working in very different settings, each author reoriented the planning conversations in their communities by shifting the narrative from planning by and for elites to planning by and for the deprived residents of the city. They set out to improve the quality of life for poor and near-poor residents by rebalancing the scales in land-use and development decisions to benefit those who have been negatively impacted by the political, economic, labor, housing, and health-care systems that continue to disadvantage these city residents, effectively locking them in "low-status" neighborhoods without access to political power or resources.

All used some variation of the traditional equity planning strategies of coalition building, leaking, and framing to move their agendas forward—sometimes successfully, and sometimes not. Lisa Bates describes the initial setbacks Portland's equity advocates faced in their attempts to include affordable housing and displacement as central platforms of the city's developing comprehensive land-use plan. She chronicles how she worked with community organizations to bring their own plan for affordable housing to the table and negotiated its inclusion into the official land-use plan. Yet, despite being presented with extensive data and analysis of increasing gentrification to help them make their case, city officials and planners were not on board. Equity advocates eventually succeeded in including measures to protect existing low- and moderate-income residents from gentrification by aligning with the statewide advocacy organization, 1000 Friends of Oregon, to argue for more affordable housing. They reframed the issue as a way to prevent displacement of existing residents and to preserve the Urban Growth Boundary. Joining with 1000 Friends amplified the voices and political clout of the equity advocates by giving them access to 1000 Friends' professional organizers, legal expertise in land use, and other needed resources to pressure reluctant city leaders and planners and, in some cases, give them the cover they needed to include equity in the land-use plan.

Mark McDermott documents the growth and maturation of the community development industry in Cleveland through his firsthand account of his own career as one of Cleveland's leading equity planners. As in Portland, community developers in Cleveland were focused on affordable housing and stability as a platform for achieving greater equity. They were also focused on race and acknowledged the role that decades of discriminatory race-based housing policies had in marginalizing poor city residents. Community developers were most successful when they formed strategic coalitions and partnerships with local officials, philanthropy, nonprofits, and universities; they also included local residents and did their homework, drawing on quality data and analysis with the understanding that research informs policy.

Majora Carter also uses as her starting point the intertwining of race and poverty. Her insights are especially revealing as she had grown up in and later returned to the South Bronx. She uses the term "low-status" communities to describe places like the South Bronx, where inequality is assumed as a given, even by those who live there. She offers a different perspective on the future of the neighborhood, now facing pressures brought on by gentrification. Although not a planner by profession, she thinks like a planner and takes the long view that neighborhoods are constantly changing.

Her place-based approach to managing that change utilizes a social entrepreneurship model of "self-gentrification" to promote a more economically diverse, equitable community that gives residents hope for a better future by staying in their own neighborhood. She uses surveys of residents and other organizing and engagement strategies to bring community voices to the table and raise awareness and to better frame issues in a way that resonates with residents. After learning what residents wanted and needed, she advocated for developing amenities and services that appealed to a range of income groups, thereby serving current residents while making the neighborhood attractive to new residents. She proposes a three-pronged strategy that involves reclaiming neighborhood control of land use, structuring real estate deals so that long-time neighborhood owners retain financial equity and benefit from any increasing property values, and promoting environmental equality. Like McDermott, her goal is to help minority communities build wealth and ownership and improve the quality of life.

Regional

Section 2 of the book widens the lens of equity planning from the neighborhood/ local/nonprofit perspective to the regional perspective. Even neighborhood planners and those working for neighborhood-based nonprofits must be cognizant of the regional dynamics influencing the equity landscape. When central city neighborhoods and inner-ring suburbs become increasingly cut off from access to regional economic opportunities in jobs, housing, health, etc., the economy of the region declines as a whole. In short, regions with high levels of income inequality are less economically competitive.

Drawing from their experience of working in and studying seventeen metropolitan areas, Christopher Benner and Manuel Pastor offer insights for equity planning at the regional scale, while Todd Swanstrom offers an example of a successful transit-oriented development project that brought together twenty-four suburbs of the Normandy School District in St. Louis County and provided affordable housing for working-class households with access to a light rail line.

Benner and Pastor's chapter focuses on process. In the absence of a formal metro government structure or regional land-use and development planning organization, equity planners need to turn to the process of building "epistemic communities." This is a concept borrowed from international policy development that uses conversation and consensus building to work toward common solutions based on the identification of shared cultures, norms, and practices. They take the concept further, however, to describe communities that are diverse—able to include different ways of knowing—as well as dynamic—able to shift to address various challenges as they arise.

They cite several regions (e.g., Seattle, Salt Lake City, San Antonio) where such a process has resulted in policies designed to promote greater equity (such as a $15 minimum wage), incentivizing development of affordable housing with transit access across the region, a fair-share affordable housing plan, and, perhaps most importantly, a set of regional indicators to track progress on equity. In addition, these successful regions also had a strong advocacy organization that served as a trusted source for information and policy analysis for various constituencies in the region (for example, the North Carolina Justice Center).

Swanstrom offers an example of a successful collaborative equity planning effort that involved the twenty-four high-poverty suburbs comprising the largely minority Normandy School District in St. Louis County, Missouri (including, notably, Ferguson). This is a case where none of the cities had a full-time planner on staff, so leadership on equity planning was provided by a nonprofit, "Beyond Housing"—another example of a strong advocacy organization, in this case one that was established to address the foreclosure crisis. Funded with a multimillion-dollar gift from an anonymous donor, Beyond Housing is a high capacity, trusted nonprofit. It commissioned a study, identified the need for housing for working families, and planned and developed a transit-oriented development project around a light rail station. The design of the development and the type of housing developed adapted in response to community input through a process facilitated by planners and organizers working for Beyond Housing. Although ultimately successful, the effort had its challenges, as it had to:

- Work across a highly fragmented local public sector that had little public money to invest.
- Institutionalize collaboration in fragmented suburbs and form alliances with central cities.

As efforts to address growing inequality increasingly turn to the regional scale and as poverty rates increase in suburban areas, equity planners are just as likely to be working at the regional scale. As noted above, the focus on sustainability, which views equity as its core foundation, along with economic and environmental concerns can be an effective way to bring equity into regional discussions. Recent regional planning efforts, including those led by the Obama administration to encourage cross-agency and cross-sector collaborative planning, have focused on fair and affordable housing, land use, transportation, jobs, and environmental considerations with mixed results.

National

The four chapters in this section offer a national policy perspective on issues of equity in transportation, workforce, housing, and planning for an aging population. Joe Grengs argues for the primacy of access over mobility with regard to transportation planning as a way to expand opportunity and promote a wider range of living and working choices for those who have few. Robert Giloth addresses the ever-present need for a more equity-oriented approach to increasing the number and quality of employment opportunities for black men and communities of color, even as wages and the quality of jobs are being eroded. He calls for shifting the focus from the traditional growth model to a focus on access to good jobs, the retention of manufacturing, neighborhood economic development, and investment in human capital and workforce training. Patrick Costigan offers an instructive case study of how the federal government, faced with a failing public housing system resulting from decades of disinvestment and indifference to the conditions in which residents were living, sought to restructure the system to infuse much-needed capital into revitalization and to make a wider array of choices available to public housing residents. In the final chapter of this section,

Deborah Howe makes a compelling case for planners to take a much more active role in providing meaningful housing, transportation, and lifestyle choices for the rapidly growing aging population.

In these cases, providing valid choices for those who have few means understanding the needs of the population in need, adopting public policy based on that understanding, and building that need into public policy. In the area of transportation planning, Grengs provides a way to target transportation services to compensate for disadvantages in other areas. He prioritizes serving the least advantaged first by designing transportation systems to provide them with the freedom and capacity to choose among a variety of options to gain access to jobs and other necessities such as health care. He offers a range of strategies to accomplish this:

- Strengthen public engagement, especially of marginalized populations.
- Replace a mobility-based framework with an accessibility framework; promote accessibility to be the fundamental metric and demote mobility in the hierarchy of importance. Mobility matters, but merely as one among several means to accessibility, which should be the end goal.
- Adopt a more explicitly normative position to seek to redress preexisting disadvantages by strategically redirecting transportation benefits to those in greatest need; bring transportation analysis in line with the Federal Transportation Law adopted by Congress in 2012 that treats accessibility as the primary and only measure of effectiveness.
- Improve analytic capabilities to reframe decision making to achieve higher levels of access.
- Develop measurement tools that link social equity and the built environment; look outside the box to new transportation solutions, such as driverless cars and shared mobility, as well as nontransportation solutions, such as changing land-use regulations to improve not only the proximity of destinations but also individual characteristics, such as income or an individual's capability of using a car, for example, to get where you need to go. Accessibility is an attribute of people or households, not places or infrastructure; the onus is on the planner to identify those people and places most in need and redirect resources.
- Advance transportation policies that broaden the scope of choices.

In the workforce arena, equity planning has always included a focus on jobs and opportunity but discrimination persists. In fact, Giloth calls for a new civil rights movement with a focus on jobs and careers as a foundation of full citizenship. How can equity planners change entrenched, discriminatory systems to open up labor markets and improve job quality (i.e., jobs with family supporting incomes and a career pathway)? They cannot do it on their own. It requires progressive political leadership at the state and local level along with supportive federal policies. He proposes a multipronged strategy—working at levels of system change, policy, planning, and organizing that involves the traditional "workforce" areas of manufacturing retention, neighborhood economic development, human capital, and workforce investment as well as education, transportation, and affordable housing so that transit dependent populations can reach job centers or afford housing near job centers. Giloth offers a number of examples of places that have used Community Benefit Agreements (CBAs) and economic inclusion plans, micro lenders, cooperative businesses, and impact investing to achieve greater equity in workforce systems at the regional scale. He also gives examples of successful long-term civic collaboration and leadership from sector partnerships (work groups of companies to spread risk across firms) and anchor institutions ("eds and meds")—changing hiring practices, using CBAs for construction projects, using local purchasing to grow local jobs in local businesses, promoting small local businesses and entrepreneurship, and working toward greater equity at the regional scale.

In the area of federal housing policy, Costigan traces the development and implementation of the Rental Assistance Demonstration program to address funding shortfalls in public housing. In 2009, faced with decades of declining funding, legislative indifference, and a structural $26 billion backlog in public housing capital repairs, the U.S. Department of Housing and Urban Development pursued change that would enable it to provide more housing options for public housing residents. The recession that triggered the collapse of the housing market also resulted in the greatest stripping of wealth from African American homeowners (most of whom have still not recovered) and provided the impetus to advance an equity-oriented public housing agenda. It took a crisis, committed and determined leaders, and the patient building of a diverse constituency to reform public housing. Using the traditional equity planning skills of vision, careful analysis, advocacy, and coalition building, HUD's leadership was able to implement a pilot program, the Rental Assistance Demonstration (RAD), that leveraged $19 of private capital for every $1 of HUD funding to revitalize eighty-three thousand units of public and assisted housing. Equally importantly, RAD gave participating public housing authorities the ability to budget and maintain long-term replacement reserves that can be used to upgrade properties and slow demolition.

As our population rapidly ages, Howe makes the case for using public dollars, building codes, accessory dwellings, universal design, transportation alternatives, and road design to transform the built environment to be aging supportive. In this way communities will be better positioned to meet the needs of elderly and nonelderly residents. Following a basic tenet of equity planning, she argues for including the elderly in planning decision making (however, avoiding pitting one generation against another) and building coalitions with advocates and experts (e.g., AARP, Robert Wood Johnson Foundation).

As these authors point out, changing entrenched systems at the national level is difficult work. There are powerful interests that benefit from the status quo. Funding for programs that benefit the most disadvantaged is declining, and the political landscape is in flux. The chapters in this section offer ways to work within existing systems, as well as ways to change the systems.

It is the planner's job to take the long-term view. For the aging, this necessitates not only building aging issues into plans but also implementing those plans to address the special challenges of aging (e.g., lifecycle communities or lifelong communities). For workforce, it involves embracing technological change and more transformative discussions about the future of work which call into question whether employment as an equity goal is even plausible. Future planners will need traditional planning skills, such as community organizing, coalition building, and conflict management. As they plan for today's workforce, they will also need vision and imagination to conceive of new and innovative "on-ramps" for individuals seeking employment (such as social enterprises) and a new social compact of income and work supports for a postwork society.

The Future

The final section of this book looks to the challenge of preparing future generations of equity planners to respond to rapidly changing urban environments and to new technology. Reardon and Forester draw from their forty years of experience teaching equity planning to offer some best practices, including exposing students to hands-on learning opportunities and offering tools and techniques to prepare future planners to prioritize equity in their professional careers. Thompson and Arceneaux provide a case study of planners using technology-enhanced tools such as public participation geographic information systems (PPGIS) to enable citizens to participate more effectively in planning for their own neighborhoods.

In educating future planners, it is not enough to offer equity planning courses or to include considerations of equity in the curriculum. Forester and Reardon describe effective techniques and enhancements to explicitly prepare students to prioritize the needs of disadvantaged populations. Students need techniques for promoting joint problem solving, such as co-generated research (providing expert analysis not FOR users but WITH users), urban ethnography (which encompasses a close and respectful working relationship with the community), internships to incorporate hands-on learning opportunities, participatory action research, experience organizing for resident-driven problem solving or community responsive public planning processes, coalition and network building, and social media usage to promote citizen participation. Curriculum enhancements include incorporating area studies of cultural identity groups, providing a more rigorous introduction to urban and metropolitan politics and community organizing, strengthening the commitment to diversity in students and faculty as well as in scholarly publications, and addressing unexamined white privilege and institutional racism and how it has shaped urban areas.

As Reardon and Forester point out, the good news is that, in the forty years since Krumholz and his colleagues wrote the first equity plan, equity planning has become an essential element of mainstream planning education. Yet, over that same time period, America's cities have changed dramatically, becoming even more segregated and unequal. And they are poised for a major transformation in the future as driverless cars and other smart technologies change the form and function of the urban landscape. At the same time, at least for the foreseeable future, fewer public resources will be available. Under these circumstances, ensuring that those with the fewest choices are not harmed further and preferably benefit from these changes will be a significant challenge facing future planners.

Another trend that is shaping how planners work is the increasing availability of open source data. According to an article in *CityLab* (Bliss 2017), more than one hundred American cities host online open data portals where planners and citizens can find data on crime, housing, transit, etc. Ideally, this data offers citizens a way to plan for their own neighborhoods and to hold governments accountable for outcomes. In practice, it is quite difficult for nonexperts to access this data and make sense of it. Planners are uniquely positioned to serve as intermediaries and to use their expertise in data and geospatial analysis to work with community organizations and residents to help them visualize the geographic implications of data and develop community plans.

Thompson and Arceneaux's chapter describes how they used one such geospatial technique, Public Participation Geographic Information Systems (PPGIS), to enable neighborhood residents to have a greater voice in planning for their New Orleans neighborhoods, post–Hurricane Katrina. In 2011, the authors—part of a group of professional and student volunteers from the University of New Orleans's Department of Planning and Urban Studies—began to use PPGIS to work with neighborhood associations to enable them to collect, map, and quantify quality-of-life challenges faced by residents. They used PPGIS to facilitate the use of big and small data by nonprofits. This tool gave neighborhood residents control over their own community narrative to guide equitable neighborhood recovery.

Their chapter points out the promise of democratizing data, as well as its challenges: local political agendas that may not coincide with citizen agendas; sustaining citizen participation over the long term; finding volunteers who live in a neighborhood, especially one that has been devastated by natural (hurricanes) or man-made (foreclosures) disasters; and concerns with the accuracy, validity, and utility of crowdsourced data. Furthermore, local government can pose a barrier by not sharing data either within the city across departments or with the public. Finally, PPGIS can be a resource for citizen decision making but does not necessarily provide a platform to catalyze policy change. Planners need to understand data management and ethics, share their expertise, and work with residents to provide ongoing support to track progress as plans are implemented to keep public officials accountable.

Barriers to Equity Planning

Equity planners need to be realistic. A frequent critique among planners is that even if they are able to prioritize benefits to disadvantaged populations in their plans and policy recommendations, they have little influence over whether or not plans are implemented; the adoption and implementation is often in the hands of politicians. The lack of political support and other external factors can be barriers to equity planning, but other barriers are internal to the planners' personal approach. Equity planners need motivation, confidence, and the will to change prevailing ideas, especially in cities without progressive political leadership.

They also need a firm grasp of the tools (illustrated throughout this book) that can be used to build constituencies for adopting and implementing plans and used to give politicians the cover they need to make the decisions that many of them would like to make—specifically, data-driven analysis, organizing and public engagement, coalition building, leaking, framing, and holding public officials accountable.

These tools will be especially useful during this time of retrenchment of federal funds and programs. Changes to policies and regulations that protect the poor and threats to immigrant and religious and ethnic minority communities and the full array of destabilizing forces will result in increasing inequality.

Since the 1970s, the equity-oriented work of city planners has some produced tangible benefits for poor and working-class city residents. It has done so even in the face of increasing levels of inequality, prevailing norms, institutional bias, and the complicated issues of race and diversity. However, much more needs to be done.

This book illustrates that equity planners no longer work exclusively for local governments. They can be increasingly found working for nonprofits, at philanthropies with public interest agendas, and in state and national government. They are also no longer exclusively involved in developing city plans. For all those who see their work as equity planning or who aspire to be equity planners—at every level and in every sector—this book is as much a "call to action" as it is a "how to."

It seems clear that the most effective contemporary planning for social equity is taking place within the community planning field. This is not true for all community-planning organizations, as they retain a spotty track record across geographies and organizations. Yet there are many community-planning organizations that are creating the space for the nexus of equity planning and equity implementation. These high-performing organizations are inviting authentic resident participation, leading coalitions and partnerships with state and local governments, creating new capital solutions that are reliant on multiple sources of funding, and driving policies focused on localized community benefit. None of these functions are new to the world of planning and community development. But it seems clear that the evolution of community planning is built on the foundation of social equity as its principal intention, and this evolution is moving faster and reaching deeper than realized, promising an upsurge of equity planning in the future.

It also seems clear that the boundaries of community-based planning are expanding rapidly. Trying to make the most of their limited resources, CDCs are turning to large, specialized, nonprofit national corporations like BRIDGE Housing and the Community Builders as a means of going to scale. Others, like the well-known Harlem Children's Zone in New York City, have education at their core; health care, as in Boston's Codman Square Health Center, is another entering wedge for community development.

At the same time, there is evidence of renewed attention to equity in cities across the country. Recently, for example, the mayor of Houston, Texas, created an equity task force to make recommendations for rebuilding the city after Hurricane Harvey (2017). The recommendations include setting goals and metrics for tracking progress in broad areas such as minimum wage, housing, transportation, and employment. The National League of Cities has a tactical team in place to provide cities with technical assistance and training in support of a racial equity plan.

What's Next for Equity Planning?

There are three reasons to expect a new upsurge of equity planning in the future: (1) the evolution of the environmental sustainability movement in the context of urban planning and development; (2) the increasing concern for socioeconomic inequalities; and (3) changes in national demographics.

Social equity is one of the "Three Es" that are central to the sustainability movement; the others are environmental integrity and economic prosperity. Sustainability is a well-known concept in urban planning, but it is now conceived with new urgency—the idea being that everyone in the community needs the opportunity to participate and thrive for that community to sustain itself.

Until the 1990s very little of the sustainable development literature focused on cities or patterns of urban development. Instead, writers discussed the crisis caused by the exponential explosion of the population worldwide, the global environment, and the need for a transformation of values favoring conservation over growth. However, in more recent years, planners and architects have begun looking more specifically at how the "Three Es"—economic development, environment, and social equity—translate into patterns of city and metropolitan development (Wheeler 2013). Some authors have emphasized urban design and physical planning and development. Others have focused on environmental planning concerns having to do with the quality of air, water, and natural ecosystems. But a significant number have also noticed the need to address social problems and inequities within the urban community, and they have emphasized the point that environmental and social issues are inextricably linked. In all of these categories, urban sustainability advocates can be seen as building on the work of past planning visionaries such as Patrick Geddes, Ebenezer Howard, Jane Jacobs, and RPAA members Lewis Mumford and Ian McHarg. We see this both in the movements for sustainability and the related push for green cities.

Some of the main directions for urban sustainability include the following: efficient land use, efficient resource use, sustainable economics, good housing and living environments, the lessening importance of the automobile, a healthy social ecology, and community participation. As noted above, these elements have been simplified into what is generally referred to as the "Three Es" (Campbell 1996). In practice, the application of sustainability is often full of intractable conflicts with implementation that favors one principle over the others—often with social equity having a lower priority (Conroy 2006). It is often called the "stealth" principle. But urban planners should always advocate for social equity. It is their unique contribution to public policy and a mandate of the profession. If planners wish to change the world for the better, social equity should be their highest priority, even if it clashes with other important values (Beatley and Manning 1997).

Green urbanization is also not a new idea. Before World War I, Patrick Geddes had classified the environmental needs of different ecological systems and developed a systematic approach to building cities that respected natural systems. Ian McHarg's book *Design with Nature* (1969) inspired the environmentally conscious generation of the 1960s. Today, respect for the natural environment is the cornerstone of the New Urbanism movement. The future will see the evolution of green development standards having to do with compact land-use patterns, regional green space designs, solar installations, and green roofs to conserve energy. Environmental justice issues will also be in the mix to ensure that the needs of the poor are taken into consideration. This is especially true in light of Pope Francis's important 2015 encyclical *Laudato Si* that points out the deleterious impact of global warming on poor populations around the world. The Pope's message is an unusual melding of science with faith and calls for a radical transformation of politics, economics, and individual lifestyles to confront environmental depredation and climate change. It is a powerful message in support of a more sustainable and equitable world.

Just as the Three Es of the sustainability movement provide support for the assumption that more equity planning is likely for the future, so too does the rising concern for socioeconomic inequality. Inequality of income, wealth, and opportunity in the United States is high compared to other developed democracies, and the gap appears to be growing.

Perhaps most significant for an expanded equity planning practice in the future is the change in our national demographics, making for a more pluralistic society. A recent census bureau report makes clear that by 2044, whites will no longer make up a racial majority in the United States (Frey 2015). By then, the nation—like today's Los Angeles—will be made up of a kaleidoscope of racial groups, including Latinos, blacks, Asians, Native Americans, and multiracial Americans. In just sixteen years from 2015 there will be minority white populations in twelve states, including California, Texas, Florida, New York, Georgia, and New Jersey (Teixeira et al. 2015). It is a change that does not depend on immigration; it is already here and thriving among children younger than five and among all students in the nation's public schools. It is a change that should be welcomed since it will help our country to prosper.

This diversity boom is a godsend, occurring in time to counterbalance the aging of our white population; this may give the United States a chance to avert the problems of a stagnating and aging population which Japan, Italy, and other European nations are already facing. We are gaining a competitive advantage, and our priority should be to integrate immigrant and native-born minorities, provide necessary social and education services, and prepare the younger members for success.

This increased diversity will produce political conditions that make a more liberal response possible, not only in planning, but in all the institutions of American society. Our diversifying population has already elected more minorities at every level of government than ever before. This process seems likely to continue as political leaders see the potential for a new and more liberal coalition to upset traditional alignments. This coalition will come under powerful pressure from the opposition trying to hold onto its power. The opposition will attempt to keep coalition members from voting while trying to subvert and scatter its membership. They will do so through voter ID laws, racial gerrymandering, mass disenfranchisement through the criminal justice system, and other devices. They will try to exploit the divisions of culture and class that exist between ethnic groups which are acute in some cities like Los Angeles (Jackson and Preston 1994). But leaders will be found to overcome these powerful impediments.

The elected leaders of this coalition will not govern in the same way, but they will all try to hold their coalition together and do more for their political base. They will work to increase voter participation, broaden the range of opportunities available to all, moderate inequality through a redistributive tax system, encourage union representation, and implement large-scale initiatives in infrastructure, education, and research. With stronger political support, planners will rediscover the concepts of advocacy, pluralism, and justice and relearn the progressive lessons of their own history.

The editors and contributors to this volume assumed that while leadership at the federal level would change from time to time, it would continue to be, if not supportive, at least tolerant of the ideas put forward by equity planners. But what if this assumption proved to be incorrect, and planners could no longer count on a benevolent federal government? The possibility of a hostile federal government was apparent to at least some observers as indicated by a passage from Richard Rorty's 1998 book, *Achieving Our Country*. Rorty, a philosopher who died in 2007, predicted that the neglected working class would not tolerate its marginalization for long. "Something will crack," he wrote:

> The non-suburban electorate will decide that the system has failed and start looking around for a strongman to vote for—someone willing to assure them that, once he is elected, the smug bureaucrats, tricky lawyers, over-paid bond salesmen, and postmodernist professors will no longer be calling the shots. . . . One thing that is very likely to happen is that the gains made in the last forty years by black and brown Americans, and by homosexuals, will be wiped out. Jocular contempt for women will come back into fashion. . . . All the resentment which badly educated Americans feel about having their manners dictated to them by college graduates will find an outlet. (Rorty 1998)

In November 2016 the neglected working class found their man in Donald J. Trump and reacted with an impact that will pass through legal and administrative systems, changing the way planners and others approach their responsibilities. Once in office, President Trump and his party immediately began to try to turn back the clock.

What strategies should progressive planners and others follow given this event? First, they should try to do everything possible to protect their cities from crucial budget cuts. This means fighting to maintain adequate levels of funding for housing, education, public transit, infrastructure, and the social safety net, all of which contribute to a functioning, cohesive society. Second, they can organize protests, support investigative reporting, and write op-eds exposing counterproductive policies. Third, planners can join the people in the streets. Given President Trump's history with African Americans, Muslims, Latinos, unionized labor, gays, people with disabilities, and other groups, there is likely to be plenty of protest; it may be that democracy will thrive in the streets as it did in the 1960s.

It would also seem that turning to institutions closer to home would constitute a proper reaction. To a large extent, these institutions are what secure and sustain our values. It is time to strengthen these institutions. Most Americans believe in and support fair-minded journalism, scientific discovery, scholarship, and the arts. Many local municipalities and state governments are eager to work on the hard problems—whether it's making sure people have a roof over their heads and enough to eat, or get proper care when they get sick, or that wages are lifted, or that the reality of climate change is addressed. States like Massachusetts will continue to implement its popular comprehensive health insurance plan, and California, with its determination to address climate change, will persevere regardless of federal resistance. Other states will follow their lead.

Closer to our daily lives are institutions like hospitals and schools. These institutions have evolved their own ethics in keeping with American ideals and will continue to protect their values regardless of the changes that take place at the federal level. If the people in Washington make bad judgments, these smaller-scale institutions that directly impact people's daily lives will check the consequences of those choices. The test is whether the gap between what we preach and what we practice shrinks or expands. The job of equity planners and others of good conscience will be to hold those in power to account for that result, and that includes the future of all those left out and left behind. Reason and compassion demand no less.

REFERENCES

Beatley, Timothy, and Kristy Manning. 1997. *The Ecology of Place: Planning for the Environment, Economy, and Community*. Washington, DC: Island Press.

Bliss, Laura. 2017. "An Open Data Hub That Builds Better Citizens." *CityLab*. https://www.citylab.com/solutions/2017/07/an-open-data-hub-that-builds-better-citizens/533217/.

Campbell, Scott. 1996. "Green Cities, Growing Cities, Just Cities? Urban Planning and the Contradictions of Sustainable Development," *Journal of the American Planning Association* 6 (2): 3.

Conroy, Maria Manta. 2006. "Moving the Middle Ahead, Challenges and Opportunities of Sustainability in Indiana, Kentucky and Ohio," *Journal of Planning Education and Research* 26 (1): 18–27.

Curry, Robert. 2015. Personal correspondence with the author.

Dill, Jennifer. 2009. "Bicycling for Transportation and Health: The Role of Infrastructure," *Journal of Public Health Policy* 30 (Suppl. 1): 95–110.

Duany, Andres, Elizabeth Plater-Zyberk, and Jeff Speck. 2000. *The Rise of Sprawl and the Decline of Nation*. New York: North Point Press.

Executive Order 12898. Federal Actions to Address Environmental Justice in Minority Populations and Low-Income Populations. 1994. 59 FR 7629 (February 16). https://www.epa.gov/laws-regulations/summary-executive-order-12898-federal-actions-address-environmental-justice.

Frey, William F. 2015. *Diversity Explosion: How the New Racial Demographics Are Remaking America*. Washington, DC: The Brookings Institution.

Grengs, Joe. 2002. "Community-Based Planning As a Source of Political Change: The Transit Equity Movement of Los Angeles' Bus Riders Union," *Journal of the American Planning Association* (68) 2: 165–78.

Huang, Joyce. 2015. "National Scan of Existing CBAs." Unpublished document. Center for Community Planning and Development, Cleveland State University.

Jackson, B. O., and M. B. Preston. 1994. "Race and Ethnicity in Los Angeles Politics." In *Big City Politics, Governance, and Fiscal Constraints*, edited by G. E. Peterson. Washington DC: Urban Institute Press.

Kaufman, Jerome L. 2004. "Introduction," *Journal of Planning Education and Research* 23 (4): 333–34.

Kerner, Otto et al. 1968. *Report of the National Advisory Commission on Civil Disorders*. New York: Bantam Books.

Krumholz, Norman. 1997. "The Provision of Housing in Cleveland: Patterns of Organization and Financial Support." In *Housing and Urban Development in the United States*, edited by Willem van Vliet. Thousand Oaks: Sage.

Krumholz, Norman, and Pierre Clavel. 1994. *Reimagining Cities: Equity Planners Tell Their Stories*. Philadelphia: Temple University Press.

Labor/Community Strategy Center v. Los Angeles County Metropolitan Transit Authority. 1996. 2:94-cv-5936 (C.D. Cal.), Consent Decree.

Levine, Amy. 2009. "Community Benefits Agreements." Accessed October 2009. http://www.communitybenefits.blogspot.com.

Rees, W. E. 1995. "Achieving Sustainability: Reform or Transformation?" *Journal of Planning Literature* 9 (4): 343–61.

Rorty, Richard. 1998. *Achieving Our Country*. Cambridge: Harvard University Press.

Teixeira, Ruy, William H. Frey, and Rob Griffin. 2015. *"States of Change: The Demographic Evolution of the American Electorate, 1974–2060,"* Center for American Progress.

Tietz, Michael, and Karen Chappel. 2012. "Planning and Poverty: An Uneasy Relationship." In *Policy, Planning, and People: Promoting Justice in Urban Development*, edited by Naomi Carmon and Susan Fainstein. Philadelphia: University of Pennsylvania Press.

Wheeler, Stephen. 2013. *Planning for Sustainability: Creating Livable, Equitable, and Ecological Communities*. New York: Routledge.

Wolf-Powers, Laura. 2010. "Community Benefits Agreements and Local Government," *Journal of the American Planning Association* 76 (2): 141–59.

Notes on Contributors

Brittany N. Arceneaux

As a native of New Orleans, **Brittany N. Arceneaux** has been working with Hurricane Katrina recovery efforts since 2010. In 2013 Ms. Arceneaux received her bachelors of science in urban and regional planning from the University of New Orleans (UNO). During her time at UNO, she worked with a group of professional and student volunteers as the program operations manager of WhoData .org. After graduating from UNO, Ms. Arceneaux began working at Pond & Company as a planner and geographic information systems (GIS) analyst. She maintains her relationship with Whodata.org as a volunteer assistant director. Her roles in project management include work in neighborhoods such as the Lower Ninth Ward and Hoffman Triangle. Along with field research, Ms. Arceneaux works with neighborhood organizations to provide GIS training and methods of data collection. She has presented her research at conferences such as the 2012 New Orleans Housing Community Development Conference and the 2012 National Reclaiming Vacant Properties Conference. Ms. Arceneaux has dedicated years to community technical support and outreach.

Lisa K. Bates

Lisa K. Bates, PhD, is associate professor in the Toulan School of Urban Studies and Planning at Portland State University. Her scholarship focuses on housing and community development policy and planning. She engages in research and practice with the aim of dismantling institutional racism, and in 2016 she was awarded the Dale Prize for scholarship on urban planning for community self-determination and racial justice from Cal Poly Pomona.

Dr. Bates has participated in research, planning, and policy formulation and evaluation with a variety of government and nonprofit partners, including ACORN Housing Corporation, the city of Portland's Bureau of Planning and Sustainability and the Portland Housing Bureau, the Urban League, Multnomah Youth Commission, PolicyLink, and the Portland Housing Center. Her work to describe gentrification and displacement in Portland has been widely cited and continues with current research on the impact of new transit investment on neighborhood housing.

Chris Benner

Chris Benner, PhD, is the Dorothy E. Everett Chair in Global Information and Social Entrepreneurship, director of the Everett Program for Technology and Social Change, and a professor of environmental studies and sociology at the University of California, Santa Cruz. His research examines the relationships between technological change, regional development, and the structure of economic opportunity, focusing on regional labor markets and the transformation of work and employment. He has authored or coauthored six books and more that seventy journal articles, chapters, and research reports. He received his PhD in city and regional planning from the University of California, Berkeley.

Majora Carter

Majora Carter is a leading urban revitalization strategy consultant, real estate developer, and Peabody Award-winning broadcaster. She is responsible for the creation and implementation of numerous green infrastructure projects, policies, and job training and placement systems. After establishing Sustainable South Bronx and Green For All (among other organizations) to carry on that work, she opened a private consulting firm which was named Best for the World by B Corp in 2014. Carter was named one of 100 Most Intriguing Entrepreneurs by Goldman Sachs. Her talent retention strategies for neighborhood development are changing how low-status American communities leverage re-urbanization, wealth creation, and quality of life.

Patrick Costigan

Mr. Costigan served as a senior advisor to U.S. Department of Housing and Urban Development Secretary Shaun Donovan from 2011 to 2014, where one of his principal responsibilities was to help frame and secure Congressional authority and guide the initial implementation of the Rental Assistance Demonstration. Previously, he held senior management roles at the Community Builders, Inc., and the Enterprise Foundation (now Enterprise Community Partners). At the outset of his thirty-plus year career in affordable housing and community development, he worked for five years at the Center for Neighborhood Development under the direction of Norman Krumholz at Cleveland State University.

John Forester

John Forester, PhD, is a professor of city and regional planning at Cornell University. He received his BS (1970) and MS (1971) in mechanical engineering and his MCP (1974) and PhD (1977) in city and regional planning from the University of California, Berkeley. Dr. Forester's research has focused on the micropolitics of planning with particular attention paid to issues of power and conflict; negotiation and mediation; and practices of organizing, deliberation, and improvisation. Dr. Forester's best-known books are *Planning in the Face of Power* (University of California Press, 1989), *The Deliberative Practitioner* (MIT Press, 1999), and *Dealing with Differences: Dramas of Mediating Public Disputes* (Oxford University Press, 2009). His recent publications include *Planning in the Face of Conflict* (APA Press, 2013), *Conflict, Improvisation, Governance* (with David Laws; Routledge, 2015), *and Rebuilding Community After Katrina* (with Ken Reardon; Temple University Press, 2016).

Robert Giloth

Robert Giloth, PhD, is vice president of the Center for Economic Opportunity at the Annie E. Casey Foundation in Baltimore. He oversees national grant making for economic opportunity programs related to workforce, adult education, community colleges, and financial stability. He has written widely on philanthropy and economic, workforce, and community development and recently coedited *Connecting People to Work: Workforce Intermediaries and Sector Strategies* with Maureen Conway of the Aspen Institute.

Joe Grengs

Joe Grengs, PhD, is chair and associate professor of urban and regional planning at the University of Michigan. His research focuses on transportation planning and how metropolitan land-use patterns contribute to uneven economic development and social inequalities. He was appointed by the Obama administration to serve on the Federal Advisory Committee on Transportation Equity at the U.S. Department of Transportation. He is a member of the American Institute of Certified Planners (AICP) and a licensed professional engineer, with work experience in the private and public sectors and in international settings.

Deborah Howe

Deborah Howe, PhD, is past president and CEO of the Oregon College of Oriental Medicine; professor emerita of community and regional planning at Temple University; and former professor of urban studies and planning at Portland State University. She was an early proponent of the importance of community planning for the aging, serving in the late 1980s as the principal investigator on a federal training grant to educate planners and local policy makers about the importance of creating aging-sensitive communities. Professor Howe has been publishing and giving presentations on this topic ever since. She has also conducted funded research on land-use and transportation policy innovations that support the creation of built environments to encourage active, healthy lifestyles through walking, bicycling, and other physical activity.

Kathryn Wertheim Hexter

Kathryn Wertheim Hexter is an associate of the university at Cleveland State University (CSU). She recently retired as director of the Center for Community Planning and Development and as founding director of the Forum Program at the Levin College of Urban Affairs at CSU. A planner and public policy analyst, she has more than thirty-five years of experience working in the areas of housing policy, foreclosures, community and neighborhood development, sustainable development, city and regional planning, and civic engagement. She has conducted national studies and published in the areas of regional sustainability, suburban poverty, distressed suburbs, and capacity building of distressed cities through urban fellowships. Most recently, she led the evaluation of the Greater University Circle Economic Inclusion Initiative, a long-term collaboration harnessing the economic power of anchor institutions to benefit neighborhood residents in Cleveland, Ohio.

Norman Krumholz

Norman Krumholz is professor emeritus in the Levin College of Urban Affairs, Cleveland State University (CSU). Professor Krumholz earned his planning degree at Cornell University. He is widely regarded nationally and internationally as a planning "legend" for promoting the practice of equity planning. Among his many publications, his book *Making Equity Planning Work* with John Forester won the 1991 Paul Davidoff award of the Associated Collegiate Schools of Planning for book of the year. Upon publication, Harvard University Professor Alan Altshuler has said of this book that *"No planner, I predict, will be able to consider his education complete during the next decade or so who has not grappled vicariously with the dilemmas Krumholz faced."*

Prior to joining the faculty at CSU, he served as planning director of the city of Cleveland from 1969 to 1979 under three mayors: Carl B. Stokes, Ralph J. Perk, and Dennis Kucinich. He also worked as a planning practitioner in Ithaca and Pittsburgh. He served as the president of the American Planning Association (APA) (1986–1987), received the APA Award for Distinguished Leadership in 1990, and in 1999 served as the president of the American Institute of Certified Planners. He was awarded the Prize of Rome in 1987 by the American Academy in Rome. Professor Krumholz was recently appointed an AICP fellow, and his Cleveland Policy Plan was declared a "Planning Landmark" by the APA. In honor of his ninetieth birthday, the city of Cleveland renamed a section of East Eighteenth Street as "Norman Krumholz Way."

Mark McDermott

Mark McDermott is a lifelong Cleveland area resident, having lived in the city of Cleveland since 1979. For the past twenty years Mr. McDermott has worked for

Enterprise Community Partners and is currently vice president and Ohio market leader for Enterprise. He also serves on various local and statewide boards and co-alition leadership positions. His research is observation of people and power; the result of that observation has always been hope.

Manuel Pastor

Manuel Pastor, PhD, is professor of sociology and American studies and ethnicity at the University of Southern California (USC). He directs the Program for Environmental and Regional Equity (PERE) and USC's Center for the Study of Immigrant Integration (CSII). Dr. Pastor holds a PhD in economics from the University of Massachusetts Amherst and is the inaugural holder of the Turpan-jian Chair in Civil Society and Social Change at USC. His research has generally focused on issues of the economic, environmental, and social conditions facing low-income urban communities—and the social movements seeking to change those realities. His most recent book is *State of Resistance: What California's Dizzying Descent and Remarkable Resurgence Mean for America's Future* (The New Press, 2018).

Kenneth Reardon

Kenneth Reardon, PhD, is a professor and director of the urban planning and community development program at the University of Massachusetts Boston. He recently coedited *Rebuilding Community After Katrina: Transformative Education in the New Orleans Planning Initiative* (Temple University Press, 2016) with John F. Forester.

Todd Swanstrom

The Des Lee Professor of Community Collaboration and Public Policy Administration at the University of Missouri–St. Louis (UMSL), **Todd Swanstrom,** PhD, is a coauthor of *Place Matters: Metropolitics for the Twenty-First Century*, 3rd ed. (University Press of Kansas, 2014), which won the Michael Harrington Award from the New Politics Section of the American Political Science Association. He is the author of *The Crisis of Growth Politics: Cleveland, Kucinich and the Challenge of Urban Populism* (Temple University Press, 1985) and coedited *Justice and the American Metropolis* (University of Minnesota Press, 2012) with Clarissa Rile Hayward. Professor Swanstrom's current research focuses on neighborhood change in older industrial cities. He uses the resources of his endowed professorship to support the Community Builders Network, a coalition of community development corporations, banks, foundations, and governments who work to build better neighborhoods in the St. Louis region.

Michelle M. Thompson

Michelle M. Thompson, PhD, is a geographic information systems professional and associate professor in the Department of Planning and Urban Studies at the University of New Orleans. Professor Thompson's research focuses on the application of public participation geographic information systems in community development and reinvestment. Professor Thompson is also the project manager of the web-based community mapping service, WhoData.org, an organization that combines parcel level neighborhood condition information with public data to monitor socioeconomic and land-use changes. Since 2009, Professor Thompson has served Cross World Africa, Inc. (CWA; www.crossworldafrica.org) as a volunteer and vice president; CWA provides cultural and economic support to families in East Africa. Professor Thompson is also the principal of Thompson Real Estate Consultants LLC, a real estate research and education firm. She has worked in both public and private companies with regard to the financing of residential and commercial real estate. In June 2017, Professor Thompson joined New America as a public interest technology fellow, focusing on financial inclusion and citizen participation.

Index